About the Author

He is 58 years old, married to Julie for thirty-seven years, with a thirty-seven-year-old daughter, Sarah. He has two grandsons, eight-year-old Austen and one-year-old Cooper, born February 2022. He retired from Rolls-Royce in 2020, just shy of 40 years' service. His sporting passions are football, cricket and running, having completed 20 marathons, including the London Marathon five times. Aside from sport, he loves gardening and travel.

50 Years 'Not Out'

John Taylor

50 Years 'Not Out'

Olympia Publishers
London

www.olympiapublishers.com
OLYMPIA PAPERBACK EDITION

Copyright © John Taylor 2023

The right of John Taylor to be identified as author of
this work has been asserted in accordance with sections 77 and 78
of the Copyright, Designs and Patents Act 1988.

All Rights Reserved

No reproduction, copy or transmission of this publication
may be made without written permission.
No paragraph of this publication may be reproduced,
copied or transmitted save with the written permission of the
publisher, or in accordance with the provisions
of the Copyright Act 1956 (as amended).

Any person who commits any unauthorised act in relation to
this publication may be liable to criminal
prosecution and civil claims for damage.

A CIP catalogue record for this title is
available from the British Library.

ISBN: 978-1-80074-552-0

This is a work of fiction.
Names, characters, places and incidents originate from the writer's
imagination. Any resemblance to actual persons, living or dead, is
purely coincidental.

First Published in 2023

Olympia Publishers
Tallis House
2 Tallis Street
London
EC4Y 0AB

Printed in Great Britain

Dedication

To my mum and dad, who made great sacrifices in their lives to support me in my love of sport. To my wife Julie, who's 'put up with me' over the last thirty-seven years following Derby County Football Club! To all the supporters of our great football club who have followed the team over the years through the good times and the not so good. Stay patient, the good times will come again.

Acknowledgements

I would like to thank some of my friends and family for taking time to read the manuscript and offering their feedback and recommending additional items to be added in.

Contents

Foreword By Martin Fisher 15
Introduction 17
Chapter 1 19
    Champions Of England And European Nights ....
Chapter 2 60
    The Colin Murphy And Tommy Doc Years ....
Chapter 3 71
    Falling Through The Trap Door – Twice! ....
Chapter 4 107
    Revival Under Arthur Cox And The Double Promotion ......
Chapter 5 136
    Back In The Big Time And The Maxwell Years ....
Chapter 6 168
    The Dream Team, Lionel Pickering, The End Of The Cox Era And Play Off Pain ....
Chapter 7 196
    McFarland Gone, Jim Smith In, The Croatian Influence And Goodbye To The Baseball Ground ....

Chapter 8 220
   Pride Park Stadium, The Italian Job And Mcclaren Departure ....

Chapter 9 232
   The Fuertes Fiasco, The £3 Million Men And Taribo West.

Chapter 10 246
   Smith Out, Todd In And Out, Gregory And The Dreaded Drop..

Chapter 11 259
   The George Burley Years, Lionel Pickering's Sad End And The 'Three Amigos' ....

Chapter 12 280
   Phil Brown, The End Of The 'Three Amigos', Peter Gadsby, Billy Davies And Play-Off Success At Last...........

Chapter 13 298
   GSE, 11 Points And 'Worst Team In History' ....

Chapter 14 306
   Jewell Out And The Nigel Clough Years............................

Chapter 15 338
   McClaren, Play-Off Heartache (With A Capital H), Mel Morris And The Crazy End To 2014/15................................

Chapter 16 359
   McClaren Out, Clement In And Out And Wassall In...........

Chapter 17 367
   Four Managers In One Season ....

Chapter 18 383

Rowett Leaves And Super Frankie Lampard ....

Chapter 19 396

Lampard Back To Chelsea And Derby's First Continental Manager Phillip Cocu..

Chapter 20 406

Fifty Years Of Watching Derby County Completed, 'Survival Saturday' And The Euro 2020 Bonus....................

FOREWORD BY MARTIN FISHER

My love for Derby County goes back to the distant days of Clough and Taylor. Whilst my dad and brothers were regular visitors to the Baseball Ground, I was considered too young and had to make do with the occasional glimpse of games on ITV's Star Soccer.

By the time I started Ravensdale Junior School, that interest had become a passion. On my first morning I was plonked on a desk next to a lad called John. Initial shyness quickly vanished as we discovered a shared love of football, and more specifically The Rams. I was SO impressed when he revealed he had actually been to the BBG!!

During lessons we would talk incessantly about our team, while in the playground we became them. Mini-McFarlands and Hectors as our gang chased a tennis ball around, scattering bemused girls and dinner ladies to all corners. I was probably commentating as we did it. A particularly high-pitched Hugh Johns.

By the fourth year we had graduated to the school team. John was our top scorer. An old-fashioned number nine. Fearless. He scored many a diving header. That year we won the League and so did Derby County. Happy boys.

As we got older trips to the BBG had become commonplace. By the time we were teenagers, a group of us had started venturing further afield. Away grounds in the 1980's. Oh what joy!! Famously once to avoid being beaten up outside Villa Park, John and I ran all the way to Perry Barr. It was the first and last time that I came close to completing a four-minute mile. Meanwhile John had discovered a new hobby!

Inevitably we lost touch over time but recently, thanks to the wonders of WhatsApp, a group of us have reconnected. Most of the 'Michigan Old Boys' are season-ticket holders. They meet up for a social drink or two before or after games. Occasionally both! Sometimes I'm able to make it too. Frequently the football is incidental, but it's always the bond. The glue that holds us all together. And whenever we can't recall a particular game or goal scorer from the past, we ask John to delve deep into his memory bank......

Out of us all, he's clocked up the most miles. Hundreds of games. The highs and the many lows. Whether it's players or play-offs, managers or owners, promotions or relegations, it's all here.

So, pick up a copy and revisit the ups and downs of Derby County's history through the eyes of one of your own.

Martin

INTRODUCTION

On Saturday 3 April 2021, it was fifty years since I first saw Derby County play a League match at the Baseball Ground as a six-year-old, two months before my seventh birthday. What a white knuckle ride those fifty years have been. I doubt whether any other club in England has witnessed such a chequered history of up and downs both on and off the field.

In this time, Derby have been Champions of England twice, FA Charity Shield winners, European Cup semi-finalists, played in the UEFA Cup twice, FA Cup semi- finalists, League Cup semi-finalists, relegated to the second tier four times, survived a battle in the High Court, relegated to the third tier, promoted to the second tier once, promoted to the top tier three times, second tier play-off finalists four times (winning once and losing three), and second tier play-off losing semi-finalists four times. One of the major developments was the move from the atmospheric but dilapidated Baseball Ground to the 33,000 plus all seater stadium Pride Park, which was opened by Her Majesty the Queen in July 1997. Remarkably, I've seen twenty-four managers that have been through the revolving doors of both the Baseball Ground and Pride Park, which probably confirms the reason why Derby have had this chequered history. But it's never been dull; it's been crazy at times, with very few seasons resulting in mid-table mediocrity.

All the opinions in the book are my own, some you will agree with, some you won't agree with. My story is possibly typical of a young boy obsessed with sport, especially football, growing up through the late 1960s and early 1970s in the days when parks were full of boys playing football every night as their main interest, without the distraction of things like social media and computer games. The majority of my school friends and I had a fantastic childhood.

Life would be boring if everyone liked the same thing. There is a sprinkling of cricket and running in the book, which are two other sporting passions of mine. There's also some travel as it has links to some of the games. I'm not a fan of other sports like Formula One, as I've never ever watched a Grand Prix, or any American Sports as I hate all the razzmatazz. So here is my season-by-season account with some fantastic memories and some not so good. The focus is mainly on memorable home games and all the away games I've been to during this time. I've seen Derby play at eighty of the other current ninety-one League clubs.

CHAPTER 1

CHAMPIONS OF ENGLAND AND EUROPEAN NIGHTS

1970/71

My dad fortunately was a big football fan. Apparently, I was always pestering him to let me go with him to watch Derby County. So, on Friday 19 March 1971, we went to see Derby Reserves v Liverpool Reserves at the Baseball Ground in the Central League, as it was called in those days. We sat in the C Stand for the game, under floodlights. I later found out that the attendance was around 11,000, quite remarkable for a reserve game. I recently managed to obtain the match day programme for this game which would have cost me two pence on the night. I found out there were some big names playing in the game; the late John Robson, Peter Daniel and Alan Durban for Derby. Tommy Lawrence, Roy Evans and Ron Yeats lined up for Liverpool. Unfortunately, I cannot find out the score and sadly my dad is no longer here to ask.

This whetted my appetite for more, so a couple of weeks later on Saturday third April, I made my League debut at the Baseball Ground, standing on the Vulcan Street pop side for the visit of Huddersfield Town, who were in the bottom five of

Division One. To ensure we got a decent view we had to get to the ground at one p.m., two hours before kick-off. That's unthinkable in this day and age of all seater stadiums, when most people take their seats as the players run out, five minutes prior to kick-off. Like most other kids of my age group, I had to take a box to stand on so I could see through the bottom of the pop side railings. Derby, who were mid-table, won the game 3-2 with two goals from Alan Hinton and one from Kevin Hector. Notable names in the Huddersfield line up were goalkeeper, David Lawson, who later moved to Everton, the late Trevor Cherry who played for Leeds United and England, and the mercurial late Frank Worthington, who notably played for Leicester City and Bolton Wanderers amongst a host of other clubs and gained eight full caps.

The next match I went to was the last match of the season against West Bromwich Albion on the first Saturday in May. The significance of this game was that it was the last game of the late Dave Mackay's Derby career at the age of thirty-six, before becoming player/manager at Swindon Town. Obviously at the time, I was far too young to appreciate his legendary status in the game. The highlight for him was being part of the Tottenham Hotspur double winning side of 1960/61. He also won the European Cup Winner's Cup with Tottenham and gained twenty-two full Scotland caps.

The finale of the 1970/71 season was the first FA Cup Final I can remember on the following Saturday between Arsenal and Liverpool. This was my first taste of the live TV coverage on both BBC and ITV, starting early in the morning, following the teams from their hotel on the bus to Wembley and mapping out the road to Wembley for the two teams. There was a special edition of It's a Knockout too. I absolutely loved it, as this was one of the very few live games on television in those days. As for the game, I remember it vividly. Steve Heighway put Liverpool ahead in extra time, beating Bob Wilson at the near post from a very acute angle, only for Eddie Kelly to equalise. Then Charlie George, who was to become one of Derby's greatest players, hit the winner from outside the box past the late Ray Clemence. I didn't know it at the time but the next few years were going to be the most successful in Derby's history.

1971/72

When I did the research for this book, I looked back through the fixture list for the 1971/72 season and I have very few recollections of the games that season. My only memory of a game I went to was the fourth round FA Cup 6-0 victory over Jimmy Sirrel's Notts County at the Baseball Ground. This win resulted in a tie against Arsenal in the fifth round which went to a second replay at a neutral ground Filbert Street, Leicester. This game at Leicester was played on a February midweek afternoon due to power cuts. I can remember the 'finale to the season' which lead to Derby being crowned Champions of England for the first time in their history. Derby had beaten Liverpool 1-0 thanks to a John McGovern goal in their final game and they then jetted off to Majorca with their fixtures complete. During the following midweek, Liverpool and Leeds United played at Arsenal and Wolverhampton Wanderers, respectively. To overtake Derby, Liverpool needed to win but only drew 0-0 at Arsenal. Leeds United needed a draw, but lost at Wolverhampton. Derby were Champions without kicking a ball. This would never happen in modern day football as all the final games are played simultaneously to suit the needs of satellite television. Derby were in the European Cup for the first time! We started a family tradition on FA Cup final day that was sadly short lived. My dad and I went to my Auntie Win and Uncle Les' house on Fleet Street in Normanton to watch the game, getting there about 2.45 p.m. This tradition only lasted for three years as Les died of a heart attack in 1975. He worked at Rolls-Royce and had a lovely bubbly character, and is sorely missed.

1972/73

So, the Champions of England were now in the European Cup with some of the biggest, iconic names in club football. Derby were in the hat along with the likes of Ajax, Bayern Munich, Juventus, Benfica, Real Madrid and Celtic. I much preferred the format of the European Cup to how it is nowadays as the Champions League. The purists say all of the best teams in Europe are involved, but I just see a lot of meaningless group games in the first stages, it's obvious who's going to qualify for the last sixteen and it's just a money-making exercise. Don't get me started on the Thursday night Europa League with again it's meaningless group games. Teams who play Thursday nights then have to play on Sundays which is a nightmare for the traditionalists who like their football mainly on a Saturday afternoon. If the tournament was a straight knockout like the old UEFA Cup, I would be fine with that.

Derby's first opponents were Zeljeznicar Sarajevo from the

former Federal Republic of Yugoslavia in the first round. This was a two-legged tie with the first leg at the Baseball Ground. As usual we had to arrive at the Baseball Ground two hours before kick-off to enable us to get a good vantage point. My dad and I stood on the Normanton Paddock. We were at the front, with my head just above the small white wall that ran along the length of the terrace that ran along from the corner flag to the players tunnel at the halfway line. The atmosphere and anticipation in the crowd rose as both teams took to the field with flag bearers with the Union Jack and Yugoslavian flag, leading out the teams as was the tradition with European football nights. Derby won the first leg comfortably 2-0, with goals from captain Roy McFarland and Archie Gemmill. Derby won the away second leg 2-1, in front of a crowd of nearly 60,000, a fortnight later and went through to the second round. Derby were then handed a plum draw in the second round. The Portuguese Champions, Benfica, with the legendary Eusebio in their team, were put to the sword by the rampant Rams who took a half time 3-0 lead with goals from Roy McFarland, Kevin Hector and John McGovern. We had our spot in the Normanton Paddock again in what the late Brian Clough called one of the greatest nights of his managerial career. The game finished 3-0 and the second leg at Benfica's Stadium of Light ended 0-0.

Derby were in dreamland and through to the European Cup quarter-finals at the first attempt! The quarter-final draw paired Derby with the former Czechoslovakian Champions Spartak Trnava, who had received a bye in the first round and beaten Belgian Champions Anderlecht to progress to the quarter-finals. The second-round ties were completed in

November and the quarter-finals wouldn't take place until March. The first leg was played in Trnava with the Czechs taking a 1-0 slender lead. Again, we stood on the Normanton Paddock in our usual spot, two goals either side of half time from Kevin Hector saw Derby home. My memory of his second goal was Hector swinging on the crossbar after the ball went in, something I've never seen a Derby player do since. More importantly Derby were 180 minutes away from the European Cup Final.

The draw for the semi-final paired Derby with the Italian giants Juventus, who included 1982 World Cup winning captain and goalkeeper Dino Zoff in their ranks together with the former England manager Fabio Capello, with the first leg to be played at the Stadio Comunale in Turin. Juventus took the lead in front of the 72,000 crowd, only for Kevin Hector to equalise two minutes later, so the teams went in at the break level, at 1-1. Two goals in the second half saw the hosts win the game 3-1. It was a controversial match, which was subject to subsequent allegations that the Italian club had bribed the match officials, leading Brian Clough to call the Italians "cheating bastards". So, Derby had it all to do in the return leg at the Baseball Ground, but had that all-important away goal in Turin. For the fourth successive match my dad and I took our place in the Normanton Paddock. What an atmosphere it was at the Baseball Ground as the teams took to the field with Derby players wearing red track suit tops pre-kick off. There was a huge Juventus support in the ground. I can remember massive Juventus black and white flags at the Osmaston End of the ground together with flares, with their billowing smoke, filling the dusky skies. I'd never seen anything like it! Derby had the majority of the possession but only created half chances in their search for an early goal that would ignite the crowd into a frenzy. They huffed and puffed but couldn't find that all important breakthrough. Their best chance was when Kevin Hector was hauled down in the box in the second half, only for the usually reliable Alan Hinton to hit his penalty past the left hand upright and into the Normanton End crowd. Roger Davies then carelessly got himself sent off, dubbed "disgraceful" by Clough for head butting Francesco Morini and Derby's chance had gone. Juventus played Ajax of Amsterdam, with the likes of Johan Cruyff, Johan Neeskens and Rudi Krol in their line-up, in the final in Belgrade. Johnny Rep scored the only goal in a 1-0 win for the Dutchmen, which was their third successive win in the tournament. My dad would have gone or at least would have tried to get a ticket for the final. I'm not sure if he would have taken a near nine-year-old with him!

Domestically as defending League Champions, by the end of November, the Rams were great at home with seven wins from nine games but had lost seven of their ten away games. This seemed to be a regular trend in the early 1970s, invincible at home but suspect away from home, with a 5-0 defeat at Elland Road against great rivals Leeds United confirming this. The most memorable home game of the 1972/73 was the 5-0 home win against the mighty Arsenal, managed by Bertie Mee. Derby were 4-0 up at half time with goals from John McGovern, Alan Hinton, Roy McFarland and Kevin Hector. Roger Davies with his first ever League goal in the second half completed the scoring. Alan Hinton, with his white boots, was magnificent that day.

The finest winger I've seen in my time at Derby, two great feet and a real dead ball specialist. He could put the ball on a sixpence. At the time of this game in late November, Arsenal were third in the League but Derby were off to a slow start to the season and were mid-table. At this stage, eight defeats suggested that the Championship this season was out of reach. We stood on the Normanton End terrace for this match.

In the next three months Roger Davies experienced an incredible high and low in his first full season following his £15,000 transfer from non-League Worcester City. It is very rare for a player to come straight from non-League to play in the top-flight English football, never mind the Champions of England. In the away game at Chelsea on the penultimate day of 1972, Davies rounded John Phillips in the Chelsea goal only to inexplicably run the ball out of play with an open goal in front of him. Davies more than made up for it with a hat-trick in the FA Cup fourth round replay at White Hart Lane against Tottenham Hotspur in front of a crowd in excess of 52,000, in one of the most remarkable matches in Derby's history. Derby came back from 3-1 down to win 5-3 after extra time. Kevin Hector scored the other two to give the Rams a famous victory. One abiding memory of the night was Derby's away kit of yellow shirts, white shorts and yellow stockings. I also went to the first game at the Baseball Ground which finished 1-1. I can remember the Tottenham keeper Pat Jennings heading the ball during the game, something I'd never seen before! The fifth-round saw Derby draw second tier Queen's Park Rangers at home, a game I also went to. Derby won 4-2, and we stood in front of the floodlight on the Vulcan End Pop side. A hat-trick from Kevin Hector saw Derby through to the sixth round. The draw for the sixth round paired Derby at home to arch rivals Leeds United. Strangely Derby played in all blue and Leeds in all red. I didn't go to the match but watched it on BBC's Match of the Day. The late Peter Lorimer's first half strike saw Leeds through to the semi-final.

I started to tune into Musical Grandstand on BBC Radio Derby around this time. This program covered midweek Derby games. The show which started at 7.25 p.m. was presented by Mike Ingham, who later became the BBC football correspondent and an ardent Plymouth Argyle fan, who sat in the BBC Radio Derby studio. The reporter at the ground was the late Barrie Ecclestone. The format of the show was to play music, and then if there was a significant piece of action or a goal in the game, Mike Ingham would cut in and go over to the ground for an update from Barrie Ecclestone. As I have previously stated, Derby were a bit suspect away from home. I used to fear the worst when Ecclestone gave his update. "It's bad news for Derby County" was his common opening line. My dad and I used to look at each other with wry smiles. "I knew that that was coming," my dad said. "It happens every time they go across to him".

The Derby Evening Telegraph and Saturday night 'Green Un' were great sources of in-depth information. The late Gerald Mortimer was a fantastic journalist reporting daily on all matters Derby County and my other love Derbyshire County Cricket Club. It was a sad day when Gerald died in December 2013. I followed his reports and stories for over forty years. He hardly missed a Derby County or Derbyshire match home or away. I thought what a great job to have! His knowledge of both clubs was second to none. I loved his style of reporting and I couldn't wait to get hold of the Derby Evening Telegraph when I got home from school and immediately turned to the back pages.

Also, I loved listening to BBC Radio's Sport on 2, which came on air on Tuesday and Wednesday evenings at 8.02 p.m. I used to go to bed and hold a small blue transistor radio on medium wave to my ear to listen to the coverage. It covered games from up and down the country, either in the League or in the domestic or European cup competitions. The presenter more often than not was the then BBC football correspondent the late Bryon Butler. Midweek games in those days started at 7.30 p.m., so the aim of the program was to go around the grounds up to half time, to get an update of the games' progress, and then they would announce which game would be selected for second half commentary. It was quite a coup in those days to be selected for the commentary. The commentators were the great late Peter Jones, who to this day is the best radio commentator I've heard, and Alan Parry, who is still going strong at the ripe old age of seventy-two. Peter Jones sadly died in 1990 at the age of sixty. I still remember now his very moving commentary as the horrific events at Hillsborough unfolded on that awful day in April 1989.
I loved the match day experience. We tended to park around the Cameron Road area near the Cavendish pub. The walk to the ground through the streets of Normanton was magical with the throbbing crowds, old men in their flat caps, programme sellers and badge and scarf sellers, the whiff of cigarette smoke, the smell of burgers and hot dogs, and for night games, seeing the first glimpse of the footlights down Shaftesbury Crescent. I couldn't wait for Saturday afternoons or

Wednesday nights whether I was going to the ground, or following via the radio and the teleprinter on BBC's Grandstand at around 4.40 p.m. when Derby were away. After the match, my dad and I would always visit my grandma's, my dad's mum, who lived on Peartree Street just up the road from the Portland Arms. I didn't really enjoy going there if I'm honest. It was a small terraced house which only had an outside toilet and a very small yard. I can still visualise her room now, with the TV in the corner and a carriage clock on the fireplace with my grandma sitting in her armchair. ITV's World of Sport with the late Dickie Davies was always on when we arrived, so we could watch the football results.

For some reason I felt a bit intimidated by her and have still got the vision of her looking a bit like Ena Sharples from Coronation Street! My sister Irene, who's older than me, who obviously knew her better than me, says she was a lovely kind-hearted lady. My analogy to Ena Sharples made her laugh, as she said she couldn't see the resemblance! Her house and the pub are no longer there, replaced by grass field that is now part of the Pear Tree School playing field. Even now when I infrequently visit the area, it always reminds of those visits when I couldn't get out of the house quick enough! The 1972/73 season saw Derby finish seventh in Division One and lose in the European Cup semi-finals. The Rams were also knocked out of the FA Cup sixth round in a season that promised so much but failed to deliver a trophy. What we didn't know at the time was the bombshell and the traumatic events about to unfold two months into the 1973/74 season.

1973/74

My first memory of the 1973/74 season was the home 6-2 win against Southampton towards the end of September. The Southampton side included goalkeeper Eric Martin with his flock of distinctive red hair, Terry Paine, who in eighteen seasons played over 800 games for the Saints, England striker Mick Channon, and the late Bobby Stokes, who scored the winning goal in the 1976 FA Cup Final against Manchester United. Kevin Hector scored another hat-trick for the Rams with the win moving them up to second in the table.

All was not well though behind the scenes, as tensions were rising between manager Brian Clough and the chairman, the late Sam Longson, who brought him to the club in 1967 from Hartlepool United. Longson was increasingly unhappy with Clough over his media commitments and TV appearances. He thought Clough was spending too much time on these commitments, to the detriment of the club. He didn't like that Clough allegedly was critical of football administrators, and also didn't like his verbal attacks on the likes of Don Revie, manager of arch rivals Leeds United. Longson feared his behaviour would cause Derby to feel the wrath of the Football Association. Longson was a great admirer of Clough's management skills and was prepared to offer him a long-term deal in exchange for Clough giving up these media commitments, but Clough would not agree. One move that angered Longson was the signing of David Nish for a British record fee of £250,000, without Clough liaising with the board of directors over this move. Clough and his assistant Peter Taylor resigned on the 16 October. The fans were in uproar over this and demanded Clough and Taylor be re-instated and wanted Longson to resign. There were protests around the ground and in the town. But Clough was gone and Derby had lost their most successful manager in their history.

To try and appease the club's supporters, Longson appointed ex-player Dave Mackay, who was the manager of our bitter rivals, Nottingham Forest. Obviously at the time, I wasn't aware of the significance of this upheaval. My dad was very disappointed with what had happened. He told me what a top player Clough was before a ruptured anterior cruciate ligament ended his playing career. In two-seventy-four appearances for Middlesbrough and Sunderland, he scored two-fifty-one goals, which is an absolutely phenomenal record. Alan Shearer, who I regard as the best striker I've ever seen in my life, scored two hundred and sixty Premier League goals in four hundred and forty-one games for Southampton, Blackburn Rovers and Newcastle United. That tells me how good Clough was. The great late Jimmy Greaves was also around at this time, so there was massive competition for places. I never saw Jimmy Greaves play live, but my dad raved about him though. It's said that great players don't make great managers. That's certainly not true of Brian Howard Clough, who went onto win the Championship and two European Cups with, dare I say it, Nottingham Forest. The best manager of his generation?

If you asked him, he was the top one!

How he never managed England is one of life's mysteries…
The day after Clough resigned, he was a pundit for ITV's coverage of the England v Poland World Cup qualifier at Wembley. This was the first time I ever watched England. The atmosphere at Wembley was raucous but tense. In those days

the only live games on TV were the FA Cup Final and crucial England games. England had to beat Poland to qualify for the 1974 World Cup Finals in West Germany. This was the night Clough called the Polish goalkeeper Jan Tomaszewski a 'clown', but he kept England at bay and they could only manage a 1-1 draw. Kevin Hector came on as a late substitute for England and had a header cleared off the line with his first touch of the ball in the last minute. Hector strangely only played for England twice.

Mackay had a massive job on his hands to continue the work Clough had started. One advantage he did have was that he was popular with the supporters during his playing days at the club. Clough also called him Tottenham Hotspur's greatest ever player. Praise indeed! Leicester City were the visitors for Mackay's first game. Kevin Hector gave Derby the lead in the first half, with Frank Worthington levelling for the Foxes. John McGovern's far post looping header gave Derby the win, so Mackay was off to a good start. During November, Mackay made his first signing with experienced Welsh international full-back Rod Thomas joining Derby from Swindon Town for £100,000. I was pestering my dad to take me to an away match, so after much deliberation on which game to go to, we set off for the away match at Molineux against Wolverhampton Wanderers on Saturday 1 December.

It was a really cold frosty day when we set off for the three p.m. kick off. As usual, we had the radio on in the car listening to BBC Radio's Sport on two. We must have got halfway there when we heard the game was postponed due to a frozen pitch! In those days there was no undersoil heating, so I was left very disappointed. One thing I remember heading back was that Bristol Rovers remarkably won 8-2 away at Brian Clough's Brighton and Hove Albion in a Third Division game. Bruce Bannister and Alan Warboys, who were known as 'smash and grab' scored seven of the goals between them for the 'Gas'. The game at Molineux was re-arranged for April. We sat opposite the stand with the 'concertina' type roof, with the massive South Stand terrace to our left. One thing I can remember from the night was that Phil Parkes the Wolves goalkeeper wore a red top. I'd only seen goalkeepers wear green in domestic games. Derby were not great away even in this era and were hammered 4-0! We left with five minutes to go at 3-0 only to get back in the car to find it ended up 4-0. Wolves were a decent team in those days with Geoff Palmer, Derek Parkin, Kenny Hibbert and John Richards in their line-up. They won the League Cup too that season. The next two home games I attended were the FA Cup third round tie against non-League Boston United from the Northern Premier League, who included ex-Derby full-back Phil Waller in their ranks and the League game at home to Burnley. Boston bought a huge 4,000 following with them from Lincolnshire. The game finished 0-0, and I can remember Boston hitting the inside of the post at the Osmaston End late in the second half with the ball rolling along the goal line before being hacked clear by a Derby defender. The replay four days later at York Street on the Wednesday afternoon saw the Rams run out 6-1 winners with a rare hat-trick from Archie Gemmill and a brace from the late Jeff Bourne. The home game against Burnley saw Kevin Hector bag another hat-trick in a 5-1 win and another brace for Jeff Bourne, the reserve striker, who was proving a more than adequate replacement for the injured Roger Davies.

The fourth round of the FA Cup paired Derby against Coventry City at Highfield Road with the game being played on Sunday 27 January. This was Derby's first ever fixture to be held on a Sunday, which attracted a crowd of over 41,000. The game finished 0-0, so it was back to the Baseball Ground for a Wednesday replay. A late Tommy Hutchinson goal gave Coventry victory in their distinctive green and black stripes away shirt. I don't know why but I always felt Coventry were the Rams' bogey side in the early seventies and we never seemed to beat them. Dave Mackay made his first significant signing in February 1974, with Bruce Rioch joining the club from Aston Villa for £200,000. Derby ended up finishing third in Division One, a good return considering the unexpected change of management, therefore qualifying for next season's UEFA Cup for the first time.

After the League season finished in May, club captain Roy McFarland was playing for England against Northern Ireland at Wembley in the home internationals, when he snapped his Achilles tendon and would face a year on the sidelines. What a blow to the club and to Dave Mackay, ahead of him starting his first full season as Derby manager.

In the summer of 1974, I had my taste of the World Cup that was being held in West Germany. I loved it as live football was on the TV most afternoons when I got home from school, and then again in the evening. My mum worked as a nurse at the old Manor Hospital in Derby from five o'clock until eight o'clock every evening, so I had license to watch as many games as I wanted as my dad was interested too! England failed to qualify following their failure to beat Poland in their final group game, so the only British interest was Scotland's involvement. They had some quality players in their squad with the likes of David Harvey, the late Billy Bremner, Gordon McQueen, Peter Lorimer, Joe Jordan, Kenny Dalglish, Tommy Hutchinson and Denis Law in their ranks. I can remember them beating Zaire in the group stage, but they failed to qualify for the second stage after draws against Yugoslavia and Brazil. The star team in the tournament in my opinion were the Netherlands, with most of their team coming from Ajax, who won the European Cup three times in a row in the early 1970s. The star man was the late Johan Cruyff, who will go down as one of the greats of the modern era. At that time, I was in my third year at Ravensdale Junior School. In the school playground all the budding footballers were trying to replicate the 'Cruyff turn'! West Germany won the tournament beating in the Netherlands 2-1 in the final with their goal machine the late Gerd Muller scoring one of the goals, with the late Jack Taylor from Wolverhampton refereeing the game. West Germany had great strength with the likes of Sepp Maier, Franz Beckenbauer, Paul Breitner and Gunter Netzer in their team. I loved the idea of all this live football and was already looking forward to the World Cup in Argentina in 1978.

1974/75

Apart from the World Cup, the summer of 1974 was memorable for me on three counts. Firstly, Derby signed Manchester City and former England striker Francis Lee for £100,000 who became Dave Mackay's major signing of the pre-season. Secondly, my dad bought us both season tickets in the Osmaston End middle tier seating on row M seats five and six. We sat close to the end of the row, next to two other men who were probably the same age of my dad. One of the men was a bit grumpy and my dad nicknamed him 'Happy'. The other man was very talkative and more friendly so dad nicknamed him 'Chatty'! Thirdly, I was picked to play for Ravensdale Junior School team for the season along with BBC's Match of the Day commentator Martin Fisher, Nigel Lee and Derek Lee. I'm still good friends with these three still today forty-six years later. Football was dominating my life. I just loved to go Bramblebrook Park in Mickleover in the evenings with my school mates when it was light enough; using coats for goalposts, we played until it was dusk. One bonus was to be allowed to play on the Ravensdale School pitch, courtesy of Jack Skertchley, the teacher who ran the football team who lived about a hundred yards from the school pitch.

Following Francis Lee's arrival, Mackay bought in Irishman Tony Macken from Waterford for £30,000. Macken though played the entire season in the reserve team. Derby's first opponents were Everton away, in a game that ended 0-0. I was travelling back from a family holiday in Scotland with my mum and dad, so fortunately, as far I was concerned, it wasn't a home game we missed as we now had season tickets! The first game we went to was the 1-1 draw with Coventry City on the following Wednesday night, a game in which Francis Lee scored on his home debut. Peter Daniel also played as he deputised for the injured captain Roy McFarland, who looked likely to miss the majority of the season due to his snapped Achilles tendon injury he suffered playing for England. Derby had a slow start to the season though only winning one of their first seven games. Derby's first opponents in the first round of the UEFA Cup were the relatively unknown Swiss outfit Servette. A couple of goals from Kevin Hector gave Derby a first leg lead of 4-1 to take to Geneva for the second leg which they duly won 2-1, moving comfortably through to the second round.

In the League Cup, Derby won 5-1 away at Portsmouth in the first round, only to get thrashed 5-0 at Southampton in the second round. The next round of the UEFA Cup saw Derby draw Spanish giants Athletico Madrid, with again the first leg being played at the Baseball Ground. The game finished 2-2 with Argentina striker Ruben Ayala, with his long black flowing locks, starring for Madrid. The second leg at the Vicente Calderón Stadium also ended 2-2 after ninety minutes and extra time. This resulted in Derby going to their first ever penalty shootout in their history. This ended going into sudden death with Colin Boulton saving a penalty, giving Derby a 7-6 victory. The home game between the two games against Athletico Madrid was against Middlesbrough, who were promoted as Champions from Division Two, under the guidance of the late Jack Charlton, who was part of the England team that won the 1966 World Cup. I loved the Middlesbrough kit of all red with the distinctive white sash across their shirt. I can remember they brought fanatical support that day with their masses stood on the Colombo End pop side. I was intrigued by some of the names in their line-up like, John Craggs, Stuart Boam, Willie Maddren, Frank Spraggon, Alan Foggon and John Hickton to name a few! Middlesbrough won the game 3-2 inflicting Derby to their first home defeat of the season and fourth overall.

At Ravensdale everything was going well and we were unbeaten in the League and had progressed in the Heath Smith Cup. We had a friendly at home to Allestree Lawn on a Friday afternoon around this time. The significance of this was Brian Clough rocking up in his silver Mercedes. Clough's son Simon, who I was to play against many times in my teenage years, was in the Lawn team. This caused quite a stir around the school as news of his arrival spread. On his walk from his car to the pitch, in his overcoat and wellington boots, he was followed by loads of school kids, paparazzi style, hoping to get a glimpse of his celebrity appearance. The game finished 1-1, my main memory was the huge crowd made of pupils and teachers watching.

In the following week, Derby travelled to Elland Road, Leeds for a game with their arch rivals, now managed by the late Jimmy Armfield who had replaced Brian Clough after his infamous forty-four days stint as their manager. A Francis Lee goal gave Derby a very rare but welcome win. The next home game was against the late Bobby Robson's Ipswich Town with Derby winning 2-0. My memory of that game was Bruce Rioch scoring Derby's second with a left foot cross shot that beat Laurie Sivell in the Town goal at the far post. Rioch wheeled away after scoring, celebrating with a somersault just down in front of us at the Osmaston End.

In the third round of the UEFA Cup, Derby were drawn against Velez Mostar from the old Yugoslavia. The first leg at the Baseball Ground on a very heavy pitch saw the visitors take a first half lead with an all-important away goal. In the second half Derby scored three with substitutes, the ever-reliable Jeff Bourne bagging two, and Alan Hinton hitting the other. In the evening when we got home, we watched the highlights of the game on Sportsnight on the BBC. Derby in this era of European football nights were regularly featured on Sportsnight and The Big Match on ITV as a highlights package. The second leg in Mostar saw Derby being knocked out losing 4-1 with a controversial penalty against a Colin Todd handball contributing to Derby's downfall. In 2014 my wife Julie and I visited Mostar with our good friends Steve and Dawn Hallam, whilst we were on holiday in Dubrovnik. We had a day trip there mainly to see the bridge, spanning the Neretva River, that had been rebuilt in 2004 following the Balkan War in the early nineties. Mostar now is part of Bosnia and Herzegovina and is a beautiful city full of cobbled streets with a mountainous background and is well worth a visit. As usual when I visit a town or city I try and find the football ground. Unfortunately, in Mostar I couldn't find it!

Derby at this stage were building some momentum, but away defeats at Everton and Luton Town just before Christmas set the Rams back in their charge up the League. The Christmas fixture at Manchester City provided me with one of my greatest memories in this era. Derby won 2-1; Henry Newton gave Derby the lead with a fine half volley strike from the edge of the box only for the late Colin Bell to equalise. Francis Lee then scored the winner in a game that was featured on BBC's Match of The Day. Barry Davies's commentary is the abiding memory. After Lee picked the ball up on the corner of City's box, Davies took over, "Lee, interesting, very interesting, look at his face, just look at his face", as the ball screamed in to the top corner of Joe Corrigan's net. I really liked Barry Davies on commentary. He and the late David Coleman were in my opinion the top TV commentators at this time. The New Year opened with a trip to Second Division Orient at Brisbane Road in the east end of London in the third round of the FA Cup in another game with extended highlights on BBC's Match of the Day. Orient went into a 2-0 lead early in the first half, but two rare goals from Colin Todd, his second only eight minutes from time, earned Derby a replay, as the away from home form continued to give them reasons for concern. Derby won the replay 2-1 to set up a fourth-round tie against Bristol Rovers, another Second Division outfit, who had just been promoted from the Third Division and a meet up with prolific lower League marksmen Bruce Bannister and Alan Warboys. In the League Derby started the year with five wins from eight games, but included two heavy away defeats at Queen's Park Rangers and Ipswich Town. Progress in the FA Cup was halted by old adversaries Leeds United, who won by the solitary goal in the fifth round at the Baseball Ground. Arsenal visited the Baseball Ground in February in a game that Derby won 2-1 with Steve Powell scoring twice. The game will be remembered though, for Arsenal having a very rare double sending off. England 1966 World Cup winner the late Alan Ball was sent off early in the first half, and left-back Bob McNab received his marching orders halfway through the second half. In mid-March Derby lost 2-1 at home to Stoke City on a quagmire of a pitch and it looked as if their title hopes had gone up in smoke. Four successive wins though put them right-back in the mix. A 2-0 win at Newcastle United was the forerunner to quite a remarkable Easter. On Easter Saturday,

Derby hammered Luton Town 5-0 with all five scored by Roger Davies who also had two disallowed. On Easter Monday a trip to Turf Moor, Burnley, saw the the Rams run out 5-2 winners with two goals from Hector, and a goal each from Rioch, Nish and Davies. Their third game in four days, unheard of these days of modern football, at Manchester City saw the Rams win 2-1 with two goals from Bruce Rioch who was certainly repaying the faith put in him by manager Dave Mackay following his big money move from Aston Villa. Derby fielded the same team in all three games which was a great testament to their fitness.

An away draw at Middlesbrough was followed by two crucial 1-0 home wins against Wolverhampton Wanderers, the game which saw the return Roy McFarland to the starting line-up following his injury layoff and West Ham United. A 0–0 draw away to Leicester City on the penultimate Saturday of the season in a game I went to with my dad and brother-in- laws Pete Birks and the late John Russell, which was my third ever away game. We stood on the East Stand terrace at Filbert Street, level with the eighteen-yard box with a double decker stand to our left and to the right there were executive boxes at the back of a small seating area of orange seats. One minor detail I can remember is that Derby wore red socks with their white shirts and navy shorts to avoid a clash with Leicester's white socks. This result combined with Ipswich Town's draw at Manchester City a few days later, confirmed the Rams as Champions for the second time in four years. The final game of the season against already relegated Carlisle United was an anti-climax and finished 0-0. Dave Mackay and his assistant Des Anderson lead the team out in front of stand in skipper for the season Archie Gemmill onto the Baseball Ground pitch in the April sunshine. The players proudly donned their white tracksuit tops with the words 'CHAMPIONS' emblazoned on the back. It was double delight for Derbyshire that day as Matlock Town beat Scarborough 4-0 in the FA Trophy final with the three Fenoughty brothers Tom, the late Mick and Nick in their line-up.

So, after all the turmoil of October 1973 with the acrimonious departure of Brain Clough, Sam Longson had the last laugh with the appointment of the infectious Scotsman Dave Mackay as manager. Derby were Champions of England for the second time in four years. Colin Boulton was a top goalkeeper who probably would have played for England if he'd not played in the same era as Peter Shilton and Ray Clemence. The full-backs complimented each other, the ever-reliable Ron Webster and classy England international David Nish. The admirable centre-half Peter Daniel who was named Player of the Year as he deputised for Roy McFarland. He partnered Colin Todd who was named PFA Player of the Year. He was one of the great players of his era and it still baffles me on how he only managed twenty-seven England caps. The midfield trio of Archie Gemmill, with his tremendous work ethic, great balance and lovely left foot, the unsung hero Henry Newton and Bruce Rioch, a goal scoring powerhouse who despite his left foot played on the right side of the three. Francis Lee added an experienced head in the twilight of his career, together with the workhorse Roger Davies who created a lot of goals for the 'King' Kevin Hector whose League record of one hundred and fifty-five goals in four hundred and eighty-six games speaks for itself. This first eleven was backed up by Jeff Bourne who scored vital goals when he deputised for one of the strikers, and thirty-three-year-old winger and fans favourite Alan Hinton, who was in the final year of his Derby career.

One observation was Derby's record as Champions, bearing in mind it was two points for a win back in those days:

Played 42 Won 21 Draw 11 Lost 10 Points 53

It's remarkable that you could win the League losing ten games. Comparing Derby's record with Manchester City winning the Premier League in 2018-19 record of:

Played 38 Won 32 Draw 2 Lost 4 Points 98

And Liverpool winning the Premier League in 2019-20 record of:

Played 38 Won 32 Draw 3 Lost 3 Points 99

This just confirms the 'Big Six' domination of modern-day football and the impact of financial clout dominating (and arguably ruining or having ruined) the game as it currently stands. The top teams have massive squads full of international stars. In the early seventies the top players were distributed more fairly around all the teams and it was a lot harder to predict who would claim the League honours. Only Blackburn Rovers and Leicester City have won the Premier League outside the 'Big Six' since its inception in 1992. Manchester

United and Tottenham Hotspur were relegated from the top tier in 1973/74 and 1976/77 respectively. It's hard to imagine that this will ever happen again.

On a personal note, Ravensdale School team won the League and Cup double under the guidance of Jack Skertchley who selected an unusual 3-4-3 formation, which Martin Fisher described as being 'ahead of his time' when we were reminiscing recently! I loved playing in our kit of blue shirts with white sleeves, white shorts and blue and white hooped socks. It was a great thrill to play with a white Mitre match ball and play with goal nets, which was a rarity in those days. The white Mitre match ball was certainly an upgrade on the laced brown leather ball we used during training and practice games. For energy, we took dextrosol energy tablets to keep us going! In the League we won all our League games home and away against Ashgate, Brackensdale, Reigate, Silverhill, Portway and Wren Park. We drew the two games 1-1 against our local rivals Mickleover, with both games drawing big crowds to watch. We ended up Champions as Mickleover matched our results but lost 2-0 in a game against Reigate. We also won the Heath Smith Cup with a 4-2 win against Cherry Tree Hill in the final, which was held at Brackensdale School. We beat St James' and Springfield on the way to the final. Great memories that will last forever!

The team was:

Keith Wilshere
Nigel Lee, Martin Clarke, Mark Bowden
Neil Dunn (c), Gordon Lamb, Derek Lee, Michael Kean

Shaun Skelton, John Taylor, Martin Fisher

Sub: Graham Stevenson

Squad Player: Roger Page

Reserve Goal Keeper: John Dorrell

I cannot believe schools nowadays do not play competitive League games and only friendlies. What's that all about? You need that competitive edge as young as possible to help you develop through the ages as a player or surely, you'll struggle when you get older. I think this is so poor and a sad indictment of the world we live in today.
It was time for Derby to have another crack at the European Cup and the bonus of a trip to Wembley for the FA Charity Shield to play West Ham United in the curtain raiser for the 1975/76 season. They had beaten Fulham in the FA Cup Final in a game that I missed, as I went on a school trip to Chamonix in France.

1975/76

In preparation for the 1975/76 season, Dave Mackay pulled off a master stroke by signing Charlie George from Arsenal, who was now supporting a 1970's style perm instead of his long hair, where he'd scored thirty-one goals in one hundred and thirty-three games for the North London outfit. Alan Hinton left Derby having a short spell in North America for Dallas Whitecaps and Vancouver Whitecaps. I suffered a major disappointment before the season and I was left absolutely gutted. My mum and dad always booked our summer holiday quite early in the year to avoid the disappointment of missing out on where they would like to stay, but I wish they'd not booked it! They'd booked for the three of us to have our annual trip to Kirkcudbrightshire in south west Scotland for a week starting on Saturday 9 August. What we didn't realise at the time that this was the day of the Charity Shield at Wembley. Obviously, I wanted for us to cancel the holiday and go to Wembley but my mum was having none of it. So, on a hot sunny morning we were on our way to Scotland and not London. I hate it now if anybody asks me if I went. It brings back bad memories, even though Derby won 2-0 with goals from Kevin Hector and Roy McFarland! Derby's home shirt for this season is one of my two favourites. A plain white shirt with an open vee neck but with a navy-blue collar and a blue trim on the sleeves. They kept with the blue shorts, which they changed from black at the start of the 1971/72 season, with white socks too. The goal nets at the Baseball Ground also changed from white to green for some reason.

Derby made a fairly inauspicious start to the League season. After away draws in the opening two games, Queen's Park Rangers won 5-1 at the Baseball Ground which was Charlie George's home debut. Rangers, under the late Dave Sexton, were a top side in those days with Phil Parkes, the late Dave Clement, Ian Gillard, England captain Gerry Francis, Dave Thomas, Don Givens and Stan Bowles, who scored a hat-trick in their squad. Bowles was a great player to watch, lovely poise and balance and a very cultured left foot. One of the games great characters, it was very sad to hear that he was reported to be suffering from Alzheimer's disease. Gerry

Francis scored BBC's Goal of the Season on Match of the Day finishing off a passing move that started in their own half in their home game against Liverpool. The first round of the eagerly awaited European Cup saw Derby being pitted against Slovan Bratislava from the old Czechoslovakia. The first leg was away with Derby slipping to a 1-0 defeat with a goal from Czech international striker Marian Masny, who was part of Czechoslovakia's 1976 European Championship winning team. My next away game, and my third away ground, was a visit to the Victoria Ground for the game against Stoke City at the end of September.

Stoke were a pretty strong side in those days with Peter Shilton, Denis Smith, Mike Pejic, Alan Hudson and Jimmy Greenhoff playing for them. Derby's form away from home again deserted them, with Greenhoff scoring the only goal to give Stoke the points. Three months after this game I can remember that a powerful storm hit the Stoke area, and one of the stands had its roof blown off by the strong winds and the ground this was closed while repair work was carried out. I spoke to Steve Hallam, my friend of thirty-five years, who despite living in Derby all his life is an avid Stoke City fan. He told me their bitter rivals Port Vale had offered Stoke the use of their Vale Park ground whilst the stand was being repaired. Stoke took up the offer for one game and they beat Middlesbrough 1-0 with a goal from the late Ian Moores. I couldn't imagine Port Vale offering Stoke use of their ground nowadays!

In the return leg of the European Cup game against Slovan Bratislava, the Rams dominated the game in front of a capacity crowd of 38,000 to win 3-0 with goals from substitute Jeff Bourne and two from Francis Lee, who also had a penalty saved. As usual when we arrived home, we watched the extended highlights which were on ITV Sports Midweek Soccer Special with commentary from the late Hugh Jones, who was also the regular commentator for ITV's Star Soccer which covered games from the Midlands on Sunday afternoons. Johns was also a fine commentator in his own right. In the second round of the European Cup, Derby received an absolutely plum draw with Real Madrid the Spanish Champions, arguably the biggest club side in the world. This night was probably my highlight of fifty years supporting Derby. Real Madrid included Paul Breitner who was part of the West Germany 1974 World Cup winning team. We took our usual seats in the Osmaston middle tier with an electric atmosphere in the ground. Charlie George gave Derby the lead inside ten minutes with a superb left foot strike from the edge of the box, with the ball screaming into the back of the net and was past Miguel Angel before he could move. It was fantastic technique and we were fortunate to be right in line with the strike. It will go down as one of the finest goals I've seen Derby score live with Barry Davies again on commentary, "Todd, all bar Boulton in the Real half, here's David Nish, Gemmill, George, oh what a cracker, applause all around the ground and my word he deserves it. That's as good a first time shot as you'll ever see. Really, brilliant goal." Five minutes later Francis Lee was brought down in the box and George scored his second, converting from the spot. Pirri pulled one back, giving Real an all-important away goal, but David Nish restored Derby's two goal advantage just before half time. George completed his hat-trick with a second penalty in the second half giving Derby a 4-1 lead to take into the second leg in Madrid. What a famous victory! My memory of the night was the whole ground singing "Oh, when the Rams go marching in." I had to pinch myself when I woke up in the morning and went off the school with a spring in my step and a smile from ear to ear. It doesn't get much better than that.

Before the second leg in Madrid, on Saturday 1 November, arch rivals Leeds United visited the Baseball Ground in what turned out to be a very fiery, infamous afternoon. As usual, the Leeds travelling fans packed out the Columbo pop side with their trademark of swinging their white, blue and yellow scarfs above their heads. As the years passed by, I began to hate this! I was probably envious of their away following, because at midweek games at places like Southampton, they would always sell their allocation of tickets without any problem at all. As far as the game was concerned Trevor Cherry put Leeds ahead with a free header from a Peter Lorimer corner. Derby equalised when Archie Gemmill slid in to shoot home, following David Harvey in the Leeds goal parrying a cross shot from Charlie George. George then converted from the spot following a Norman Hunter trip on Francis Lee that was the start of an ongoing feud between the two players that lead to a fight between the two inside the Leeds penalty area at the start of the second half. After referee the late Derek Nippard had dealt with the situation and booked Hunter and Lee, the fight continued near the touchline in front of the Normanton Paddock. A melee between most of the players ensued and the two players were finally sent off, with the late Gordon Guthrie, the Derby physiotherapist, running on the pitch to restrain Lee and get him off and down the tunnel to avoid any further misdemeanours. This was the first time in watching Derby in a domestic League game that I'd seen players fighting on the pitch and subsequently getting sent off. The only previous incident was Roger Davies getting sent off in the European Cup semi-final against Juventus. The game continued to ebb and flow, with the Leeds pressure resulting in Duncan McKenzie levelling. But with two minutes to go, substitute Roger Davies cut in to the box from the right and drilled a left foot shoot past David Harvey's right hand to give Derby a famous 3-2 victory. For Roger Davies this was the start of him earning the nickname 'super sub' from the Derby faithful.

Onto to the world famous Bernabeu Stadium in Madrid. Could Derby preserve their 4-1 advantage from the first leg in front of 120,000 fans in a deafening noise, which is the highest attendance they had ever played in? I was listening to Musical Grandstand on BBC Radio Derby with Mike Ingham in the studio and Barrie Ecclestone out in Madrid, on what was going to be a long, tense night. Real shot into a three-goal lead with two goals from Roberto Martinez, before Charlie George pulled a goal back on the hour to give the Rams hope. A soft penalty though which was converted from Pirri restored parity for Real and ensured the game went into extra time. Derby were out on their knees when Santillana put Real 5-1 up on the night, and 6-5 on aggregate.

It was so heart breaking to go out after having the 3-goal advantage from the first leg. This turned out to be Derby's last ever fixture in the European Cup. I doubt if I will ever see them playing in the Champions League in my life time. Before the end of the month, Derby signed Welsh international winger

Leighton James, in a £300,000 deal from Burnley. In the last game before Christmas, Derby beat Sheffield United at the Baseball Ground. I can remember it being very cold and watching the sleet and snow showers coming over the Osmaston End roof. The Rams won the game 3-2 with Charlie George yet again on the scoresheet. Alan Woodward who played on the right wing, with his distinctive silver hair and England player Tony Currie were United's two best players. The previous season, Currie scored in United's 1975 game against West Ham United. The game was on BBC's Match of the Day with commentator John Motson producing his famous line: "A quality goal, from a quality player," as Currie picked the ball up just inside the West Ham half, went on a mazy run, before beating Mervyn Day with a low shot from the edge of the box.

As always, I was looking forward to the FA Cup in January. Derby had drawn Everton at home in the third round, in what was a really tough encounter. Charlie George scored his fifteenth and sixteenth goals of the season, but Everton still put Derby under a lot of pressure, yet they didn't convert their chances, until a Gary Jones goal was far too late. Liverpool were Derby's opponents in the fourth round and Derby had home advantage again. Liverpool, managed by the late Bob Paisley who had replaced the late Bill Shankly, would be a tough nut to crack. This was the time when they started to dominate domestic and European football. What a line-up they had, which was full of household names. Ray Clemence in goal. A back four of the late Tommy Smith, the late Emlyn Hughes, Phil Thompson and Phil Neal. The midfield trio of the late Ray Kennedy, who had suffered from Parkinson's disease for over thirty years, Ian Callaghan, who holds the record for most appearances for Liverpool and Jimmy Case. Steve Heighway played wide left with John Toshack and Kevin Keegan, who were as good as any front two in the country. Derby managed a great 1-0 win with 'super sub' Roger Davies bundling in the winner from close range following a strong run down the wing and cross from Bruce Rioch. The fifth-round draw was again kind to Derby with another home draw. This time their opponents were Division Three Southend United who had beaten Swansea City, Dover Athletic, Brighton and Hove Albion and Cardiff City to progress to this stage. It was a scrappy game, but Bruce Rioch's goal gave Derby a 1-0 win and a place in the last eight of the FA Cup. I was dreaming of the twin towers of Wembley. Could it be our year? Luck was with Derby and yet again the draw was favourable with yet another home draw.

Newcastle United were the visitors for the sixth round. The game turned out to be a classic encounter and one of my favourite games of all time. Newcastle suffered a blow in the week before the game with their Northern Irish goalkeeper Ian McFaul injured. He was replaced by Eddie Edgar in what would be his only ever appearance for the club. Bruce Rioch was again in the goals and he scored twice after only fifteen minutes. His second goal was a thunderous strike from a free kick on the edge of the box. Even if there had been three goalkeepers, none of them would have saved it. Alan Gowling pulled one back before half time before Henry Newton's twenty-five-yard strike restored Derby's two goal advantage. Then Charlie George scored another of my all-time Derby favourite goals. A long kick from Derby keeper Graham

Moseley, who had replaced Colin Boulton ironically after Derby's 4-3 defeat in February in the League game at Newcastle, was headed on by George to Kevin Hector who back-heeled the ball into George's path, who then strode into the box before steering the ball past Egdar to make it 4-1. Alan Gowling added a second for Newcastle late on but Derby had done it and reached the FA Cup semi-final.

One strange thing I remember from the evening of the Newcastle game, Cilla Black hosted a series on the BBC during this time that was aired around eight p.m. The Derby v Newcastle game was on Match of The Day, so obviously the TV cameras were in the Derby area. One of the themes of the Cilla show (as it was called) was for Cilla Black to pay a surprise random visit to someone's home. On this occasion she visited a house in Harrington Street which was a road leading down to the Normanton End and Ley Stand corner at the Baseball Ground. I said to my mum and dad before the show, as we were regular viewers, that she would carry out the visit in Derby beforehand as it tended to happen in towns or cities where the Match of the Day cameras were! I couldn't imagine that happening nowadays. Just to confirm this program wasn't Surprise Surprise, which was also presented by Cilla Black, but was on ITV and didn't start until 1984! On Monday, it was the semi-finals draw. The other teams involved were the late Tommy Docherty's Manchester United, Division Two Southampton and Division Three Crystal Palace. I took my transistor radio to school to listen to the draw at 12.30 p.m. that was conducted very professionally by the late Ted Croker who was secretary of the Football Association. "The next item on the agenda is the draw for semi-finals of the Football

Association Challenge Cup," he said in his dulcet tone. I much preferred how the draw was done then compared to now in its 'razzmatazz' style for television.

I had now left Ravensdale Junior School and had started Mickleover Senior School which is now Murray Park Community School. The main school buildings were still incomplete, so the four forms of one hundred and twenty pupils were taught in temporary buildings at the junction of Western Road and Uttoxeter Road adjacent to the bridge over the A38 road. At 12.30 p.m. the draw took place, with the main objective to avoid Manchester United and be drawn against one of the two clubs from the lower divisions. Unfortunately, lady luck wasn't on our side and Derby drew Manchester United. The game was to be played on neutral ground at Hillsborough, the home ground of Sheffield Wednesday. In the other game Southampton would play Crystal Palace at Stamford Bridge, the home ground of Chelsea. My two brothers-in-law queued up all night at the Baseball Ground in an attempt to secure tickets for the semi-final. Thankfully they succeeded in getting four tickets so we were off to Sheffield on Saturday 3 April.

Derby's League form was good since the turn of the New Year with six wins, three draws and two defeats in their eleven games whilst progressing in the FA Cup. They were fourth in the League table only two points behind leaders Queens Park Rangers with seven games left before Stoke City visited for a midweek game towards the end of March. It turned out though a very significant evening for all the wrong reasons. The game finished 1-1, but more importantly Charlie George suffered a dislocated shoulder following a collision with Stoke skipper Denis Smith in front of the Normanton Paddock. George was subsequently ruled out for the season and would miss the FA Cup semi-final in ten days' time. Stoke midfielder Alan Hudson broke his leg in the same match but managed to walk off the pitch. Onto Hillsborough for the most important match of the season. We went to Sheffield on a coach from Rolls-Royce where my dad worked. We saw some shocking scenes, with fights and scuffles breaking out on the walk to the ground from the coach park. It was all quite intimidating and the first time I'd witnessed this type of thing. I was amazed when we walked into the 55,000-capacity stadium, everyone standing on the terraces were packed in like sardines. It was only the fifth ground I'd been to and was by far the best. There was a massive cantilever stand to the left and the Main Stand on the right. Opposite was the Spion Kop which was divided equally between the two sets of fans separated by a central gangway. We were sat in the Upper Stand of the Leppings Lane End with fellow Derby fans with Manchester United fans stood below us on the terracing. The atmosphere was electric but very tense as the players emerged from the tunnel to a crescendo of noise, with the Derby fans releasing their blue and white balloons. Derby were a very experienced side, with Roger Davies picked to replace Charlie George, partnering Kevin Hector up front with Leighton James on the left wing. United were mainly a young and up and coming side with a sprinkling of experience with Alex Stepney, Stewart Houston and Martin Buchan the older heads amongst the younger players, such as Gerry Daly, Gordon Hill, Steve Coppell and Stuart Pearson. 1974 World Cup referee Jack Taylor from Wolverhampton was the man in charge as Derby kicked off playing towards the Leppings Lane End. United dominated early on and after a Derby move broke down in the United half, it was no surprise when winger Gordon Hill gave United the lead with a superb curling left foot shot from the edge of the box into the top corner of Graham Moseley's net in the Derby. We were right in line with it and Moseley stood no chance. Barry Davies again was the commentator on BBC's Match of the Day and I can recall his commentary. "Hill tries to curl it and does, Gordon Hill." The United fans all around the ground went wild with delight and there was a deafening noise. Derby were struggling to impose themselves on the game. David Nish scored a goal that was disallowed when he chipped the ball over the United defence, chased it through to pick the ball up himself to shoot past Alex Stepney. There were Derby players in an offside position who weren't interfering with play but the goal was ruled out. Derby protested to no avail. With the modern-day use of the Video Assistant Referee, the goal nowadays would probably have stood, but this was 1976!

United were the better side and Gordon Hill's deflected shot that struck Steve Powell six minutes from time sealed Derby's fate. I hardly ever saw Derby lose in this era and this was hard to take. The Charlie George injury was a major factor as he was arguably in the best player in the country at the time. This defeat is regarded by many supporters of my age and older as a major watershed in Derby's history. If they had won and gone on to win the FA Cup their whole subsequent history may have been different. This day still haunts me today and each year when 3 April comes around it brings back painful memories. I was obsessed with the FA Cup which in those days was the best tournament in the world. It really saddens me in modern times that the tournament isn't taken seriously as it should be. The financial rewards of the Premier League are so great that the FA Cup is now of secondary importance. Teams field below strength teams now and attendances have suffered greatly. The FA Cup Final is now just another match with the obscene amount of live football now available on satellite television. We left the ground under a massive crush, as I was carried along with my feet off the ground, and my dad and brothers-in-law got quite frightened, as they thought we would lose each other. It was if there were too many spectators at that end of the ground. The events of the Hillsborough disaster of 1989 when ninety-six Liverpool fans lost their lives at the Leppings Lane End of the ground was one of the most upsetting scenes I've seen and didn't come as a surprise. Sadly, this has now risen to ninety-seven lost lives.

As the events of that day unfolded my dad and I recalled our day there and what we had witnessed thirteen years earlier. The Rams ended the season with a remarkable 6-2 win against Ipswich Town at Portman Town in what was Francis Lee's final match of this career. Lee, Bruce Rioch and Kevin Hector all scored twice as the curtain came down on the season. Liverpool were League Champions with Derby finishing fourth and therefore qualifying for the UEFA Cup. The FA Cup was won by Lawrie McMenemy's Southampton who surprisingly beat Manchester United 1-0. As usual I watched the coverage of the whole day only to miss the goal as I needed the toilet. Oh well!

1976/77

Derby sold Roger Davies to Club Bruges for £135,000 before the start of the season. Davies had been a good servant to Derby following his £15,000 move from non-League

Worcester City in 1971. He had scored thirty-one goals in one hundred and fourteen appearances. In their third game of the season, Derby entertained Manchester United at the Baseball Ground in a game that ended goalless. This was the first time I'd witnessed hooliganism inside a ground, as the United fans from the Colombo pop side spilled onto the pitch during the game to confront the Derby fans who were stood on the Osmaston terrace. I had seen it at Hillsborough in April and United had a growing reputation for hooliganism which was becoming part and parcel of football in this era. Order was eventually restored but it was an ugly sight for a twelve-year-old boy.

It was Derby's second venture into the UEFA Cup. Their first-round opponents were Irish part timers Finn Harps. I stood on the Osmaston terrace for this game with Chris Stevenson, as my dad was away with work. Finn Harps were extremely poor and out of their depth as Derby went into a 9-0 lead at half time, eventually running out 12-0 winners. Kevin Hector scored five, Charlie George and Leighton James bagged hat-tricks with Bruce Rioch completing the scoring. Derby won the second leg 4-1 at Finn Park to book their place in the second round. Derby suffered an embarrassing 5-1 defeat to Birmingham City, with Kenny Burns scoring four. Burns played as a striker in those days before Brian Clough converted him into a central defender when he joined and had great success at Nottingham Forest in the late 1970s and early 1980s. I went to Meadow Lane for a second round League Cup replay against Notts County. We stood on the open terrace behind the goal with the Main Stand to our right. Bruce Rioch scored twice as Derby progressed though. My memory of that night was Derby wearing an away kit of red shirts, white shorts and green socks.

Derby recorded on one of the biggest wins in their history in October. They beat Tottenham Hotspur 8-2, who would end the season bottom of the League, with Bruce Rioch scoring four. Remarkably this was Derby's first League win of the season. This was the first match my nephew, Matt Birks, who was only four years old at the time, attended. What a start! I would go with Matt to a lot of away games in the early 1990s, as he accumulated his away ground collection. Derby travelled to Athens to play AEK in the second round of the UEFA Cup and lost 2-0. The return at the Baseball Ground wasn't much better as Derby's poor start to the season continued as they lost 3-2 in front of a fanatical travelling support decked in gold and black. Sadly, this turned it to be Derby's last ever match in the major European competitions. Following the defeat at Everton, Dave Mackay asked the board for a vote of confidence, but this was not forthcoming and was sacked by chairman George Hardy who had replaced Sam Longson. They were seventeenth in the League having only won two games with seven draws and eight defeats. I thought this was quite harsh on Mackay as his record in the three years since he replaced Brian Clough was pretty good. Remarkably, as with Clough, Mackay lasted just eighteen months at Derby after winning the title. Bruce Rioch also played his last game for the club at Everton, before ironically joining them for £200,000. I loved Rioch with his pace and power and fantastic goal scoring ability. Together with Peter Lorimer, he probably had the hardest shot at that time in English football.

CHAPTER 2

THE COLIN MURPHY AND TOMMY DOC YEARS

Who would take over? George Hardy tried to entice Brian Clough back from Nottingham Forest. He was invited for talks but Clough eventually declined the offer and stayed at Nottingham Forest, much to the disappointment of the fan base. Hardy surprisingly decided to appoint Colin Murphy as the new manager, who was the reserve team coach. In my opinion this was a major mistake. Experience was needed. The squad was ageing and in need of two or three younger quality players. Murphy appointed Dario Gradi as his assistant, who went on to have a wonderful career at Crewe Alexandra producing player after player and selling them on to higher League clubs. Gradi did however apologise following an independent review for 'not recognising the signs of child sex abuse' at the club carried out by convicted paedophile Barry Bennell who was coaching at the club at the time. Derby beat Sunderland 1-0 in Murphy's first match in charge with a goal from Leighton James. They made good progress in the League Cup but suffered a 2-1 home defeat in the quarter-final at home to Bolton Wanderers at the start of December, who included Sam Allardyce and Peter Reid in their line-up.

Murphy signed Charlton Athletic striker Derek Hales for £330,000 and he made his debut in the 0-0 draw against Arsenal in mid-December. Hales had scored a remarkable seventy-two goals in one hundred and twenty-nine appearances for the Second Division South London outfit. Hales failed to live up to his reputation at Derby. I felt sorry for him really. I believe a lot of the supporters expected him to solve all the club's problems, but they were deeper than that. He only scored four goals in twenty-three appearances and was quickly sold to West Ham United for a cut price £110,000 ten months later. Derby only won two of their next fifteen games following the win against Sunderland, beating both Leicester City and Newcastle United 1-0 and 4-2 respectively at the Baseball Ground. They also suffered five successive defeats against Manchester United, Leeds United, Liverpool, Aston Villa and West Bromwich Albion. One ray of light in the Leeds game was the debut of young Irishman David Langan, who had progressed through the youth system. Derby also signed Irish international Gerry Daly from Manchester United for £170,000. Daly fell out with United manager Tommy Docherty and Murphy did well to snap him up. I was very impressed with Daly at Hillsborough in the FA Cup semi-final.

In the FA Cup third round, Derby drew 0-0 away at Bloomfield Road, Blackpool, winning the replay 3-2 at the Baseball Ground with Hales scoring one of the goals. In the fourth round Derby were drawn away to Colchester United at Layer Road. Derby, playing in the away kit of red shirts, white shorts and green socks, took the lead with Hales scoring again, only for Colin Garwood to earn the home side a replay with a goal deep into added on time. Leighton James scored the winner for

Derby in a very scrappy game in the replay. In the fifth round, Derby beat Blackburn Rovers 3-1, which earned them a really tough draw in the sixth round away to Everton. On the day of the cup tie I had my first ever trip to Wembley, organised by school, to watch England schoolboys play Scotland schoolboys. Players of note who played for England that day were Gary Mills who played for both Nottingham clubs and Derby, Mark Chamberlain formerly of Stoke City and Portsmouth and the late Tommy Caton, formerly of Manchester City and Oxford United. Former Celtic player Willie McStay, brother of Paul, captained Scotland on the day. Former Nottingham Forest and Charlton Athletic midfielder Colin Walsh was also in the Scotland line-up. My mind though was on events at Goodison Park and trying to get score updates. Derby lost 2-0 as Bob Latchford and Jim Pearson sent the Toffees through to the semi-final.

Derby's most memorable match in the remainder of the season was the April 4-0 victory against high flying Manchester City who were second in the table behind leaders Liverpool. Derby were only four points above the relegation zone with three games left and had a striker shortage through injury, so Murphy played Archie Gemmill as centre forward alongside Kevin Hector. Gemmill had an outstanding game, giving England centre-half Dave Watson a torrid time. The goals were shared by Gemmill himself, Peter Daniel, Hector and a Gerry Daly penalty. The pitch was so devoid of grass that the penalty spot 'disappeared'. There was a delay in the game as groundsman Bob Smith had to come onto the pitch with his tape measure and tin of paint to re-insert the penalty spot. The win virtually saved Derby from relegation but it had been a season to forget, with a lot of uncertainty surrounding the club going into the following season.

1977/78

During the close season, the Rams signed experienced Scottish striker Billy Hughes from Sunderland initially on loan. Hughes had won an FA Cup winners medal, being part of the Sunderland team in 1973 as Colin Murphy looked to bolster his squad. My dad decided to relinquish our season ticket as he was unhappy with the decision to sack Dave Mackay.
He thought the board were pressing the self-destruct button again, by sacking him and Brian Clough in the space of just over three years after they had both won the Championship. Before the season started, Derby were the first ever League club to sign a sponsorship deal. It was with Swedish car manufacturer Saab, who would supply the club's players with Saab cars. Shirt sponsorship at this time though, was still vetoed.

Derby only took three points from the first six League games of the new season, which included a 3-0 defeat against Nottingham Forest at the City Ground, when chairman George Hardy decided to sack Murphy, who had been in charge for only ten months and was replaced by former Manchester United manager Tommy Docherty, who would be assisted by Frank Blunstone. Derby lost to Champions Liverpool 1-0 at Anfield in his first match, but then beat Middlesbrough in his first match in charge at the Baseball Ground. Billy Hughes scored one of the goals and Docherty made his move permanent after agreeing a £30,000 fee with Sunderland. The wheeling and dealing continued with Archie Gemmill moving to Nottingham Forest in exchange for their goalkeeper John Middleton. That decision didn't go down too well with the supporters, with Gemmill never playing a game under Docherty at Derby. Other players from Derby's golden era also departed over the next few months including Colin Boulton, Colin Todd, Charlie George, Kevin Hector and Leighton James. The squad needed an overhaul, but the speed of it was far too quick over a short space of time and Docherty didn't endear himself to the supporters, but the revolution had started. Arrivals included Don Masson from Queen's Park Rangers who was exchanged for Leighton James, Gerry Ryan from Bohemians, the return of Bruce Rioch for a second spell from Everton, Terry Curran from Nottingham Forest and Steve Buckley from Luton Town. Ryan lasted less than a year before being sold to Brighton and Hove Albion, citing that everyone fell out with Docherty. Ironically, Curran too lasted less than a year only playing twenty-six times, before being sold to Southampton in the summer of 1978. After the Middlesbrough home win, this was followed up with a couple of 2-1 away wins at Wolverhampton Wanderers and Newcastle United. The next home game was against West Bromwich Albion in their green and yellow striped shirts. Their team was full of quality, with John Wile and Alistair Robertson in central defence and Derek Statham at left-back.

Future England captain Bryan Robson in midfield, with the late Laurie Cunningham, the late Cyrille Regis and Scottish winger Willie Johnson as their attacking options, with the game finishing 1-1. The 3-1 defeat at Bristol City was Kevin Hector's final game in his first spell at the club before he started an exodus of players moving to the North American Soccer League, joining Vancouver Whitecaps. Billy Hughes was making quite an impact scoring eight goals in nineteen games. I can remember Docherty singing his praises, stating he was a certainty for the Scotland squad for next year's World Cup in Argentina, then the next week in explicably selling him to Leicester City for £45,000 only three months since signing permanently for Derby. What was all that about? I was fuming! By mid-December things seemed to be settling down quite well, with four wins and a draw in five games. The wins were 2-1 at home to West Ham United, 3-1 away at Arsenal, 2-1 at home to Manchester City and 1-0 against Bristol City. The 1-1 draw came in the away game at Leicester City. Nottingham Forest, promoted from the Division Two, were setting the pace as League leaders. The game against bitter local rivals Forest at the Baseball Ground ended in a 0-0 draw, in a game in which Steve Buckley made his League debut. Since I had started watching Derby in 1971, we hadn't really played Forest in the League as they were relegated from the top flight in 1972 and remained in the second tier until their promotion in 1977.

In the FA Cup third round, Derby drew Southend United again only two years after playing them in the fifth round. A 3-2 victory saw Derby through to the fourth round against Birmingham City at home, which resulted in a 2-1 victory. Derby drew West Bromwich Albion in the fifth round in a game that was played in midweek on 22 February, following the Saturday postponement. Derby included Jeff Blockley, who was on loan from Arsenal. This was Blockley's only appearance during his loan spell. West Brom won 3-2 before eventually being beaten by eventual winners Ipswich Town in the semi-final at Highbury. The most memorable home game in the second half of the season was the midweek game in March against Champions Liverpool. Liverpool had knocked Derby out of the League Cup with a 2-0 win at Anfield.

Derby though, who were outstanding on the night, won 4-2 with a debut goal for Andy Crawford, a Gerry Daly brace and Charlie George completing the scoring for Derby. Steve Ogrizovic, who played over 500 career games for Coventry City, made his Liverpool debut in goal. They also had Kenny Dalglish. Graeme Souness, Terry McDermott and Alan Hansen in their line-up. My next away game was the trip to Aston Villa. I went with my dad and brothers-in-law. We sat in the North Stand upper tier behind the goal, opposite the Holte End vast terracing. We were right near the back of the Stand. It was a very uninspiring game that finished 0-0. John Gregory and Gordon Cowans, who played later for Derby in their careers, were in the Villa line-up. In April, Derby signed goalkeeper David McKellar from Scottish junior side, Ardrossan Winton Rovers for £2,500 and pulled off a major coup by signing Manchester United winger Gordon Hill for £250,000, in a move that upset a lot of United fans. In the remaining thirteen League games Derby won four, drew four and lost five, including three successive away defeats at Leeds United, West Ham United and West Bromwich Albion. Derby finished twelfth in the League which was an improvement from the previous season. Nottingham Forest under Brian Clough were the League Champions, finishing seven points ahead of Liverpool. It is inconceivable nowadays that a team can win the Premier League straight after being promoted from the second tier. I didn't go to that many games in the season with not having a season ticket. I was hoping to see more games in 1978/79.

1978/79

Derby had a new shirt manufacturer for the 1978/79 season with Le Coq Sportif replacing Umbro. The away kit was now orange shirts, black shorts and orange socks. Goalkeeper Colin Boulton, who was the only player to play in all of the eighty-four games in the two League Championship campaigns, left to play for Tulsa Roughnecks in the North American Soccer League. The most staggering statistic though at this time was the remarkable number of players that joined Derby. Derby made four more signings around the start of the new campaign as Docherty continued to ring the changes. They signed Notts County winger Steve Carter, who came in exchange for Don Masson, who failed to make an impact following his move from Queen's Park Rangers. He only made twenty-three appearances in the previous season. Centre-half Aiden McCaffrey signed for Derby for £60,000 from Newcastle United. Striker Billy Caskey and defender Vic Moreland joined from Northern Ireland outfit Glentoran for a combined fee of £90,000. In September, three players arrived. The late John Duncan a striker joined from Tottenham Hotspur. Midfielder Jonathan Clarke made the move from Manchester United after making one substitute appearance for £50,000, and nineteen-year-old winger Paul Emson joined Derby from non-League Brigg Town. Colin Todd, who was a major player in both League Championship sides, moved onto Everton for £300,000 as Docherty was determined to move on the senior players. Todd would certainly be a player that supporters would put down in their greatest ever XI.

In December, veteran defender David Webb, who had enjoyed

a glittering career at Chelsea, joined the Rams from Leicester City. Derby signed Steve Wicks from Chelsea for £275,000 and Roy Greenwood from Sunderland in January. The first home game I saw was Derby's first win of the season in September against Ron Atkinson's West Bromwich Albion. Albion had very much an unchanged squad from the previous season, so I expected a tough game. The Rams raced into a 3-0 first half lead with goals from Duncan, Powell and Daly. Albion fought back in the second half with goals from Cyrille Regis and Laurie Cunningham, but Derby held on to win 3-2. In the League Cup, Derby won in the second round with a 1-0 victory at Leicester City, but lost at Southampton to a Phil Boyer goal. Boyer was in Derby's Youth team but never played a senior game. Terry Curran was also in the Southampton line-up. A 5-0 defeat against Liverpool at Anfield in October was the game in which Charlie George's reign at Derby came to an end. George was injured in that match and was sold to Minnesota Kicks in the North American Soccer League. George admitted his time at Derby wasn't the same after Dave Mackay had been sacked. I loved watching George play and I still regard him as the greatest player I've seen in a Derby shirt. A sad day for me, but what memories he gave the supporters. Derby's next opponents were Tottenham Hotspur at home, who had just been promoted on goal difference. They had very much surprised the football world by signing Argentinian 1978 World Cup stars Osvaldo Ardiles and Ricardo Villa for a combined fee of £750,000. The game finished 2-2 with Glenn Hoddle playing for Tottenham also that day. I rate him as the best midfielder of his generation. Very two footed and the best passer of a long ball I've ever seen. He was an absolute joy to watch and he had a fantastic career. Steve Buckley scored one of the goals for Derby and without doubt, was by far the best of Docherty's signings, making over 300 appearances in nine years at the club. John Duncan also scored against his old club with Peter Taylor and Don McAllister, replying for the North Londoners. The first East Midlands derby of the season against the reigning League Champions Nottingham Forest was at the City Ground on Boxing Day. Derby took the lead in the first half through a Gerry Daly penalty, with Tony Woodcock levelling up during the second half. Going into the New Year, Derby were fifteenth in the League and Forest were flying high in third place.

In the third round of the FA Cup, Derby were drawn away to Preston North End from the second tier in a game that was postponed twice, and had to be played in midweek due to the inclement weather. It was a night for Derby to forget as they lost 3-0, with Alex Bruce hitting two of North End's goals. The League games following the cup exit gave supporters more cause concern with five successive League defeats during late February and early March. The defeats were 2-0 at home to Liverpool, a game in which Ray Kennedy scored a goal that won BBC's Goal of the Season competition, 1-0 at home to Ipswich Town, 2-0 at Tottenham Hotspur, 1-0 at home to Leeds and 3-0 at Middlesbrough. That losing streak ended in the next game, a midweek game I went to, a 3-0 victory over Bolton Wanderers with two goals from Roy McFarland and one from Gerry Daly. The Rams though were to win only one more game that season, which was a 2-0 home win against Arsenal at the end of April. This was just a few weeks before Arsenal won the FA Cup with a 3-2 victory over Manchester United. Derby finished a very disappointing season in nineteenth position, only six points above the relegation zone, with a really poor 3-0 home defeat against Middlesbrough. The turnaround in players was astonishing and supporters were getting restless with the alarming slump. The Middlesbrough match saw the end of the Tommy Docherty era. He resigned and took over at Queen's Park Rangers. Derby were searching for a new manager yet again. In hindsight why didn't they stand by Dave Mackay?

CHAPTER 3

FALLING THROUGH THE TRAP DOOR – TWICE!

1979/80

Derby appointed former Hereford United and Newport County manager Colin Addison as their new manager in July 1979. He joined Derby from West Bromwich Albion where he was assistant to Ron Atkinson. He appointed John Newman, the Grimsby Town manager, as his number two. Derby started the season with a 0-0 draw against West Bromwich Albion, with the squad Addison had inherited from Tommy Docherty. Goals were hard to come by, with Derby not scoring in their first four games losing three of the games including a heavy 4-0 defeat at Crystal Palace. Derby beat Arsenal 3-2 in their fifth game of the season. Derby were 2-0 down at half time, but rallied with three second half goals from David Langan, Aiden McCaffrey and John Duncan.

In the midweek following the Arsenal game, I went to Wembley on a school trip to see England play in a full international for the first time against Denmark in a qualifying match for the 1980 European championships. It proved to be an eventful evening and not because of the football. Myself,

Nigel Lee, Nigel Yeomans, two school mates of mine, plus a couple of others, naively decided to take some cans of Carling Black Label on the bus for the journey down to London. We sat at the back of the bus, but John Wright, the teacher supervising the trip was made aware that the beer was on the bus. He come down the bus and confiscated the beer. I think, he expected a couple of cans or so to be handed over but about twenty cans were thrown into the bag he provided much to his surprise! We thought we would be summoned to the headmaster's office the next day to explain our actions but strangely there was no repercussions! More importantly, we never did see that beer again as John Wright must have drunk it! Looking back, it was a really stupid for us thing for fifteen-year-olds to do. What were we thinking? For the record England won the game 1-0 with a goal from Kevin Keegan who was the 'golden boy' of English football in this era.

Colin Addison's first signing was Australian goalkeeper Yakka Banovic from Heidelburg United, who was then followed by midfielder Steve Emery from Division Four outfit Hereford United for £100,000. At the end of September, Derby lost 4-0 at the Dell against Southampton. Phil Boyer again came back to haunt the Rams, as he scored a hat-trick for the Saints. I think even at this stage of the season, it appeared that it would be along hard winter for Derby who had a lack of quality all over the pitch. The week after the Southampton game, Derby beat Bolton Wanderers 4-0, with John Duncan and Paul Emson scoring two goals each. Keith Osgood made his debut as a central defender, following his £150,000 move from Coventry City. Duncan was looking to be a decent acquisition in a poor side. Derby drew away at Wolverhampton Wanderers and then lost three on the spin at Tottenham Hotspur, at home to Aston Villa, which was the first game of the start of Roger Davies' second spell at Derby following his move from Alan Hinton's Tulsa Roughnecks in the North American Soccer League, and away at Stoke City. Addison's next signing was Barry Powell, who joined Derby from Coventry City for £350,000. Derby's team three years on from Mackay's last match at Everton in November 1976 was now completely unrecognisable. An ageing team full of internationals had been replaced with very honest players, but massively lacking quality and experience at this level, together with a manager who had only managed in the lower divisions. It was a very worrying time for all supporters. Saturday 24 November though will be regarded as the best day of the season, with the visit of reigning Champions Nottingham Forest to the Baseball Ground. I stood on the Vulcan End pop side that day. High flying Forest had a formidable side. England 'keeper Peter Shilton was in goal, England full-back Viv Anderson played at right-back, Scottish international Frank Gray played left-back with Larry Lloyd and David Needham the central defenders. Martin O'Neill, Gary Mills and ex-Derby player John McGovern lined-up in midfield. John Robertson started on the left wing, with Garry Birtles and Britain's first million-pound footballer, Trevor Francis, as the strikers. Derby took a 1-0 lead when Gerry Daly pounced to score after Peter Shilton failed to hold onto a Steve Buckley cross. Graham Richards, who was commentating for BBC Radio Derby, had a field day describing the action as it unfolded. After John Duncan's close range header Richards went on the rampage with a classic piece of commentary;

"Incredible, Forest all over the show, Forest absolutely chaos and Derby are two ahead. And as I speak Emery's through and he's scored, Emery's clean through, Forest are in absolute ruins and Derby are three up. And manager Brian Clough, I've never seen such an expression of disgust on his face." Richards' voice was going hoarse at this stage, but this was him at his brilliant best. His commentary was legendary, and he has provided some great entertainment over the years. John Robertson pulled one back from the penalty spot, but John Duncan added his second and Derby's fourth to give them a famous win against all the odds.

This sadly though was a false dawn. Derby went winless in the next twelve games which included three draws and nine defeats, as they slipped to second bottom of League, seven points from safety. During this spell of games, Derby signed former England striker Trevor Whymark from Ipswich Town on loan, just before Christmas. He only played two games when he contacted glandular fever and never played for Derby again. In December the Rams signed Kevin Wilson from non-League Banbury United for £20,000, and also signed striker Alan Biley from Cambridge United for a reported fee of £450,000. He made his debut in the 2-1 home defeat at Crystal Palace the week after the ill-fated FA Cup defeat at Bristol City. It was hoped the FA Cup third round would give Derby's season a much-needed lift. But how wrong I was, as Derby were thrashed 6-2 against Bristol City at Ashton Gate. The day didn't start well as Republic of Ireland international David Langan missed the team bus, as he didn't want to be cup-tied if or when he moved to another club. A good friend of mine Paul Cannon and Martin Fisher, who had gone to the match, actually saw and spoke to Langan at Bristol train station after he had made his own way down to the south west. Looking a bit dishevelled, all he said was that the club had sent him home.

The club naturally came down hard on him with a heavy fine and he was also not selected for a couple of games. Derby's next win was 2-1 against Tottenham Hotspur, with Biley scoring his first goal for the club. Derby signed David Swindlehurst initially on loan from Crystal Palace and he made his debut in the away game at Aston Villa on Saturday 1 March. I went to this game at Villa Park with my school friends Martin Fisher, Dave Hudson, Nigel Lee and Nigel Yeomans. This was the first away game my parents let me go to with my schoolmates, as I was three months short of my sixteenth birthday. Naively, we all took a packed lunch, as you did on school trips in those days! We went on the service train and arrived at New Street Station around eleven a.m. for a three-p.m. kick-off! What were we thinking! We wandered around a Birmingham suburb trying to kill time when Nigel Yeomans started chanting Derby songs after we had just bought some fish and chips in what looked like an undesirable area. All of a sudden, we were being chased by some Villa fans. Nigel Lee was struck with part of a concrete slab on his back. We all split up and ended up in different parts of the city! It was quite a terrifying experience with hooliganism rife in those days. We all eventually met back up at the ground, luckily unscathed. We stood on the North Stand terrace. We didn't have a great view as the terrace was quite shallow and this was the time when supporters were 'fenced in' to stop encroachment onto the pitch. Derby lost 1-0 to an Allan Evans goal in the first half. Villa were a very strong side that went on to be League Champions a year later with Jimmy Rimmer in goal, Kenny Swain and Colin Gibson as the full-backs, Evans and Ken McNaught in central defence. The midfield trio was Des Bremner, Dennis Mortimer and Gordon Cowans. Up top they had Brian Little, Gary Shaw and Tony Morley. I really rated Gary Shaw, who was a really top player and destined for big things when his promising Villa career effectively ended after sustaining a knee injury at the age of twenty-two. Alan Biley gave Derby a ray of hope scoring in three successive goals in the home games against Stoke City and Bristol City and the away game at Bolton Wanderers. But wins were hard to come by. I went to the away game at Coventry City at Highfield Road on Easter Monday. My dad drove my good friend Mark Jarrett and myself to the ground and picked us up afterwards. Derby lost 2-1 and were looking odds on for relegation. By the time of Derby's next win, 3-0 against Brighton and Hove Albion, there were only three games left and Derby were second from the bottom and four points away from safety.

The return fixture at Nottingham Forest was the week after. They got their revenge with a Frank Gray goal sending Derby to a 1-0 defeat. Derby were as good as relegated, still second from the bottom and still four points away from safety with an inferior goal difference. The following Saturday before the Manchester City game, David Swindlehurst converted his loan spell into a permanent transfer in a £400,000 deal. Biley and Swindlehurst scored in a 3-1 win but Derby were relegated as Stoke City won away at West Bromwich Albion. It had been a really poor season, but at least the Biley and Swindlehurst partnership showed signs of promise. It was a pity that Derby couldn't have signed them earlier on in the campaign. The season ended with a 4-2 loss at Norwich City. The travelling faithful though were full of hope though. "We'll be back in 81" was the song. It was the first time Derby had been in the second tier since the season 1968-69.

1980/81

From leaving Ravensdale Junior School and moving up to Mickleover School, I was always in the school football team, from under twelves all the way up to the under sixteens. I was also in the Derby North End team during this period. We played in the Derby Parks League on Sunday mornings against teams like Littleover Dazzlers, Mitre, Matlock, Belper Phoenix, Sherwin and Redwood. My dad used to ferry me around everywhere, whether it was the Racecourse, Darley Fields or Alvaston Park. He hardly missed a match, come rain or shine, in five seasons I was with Derby North End. It was extremely competitive, and we managed to win the League twice under manager the late Roy Bishop. All the players who were involved with Derby Boys played in the League. I managed to get into the Derby Boys squad on two separate occasions.

It was very difficult to get a place in the team. I only managed it twice, once against Burnley Boys at Littleover School on Pastures Hill in a game we won 2-0, and then in an away game with Nottingham Boys that finished 3-3.

I started work at Rolls-Royce on a four-year Craft Apprenticeship on Monday 1 September 1980. My first year was based at the training school in Mickleover, just down the road from where I lived on Edale Avenue. At the start of the 1980/81 season, I signed for Mickleover Sports who played in the Derby and District Senior League on Vicarage Park, which meant playing on Saturday afternoons, so it restricted me watching my beloved Derby. It was worth it, though. It was my first transition into men's football from youth football. It was quite intimidating at first, as I was only five foot eight inches tall and ten stone but I soon found my feet. I played the whole season in the reserve side in Division Three. My good friend Derek Lee, who I also played with at Ravensdale and Mickleover, went straight into the first team. He was an excellent player. His brother Nigel also joined the club the following season. Both of them had the capability to play at a higher level. My brother-in-law Pete Birks was manager of the reserve side and he played me on the right wing, a position I'd not played before. I scored twenty-five goals in a team that finished runners-up in the League and winning the League Cup against Hemington, who had won the League. The final was held on 'The Municipal Bowl' as it was known at Moorways, at the end of March. It was the dream of most local footballers in those days to play there. I scored the first goal, cutting in from the right and firing in with a left foot shot to give us the lead with ten minutes to go. Pete Birks then for some reason took me off and I was gutted, as I thought I was having a good game. Hemington equalised almost immediately and the game went into extra time, but we eventually ran out 3-1 winners.

Around February time Steve Cattrell, who was in the Mickleover Sports first team, asked me if I fancied playing Sunday morning football for Personal Service Station who played in the Derby Taverners League, with their home ground at the Rowditch. I knew quite a few of the players, like Keith Wilshere who was goalkeeper in our team at Ravensdale, and John Richards, who was about three years older than me who I knew from being in and around Mickleover. I played a handful of games and scored a few goals and I quite enjoyed it. They asked me to sign on for the following season, which I agreed to. BBC Radio Derby's Devon Daley was also in the side. It meant I could only attend midweek games, but I felt it was much better to play than watch.

Derby only made two signings ahead of the season. Experienced goalkeeper Roger Jones joined for £20,000 from Stoke City and Alan Ramage signed from Middlesbrough. Ramage was one of the rare breeds of professional footballer/cricketers in the late 1970s and early 1980s along with the likes of Jim Cumbes, Ted Hemsley, the late Chris Balderstone and Phil Neale. Ramage was a quick bowler for Yorkshire. Incidentally, Chris Balderstone made history in 1975. He played for Leicestershire in a County Championship against Derbyshire at Queen's Park, Chesterfield. He was not out at stumps, then he was driven up to Belle Vue by manager Stan Anderson to play for Doncaster Rovers against Brentford. The following day he carried on batting and made a hundred. What a great achievement!

The first game of the season I saw was the first home game of the season against Chelsea. Derby had got off to a horrendous start to the season losing, 3-0 away at Cambridge United. Derby played well on the night against Chelsea, running out 3-2 winners, with goals from Alan Biley, Barry Powell and a Gary Chivers own goal. Derby then went on a good run of three wins and two draws, with good away wins at Luton Town and Grimsby Town. At Blundell Park, midfielder Glenn Skivington made a fine debut following his signing from non-League Barrow. The Rams then lost two games on the bounce at home to Wrexham, in a game that Keith Edwards scored an outstanding cross shot volley from the corner of the box, and away at Orient. Derby drew four games on the trot, including a 3-3 draw at Queen's Park Rangers, in a game that debutant Frank Sheridan scored twice. Sheridan had progressed through to the first team via the club's youth system. Young striker Kevin Wilson also made his debut in this match. He scored in the 2-2 draw at Bristol City and then again in the fine 3-1 win at Chelsea. He was making a good impression will his willing running and great enthusiasm. Tony Reid also scored on his debut in the win at Chelsea, as Derby moved up to eighth place in the table. Up to the New Year, Derby played nine more games, winning four, drawing three and losing two. One of the wins was an impressive 3-0 away win at Preston North End, in a game where Kevin Hector made his 'second debut' and scored following his return to the club from Vancouver Whitecaps, which included two loans spells at non-League Boston United and Burton Albion. The other win was 2-0 at Newcastle United, who included Mick Harford and a young Chris Waddle in their line-up. The FA Cup draw revoked bad memories from the previous season, with Derby again pulling Bristol City out of the hat. The first game at the Baseball Ground ended 0-0, with the Robins winning the replay at Ashton Gate 2-0. From the first ten games in the New Year, Derby won three, drew four including three successive draws at home to Orient and away at Wrexham and Sheffield Wednesday. I went to the midweek home game at home against Swansea City at the end of March. I was still limited to games I could go to, due to my playing commitments. Derby lost the game 1-0 to the Swans and slipped to tenth in the table. The last six games of the season ended with a mix of two wins, two draws and two defeats. The final game of the season was a 2-1 home defeat at the hands of Preston North End. More significantly, this was the last game of Roy McFarland's Derby career, before his departure to take over as player-manager of Bradford City. He was signed by Brian Clough from Tranmere Rovers in 1967 for £35,000 and made four hundred and thirty-four appearances, scoring thirty-four goals. He was a key player in the Second Division 1968/69 promotion winning side, as well as the 1971/72 First Division Championship side. He only played four games in the 1974/75 Championship side due to the injury he suffered playing for England. He also won the FA Charity Shield. For England he won twenty-eight caps, this tally would have been a lot more if it had not been for injuries. Together with Colin Todd, he formed the most formidable central defensive partnership in the club's history. It was an absolute pleasure to watch him play. Derby ended the season in sixth place; on reflection, it was quite a reasonable season. With the right additions to the squad, could they go one step further the following season?

1981/82

I continued playing for Mickleover Sports Reserves in the Derby Senior League, following our promotion to Division Two. My school friends from Mickleover School and I decided to form a team that would play on Sunday afternoons in the Derby City League. Dave Hudson, Nigel Lee, Derek Lee, Mark Jarrett, Martin Fisher, Nigel Yeomans, Richard Tansley, Richard Tapping, Chris Stevenson, Mick Brown, Graham Stevenson, Graham Cunningham and Paul Cannon, together with Dennis Ceranic, Andy Nickels, Andy Mellor, Simon

Ratcliffe, Mark Snape, Gary Parkin, Alan Ottewell, Jeff Ottewell, John Luke and Anthony Greatorex would all form the backbone of Michigan Dynamo Football Club for the next fifteen years. The formation of Michigan Dynamo meant I had to end my short spell at PSS, as I couldn't manage two games on a Sunday, as well as Saturday afternoon football.

Before the start of the 1981/82, Derby sold striker Alan Biley to Everton for £300,000. This was a major blow to the supporters, as he had formed a good striking partnership with David Swindlehurst. Derby also signed experienced right-back Mick Coop for £20,000 from Coventry City. Coop had made 425 appearances in fifteen years for the Sky Blues. The season started poorly with a 2-1 defeat at home to Orient. A week later though, Derby had their first victory with a 2-1 win at Cambridge United. The week after on Saturday 5 September, I had one of the best sporting days of my life. Cricket is also a great passion of mine too. I went to Lord's to watch Derbyshire play in the NatWest Trophy final against Northamptonshire with Mark Jarrett, Richard Tapping and Nigel Lee, with Derbyshire winning off the final ball, by losing fewer wickets as the scores were tied. Derby were hammered 4-1 at Shrewsbury Town, but it didn't tarnish the day. Frank Gamble, who Derby had signed from non-League Burscough in May following a loan spell, made his debut in the home win against Queen's Park Rangers at the end of September.

From the next ten League games, there were four wins, four defeats and two draws, with West Ham United defeating Derby 5-2 on aggregate in the League Cup two-legged affair. Following the 4-1 defeat at Norwich City towards the end of

November, Derby slipped to seventeenth in the table and another long hard winter was looming. Derby only managed three more home games in the period up to the end of the year. They only played one game in December, as the harsh winter weather set in. In those days, not many clubs in the second tier had the luxury of their pitches having under soil heating. Derby were the hoping the FA Cup would give them a much-needed confidence boost. They were drawn away to fellow Division Two club Bolton Wanderers at Burnden Park. Derby had signed Liverpool reserve player Richard Money on loan to bolster their back four, and he made his debut, together with youngster Ian Dalziel. This game was Mick Coop's last game in a Derby shirt. Jeff Chandler, who was later to join Derby, gave Coop a torrid afternoon. Coop had failed to make an impact in his five months at the club and it was to decided that both should part company. The pressure was certainly mounting on manager Colin Addison, and the club decided to part company with him on 25 January, the day before the Watford away match. I can recall a radio interview with Addison following his departure which he described in three words. He said, "Sadness, disappointment, relief." I thought it was a strange appointment in the first place, following the resignation of Tommy Docherty. Derby needed an experienced manager who knew Division One, not a rookie manager from the lower Leagues. I couldn't fault Addison for his commitment and found him to be honourable and honest, but it wasn't the right time for him to take over at Derby. I will remember him though as a player in the non-League Hereford United team who beat Newcastle United in the 1972 FA Cup, with that goal from Ronnie Radford.

Derby appointed Addison's assistant John Newman as his

successor. His first game in charge at Vicarage Road couldn't have been worse. Watford, third in the League under Graham Taylor, ran out 6-1 winners. This also signalled Roger Jones' last game for Derby before he was transferred to York City. Derby made a good recovery in the next game with a 3-1 win at home to Sheffield Wednesday. Kevin Wilson scored twice, with goalkeeper Yakka Banovic making his League debut. John Newman then signed veteran defender John McAlle from Sheffield United, who had played over 500 games for Wolverhampton Wanderers, and Brian Attley from Swansea City. Derby drew three and lost four of their next seven games. The first of these seven games ended in a 2-1 defeat at Rotherham United with striker Andy Hill scoring on his League debut.

The game was overshadowed, though, with a possible career-ending tackle by Gerry Gow on Steve Emery, which resulted in a broken leg for the Derby midfielder. Somehow Gow stayed on the pitch and wasn't sent off. In the last of this run of seven games, the Shrewsbury Town home 1-1 draw only attracted a crowd of 7,518 which is the lowest I can ever remember for a Derby home game in my time as a supporter. Kevin Wilson scored twice in the 4-1 home win against Crystal Palace, which halted the run of seven games without winning, but this was followed by losing at Grimsby Town in a game that Charlie George made his 'second debut', returning to the club after a very short spell at AFC Bournemouth. Three successive draws followed, against Champions elect Luton Town, Wrexham and Barnsley. John Barton made his debut against Luton following his move from First Division Everton. The season petered out with Derby finishing a very disappointing sixteenth after finishing a respectable sixth in the previous season. The final game of the season, a 3-2 win over already promoted Watford, was the final game of Kevin Hector's glittering career, in a game he scored two goals. He was signed by Tim Ward from Bradford Park Avenue in 1966 and he was a key player in the Second Division 1968/69 promotion winning side, as well as the 1971/72 and 1974/75 First Division Championship sides. He also won the FA Charity Shield. For England he won two caps, which was a travesty really. 'King Kevin' will go down as a Derby legend and a fans favourite, there's no doubt about that. Charlie George's short spell ended too, which meant only Steve Powell was left from the two League Championship winning squads.

1982/83

I passed my driving test on Wednesday 15 July 1982 at the age of eighteen, which I still class as one of most nerve wrecking days in my life! Footballing wise I decided to move to Derby and District Senior League One side Derventio, as I saw my chances of getting in the Mickleover Sports first team quite limited. Andy Nickels, who played for Michigan Dynamo also played for them and Dave Hudson joined too. Derventio were quite an ageing side, with the likes of Bryan Huckerby, Dave Holness, Trevor Nunn and Colin Fearn in the side. I enjoyed my season though, winning Player of the Year, but I knew it would only be a short-term move.

John Newman signed central defender George Foster from Plymouth Argyle and winger Mike Brolly from Grimsby

Town. In the first game of the season, a 3-0 defeat at home to Carlisle United, Foster and Brolly both made their debuts. There were two more defeats following the Carlisle game, 2-1 away at Fourth Division Halifax Town in the League Cup first round first leg, and 4-1 at Loftus Road on the Queen's Park Rangers artificial turf. A Steve Buckley penalty gave Derby a first win of the season as their impressive run of results against Chelsea continued. Buckley's goal scoring exploits continued as he bagged two in the second leg against Halifax as they overturned the first leg deficit in a game I went to. Derby then lost two on the bounce, both 2-1, away at Leeds United and at home to Blackburn, with Paul Blades making his first team debut at Leeds. Derby then went on to record four successive 1-1 draws in away games at Charlton Athletic and Grimsby Town, and home games against Cambridge United and Barnsley. At Grimsby Town, former Nottingham Forest European Cup winner Gary Mills made his Rams debut following his loan move from North American Soccer League side Seattle Sounders. Mills only played eighteen games, but he added much needed quality to the side. The following week Leicester City visited the Baseball Ground and they won 4-0 with twenty-one-year-old striker Gary Lineker grabbing a hat-trick. Former Arsenal striker Alan Smith came on as substitute to score the other goal. Derby then suffered a further two more League defeats, away at Wolverhampton Wanderers and Sheffield Wednesday in the League. It wasn't surprising when John Newman was relieved of his duties and was replaced by former assistant manager Peter Taylor, with Roy McFarland returning as his number two. He left Bradford City in controversial circumstances with allegations Derby tapped him up, and they eventually had to pay a large fine and compensation for taking him back to the Baseball Ground. McFarland later in his autobiography admitted that he should have stopped at Bradford and continued his fledgling management career at Valley Parade, but his head was turned by Taylor. Taylor's first game in charge was the League Cup third round defeat at Birmingham City. Three successive draws followed at home to Bolton Wanderers, at Oldham Athletic and away at Burnley. The game at Oldham was yet another game in which a former player made his 'second debut'. This time it was thirty-four-year-old, twice Division One Championship winner Archie Gemmill, who'd had a short spell at Wigan Athletic. John Richards, who had scored an impressive one hundred and forty-four goals in three hundred and eighty-five games for Wolverhampton Wanderers, also joined the club on loan making his debut, as Derby slipped to the bottom of the table with only one win in sixteen games. Finally, the following week, they recorded only their second League win of the season, their first win in three months, by beating Rotherham United 3-0 at home with two goals from David Swindlehurst and one from Ian Dalziel. In the final four games of the calendar year, Derby lost three of their four games, away at Fulham, away at Newcastle United and at home to Shrewsbury Town. The significant factor of the Newcastle United away match was the debut of twenty-three-year-old striker Bobby Davison, who had joined the club for £85,000 from Halifax Town.

Davison had impressed Taylor when he scored against Derby in both legs of the League Cup first round earlier in the season. Davison, later in his career, revealed he nearly joined Arsenal who were interested in him at the same time. In the 3-2 home defeat by Shrewsbury, Davison scored twice. Derby were still bottom of the League, nine points adrift of fourth-from-bottom Cambridge United. It was looking bleak for Derby as the New Year loomed.

The FA Cup third round draw remarkably pitted Peter Taylor's Derby at home to Brian Clough's Nottingham Forest. A tough game was ahead with Forest riding high in Division One in third place, eight points behind leaders Liverpool. I stood on the Vulcan End pop side in a 28,000 plus crowd. Inexplicably, Derby won 2-0 on a heavy Baseball Ground pitch with the first goal, a beautiful Archie Gemmill curling free kick that beat Steve Sutton in the Forest goal on the hour. Forest then had incessant pressure but couldn't beat Steve Cherry in the Derby goal. The second goal was scored in the last minute by Andy Hill, who was only in the side because new signing Bobby Davison was cup-tied and Wolverhampton Wanderers didn't want John Richards cup-tied. Mike Brolly carried the ball forward in the inside right position before slipping a lovely ball though to Hill who lifted the ball over the advancing Sutton.

The following week, after the euphoria of the Nottingham Forest victory, Derby lost 3-0 in the League at Brunton Park against Carlisle United. Taylor wasn't a very happy man, and he made a scathing verbal attack on the players' attitude and desire in a post-match interview. The following two Saturdays at the Baseball Ground in the 3-3 draw on the League against Leeds United and the fourth round FA Cup 2-1 win against Chelsea saw hooliganism rear its ugly head yet again. The Leeds and Chelsea fans ripped up seats from the stands and started hurling them onto the pitch, with thousands of pounds of damage caused, with a fight breaking out at the Osmaston End of the ground. Derby were found guilty by a FA commission of failing to take enough precautions by segregating the Leeds fans. By a strange twist of fate, Derby played at Stamford Bridge in the League the following Saturday. The club and police urged Derby supporters not to go, but around fifty defied the plea and went, including Richard Tapping and Dave Hudson two good friends of mine. Derby's fantastic run of results against Chelsea continued with a 3-1 win. The late Paul Futcher made his Derby debut following his move from Oldham Athletic.

In the fifth round of the FA Cup, Derby drew Manchester United in a plum draw. I managed to get a seat in the Ley Stand for this game, sitting towards the Normanton End. It was quite rare for me to sit in the Ley Stand, as I found it cold and not as atmospheric as other parts of the ground.

United, who were managed by Ron Atkinson, had quite a star-studded line up. Gary Bailey was in goal, Mike Duxbury and Arthur Albiston as full-backs. Gordon McQueen and Kevin Moran were the central defenders. Steve Coppell, Remi Moses, Bryan Robson and Arnold Muhren lined up in midfield, with Frank Stapleton and nineteen-year-old Norman Whiteside up front in their 4-4-2 formation. United won 1-0 with a Whiteside goal in front of a 33,000 plus crowd in a deafening atmosphere. United won the FA Cup that year, beating Brighton and Hove Albion 4-0 in a replay following the 2-2 draw in the first game. That first game was famous for the radio commentary by Peter Jones, "...and Smith must score," talking about a shot by Gordon Smith, which was then saved by the Manchester United goalkeeper Gary Bailey with the score at 2-2 and minutes left. That will probably haunt Smith until the day he dies.

Derby then beat Grimsby Town 2-0 with Bobby Davison on the scoresheet. They then recorded four successive draws at Leicester City, at home to Wolverhampton Wanderers, away at Cambridge United and at home to Sheffield Wednesday. I went with Nigel Lee to the away draw at the Abbey Stadium on the Road rider bus. This was on a Tuesday night in mid-March. The Abbey Stadium was a right eye-opener and by far the smallest ground I had been to. We stood on a very shallow open terrace watching the game from virtually ground level. Behind the terrace was an allotment. I can remember a very large clock behind the goal at the other end towards the corner flag. It was a very poor game, but Derby added another point to their tally and this stretched the unbeaten run to six League games. Derby then won 2-0 at Bolton Wanderers and finally moved off the bottom of the table, with goals from Mike Brolly and Kevin Wilson. Wilson and Bobby Davison were beginning to form a really good understanding. Paul Hooks made his debut following his move from First Division Notts County for £60,000. I had always rated Hooks when I'd seen him play, and it seemed an astute signing by Peter Taylor. The following Saturday, which was Easter Saturday, I went to Gay Meadow for the game against Shrewsbury Town. I drove in my purple 850 Mini with Nigel Lee, Richard Tapping and Dave Hudson, the first time I'd driven to an away match. The game finished 1-1, with Hooks scoring his first goal for the club in his second game. On Easter Monday, Derby were home to Newcastle United in a three-p.m. kick-off. In the morning, I went to the annual wheelbarrow race in Mickleover. I got there about ten a.m., but by the time we left to go to the match at two p.m. I'd had far too much to drink. I took my place on the Vulcan pop side but I didn't feel too good and regretted having the drink. Newcastle had Kevin Keegan, Chris Waddle, Terry McDermott and Imre Varadi in their side, and were fifth in the table, six points behind third place Fulham.

Former Nottingham Forest defender Kenny Burns, who was now at Leeds United, joined Derby on loan and came on as second half substitute. Waddle gave Newcastle the lead before Hooks and Kevin Wilson scored to give Derby the victory, with the unbeaten run extending to ten games.

Derby had a fantastic victory at Ayresome Park in their next match against Middlesbrough. Burns made his full debut, partnering with Paul Futcher at the heart of the defence as two goals from Bobby Davison and a penalty from Archie Gemmill gave Derby a precious victory. Derby moved up to sixteenth place on forty points, with the four teams directly below them Crystal Palace, Rotherham United, Charlton Athletic and Middlesbrough all on thirty-nine points. Second-from-bottom Bolton Wanderers were on thirty-eight points, so it was really tight, with Derby having seven games to go. That afternoon I played for Derventio at Darley Fields. After the game after removing my socks and pads, I noticed that I'd got a three-quarter inch gash down my shin that had opened up and was bleeding badly. I ended up spending the evening at the hospital having it stitched up.

Derby then drew at home against fellow strugglers Charlton

Athletic, in a midweek game I went to. It was an important match not to lose. It ended 1-1, as did the game the following Saturday at home to Barnsley, with Kenny Burns scoring for the Rams. The following week, I drove up to South Yorkshire for the game against Rotherham United at Millmoor. We sat at the side opposite the Main Stand, level with the eighteen-yard box, with a large following from Derby on the terracing to our left. The game finished 1-1, with Derby moving three points up to fifteenth place and two points above the drop zone. Bottom of the table Burnley were the next visitors to the Baseball Ground. Derby extended their remarkable unbeaten run in the League to fifteen games with a 2-0 win with goals from Bobby Davison and Kevin Wilson. We were on the Roadrider again for my fourth new ground in a couple of months, with a trip to Ewood Park to meet mid-table Blackburn Rovers. The game was played on a wet and gloomy May Day Monday evening. We stood on the Darwen End covered terrace behind the goal. Derby's fifteen game unbeaten came to a halt as they lost 2-0.

The final away game of the season was at Selhurst Park away to Crystal Palace, who following a poor run, were third-from-bottom and who occupied the final relegation spot. Derby were four points ahead of Palace, so it was imperative not to lose. Gavin Nebbling, Kevin Mabbutt and Henry Hughton fired Palace into a three-goal lead, before a Billy Gilbert own goal gave Derby hope only for Mabbutt to get his second, so Palace ran out 4-1 winners. A tense final day of the season lay ahead for sides at the bottom of the League.

Derby were fifteenth, two points ahead of Middlesbrough who

were in the final relegation place with four clubs in between Derby and Boro. Derby were at home to Fulham who were in fourth place level on points with third-place Leicester City. Leicester had a far superior goal difference, so only had to match Fulham's result to gain promotion. In the first half Fulham were on top, but Derby took the lead midway through the second half with a superb Bobby Davison volley. Following the goal, a minor pitch invasion by celebrating fans was soon cleared, but the crowd were lined around the edge of the pitch, five or six fans deep. Fulham midfield player Robert Wilson, was kicked by a spectator while the ball was in play close to the edge of the pitch. The touchlines were no longer visible. Referee Ray Chadwick did his best to keep the game going in difficult circumstances. He blew his whistle for an offside and the fans invaded the pitch assuming that the game had finished with Derby the victors and safe from the dreaded drop. However, the referee's watch showed seventy-eight seconds still to play, but as the teams left the field Jeff Hopkins was punched by a Derby fan. The referee did not take the players back on to the pitch. Fulham manager Malcolm MacDonald was fuming and felt the game should be replayed, and he was actually supported in this by Derby chairman Mike Watterson. He complained that the crowd invasion was nothing to do with Fulham and that it wasn't their fault that the crowd had invaded the pitch and cut the game short. Derby were well on top when the game was halted, and the chances of Fulham scoring two goals in the last seventy-eight seconds were minimal. The Football League ruled against any replay and said that the result should stand. Fulham appealed to the Football Association but they would not alter their decision. Crowd trouble at the Baseball Ground had reared its ugly head since the turn of the year. Security at the ground was improved with the erection of ugly perimeter fencing all around the ground, to avoid any repetition of the events of during the Chelsea, Leeds United and Fulham games. This fencing would be place at stadiums up and down the country for six years, until the tragic events of Hillsborough in April 1989 changed things forever. Derby survived for another season following their remarkable run of results since the Carlisle debacle in January. The signing of Bobby Davison, who had scored eight goals since his debut at Newcastle, was a major factor. His partnership with Kevin Wilson flourished and gave the club hope for next season.

The next day, on Sunday 15 May, Nigel Lee, Dave Hudson and I took part in the first ever Ramathon that was sponsored by Kennings. To be honest we didn't do that much training in our pursuit of completing the 26.2-mile course. We were only eighteen and very naïve when it came to marathon preparation. I probably did more training than Nige and Dave. My longest run was from Mickleover to Ashbourne and back one evening in April that took me about four hours. When I got home, my dad went barmy at me for doing this without any drinks or method of communication if I'd got into trouble in anyway. All three of us were playing football regularly at this time and hopefully this would see us through. On the day sadly Nige had to pull out at about halfway. Dave finished in four thirty and myself in four ten. It was one of the toughest things I'd done in my life. At around twenty-two miles, I passed a guy standing outside the Sinfin Moor Social Club who was watching the race and drinking a pint of Guinness. I asked him I could have a sip. He obliged and I ended up drinking three quarters of it as I was out on my knees! He was fine about it and we had a bit of a laugh about it and he wished me good luck on the last part of the race. I would love to trace him and buy him a drink back!

1983/84

Personally, I decided to concentrate on Sunday afternoon football only with Michigan Dynamo, but said to Derventio I would play if they were short of numbers. Derby made three major signings ahead of the season in a bid to strengthen their squad. Northern Ireland and Bradford City striker the late Bobby Campbell made the move to the Baseball Ground for £70,000. Campbell had scored seventy-six goals in one hundred and forty-eight games for the Bantams. Winger Calvin Plummer signed from Chesterfield. The most controversial move though, was John Robertson's free transfer from Nottingham Forest. Robertson signed for Derby with neither him or Peter Taylor letting Clough know in advance of the deal. When Clough heard of this 'deception', he vowed to never speak to Taylor again.

Derby were full of confidence as they went into their first game of the season, against old adversaries Chelsea at Stamford Bridge. On a hot, sunny late August Saturday afternoon, Derby gave debuts to summer signings Campbell, Plummer and Robertson, while Chelsea gave debuts to goalkeeper Eddie Niedzwiecki, defender Joe McLaughlin, midfielder Nigel Spackman and striker Kerry Dixon, following their disappointing campaign the previous season. It turned out to be an uncomfortable afternoon for the Rams, who went behind to an early Spackman goal. Four more goals in the second half from Clive Walker, Chris Hutchings who later in his career was to become Derby assistant manager to Paul Jewell and a brace from Kerry Dixon, gave Chelsea a thumping 5-0 win. Derby then drew 1-1 at home to Sheffield Wednesday, with Bobby Davison on the scoresheet. Davison scored again, with Bobby Campbell scoring his first for Derby in the 2-1 home win against Swansea City. In that game Ray O'Brien made his debut following a move on loan from Notts County. Assistant manager thirty-five-year-old Roy McFarland was yet another player with a League Championship winner's medal to make his 'second debut'.

On Tuesday 6 September, I made the trip to the Brighton and Hove Albion for a midweek League game. I went on the Roadrider bus with Nigel Lee, Paul Cannon and Chris Stevenson. The bus left Derby at one p.m., but we didn't reach the south coast until seven p.m. In those days before the M25 was built, it was a nightmare getting through central London. It was a really poor performance from Derby at the Goldstone Ground which they lost 1-0. Derby were without the injured Bobby Davison, who was replaced by Andy Hill. This turned out to be Hill's final appearance in a Derby shirt before he was transferred to Carlisle United. Derby conceded five goals on the road again when they visited Blackburn Rovers in the next game, with striker Simon Garner scoring all five goals. He was always a thorn in Derby's side during this era. Bobby Campbell scored Derby's only goal in the 5-1 defeat. It was early days, but Derby were already eighteenth in the League table. Campbell scored two more in the next game a 2-2 draw at home to Oldham Athletic. Centre-half Dick Pratley, who was a summer signing from non-League Banbury United, made his League debut.

Derby then signed thirty-seven-year-old former England, Sunderland and Manchester City defender Dave Watson from Vancouver Whitecaps. He made his debut at the Valley in the next match against Charlton Athletic, which Derby lost 1-0. On that day Graham Harbey also made his debut at left-back. I'd played with Harbey for a couple of seasons for Derby North End in the Derby Parks League as a fourteen-year-old, when he was more of a central defender. He was from Matlock, and came through the ranks at Derby. He was an exceptionally good player at that junior level and went on to have a fine career, joining Ipswich Town and West Bromwich Albion when he moved on from Derby. There were other players at junior level who were on a par ability wise with Harbey who didn't make it into the professional game. It just goes to show the fine dividing line of making it or not. Following the defeat at the Valley, the Rams lost four of their next five League games, 4-1 at home to Carlisle United, 2-0 at home to Barnsley, 3-0 at Huddersfield and 2-1 at home to Grimsby Town. Following the Grimsby match, Derby slipped to second bottom in the table with eight points from twelve games with only Swansea City below them. It was also the end of Bobby Campbell's Derby career as he struggled to make an impact, and he returned for a second spell at Bradford City. The only success was a 1-0 win at rain drenched Selhurst Park against Crystal Palace, with John Robertson scoring the late winner. Derby also crashed out of the League Cup, going out 7-0 on aggregate to Birmingham City. Derby then won two games 1-0, away at Cambridge United and at home to Middlesbrough, with Bobby Davison scoring in both games. Eamonn Deacy made his debut at Cambridge after joining on loan from Aston Villa.

I went to the next away game against Manchester City at Maine Road, with Richard Tapping and Dave Hudson. It was the first time I had ever travelled on a football special train to an away game. When we arrived at Victoria train station, I couldn't believe how many police, police horses and police dogs were waiting to escort us to the ground. I was quite glad to be honest. Near the ground there were so many adjacent alleyways and streets that could be fraught with danger for the away fan, because it was ideal for ambushes. This was a time when football hooliganism was at its worst and pretty intimidating. We stood at the side on the massive Kippax terrace. It was a fantastic atmosphere inside the ground. Former Glasgow Rangers striker Derek Parlane gave City the lead, with Derby levelling late on with Calvin Plummer's first goal for the club. Maine Road was up there with Hillsborough as the best grounds I'd been to so far.

On the first Saturday in December, Newcastle United were the visitors to the Baseball Ground. I always looked forward to games against Newcastle because no matter where they were in the League table, they always bought down a large contingent of supporters and there was always a terrific atmosphere. Kevin Keegan once stated their supporters always followed the club though 'thin and thinner'. Newcastle came into the match third in the table while Derby were fourth bottom. Newcastle, playing in an all silver/grey kit which probably was the first time I'd ever seen a team playing in that, took a two-goal lead in the first half attacking to the

Normanton End. A Kevin Keegan header from a Chris Waddle cross gave the Geordies the lead, which Waddle doubled with a tremendous left foot strike from just inside the box in the inside right position. Derby though, fought back in the second half levelling with two Bobby Davison headers from two Dave Watson assists, Archie Gemmill scoring the winner from the spot following a Peter Haddock handball. My next away trip was to Craven Cottage, Fulham, on Boxing Day. I went on the Road rider with Chris Stevenson, Nigel Lee and Richard Tapping. We stood on the open terrace at the Putney End. Fulham, who narrowly missed out on promotion in that last game of the season, were struggling in the bottom three with Derby only two places ahead of them. The game finished 2-2 with Kevin Wilson bagging both Derby's goals. Derby were at home to mid-table Cardiff City the next day, something that never happens now in modern day football. I can understand the two games in two days but why not have local derbies? For these two games, the away team was had to travel over one hundred and twenty miles. Surely a bit of common sense was needed? Derby lost the game 3-2 after being two goals up. Paul Hooks and a collector's item goal from John McAlle, his only League goal in his professional career spanning 582 games.

In the first game of 1984 at home to Charlton Athletic at the Baseball Ground on a miserable wet Monday afternoon, Derby gave goalkeeper Jake Findlay a debut following his loan move from Barnsley. Like Jeff Blockley, this was Findlay's one and only appearance for the club. Derby lost 1-0 and slipped to fourth bottom of the table, only three points above Fulham. In the third round of the FA Cup Derby had a good 3-0 win against Cambridge United, who were bottom of the second division. Kevin Wilson, Calvin Plummer and John McAlle were the scorers. This was McAlle's only cup goal of his career. Two more League defeats followed, 2-1 at home to Chelsea and 3-0 away at Oldham Athletic, before Derby played non-League Telford United in the fourth round of the FA Cup in a game I went to. Telford bought a good following on the Osmaston terrace in the 21,000 crowd. A Bobby Davison hat-trick saw Derby home to a 3-2 win. Two of his goals were what becoming his trademark one-on-one finishes and his other was a header. There was extra pressure on Derby to make progress in the competition. After the game, Managing Director Stuart Webb had revealed the club had major financial problems. Derby were drawn at home to mid-table First Division Norwich City in the fifth round of the FA Cup. Striker Andy Garner made his Derby debut a month before his eighteenth birthday, in front of a crowd of 25,793 with the usual strong following from Norfolk. There were no goals in a competitive first half. However, Norwich's goalkeeper Chris Woods was lucky not to be sent off as he poleaxed Kevin Wilson outside the box, after the striker had raced through onto a long clearance from Derby keeper Steve Cherry. Derby took the lead early in the second half when John Robertson was tripped inside the box. Archie Gemmill converted the penalty, with Bobby Davison doubling the lead with yet another top one-on-one finish as he slipped the ball past the advancing Woods. Norwich piled on the pressure, with John Deehan pulling one back with four minutes to go, but Derby held on for a famous victory and a place in the sixth round for the first time since 1977. On the Monday, Derby were drawn away to Third Division Plymouth Argyle at Home Park in the FA Cup sixth round.

My next away match was the visit to Blundell Park for the evening game against Grimsby Town on Tuesday 21 February. We went on the Roadrider and got there quite early, so we went for a walk along the seafront in the dark, with a howling gale blowing. We stood behind the goal near the corner flag in the away end, with the Findus Stand across on the far side. Grimsby went ahead with a header from Paul Wilkinson from a cross from former Derby winger Paul Emson. The Rams levelled through Andy Garner, who beat Nigel Batch with a fine low right foot shot from the edge of the box. This was Garner's first goal on his first League start. The Mariners though restored their lead in the second half with a fine header from Kevin Drinkell and moved up to third place in the League with this 2-1 victory.

The two-hundred-and-fifty-mile trip to Devon for the Plymouth game was on Saturday 10 March. We went on a mini bus driven by Paul Cannon's dad Mike, leaving at seven a.m. We arrived at about two p.m., after a couple of stops on the M5 on the way down. We stood on the open terrace at the Devonport End with 8,000 other Derby fans in the crowd of over 34,000. There was a fantastic atmosphere in the ground. Derby didn't play very well on the day and were indebted to a fine display by goalkeeper Steve Cherry. He made a fantastic stop, pushing Gordon Staniforth's shot onto the left hand upright with the ball then bouncing along the line and hitting the right hand upright before the ball was cleared to safety. The game finished 0-0 with all to play for in the replay at the Baseball Ground. On Monday, the draw for the semi-final was made, with Division One Watford awaiting the winners of this match. Everton drew Southampton in the other semi-final.

More importantly the following week was arguably the most traumatic week in Derby's ninety-six-year history since they were formed in 1888. On Monday 12 March, Derby were in the High Court. They owed the Inland Revenue just under £132,000 and unpaid VAT of just over £78,000 to the Customs and Excise. Stuart Webb was trying to get a major backer involved as there was no financial assistance from Derby City Council or Derbyshire County Council. Existing and three new Directors assisted with some cash as did Webb, who bought £140,000 worth of shares. Webb spent most of the Wednesday trying to persuade Oxford United Chairman and media tycoon Robert Maxwell, who Webb had entered into negotiations with to enlist his help with financial assistance, not to back away, but he was no longer interested shortly after the High Court sitting. It was of course the day of the Plymouth replay, which ended in a disastrous 1-0 defeat. That night I stood on the Normanton terrace as Andy Rogers scored directly from a first half corner which was totally misjudged by Steve Cherry, who had played so well in the first game at Home Park. This was a genuine opportunity of reaching our first FA Cup semi-final in eight years that was missed. It was Paul Futcher's last appearance in a Derby shirt, as he left to join Barnsley. Webb returned to Derby, only to find out the result from his wife who met him at Derby train station. The day finished with Derby out of the FA Cup, but, more scarily, clinging on to their existence. Webb eventually enlisted the help of Maxwell to finally raise the £220,000 necessary to lift the petitions and Derby survived off the pitch. What a relief! The following Saturday, on the return to the League action, things continued to get worse, as Brighton and Hove Albion won 3-0 at the Baseball Ground as Derby gave a really worrying woeful performance. Steve Cherry was dropped and replaced by Yakka Banovic in goal following his error against Plymouth, and John McAlle replaced the departed Futcher. This was Calvin Plummer's last appearance before also joining Barnsley. After the game the Rams slipped into the bottom three, five points behind fourth-from-bottom Crystal Palace.

My next away game on Saturday 31 March at Barnsley turned out to be a very significant day both for Derby and me personally. I went on the train with Richard Tapping and Dave Hudson for the visit to Oakwell. It turned out to be a forgettable afternoon as Barnsley, who had Paul Futcher and Calvin Plummer in their side, romped to a 5-1 win. As we stood on the vast open terrace, there were frequent snow showers during the game to make matters worse. Peter Taylor was sacked after the match. This game also signalled the end the Derby careers of John Barton, Brian Attley, John McAlle and Yakka Banovic. It was one of the most depressing days watching Derby. In the evening, on my return to Derby, after a bit of deliberation, I went for a night out with Simon Taylor and went to the Pink Coconut in town. It was a good job I did, as this was the evening, I met my future wife, Julie Bull, so the day ended on a really good note. If I'd not gone out that night, my life would have been so been so different to what it is now.

Roy McFarland was named as manager until the end of the season. He had a massive job on his hands to keep Derby in the second tier. Following the Barnsley debacle, Derby were now seven points behind fourth bottom Crystal Palace. McFarland's first game in charge ironically was against Palace at home the following Saturday in what was a massive 'six-pointer'. It was a day of personal triumph for Andy Garner who hit a hat-trick in a confidence boosting 3-0 win. Nigel Lee always saw the light-hearted side of the programme notes on Garner. "A locally born strapping six-footer, with deceptive pace." Nige said, "Yeah he's slower than he actually is!"

After a midweek 3-1 defeat at Sheffield Wednesday, I went to the away game at Elland Road against Leeds United with Richard Tapping. Paul Blades came into the side at right-back, in a game that finished goalless. On Easter Saturday, Derby beat Fulham 1-0. On the Monday, Derby were away at Cardiff City. I didn't have a ticket for the Roadrider bus, so I took a risk and went to the bus station with Richard Tapping, to see if there was space on the bus. Unfortunately, there wasn't space, so I trudged home. Derby lost 1-0. With four games to go, Derby were still third-from-bottom, two points away from safety. The next home game against Manchester City was a must win. Dave Watson hit the winner against his former club with a strike into the roof of the net when the ball dropped to him following a corner. With three games remaining, the gap to fourth bottom Oldham Athletic was still two points.

The following Saturday, I made the trip to St James' Park with Richard Tapping for the daunting trip to promotion chasing Newcastle United, managed by ex-Chesterfield boss Arthur Cox. The Magpies were third in the table, six points ahead of Grimsby Town with a far superior goal difference, so a win against Derby would see them promoted. There was a carnival atmosphere when we arrived in the ground. The five hundred or so Derby fans were stood on the open terrace at the Leazes End opposite the Gallowgate End in the sell-out crowd. It was one of the best atmospheres I'd ever witnessed in a football ground. Kevin Keegan headed the home side into a 1-0 lead from a Chris Waddle cross. Peter Beardsley made it 2-0 five minutes later. Chris Waddle made it three after the interval. Newcastle, a joy to watch, with a rampant brilliant display of attacking football, and Derby, totally outclassed in the May sunshine. Peter Beardsley added a fourth as Newcastle confirmed their return to the top flight after six seasons. It was Kevin Keegan's final match in Newcastle's colours. Ignoring Derby for once, as a football fan, it was a pleasure to witness that. Derby were five points from safety with two games left. Their fate was sealed though on the Monday evening, as Oldham Athletic beat Grimsby Town and Derby were relegated to the third tier for the first time since they won the third Division North in 1956/57. In their final two games, the Rams beat Portsmouth 2-0 in a game I stood on the Vulcan pop side with Chris and Mark Stevenson, and then lost 3-0 at Shrewsbury Town, to end off a thoroughly depressing season. Derby had spiralled from Champions of England in 1975 to the third tier of English football in nine years. The decision to sack Dave Mackay was harsh and short sighted. The team was ageing but it needed tweaking, with a sprinkling of quality younger players. The board made a series of poor managerial appointments. The job was far too big for Colin Murphy. Tommy Docherty came in and ripped the squad apart with alarming speed. Colin Addison and John Newman, very amiable and honourable men, had no experience of top tier management. Things under Peter Taylor started to improve, especially with the great escape of 1983, but he eventually ran out of steam. Between 1971 and 1976, Derby must have only used about twenty players. I dread to think how many they used in the period after Mackay's departure and the end of this season. The only players to come out of this period with any credit were Alan Biley, David Swindlehurst, Steve Buckley, Steve Powell, Archie Gemmill, Kevin Wilson and Bobby Davison, and to a lesser extent, youngsters Graham Harbey and Andy Garner, who were experiencing their first season of first team football. The next managerial appointment needed to be one of the most important in the club's history.

CHAPTER 4

REVIVAL UNDER ARTHUR COX AND THE DOUBLE PROMOTION

1984/85

After leading Newcastle United back into the Division One, much to the surprise of the football world, Arthur Cox left the club after a dispute with the board about his contract. Before May was out Stuart Webb pulled off a master stroke by appointing Cox as the new manager of Derby. There was very little money to spend as Cox inherited a squad of ageing players. The Maxwell family had taken over the ownership of the club, with Ian Maxwell as the new chairman in what was Derby's centenary year. The rebuilding of the club started with four free transfers. The late Rob Hindmarch joined from Sunderland, a player Cox said he would have tried to sign for Newcastle United if he had been still been there. Striker Billy Livingstone joined from Wolverhampton Wanderers, right-back Charlie Palmer and experienced goalkeeper Eric Steele both signed from Watford. Cox also signed twenty-two-year-old Paul Richardson for £15,000 from non-League Nuneaton Borough. Sadly, Richardson's professional career was cut short during the season, following having trouble breathing due to blood clots in his lungs. Derby also signed midfielder

Kevin Taylor from Sheffield Wednesday.

Derby had a new kit for their centenary year. A white shirt with a blue trim on an open v-neck, with diagonal sashes in Derbyshire colours of gold, blue and chocolate extending from the left shoulder to the middle of the chest, with the sponsor Bass' logo in red, emblazoned in the middle of the chest. The opening day of the season pitched Derby on the south coast against AFC Bournemouth at Dean Court. Derby gave debuts to Steele, Palmer, Hindmarch, Taylor and Richardson as they slipped to a 1-0 defeat in front of a capacity crowd that was swelled by a massive travelling support. I didn't go that day, as Julie and I went to Hopton-on Sea in Norfolk for a week's holiday. Julie and I went down to Portman Road during the week to watch the Division One game between Ipswich Town and Luton Town. We arrived slightly late as we had to turn back, as I had forgotten my wallet! We missed the opening goal of the game scored after two minutes by Eric Gates for Ipswich, but saw David Moss equalise for Luton in the second half. Luton were a top team in those days, with Brian Stein and Ricky Hill in their side. Ipswich included George Burley, Russell Osman and Terry Butcher in their line-up. I think Julie secretly loved it and was now understanding my obsession for football! The following night Derby played Hartlepool United in the League Cup first round first leg with Kevin Wilson scoring four in a 2-1 win. No, we didn't go! We returned from Norfolk the following Saturday. We set off early and arrived back in time so I could go to the home game against Bolton Wanderers, which Derby won 3-2, with Kevin Wilson's hot scoring streak continuing as he scored a hat-trick.

In the midweek I went to Hartlepool United with Nigel Lee on the Roadrider bus for the League Cup second leg match at the Victoria Ground (for some reason the ground is now called Victoria Park). Derby won 1-0 with a late John Robertson penalty. Whilst Nige and I were stood on the away terracing, we got threatened with a knife by a guy who we assumed, but never found out, was a Hartlepool fan. We managed to lose him but it was quite a terrifying experience. There seemed to be a complete lack of police or steward presence who we could report to. Fortunately for us the bus was parked right outside the away terrace, we got on and never saw the guy again. The next game I went to was Derby's home game against Bristol City. Julie made her first ever visit to the Baseball Ground. We sat in the Ley Stand with the Rams winning 1-0, with yet another Kevin Wilson goal. We'd found out that Julie was pregnant around this time and we were discussing how to broach the subject with our parents, as we'd only been together for five months and we were unsure how they take the news. To be honest after about six weeks I knew Julie was the girl I wanted to spend my life with. The following Saturday I went to Elm Park to watch Derby play at Reading. John Burridge made his debut in goal, as Eric Steele had chipped bone in his wrist. Defender Floyd Streete also made his debut after moving from Dutch side SC Cambuur. The game finished 0-0 in a game of few chances. I arrived back home from Reading about eight p.m. When I sat down, my dad said to me, "I believe you and Julie have got something to tell us?" As soon as he said that, I knew what he was referring to. He added that Julie's parents had been here and were absolutely livid, upset and wanted an explanation. Julie was really upset with her parents' reaction. To be fair, my mum and dad were totally fine about it. I told them how I felt about Julie and that we would start to look for a place to live. At the start of October, Derby were mid-table following a defeat at Bristol Rovers. Julie and I travelled to Spain for a week in the sun at the Cala Font Hotel in Salou. Football took a back seat for a while when we returned home, whilst we were house hunting. We found a house in Killingworth Avenue in Sinfin that my mum and dad had viewed whilst we were away. We were impressed with the house. Our offer of £17,950 was accepted, and we had no problem in paying the £1,800 deposit with our combined savings. I was still at Rolls-Royce working as a machinist on three shifts and Julie worked in retail at Woolworths.

Back to the football, as Derby were now in the third tier, they had the joy of playing in the first round of the FA Cup. Ironically, they were drawn yet again against Hartlepool United with the game at the Victoria Ground. Derby suffered a very poor 2-1 defeat. After this match, an unfortunate incident took place that soured relationships between Arthur Cox and BBC Radio Derby's commentator Graham Richards, to such an extent that Richards found it necessary to make his opinion of the manager loud and clear over the air-waves.

Richards was unhappy at the slow start Derby had made to the season. Derby though, won three and drew two of their next five League games. In the first of these games, midfielder the late Mickey Lewis made his debut in the home 2-2 draw with Wigan Athletic. They also came back from three down to draw 3-3 with Newport County at the Baseball Ground on the last Saturday before Christmas, as they moved up to eighth in the table. The away form was the main issue, with six defeats in nine games whilst they were unbeaten at home with eight wins and three draws. I went on the Roadrider with Nigel Lee on Boxing Day for the trip to Kent to play Gillingham at the Priestfield Stadium. I heard a story where another fan turned up to another Gillingham in Somerset. What a way to spend Boxing Day! The form away from home continued to be a problem, as Derby lost 3-2. On Saturday 29 December, I went on the football special train to Swansea City with Dave Hudson, Nigel Lee, Mark Jarrett and Richard Tapping, that cost £5 return. Following persistent heavy rain, the Vetch Field pitch was like a paddy field and I felt the game might get abandoned. Derby played very well and won 5-1 with five different scorers; Bobby Davison, Steve Buckley, Charlie Palmer, Andy Garner and Kevin Wilson all bagged a goal each. 'The Vetch' was a ram shackled old stadium, as Swansea had hit hard times following their dramatic fall back to Division Four, following their meteoric rise up to Division One. Following this game, only Cambridge United were below the Swans in the League table.

We exchanged contracts on our house on New Year's Day and moved in on Thursday 3 January. On New Year's Day Derby beat York City 1-0 at home, to go to seventh in the table, with a Bobby Davison goal in front of a season's best 16,000 plus crowd. This was Kevin Wilson's final game in a Derby shirt before he was sold to Division One Ipswich Town for £150,000. What a good servant he had been in his six years at the club. He was a tireless worker with his endless running, and had formed a good partnership with Bobby Davison. I was sad to see him go, but he deserved a crack in the top flight. Derby signed the late Gary Ablett on loan from Liverpool and

I saw him play in the next two away games I went to. The first was a 0-0 draw at Sincil Bank, Lincoln. He then played in a very rare Friday night game against Doncaster Rovers at Belle Vue, in a game Derby lost 2-1 and slipped to twelfth in the League table. Trevor Christie made his debut following his move from Nottingham Forest as the replacement for Kevin Wilson. Another two signings, Gary Micklewhite from Queen's Park Rangers made his debut in the next game, a 3-0 defeat at Bristol City. Steve Sutton made his debut in the 1-1 home draw against Rotherham United following his loan move from Nottingham Forest. My next away game was the early March game against high-flying Hull City at Boothferry Park, who were third in the table behind leaders Bradford City and second place Millwall.

We went on the football special train to Hull, which stopped right outside the ground at the appropriately named Boothferry Halt. Derby raced into a two-goal lead through a Steve Buckley penalty and Bobby Davison strike. Hull hit back to win 3-2 with two goals from Billy Whitehurst, a big bustling centre-forward, who was the size of a Rugby League player. He certainly caused Derby some problems that day. There was a massive pitch invasion at the end of the game, with the Hull fans baiting the Derby fans. I think they thought they were already promoted. At the end of March, Derby drew 0-0 at home to Bristol Rovers. Paul Hooks made his final appearance before moving to Mansfield Town and Paul Ablett returned to Liverpool following his loan spell. More significantly, Arthur Cox signed Rovers' midfield player Geraint Williams for £40,000 as he continued to rebuild his squad using the money generated by the sale of Kevin Wilson. Williams made his debut in the next game, a 1-1 draw at Brentford. On the Sunday following the Brentford match, Julie who was eight and half months pregnant now was suffering stomach pains, so we went to the Derby City Hospital. Fortunately, it was a false alarm and was diagnosed as Braxton Hicks and to our relief she was discharged. We were quite glad as we avoided having a baby born on 1 April.

In the next five games at the start of April, Derby lost at home 2-1 to Millwall, drew away at York City and at home to Bradford City. They beat Gillingham 1-0, and then Reading 4-1 on Wednesday 17 April at home and were lying in mid-table, with fifty-nine points from forty games. On the night of the Reading match, it was also the FA Cup semi-final replay between Liverpool and Manchester United at Maine Road. Julie and I were in bed were watching the highlights on the television. Julie said she was having contractions. I said let's just hold on a bit until the game finishes. She reluctantly agreed!

Following the game, we went to the Derby City Hospital about 11.30 p.m. and on to the maternity ward. We were greeted by a nurse who examined Julie and confirmed that she was in the early stages of labour. The nurse advised me to go home and call in the morning for a progress update. I said to the nurse I was on the 6 - 2 morning shift at work, so I'd call about five a.m. I went home and went to bed. I got up at five a.m. and as agreed, I called the hospital. They told me that Julie had given birth to a seven pounds one ounce baby daughter at 3.26 a.m.! They had called me about two a.m., but I was asleep and missed the call! I couldn't believe it! I went down to the hospital to see our daughter, who we called Sarah Clare. Julie has never let me forget this! My mum was thrilled that we had called her Sarah, as she had a sister called Sarah who died as a teenager that I never knew about. On the Saturday evening, Julie and Sarah came home. Sarah was slightly jaundiced and had to have a short spell under a bili light.

The Reading game was the final appearance in a Derby shirt of Steve Powell. What a fantastic servant to the club he was in his fourteen-year association with the club and the last link to the Division One Championship squad. If you snapped Powell in two, he would have Derby County running through his veins. The biggest complement I can pay him is that he hardly ever had a bad game, even with all the ensuing chaos around him. His career was blighted by injury, but he still made over four hundred appearances for the club. He's the type of man you'd want in the trenches with you if your country went to war. In the final six games of the season, Derby won three, drew two and lost one, in a decent finish to the campaign. I went to the last game of the season, on the football special train to Newport County for the game at Somerton Park. Double decker buses shipped us to the ground. The ground was probably the worst ground I'd been to. We stood on a shallow covered terrace with a type of chicken wire restraining the fans from getting on the pitch, which also restricted the view with what appeared to be a speedway track encircling the pitch. Derby fans made up more than half of the 4,000 crowd. Derby won the game 3-1 with goals from Bobby Davison, a Trevor Christie penalty, and my old team mate Graham Harbey scored his first ever League goal. Derby finished a respectable seventh, as Arthur Cox began to make his mark in the second half of the season with further signings in the summer looking likely. On the same day, horrific events unfolded as fifty-six people lost their lives at Valley Parade, the home ground of Bradford City, following a fire which occurred during the Third Division match between Champions Bradford and Lincoln City. Eighteen days later, on Wednesday 29 May, approximately 60,000 supporters of Liverpool and Juventus filled the ageing Heysel stadium in the Belgian capital Brussels. Around an hour before the kick-off, the trouble started. Fans had been chanting, waving flags and letting off fireworks, but the atmosphere turned ugly and a thin line of police were unable to prevent a contingent of Liverpool followers from stampeding towards rival fans. A retaining wall between the Liverpool and Juventus supporters collapsed under the pressure and many were crushed or trampled on when the Juventus fans tried to escape. This led to the deaths of thirty-nine fans and a five-year ban on all English clubs in European football.

1985/86

After the consolidation of the previous season, Arthur Cox was keen to add more signings to strengthen his squad further. In came experienced thirty-two-year-old goalkeeper Mark Wallington for £25,000, who had enjoyed a fine career with Leicester City. Central defender Ross MacLaren signed for £67,000 from Shrewsbury Town. The fee was decided by a tribunal, with Town manager Chic Bates extremely unhappy with the fee, claiming Derby had got a 'steal'. Midfielder Steve McClaren, who played a big part in Hull City's promotion to the Division Two, left the Tigers to join Derby for £70,000, which was another fee decided by a tribunal.

Former Leeds and Bolton winger Jeff Chandler signed for £38,000. Meanwhile John Robertson was on his way out of the club and re-joined Nottingham Forest.

The Rams opened the season with a 3-0 opening day win at home to AFC Bournemouth, with Jeff Chandler scoring two and Trevor Christie adding the other. I missed the game as I was playing cricket for Scarsdale in the Derbyshire County League. Richard Tapping was also playing for us and he'd travelled back from the Bournemouth area where his parents lived to play in the game. I'd played for Scarsdale since I was fifteen. It was always a dilemma what to do when the football and cricket seasons clashed. Unbelievably, Derby drew Hartlepool United again in a two-legged League Cup tie. Nigel Lee and I decided not to go after our experience there. We said we'd be crapping ourselves if we saw the knifeman again! The first game I went to that season was the August Bank Holiday Monday home game versus Wolverhampton Wanderers. I stood on the Vulcan pop side as Derby ran out 4-2 winners. The following Saturday, the last one in August, I was still playing cricket, so I missed the trip to Eastville for the game against Bristol Rovers. I was disappointed to miss it as I never got to go to Eastville, before Rovers were forced to leave due to financial difficulties in 1986.

On Sunday 1 September, I went to Bolton to compete in the Adidas British Marathon. I'd watched the live TV coverage of the previous year's race and decided to give it a go. I was more prepared than I was for my marathon debut sixteen months earlier. My memory of the race is quite vague. Two things I can remember. About seven miles into the race, I was desperate for the toilet. Along this road there was a row of terraced houses that had quite long paths and gardens leading to the front door. I said to this guy outside his house watching the race, "Can I use your toilet please?" He said, "Yes mate, just at the top of the stairs." I entered the house and noticed there was no doormat. My running shoes were dirty, as it was raining. I ran up the pink carpeted stairs. My legs were trembling like jelly as I sat on the throne. There's nothing worse when running than having to stop. I ran back down the stairs and noticed black footprints on the pink carpet. I was so embarrassed! I thanked the guy and carried on with the race. I didn't have the heart to tell him about the carpet! Another thing I remember about the race was a long monotonous long hill on the aptly named Plodder Hill. I was quite pleased with my effort though, finishing in 3.56. On the first Saturday in September Julie, Sarah and I went to Scarborough, on holiday with my mum and dad, so I missed the home defeat to Blackpool and the away draw at Gigg Lane, Bury the following Saturday.

Whilst we were on holiday, Scotland were playing Wales at Cardiff, in a World Cup qualifying game that my dad and myself were watching on television. Their manager sixty-two-year-old Jock Stein collapsed and died shortly after the game in the Ninian Park medical room.

My next away game was the midweek trip in mid-September to Bristol City for the game at Ashton Gate. Bobby Davison scored in the 1-1 draw as Derby's mixed start to the season continued. Chesterfield were the visitors to the Baseball Ground on the following Saturday, this being Derby's first League meeting with their county neighbours for twenty-eight years. The game ended in a disappointing goalless draw. Derby had drawn Division One Leicester City in the second round of the League Cup, following their success against Hartlepool United in the previous round. After winning the home leg 2-0 Derby, took a large away following to Filbert Street for the second leg. We stood on the terracing opposite to the end that housed the executive boxes. Derby managed to draw 1-1 with Bobby Davison again scoring, booking their place with bitter rivals Nottingham Forest in the third round, with Derby having home advantage.

With regards to local rivalries, the East Midlands derby is the Derby County v Nottingham Forest match. No Derby or Forest fans I've asked remotely consider Leicester City as their rivals. Derby and Nottingham are fourteen miles apart and both Nottingham and Derby are about thirty miles away from Leicester. Coventry is the nearest city to Leicester, but I'm not party to what the rivalry is between those two clubs. Nottingham Forest won the League Cup match 2-1 at the Baseball Ground. I sat in the Ley Stand for the game. Derby took the lead through Jeff Chandler, only for Johnny Metgod to head Forest level, with Franz Carr scoring the winner for Forest. Forest were worthy winners with Stuart Pearce, Neil Webb, Nigel Clough and Peter Davenport in their ranks. After the Forest defeat, Derby went on a fine unbeaten run in the League and FA Cup. In the League they won seven and drew four of their next eleven League games, and had progressed to the fifth round of the FA Cup. They did however lose in the Freight Rover Trophy at home to Gillingham. I won't dwell on it, as I don't think it was high on Arthur Cox's priorities. I have no problem with the tournament, as it gives players from the lower Leagues the chance to play at Wembley.

I went to a good run of away games, beginning at Griffin Park against Brentford. It was a midweek game and I drove there with Mark Jarrett and Nigel Lee. I hated driving through London. Mark Jarrett reminded me recently that we got stuck on a roundabout in our pursuit of finding the ground. The game finished 3-3, with skipper Rob Hindmarch scoring twice. Derby then made a major signing with Queens's Park Rangers and ex-England international John Gregory dropping down two divisions to join the Rams in a £100,000 deal.

Derby then scored twelve goals in their next two home games, beating Lincoln City 7-0 in the League, and beating Crewe Alexandra 5-1 in the FA Cup first round. My next away game was at Burnden Park, Bolton. A Gary Micklewhite goal gave Derby victory in a game Jeff Chandler suffered a lot of verbal abuse from the home faithful. The following week a crowd in excess of 16,000 saw Derby hold League leaders Reading to a 1-1 draw. Derby's goal fest continued in the FA Cup second round with a 6-1 win over non-League Telford United with Jeff Chandler bagging a hat-trick. The next away game was the post-Christmas 4-0 victory at Molineux against Wolverhampton Wanderers. It was very strange that day, as all the 9,000 fans with 4,500 from Derby, were housed and segregated in the South Stand behind the goal. The relatively new John Ireland Stand to the right was unused. The North Stand and Waterloo Road Stand were deemed unfit for use following the Bradford fire. Derby won 4-0 with goals from Bobby Davison, John Gregory, Trevor Christie and Geraint Williams.

On New Year's Day, I drove one of two car loads down to South Wales with Paul Cannon driving the other car, for the three-p.m. kick off against Newport County at Somerton Park. We stopped off at Ross-on-Wye, and David Hudson, who went with us, can recall having a shepherd's pie in the pub we stopped in. About one p.m., as we approached Newport, the heavens opened and it absolutely pissed it down. The game started and Newport took the lead. More concerningly for Derby, Bobby Davison suffered an ankle injury and had to be replaced. The pitch was becoming waterlogged and the ball was sticking in the rising water. Referee Roger Milford had no choice but to abandon the game with about ten minutes to go to half time. We travelled back up to Derby with the rain unabating, and my Ford Fiesta cut out north of Birmingham after we had left the M5 Motorway. I got it going again but the following day I couldn't get it started again. It must have been a fortnight before the car was back on the road again. I've never had or will have another Ford car!

I made the long trip to Gillingham for the FA Cup third round clash at The Priestfield Stadium. I'd been on nightshift at work before getting on our minibus at eight a.m. for the trip to Kent. I'm not sure I'd do that nowadays! Andy Garner gave Derby an early lead, which Derby held onto until the late stages of the game, when Tony Cascarino earned the Gills a replay, which Derby duly won. My next away match was again a long trip, this time to AFC Bournemouth for the game at Dean Court in mid-January. Andy Garner scored again in a 1-1 draw. Derby drew Division Two Sheffield United away in the FA Cup fourth round. It proved to be a memorable afternoon for the 9,000 travelling fans who'd made the short trip to Bramall Lane.

A first goal from skipper Rob Hindmarch, who had scored a valuable contribution of goals in the season to date, sent Derby through to the fifth round, and then a home draw to United's neighbours Sheffield Wednesday of Division One. The winter of 1986 was particularly harsh and cold. This cold weather continued, as the following week I went on the minibus again to Bloomfield Road, Blackpool on the first Saturday of February. I bought a meat pie from outside the ground, bit into it, and discovered a block of ice! The queue was that long that I couldn't be bothered to go back and complain. Derby won 1-0 with another goal from Andy Garner. The ground was in serious disrepair. We stood at the side under a covered terrace with a massive open terrace to our right. There was snow on the ground the following Saturday when I drove to York City with Nigel Lee for the game at Bootham Cresent. Two goals from Gary Micklewhite gave the Rams the points in a 3-1 win as Derby surged up to third in the table, fourteen points behind leaders Reading, but with four games in hand due to their excellent progress in the FA Cup. Derby's fine unbeaten run in the League came to an abrupt end in the next away match, by Chesterfield, at Saltergate, on a snow-covered pitch. The Derby fans travelled in their droves for the trip up to the north-east of the county. A Steve Baines goal in the last minute gave the Spirits an unlikely win. Baines went on to be a League referee, one of the very few ex-players who have. To be fair to Baines, when I've seen him referee games, he was very good. His experience led him to understand the game, not just the rules. It's a pity not many other players followed his route.

On the following Wednesday night, Sheffield Wednesday were in town for the much the eagerly awaited FA Cup game that had been postponed in between the York and Chesterfield games. That night was probably the coldest I have ever been at the Baseball Ground, as I stood on the Vulcan pop side. The pitch was bone hard, and dangerous, in my humble opinion. Derby went ahead in the second half with a typical Bobby Davison one-on-one finish, slipping the ball through Martin Hodge's legs as he advanced. Trevor Christie miscued a corner into his own net to earn Wednesday a replay. Derby's next home match was the on Saturday 1 March, which ended in a 2-1 win against Cardiff City. The next day Michigan Dynamo played their first match of the calendar year due to the cold snap. Derby travelled to Sheffield Wednesday for the cup replay in midweek. But as usual the Hillsborough 'hoodoo' struck yet again with the Owls running out 2-0 winners. In their next six League games Derby won three, drew two and lost one. The defeat was a heavy 4-1 reversal at fellow promotion chasers Plymouth Argyle. Following the game in Devon, Derby were third in the table one point ahead of Plymouth who were fourth, but Derby had four games in hand. Derby signed former Welsh international Mickey Thomas on a month's loan from West Bromwich Albion and handed him his debut in the home 1-1 draw against Newport County.

My next away game was the Easter Monday match against Walsall at Fellows Parks. Derby fans again travelled in their numbers, making up half of the crowd. In a very scrappy game, Ross MacLaren's strike earned Derby a point in a 1-1 draw. Derby were now fourth in the table, two points behind

Gillingham with five games in hand. The FA Cup run, although great for club finances, was threatening Derby's promotion bid with the backlog of games that was building up. The Rams then had three successive home games. A 1-1 draw with Brentford was followed a massive 2-0 win against Gillingham with goals from Bobby Davison and Gary Micklewhite. A very jittery 2-0 defeat against bottom half of the table Bristol Rovers did nothing to help the cause. Derby had slipped to fifth in the table, a point behind third place Wigan Athletic with two games in hand. Things were getting really tense with daily scrutinising of the League table.

I went to the next away game at Lincoln City. Another decent following of Rams made the relatively short journey to Sincil Bank. A first half goal from Bobby Davison gave Derby a vital victory. The midweek game at Feethams against Darlington was postponed just over an hour before kick-off at around six p.m., due to a thunderstorm that had flooded the pitch. That did me a favour as I could now go to the re-arranged game, which would now be Derby's last game of the season. Derby then beat Bolton Wanderers at home to back up the Lincoln win and to move into second in the table on seventy-five points, ahead of Wigan and Gillingham on goal difference. Champions elect Reading were thirteen points ahead of Derby, who had three games in hand. It was squeaky bum time! The re-arranged game at Newport ended all square at 1-1. I then made the trip to Elm Park for the tough away game at Reading. Trevor Senior, who always seemed to be a thorn in Derby's side, gave the Royals a 1-0 win and with it the Division Three Championship. Reading were very worthy Champions, remarkably winning their first thirteen League games. Derby then had a massive opportunity to seal promotion with two home games against Bury and Doncaster Rovers. The tension, though, got to the team, which spread through to the supporters, and both games ended 1-1. Striker Phil Gee, who Derby had signed from non-League Gresley Rovers on the recommendation of their chairman David Nish made his debut when he came on as a second half substitute. He had scored thirty-one goals in Derby's reserve title winning side. With three games to go, Derby had slipped to fifth, five points behind third place Wigan Athletic and a point behind fourth-placed Gillingham. Both Wigan and Gillingham had completed their fixtures. The three games left were away to Swansea City on the Tuesday, Rotherham United at home on the Friday, and the re-arranged game away at Darlington on the Monday. The equation was quite easy, two wins from three games would see the Rams promoted. Anything less would see Derby spending yet another season in Division Three.

I went to the away game at Swansea City on the football special train with Nigel Lee and David Hudson. Swansea had one game left and needed to win to avoid relegation to Division Four. Derby played exceptionally well on a warm evening, a real contrast to our last visit in December 1984, and won 3-0, with two goals, including a penalty from Trevor Christie, and one from Jeff Chandler.

The night after the Swansea game, Michigan Dynamo played in the Derby City League Intermediate Cup Final against Holbrook Miners Welfare Colts at the Asterdale Bowl, home of Borrowash Victoria. Holbrook had won the League title, with us as runners-up. They were a fine side full of quality eighteen and nineteen-year-old players who were more than capable of playing at a higher level. At ninety minutes the score was goalless and went into extra time. Holbrook scored twice and won 2-0. To be fair, they deserved to win, as we didn't turn up and do ourselves justice.

Friday 9 May was D-day for Derby. A win would take them into Division Two. Rotherham United, managed by Leeds United legend Norman Hunter, were in mid-table and had nothing really to play for. I sat in the Osmaston Paddock with Mark Jarrett, Nigel Lee, Martin Fisher and David Hudson. A crowd of just over 21,000 saw substitute Phil Gee give Derby the lead after seventy-seven minutes, as he raced clear to beat Keiron O'Hanlon. Rotherham duly equalised following a mistake from Derby goalkeeper Mark Wallington.

The ground went silent and you could hear a pin drop. With six minutes to go Bobby Davison was brought down on the edge of the box by John Dungworth who was sent off. Steve Buckley's free kick was saved by O'Hanlon. Referee Tom Fitzharris inexplicably gave Derby a penalty for an infringement in the Rotherham wall. I've watched the incident hundreds of times and to this day I can't see why he gave it. Trevor Christie stepped up and slotted the ball into the net past O'Hanlon's right-hand upright. Radio Derby's commentator Graham Richards described it brilliantly, "Christie, looking as cool as custard, comes back one, two, three, four shoots GOAL, GOAL, GOAL." Derby were promoted back to Division Two. After the post-match lap of honour, we went down Normanton Road to celebrate at the Crystal Palace pub, I'm not sure how we ended up there. It's the only time I've been there and I've never been since. In fact, I don't know if it's still there!

After years of decline, Derby had stopped the rot and only spent two years in Division Three. A lot of big clubs like Manchester City, Leeds United, Sheffield Wednesday, Sheffield United, Wolverhampton Wanderers, Stoke City, Middlesbrough, Birmingham City, Nottingham Forest, Leicester City, West Bromwich Albion, Norwich City, Blackburn Rovers and Southampton have had the pleasure of the third tier. It's not easy to get out of as Sheffield Wednesday, Portsmouth and Ipswich Town are currently finding out. No team has a divine right to be in the top tier of English football. The final game of the season was up in the north-east in Feethams, to play Darlington. The Quakers were safely in mid-table following their promotion from Division Four. I went on the football special train with Mark Jarrett and Nigel Lee. Feethams was a quaint old stadium, situated adjacent to the cricket ground which is still in use, and has hosted first-class cricket for Durham homes games. We arrived at the ground and stood on some open terracing which ran from the corner of the ground to the eighteen-yard box. Next to the terracing was a covered seating area, which ran the length of the pitch to the other eighteen-yard box. Somehow, we managed to climb into the seating area from terracing without any intervention from any stewards or the local constabulary to get an improved view! The Rams lost the game 2-1 but it didn't really matter, as the match was a 'dead rubber'. Charlie Palmer, Steve Buckley and Trevor Christie all made their final appearances for the club. Buckley, who was twice voted player of the season, was a fine left-back with a lovely left foot and without doubt Tommy Docherty's best signing. He made over three hundred appearances in eight years, which sadly clashed with an era of poor Derby sides. Ask any supporter though and he will be remembered very fondly.

1986/87

s the away game at Crystal Palace at Selhurst Park. It was the football special train again, to avoid the arduous journey by car to South London. We stood on the open terracing in the corner at the Holmesdale Road End. Andy Gray scored the only goal of the game, giving the Eagles a 1-0 win. Due to the inclement weather, Derby's next game wasn't for three weeks. The away game at Boundary Park was a massive clash with second place Oldham Athletic on their artificial pitch. Derby's inactivity had left them five points behind new leaders Portsmouth with a game in hand. It was a very wintry scene as we travelled up by car to Greater Manchester. Derby produced their finest performance of the season with a 4-1 win, the goalFollowing the departure of Palmer, Buckley and Christie, Arthur Cox made four summer signings to strengthen his squad. Full-back Mel Sage, who always impressed me whenever Derby played Gillingham, signed for £60,000. Another full-back Michael Forsyth joined from West Bromwich Albion for £20,000. Experienced midfielder Steve Cross, who had spent ten seasons at Shrewsbury Town cost £60,000. Manchester City striker Mark Lillis was the costliest signing, when he signed on the dotted line for £200,000. All four players made their debuts in the disappointing opening day 1-0 home defeat against Oldham Athletic at the Baseball Ground. Division Three Chester City also won 1-0 at the

Baseball Ground in the League Cup first round first leg, as Derby's disappointing start continued. Julie, Sarah and I went on holiday to Porthmadog on the following Saturday. The second leg at Chester was in the midweek of the holiday, and I was toying with the idea of travelling the sixty miles journey to go to the game. Julie talked me out of it as it meant driving through the Snowdonia National Park in the dark on the way back. I have to agree she was right; it wasn't worth risking. The first game I went to was the home game against Crystal Palace when we got back from holiday. Derby won 1-0 through a John Gregory penalty, but the win came as a cost as new signing Mark Lillis suffered a knee injury that would keep him out of action for three months.

The following Saturday I went to my first away game of the season at Grimsby Town. A Bobby Davison goal gave Derby their first away League win of the season.
It was then a trip to Glasgow, as I was getting the running bug, and entered the Glasgow Marathon. On the Saturday, the day before the run, I went to watch Celtic play Hibernian in the Scottish Premier League. Celtic Park was a huge stadium. I stood behind the goal with the Main Stand of seating to my right. The rest of the ground had covered terracing with a running/speedway type track around the edge of the pitch. Celtic won 5-1, with Brian McClair scoring twice in front of a 20,000 crowd. The Glasgow Marathon went well, as I finished in 3.48. My memory of this run was that I passed Jimmy Saville at around the eighteen-mile mark. He was being cheered on by the vast crowds supporting the race. Little did we know back then…

The following Saturday I made the short journey to the Hawthorns for the away game at West Bromwich Albion. The injury to Mark Lillis had opened the door for Phil Gee to stake his claim for a first team place. Derby lost 2-0 in a poor display and slipped down to sixteenth place in the League, with eight points from six games. Derby did have success in the next away game I went to at Shrewsbury Town in mid-October. A Phil Gee goal was enough to give the Rams the three points. In the midweek I made the long trip down to Portsmouth with Paul Watterson, a guy I worked with, for the game against third-placed Pompey at Fratton Park. John Gregory gave Derby a first half lead. There was a howling gale behind them that was blowing towards the open terraced Milton End, where we were stood. In the second half, a Mick Quinn hat-trick gave Pompey the three points in a half that they totally dominated. They ended the evening as League leaders. I didn't realise until the following day that Mick Quinn was an apprentice at Derby in the Tommy Docherty era before he was released and started his League career at Wigan Athletic. The games were coming thick and fast, and I didn't miss an away game for the rest of the season apart from the visit to Sunderland in February. The next game was the away fixture at the Victoria Ground against Stoke City on the first day in November. Phil Gee and a very rare Geraint Williams goal gave Derby a 2-0 victory. My main memory of this game was a mass melee in the Derby six-yard box with most of the outfield players involved, that spread over into the goal net. I think George Berry of Stoke was the main perpetrator, but I may be wrong! After Derby lost at Aston Villa in the League Cup, they won three games on the bounce, 2-1 at home to Ipswich Town, 1-0 away to Barnsley and 2-0 at home to Sheffield United. My next away game was the 2-0 away defeat to Leeds United at Elland Road, with John Sheridan scoring with a great strike from a free kick to give the hosts the points.

Derby were fourth in the table with thirty points from seventeen games, four behind leaders Oldham Athletic. My next away trip was the mid-December game at Home Park against third-placed Plymouth Argyle, which was sandwiched in between the two big home wins 3-0 against Reading and 4-0 against Grimsby Town. We went on the special train to Plymouth. On this occasion we stood on the open terraced Barn Park End, the opposite end to where were stood for the FA Cup Round tie two and half years earlier. Gary Micklewhite gave Derby the lead in the first half with a low right-foot drive past Steve Cherry, who ironically was now in the Argyle goal. The Rams held on to the lead until the ninety-fourth minute, until Tommy Tynan popped up and headed in the equaliser. What a cruel blow for the two- hundred and fifty-mile return home journey! Boxing Day 1986 was a significant and emotional day in the history of Bradford City. Derby's visit was the first game at Valley Parade since the horrific fire nineteen months earlier. We stood behind the goal, with the newly built stand to our left. A John Gregory penalty two minutes from time gave the Rams a 1-0 win and up to third place on forty points, two points behind leaders Portsmouth and one point behind Oldham Athletic. The top three were threatening to pull away from the chasing pack, with Derby six points ahead of fourth place Ipswich Town. As a usual occurrence in this era, Derby played the following day with a home game against lowly Barnsley. A 3-2 win with goals from Phil Gee, Bobby Davison and John Gregory sent Derby to the top of the League following a very impressive run of nine wins, a draw and a defeat in their last eleven League games.

The first fixture of 1987 was being shared by Phil Gee, Bobby Davison, a John Gregory penalty and Gary Micklewhite. The FA Cup third round paired Derby up against Division One Sheffield Wednesday at Hillsborough on the Monday night following the Oldham game, in a game delayed again to the bad weather. I made the trip up to the north of Sheffield on the football special train. I loved the FA Cup, but I thought it would be best to get knocked out and not let it get in the way of the main aim of achieving promotion. My thoughts went back to last season when the cup run nearly derailed the promotion. Derby's record at Hillsborough was poor anyway so I wasn't under any illusions!

Derby lost 1-0 in what turned out to be Graham Harbey's final appearance for the club before he left to join Ipswich Town. Derby drew their next two home games with Birmingham City, a game in which Derby were 2-0 down before two Phil Gee goals earned the Rams a point and 1-1 against West Bromwich Albion. Winger Nigel Callaghan made his debut following his £140,000 move from Watford against Birmingham. In between they had a fine 2-1 victory at Sunderland. My next away game was the visit to Millwall at the Den, arguably the most feared away trip in the country. I went with Paul Watterson, as I did to most of the away games around this time, on the football special train. We arrived at New Cross Gate train station to be greeted by a massive police presence for the twenty-minute walk to the ground. About eight hundred Derby fans were ringed by police, dogs and horses. There were a few verbal exchanges between the two sets of supporters as we headed to the ground but that was about it. We stood behind the goal with a covered terrace, with the Main Stand to our right and a massive bank of terracing to the left which was half covered. Despite a crowd of just over 7,000 there was a terrific, intimidating atmosphere in the ground. Nigel Callaghan's first goal for the club gave Derby a vital 1-0 win, with Tony Cascarino and Teddy Sheringham playing up front for the Lions. Derby were now second in the League with fifty-four points from twenty-eight games. Fortunately, we got back to New Cross Gate unscathed and back home to Derby.

The Rams next home match on the following Saturday was against leaders Portsmouth who had opened up a six-point lead at the top of the table. A scrappy game ended goalless in front of a 21,000 plus crowd, a game in which each team didn't want to lose. Derby were winners in the next away game I went to at the Goldstone Ground, against struggling Brighton and Hove Albion who were second bottom in the table. A Phil Gee goal gave Derby victory. My memory of this day was hearing about the Zeebrugge ferry disaster on the way to the game, when the MS Herald of Free Enterprise capsized, with 190 people losing their lives. Two fine home wins 3-1 against Shrewsbury Town and 3-2 against Blackburn Rovers proved the perfect tonic before two away games at Hull City and Ipswich Town. The two home wins moved Derby to top of the table, two points ahead of Portsmouth and more importantly six points ahead of third place of Oldham Athletic. The significance of this was that this was the first ever season of the end of season play-offs. The top two teams of Division

Two would automatically be promoted to Division One. The bottom three teams in Division One would automatically be relegated. Four teams would play two two-legged semi-finals. Nineteenth place in Division One v Fifth place Division Two and Third place Division Two v Fourth place Division Two. The winners of each game would play a two-legged final with the prize a place in Division One.

I went to both the Hull and Ipswich games. A Rob Hindmarch goal gave Derby a share of the spoils at Boothferry Park. Derby put in a fantastic performance in at Portman Road, in a game I went to on a minibus organised by John Moreton from work. It was an exciting open game which fourth-placed Ipswich had to win to keep their slender hopes of automatic promotion alive. Mark Brennan put a first half penalty woefully wide before Nigel Callaghan put Derby ahead with a fine curling shoot from twenty-five yards just after the interval. Gary Micklewhite's mazy run down the right and cross was perfect for Bobby Davison to head home at the far post to send the away following wild. This was this day that I started to believe promotion could be a reality. Derby and Portsmouth were neck and neck, both on sixty-eight points from thirty-four games with Oldham on sixty-five points from thirty-four games. It was going to be a titanic battle that would possibly go right down to the wire, with eight games to go. Derby's next two games saw four points collected from a 2-0 win against Huddersfield, with Eric Steele replacing the injured Mark Wallington in goal, and a goalless draw against Stoke City. Good Friday and a trip to Blackburn Rovers. Ewood Park had become a bit of a bogey ground in recent seasons. In the Lancashire sunshine, that trend continued with

Derby falling to their first League defeat since the Crystal Palace reversal at the beginning of January. Rovers won 3-1, with that man Simon Garner scoring two. To add salt into the wound, Bobby Davison limped off injured. The Easter Monday game at home to Bradford City now took on greater significance with the Davison injury. Mark Lillis came back into the side for only his second start of the season following injury and the emergence of Phil Gee. Lillis scored a diving header from Gee's cross to give the Rams a precious three points. This turned out to be Lillis' only goal in his Derby career. After the Bradford game, Derby had stretched their lead at the top of the League to three points from Portsmouth and ten points from Oldham although the Latics had two games in hand.

Bramall Lane, Sheffield was the venue for the next away game, with four games remaining. There was another mass following for the Rams, with nearly 8,000 making the short trip up the M1. Phil Gee scored the winner as he outpaced centre-back Paul Stancliffe, before slotting the ball past John Burridge to send the fans behind that goal into raptures. Derby broke a 103-year-old record with their eleventh away win of the season. The lead over third place Oldham now extended to twelve points, but they still had a game in hand. Oldham won their game in hand by 2-0 at Stoke City so were now nine points behind Derby with three games left. Derby had a far superior goal difference so one point from three games would see Derby home. On Saturday 2 May, a crowd of 20,000 packed into the Baseball Ground for the game against Leeds United. Goals from the fit again Bobby Davison and Phil Gee gave Derby a 2-0 win and guaranteed a return to the top tier for the first time since their relegation in 1980.

With two games to go the only question to answer was who would be Champions: Derby or Portsmouth? Derby had a three-point advantage going into their last away game at Reading on May Day Monday. I went to the game at Elm Park, my third trip there in three years. Derby were surprisingly poor and lost 2-0. Portsmouth also lost 1-0 at Crystal Palace, so with one game left at home to Plymouth Argyle, Derby only needed a draw to be Division Two Champions.

On the day of the Plymouth match I travelled to London to compete in my first London Marathon, as I'd been accepted through the ballot, therefore missing the match. I went with my dad and brother-in-law, Pete Birks. I picked up my running number in the morning before we headed off to Wembley to watch Burton Albion, managed by Brian Fidler, take on Kidderminster Harriers in the FA Trophy final. Burton were in the Northern Premier League and Kidderminster were in the Conference. The game finished 0-0 but I was really more concerned with the events at the Baseball Ground. Goals from Bobby Davison, Nigel Callaghan, Gary Micklewhite and John Gregory gave the Rams a 4-2 win and a thoroughly deserved Division Two Championship. Veteran keeper Eric Steele made his final appearance for the club before moving to Southend United. It had been a remarkable couple of seasons. Arthur Cox had masterminded the two promotions and legendary status with it. The next day, I completed the London Marathon in 3.54 minutes to round off a fantastic weekend.

CHAPTER 5

BACK IN THE BIG TIME AND THE MAXWELL YEARS

1987/88

There were two major events in the summer of 1987. Robert Maxwell, who had helped rescue the Rams three years earlier, took over as chairman from his son, Ian. He also pulled off a major coup by signing thirty-seven-year-old England goalkeeper Peter Shilton from Southampton. As well as Eric Steele, Mark Wallington, who had played a major role in the double promotion also left the club, joining Lincoln City. Shilton made his debut in the opening day 1-0 victory over Luton Town, with John Gregory scoring the solitary goal to give the Rams a great start to the season. I had bought a season ticket in the Normanton End upper tier with three friends from work, Tony Clemson, Kal Bhatti and Paul Watterson. On the following Wednesday, I drove to West London for the game at Loftus Road against Jim Smith's Queen's Park Rangers on their artificial pitch. Mark Snape and Nigel Lee came with me on what was a hot mid-August afternoon. As we travelled down the M1, news was emerging on the radio about a gunman going on a killing spree in the Berkshire town of Hungerford. Frighteningly, Michael Ryan killed sixteen people by going on a rampage through the town before turning the gun on himself. At Loftus Road, Phil Gee gave Derby an early lead before Gary Bannister levelled before half time, with the game finishing 1-1. As we travelled back up the motorway, we had a two-hour delay due to a combination of roadworks and people returning from the Madonna concert at Wembley. It had been a long unforgettable day!

Derby then signed twenty-four-year-old England centre-back Mark Wright from Southampton for a club record £760,000, as Arthur Cox continued to strengthen his squad. Cox confirmed Wright would make his debut in the next game at home to Wimbledon, but he wouldn't reveal whether Rob Hindmarch or Ross MacLaren, who had formed a formidable partnership at the heart of Derby's defence, would make way for Wright. Much to my surprise it was MacLaren who was the unlucky man to drop out of the side. Derby lost the game 1-0, with John Fashanu scoring a second half winner for the Dons. Derby's first away win was on the following Saturday, when they won 2-1 at Norwich City. I listened to the game on the radio, with Bobby Davison and a John Gregory penalty earning the three points. Derby had made a sound start to the season with eight points from five games, lying eleventh place in the table.

My next away trip was the League Cup second round first leg game at Roots Hall against Division Three side Southend United. I drove the one hundred and sixty miles to the game, with Mark Jarrett, Nigel Lee and Dave Hudson. By a strange twist of fate, Eric Steele was in goal for the Shrimpers. It turned out to be an embarrassing night for the Rams as they lost to a Roy McDonagh goal, a name I'll never forget! To make matters worse, Derby had Bobby Davison sent off. On the return journey we stopped at the M1 services near Leicester. As we left the services and got back onto the motorway, I suffered a puncture on one of my back tyres, and had to stop on the hard shoulder and change it. That's the last thing you want at one a.m. after a bad defeat and a gruelling journey home! On the Saturday, Derby lost their home game 1-0 to Oxford United. This was the first game in which Robert Maxwell made a fleeting appearance in his helicopter. It landed somewhere behind the Osmaston End before he made his way to the Director's box. Maxwell certainly thrived on the limelight.

Anfield Road, Liverpool, L4 OTF on Tuesday 29 September 1987. This was the scene of the greatest performance I have ever seen by a football club live. I can still see Gerald Mortimer's headline on the back page of the Derby Evening Telegraph. DON'T FEAR REDS was Arthur Cox's message to his side. We went to the game in a minibus. We parked up on one of the side streets and made our way to the ground, past throbbing pubs, packed fish and chip shops, mobile hot dog and burger stalls, stalls selling programmes, flags, scarves etc. Nigel Lee, who was with us, wasn't impressed with the 'Scouse' pie he bought. He recalls it was cold, half-full, congealed and horrible! It reminded me of my early days of going to the Baseball Ground, but I'd not seen anything on this scale outside a football stadium before. This was even better than outside Hillsborough, Villa Park and St. James' Park, as the majority of the grounds I'd visited were in the lower Leagues. We stood in the corner at the Anfield Road end, opposite the Kop. The atmosphere was electric as 'You'll

Never Walk Alone' bellowed around the magnificent stadium. Liverpool played some magical football, hardly losing the ball with great movement off the ball. A John Aldridge penalty gave Liverpool a half time 1-0 lead. Liverpool turned on the heat even more in the second half, with Peter Shilton having a fantastic game, pulling off save after save after waves of Liverpool attacks. Bruce Grobbelaar in the Liverpool goal only touched the ball twice in the whole game and they were two pass backs! Liverpool added three more goals in the second half, with two more from John Aldridge, including a second penalty and Peter Beardsley. John Barnes and Craig Johnston were magnificent in a faultless display. The final score was 4-0. If it hadn't been for Shilton it could have been 44-0! It had been an absolute privilege and honour to be among the 43,405 crowd.

Derby then hosted Southend United for the League Cup second round second leg at the Baseball Ground, trying to overcome their 1-0 defeat in the first leg. Derby were having trouble scoring goals, which was becoming concerning. The game ended goalless, so Derby were knocked out. The eagerly awaited East Midlands derby against Nottingham Forest was Derby's next match. Forest, in the top six, had a fine side with Stuart Pearce, Des Walker, Neil Webb, Nigel Clough and Franz Carr in their ranks. In a typical bloods and guts local encounter, Paul Wilkinson's goal separated the two sides. Two days before Derby's next match against Charlton Athletic at their temporary home of Selhurst Park, a powerful storm ravaged many parts of Britain with the south-east of England bearing the brunt of the storm. Very strong winds were gusting at up to a hundred miles per hour, and there was massive devastation across the country and eighteen people were killed. Many trees fell on to roads and railways, causing major transport delays. Most people remember BBC weatherman Michael Fish just before the storm declaring, "Earlier on today, apparently, a woman rang the BBC and said she heard there was a hurricane on the way. Well, if you're watching, don't worry, there isn't!" Derby won the game in the capital with Steve Cross scoring his first goal in the 1-0 win. The following Saturday, I went to Highbury for Derby's visit to Highbury to play Arsenal. Like Anfield, Highbury had the feel of matchday being a massive occasion on the walk from the train station to the ground. We stood on the open terraced Clock End opposite the North Bank. Arsenal were a team full of international class, with Tony Adams, David O'Leary, Kenny Sansom, the late David Rocastle, Steve Williams and Alan Smith. Kevin Richardson gave the Gunners a first minute lead, with Michael Thomas adding a second from the spot ten minutes later. It looked like it was going to be a long afternoon for Derby, but they rallied and pulled one back, through Andy Garner's header. It finished 2-1 to Arsenal with nineteen-year-old Paul Merson coming on as a second half substitute. Peter Shilton put on a masterclass in Derby's next away game at Newcastle United, which was Arthur Cox's first return there since his departure in May 1984. I listened to the game on Radio Derby with Graham Richard's commentary. Newcastle, spurred on by the very gifted Paul Gascoigne, just couldn't beat Shilton. Cox asked Shilton for his autographed shirt after the game, which finished goalless. This game was also Bobby Davison's last game for the club in his first spell, before his £350,000 move to Division Two Leeds United. I must admit, Davison is one of my all-time favourite Derby players. He suffered the relegation to Division Three but was a major part of the double promotion winning team, scoring eighty-three goals League goals in 206 appearances in his five years at the club. Derby then signed twenty-two-year-old Mark Patterson for £60,000 from Division Four Carlisle United. Derby's next home game was the first time that they appeared live in a League match on television. The game, covered by the BBC's Match of the Day, was played on a Sunday afternoon at the end of November against Chelsea. Two things I remember from the day are Chelsea playing in an all-lime green kit, and John Gregory scoring Derby's second goal with an acrobatic volley in a 2-0 win. My next away game was three weeks later, against Everton at Goodison Park. I again went on the football special train. Reigning League Champions Everton were fifth in the table, so I was expecting it to be a very tough afternoon. It turned out that way, with Derby slipping to a 3-0 defeat. Everton had a terrific line up with Neville Southall, Gary Stevens, Kevin Ratcliffe, Peter Reid, Trevor Steven, Kevin Sheedy and Graeme Sharp having far too much quality for Derby. After eighteen games, Derby were eleventh in the table with twenty-four points. Derby then suffered three successive defeats before my next away game on New Year's Day at Wimbledon. The Rams lost two home games both 2-1 against Tottenham Hotspur and Norwich City, with David Penney making his first start in the Norwich game and then the customary defeat at Hillsborough by 2-1 to Sheffield Wednesday. So on to Wimbledon for the New Year's Day late morning kick off at Plough Lane. I went on the Roadrider bus to witness another defeat. Wimbledon were big and strong, with their own unique style. Former Derby apprentice Alan Cork and John Fashanu scored for Wimbledon, with Nigel

Callaghan scoring Derby's goal. Brian McCord made his League debut starting at right-back. Following five defeats on the bounce, it left Derby a worryingly sixteenth in the table with twenty-four points from twenty-two games, only three points above the dreaded drop zone. The FA Cup third round paired Derby at home to Chelsea. Dave Penney scored his first goal for the club after Kevin McAllister had put Chelsea ahead, but goals from Kerry Dixon and Roy Wegerle sent the Blues through to the fourth round, leaving Derby to focus on their efforts to climb away from any relegation danger.

Derby's alarming form continued though, with three more League defeats away at Luton Town, at Portsmouth and at home to Manchester United. Prior to the game at Fratton Park, Derby added much needed new blood to their squad, with the arrival of Scottish winger Ted McMinn from Spanish side Seville, in a £300,000 deal. McMinn scored a spectacular left foot drive in the 2-1 Manchester United defeat. Eight successive defeats had plummeted the Rams to fourth-from-bottom of the League, a point ahead of Watford. The next game was a classic 'six-pointer' at the Manor Ground, against second bottom Oxford United. Derby at last arrested the slide in a dour goalless draw in a game that was important not to lose. The following week, on the penultimate day of February, Derby recorded their first win since the end of November, with a 1-0 win over West Ham United. Ted McMinn missed a first half penalty, but a diving header from Nigel Callaghan from a Phil Gee cross gave Derby the precious three points.

In the midweek, I went with Paul Cannon and Mark Jarrett to the away game at White Hart Lane against Tottenham Hotspur.

We stopped at a pub in Harpenden, meeting up with Gary Parkin. In a fairly uneventful game, Derby secured a good point with a 0-0 draw. Tottenham included Paul Walsh in their line up following his move from Liverpool for £500,000, after seeing off Derby for his signature. Arthur Cox was a long-time admirer of Walsh. I was gutted when he chose Tottenham. I love a centre-forward who can hold the ball up and bring other players into the game. Despite Walsh only being a small man, he was a master of playing that role and had a fantastic seventeen-year career.

Derby then drew two home games against Charlton Athletic and admirably against Champions elect Liverpool, who had a fifteen-point lead over second place Manchester United with two games in hand. Craig Johnson had given the Reds a second half, before a swashbuckling run from Michael Forsyth, who received a return pass from Gary Micklewhite, before firing past Bruce Grobbelaar. Derby then had a fine 3-0 win at Coventry City, with experienced Republic of Ireland striker Frank Stapleton making his debut. Derby were desperately short of strikers, and really needed Stapleton's vast experience. I didn't know the score until after the match, as I was running in the Rhayader twenty-mile road race in mid-Wales. I was in training again for the London Marathon after being accepted through the ballot for the second successive year. The vital win at Coventry moved Derby up to sixteenth in the table, four points above the bottom three automatic relegation places and three points above fourth-from-bottom, which was the dreaded play-off position. My next away game was my first ever visit to the City Ground, Nottingham for the midweek fixture at the end of March. We stood at the Bridgford End corner next to the Brian Clough Stand, in the hostile atmosphere you'd expect in a local derby. Derby were under pressure for most of the first half, with Nigel Clough giving Forest the lead. A Colin Foster own goal gave Derby hope before Clough restored the home side's lead with the game finishing 2-1. A Brian McClair hat-trick in Derby's next away game on Easter Saturday at Old Trafford, set Manchester United on the way to a 4-1 victory. With six games to go Derby were in seventeenth place in the table only three points above the relegation zone and two points away from the play-off position. The Easter Monday home game against Newcastle United gave Derby much needed relief with a 2-1 win. Two successive defeats at Chelsea and at home to Queen's Park Rangers left Derby five points ahead of the drop zone and two points away from the play-off position, as other results went in their favour. A week prior to the crucial Southampton home game, I again competed in the London Marathon. I was gradually improving and finished in a time of 3.48. A win against Southampton would go a long way to preserving their Division One status.

Derby were strengthened by the return of right-back Mel Sage, who had been out for six months with a groin injury. Southampton included seventeen-year-old Alan Shearer in their side. A fine finish from John Gregory and a first goal for Frank Stapleton gave the Rams the vital three points as they moved up to fifteenth, six points above the drop zone and still only two points away from the play-off position.

The two games remaining were away at already relegated second bottom Watford and at home to reigning Champions Everton. I went to the game at Vicarage Road, which finished in a scrappy 1-1 draw with ex-Watford man Nigel Callaghan scoring Derby's goal. The performance was irrelevant, it was all about picking up something up from the game. A draw against Everton materialised and Derby had done it. It was a massive achievement to avoid relegation, as seven of the players were involved when Derby were promoted from Division Three. The only major signings were Shilton and Wright, with Ted McMinn joining the club for the final third of the season. Against Everton, Frank Stapleton, John Gregory and Ross MacLaren all made their final appearances for the club. Like Bobby Davison, Gregory and MacLaren had made massive contributions to the club in their meteoric rise. The trick now for Arthur Cox was to improve the squad further with backing from chairman Robert Maxwell.

1988/89

Arthur Cox did strengthen his squad. The major signing was Paul Goddard from Newcastle United for £425,000. Goddard or 'Sarge' as he was known, had been a success on Tyneside, but his family had failed to settle in the north-east and wanted to move back down south. Cox convinced him to join Derby but promised to inform him if a club nearer London came knocking. Experienced Oxford United thirty-year-old midfielder Trevor Hebberd signed for £275,000, with Mickey Lewis moving to the Manor Ground as part of the deal.

Nick Pickering, who had played for Coventry City in their 1987 FA Cup Final 3-2 win against Tottenham Hotspur, joined Derby for £250,000. Former Notts County Nigerian winger John Chiedozie joined on a free transfer from Tottenham

Hotspur. Goddard, Hebberd and Chiedozie all made their debuts in the opening day 1-0 home win against Middlesbrough, with Goddard scoring the winner with a second half header. Nick Pickering made his debut the following week in the away match at the Den against Millwall, who were playing their first ever home game in the top tier of English football. Teddy Sheringham scored the only goal to give the Lions victory. John Chiedozie suffered cartilage damage in only his second appearance for Derby, which sadly turned out to be his last. Derby recorded their second home victory against Newcastle United. A stunning left foot strike from fully twenty-five yards by Trevor Hebbard screamed past Dave Beasant, who had just joined Newcastle from FA Cup winners Wimbledon. Paul Goddard turned in Ted McMinn's cross to give Derby a 2-1 win. In the East Midlands derby the following week at the City Ground, Hebbard scored again, equalising a minute after Colin Foster had given Forest an eighty-sixth minute lead, with the game ending all square at 1-1. Derby lost their next two home games, 1-0 against both Queen's Park Rangers and Norwich City, with a 0-0 draw at Southampton in between. In the Norwich game, Mark Wright scored an own goal to give the Canaries the points, and then was sent off after throwing a punch at Trevor Putney.

Derby beat old adversaries Southend United in the two-legged League Cup second round but were struggling to score goals in the League. Arthur Cox missed the next home game against Charlton Athletic, which finished goalless, as he went on a scouting mission to find a partner for Paul Goddard to end their goal drought. The day before the next game at home to Wimbledon, Derby unveiled their first ever million-pound signing, with Welsh international striker Dean Saunders joining the club from Division Two Oxford United. The U's manager Mark Lawrenson and chairman Robert Maxwell's son Kevin had an agreement that Saunders would only be sold if Oxford failed to win promotion at the end of the season. Mark Lawrenson promptly resigned in protest. Saunders was an instant success scoring twice on his debut in the 4-1 Wimbledon home win. Derby were thirteenth in the League table with twelve points from nine games. The Rams were then dumped out of the League Cup, losing 5-0 in the third-round tie at Upton Park. My Michigan Dynamo mates had arranged a minibus to go to the game. I had to miss the game as my wife Julie was working at Peter Brown's in Sheffield that day. She got the train up there, but I didn't want her hanging around a train station in the dark and unfamiliar surroundings so I drove up to Sheffield to pick her up around tea time. Derby then had a fine 3-1 win at Tottenham Hotspur, with two goals from Ted McMinn and another for Dean Saunders. Saunders then scored again in successive games, in the 2-2 home draw with Manchester United and then in the away win at Aston Villa as his partnership with Paul Goddard began to flourish. Derby surged up the table moving up into the top six, with nineteen points from twelve games. Norwich City were League leaders, with twenty-eight points from thirteen games. Derby recorded another win against a top club, by beating Arsenal 2-1 at home. Michael Thomas gave the Gunners the lead, with Nigel Callaghan equalising following in Ted McMinn's missed penalty, with his first goal of the season. Phil Gee, who had slipped down the pecking order following Dean Saunders arrival, volleyed in superbly from Callaghan's cross.

I finally got to go to an away game on the Saturday before Christmas, with the trip to Highfield Road for the away game against Coventry City. Dean Saunders scored yet again with Ted McMinn adding the other in a 2-0 win as the Rams' rise up the League continued as they moved up to fourth in the League with twenty points from sixteen games, seven points behind leaders Norwich City. On Wednesday 21 December Derby lost at Wimbledon in the totally irrelevant Simod Cup, a knock out tournament for teams in the top two tiers that had been introduced to fill the void left by the English teams being banned from Europe following the Heysel disaster of 1985. Martin Fisher, who was reporting for BBC Radio Derby, went with Chris Stevenson, Paul Cannon and Mark Jarrett. I remember this day vividly as it is Julie's birthday, our wedding anniversary, and the day flight Pan Am flight 103 crashed over Lockerbie in south-west Scotland.

Derby then lost two games at home over Christmas, 1-0 against Liverpool with Ian Rush scoring, and also 1-0 to Millwall, with Teddy Sheringham heading home, which in all honesty Peter Shilton should have saved. Derby, though were back to winning ways in their first match of 1989, when Mark Wright's towering header gave Derby a 1-0 win at Newcastle United. I was really looking forward to the FA Cup, especially as Derby were putting a good side together, capable of beating the best teams in the country, and I fancied them to go along way if the draw was favourable. Derby were drawn at home to fellow Division One side Southampton. Chairman Robert Maxwell saw this as a chance to parade Lubos Kubik and Ivo Knoflicek, who were playing their football in Czechoslovakia with Slavia Prague, in front of the Baseball Ground crowd prior to the match. The pair had absconded from a training camp and spent five months fleeing authorities though Western Europe. Maxwell claimed they were amateur footballers and genuine refugees and they were desperate to ply their trade in England. The two, though, were not amateurs or free agents; they were under contract to Slavia Prague. Maxwell had put the pair up in hotels, claiming he could get the players for free, but Slavia Prague were having none of it. Arthur Cox was very coy about the whole deal and wouldn't be drawn in on it. The deal never materialised. Kubik finally ended up in Serie A with Fiorentina, and Knoflicek ended up in West Germany. It was all rather theatrical and a typical Maxwell publicity stunt. On the pitch, the game ended 1-1. I went to the replay at the Dell on the following Wednesday. I left my car in Carrington Street before taking the Roadrider bus to the south coast. Derby put in a tremendous performance, winning 2-1 with goals from Ted McMinn and Dean Saunders, which earned Derby a fourth-round tie at Watford. The bus arrived back in the early hours, I returned to my car only to find someone had smashed my quarter-light. Fortunately, that was the only damage and nothing missing from the car. Derby lost their next home game 2-1 against West Ham United.

The Hammers left-back Julian Dicks had a tremendous game. It was unfortunate for him that he played in the same era as Stuart Pearce. He never played a senior game for England which was quite surprising, even with his poor disciplinary record. The following week, Geraint Williams scored the winning goal at Queen's Park Rangers, with his first goal of the season. I went to the FA Cup fourth Round against Watford at Vicarage Road on a very wet day. We were stood on the covered terrace behind the goal, which was quite a distance from the pitch. The ground was in desperate need of modernisation. Rick Holden put the Hornets ahead, with Gary Micklewhite levelling with fifteen minutes to go. It looked like Derby had earned a replay, but Neil Redfearn sent Watford through with a twenty-five-yard free kick. I was beginning to think I would never see Derby in a FA Cup Final.

I drove to the next match at Norwich City, with Paul Cannon, Chris Stevenson and Mark Jarrett. We met Paul's uncle, a lifelong Norwich season ticket holder, at the Freemason's Arms just down the road from the ground for a drink before the match. Robert Fleck scored the Canaries winner, with the only goal of the game. I really like Carrow Road, it's a really good stadium with a good view from our position in the South Stand seating area. Norwich have always had a good following home and away for a place which is such a pain to get to, as England's most easterly football ground. Surprisingly Derby then sold Nigel Callaghan to Aston Villa in a £500,000 deal, reuniting him with his former boss Graham Taylor. Derby beat Everton the following Saturday in a cracking end to end game at the Baseball Ground. Dean Saunders stabbed home a Gary Micklewhite cross, but Graeme Sharp equalised just before the break, latching on to a Michael Forsyth back pass. Paul Goddard restored Derby's advantage from close range following Trevor Hebbard's cross. Wayne Clarke's powerful header from Kevin Sheedy's cross made it 2-2, before a sublime chip from Paul Goddard sent the home fans home happy. Derby were sixth in the table with thirty-eight points from twenty-four games. Derby were thrashed 4-0 against Wimbledon in the midweek, on a heavy pitch at Plough Lane, with Paul Miller bagging a hat-trick.

Dean Saunders gave Derby the lead in their next match at home to Tottenham with a fine one-on-one finish, typical of Bobby Davison. Paul Gascoigne's curling free kick, though, gave Spurs a share of the spoils. Ted McMinn's in-swinging corner was pushed into his own net by Middlesbrough's Stephen Pears, to give Derby a 1-0 win at Ayresome Park in the next away game. The much-awaited East Midlands derby between seventh-placed Derby and fifth-placed Nottingham Forest was the next game, with both clubs on forty-two points. This was the closest the teams had been in terms of League placings for a very long time. Forest though came out on top yet again, with a fine strike from Steve Hodge and Lee Chapman cashing in on a Mark Wright error.

My next away game was my first ever visit to Upton Park for the game against West Ham United. We went on the football special train on an early April sunny morning. We stood behind the goal on the South Bank covered terrace, with the East Stand that became affectionately known as 'The Chicken Run' away to our right. Gary Micklewhite gave Derby the lead, with Leroy Rosenoir equalising with the game finishing 1-1.

The following week on Saturday 15 April will go down as one of the darkest days, if not probably the darkest, in the history of British football. A crush developed on the Leppings Lane terracing at the Hillsborough stadium in Sheffield, resulting in the deaths of ninety-six Liverpool fans attending the FA Cup semi-final between Liverpool and Nottingham Forest. Football changed forever following this tragic event.

Following the report into the disaster by Lord Justice Taylor, he recommended football grounds in the top two tiers to be all-seater stadium and all perimeter fences were to be removed. That night my dad and I recalled leaving the same end of the ground in the 1976 FA Cup semi-final, and we be both mentioned the crush as we left the ground. On the same day Derby won 2-0 at Manchester United, but that was totally irrelevant following the upsetting news that filtered through from South Yorkshire. The events of Hillsborough and watching it unfold on the television gave me the shudders. How could you possibly go to a football match and not return home? It's hard to contemplate what those families have gone through in the intervening years.

Derby had six games left to consolidate their place in the top six. In fact, looking back the only Derby game I can remember from those final six games was Derby's 2-1 victory at Highbury, in their penultimate game of the season. Dean Saunders put Derby ahead halfway through the first half with an outstanding volley on the turn from Geraint Williams' cross. Saunders doubled Derby's lead when he dispossessed Tony Adams, before being brought down by the Arsenal skipper and then converting the penalty. Alan Smith pulled one back but Derby held on for a famous victory. This was a massive blow for Arsenal in their pursuit of the title. Arsenal faced Liverpool at Anfield in the final match of the season. The equation was simple – they had to win by a two-goal margin against the defending Champions to claim the title for the first time in eighteen years or Liverpool would retain the title. Manager George Graham's got his tactics spot on. Arsenal scored just after the break through Alan Smith's header. Deep into injury time midfielder Michael Thomas scored the all-important second goal to secure the title. What an unbelievable finish to a season! Derby finished fifth in what had been a fantastic season. Peter Shilton called it a 'battling fifth'. If it wasn't for Heysel and the five-year ban imposed on English clubs, Derby would have qualified for the UEFA Cup for the first time since 1976/77. The arrival of Dean Saunders was just what Derby needed. The combination of Saunders and Goddard was as good as any I had seen since I started watching the Rams. All was looking rosy ahead of the 1989/90 season.

1989/90

There were no major incomings or outgoings in the lead up to the new season, as Derby headed to play Charlton Athletic at their temporary home of Selhurst Park on the opening day. One thing that did change was Derby reverting to black shorts and socks from navy blue shorts and socks. The game ended in a draw, as did Derby's first home game of the season in midweek against Wimbledon. Derby recorded their first home win when Manchester United came to town on the following Saturday, with goals from Paul Goddard and a Dean Saunders penalty. The first East Midlands derby took place at the City Ground on the last Saturday of August. Forest's domination over Derby continued. Derby took the lead, with Steve Hodge heading into his own net following Gary Micklewhite's free kick. Forest took control in the second half, with Gary Crosby scoring from close range following Mark Wright's error. Stuart Pearce scored Forest's second, following a return pass from Nigel Clough. Pearce really was a thorn in Derby's side in this era and arguably, dare I say it, England's finest left-back I've seen in my life time. Derby were completely outplayed in their next home game against Liverpool. Three first half goals from Ian Rush, a John Barnes penalty and Peter Beardsley gave the Reds a 3-0 victory. Derby's slow start to the season left them in fourteenth place with five points from five games. Derby unveiled their new away kit in the next away game against Queen's Park Rangers at Loftus Road. It was a quite unusual with 'snazzy' grey and black stripped shirts, red shorts and red socks. Dean Saunders steered home Paul Goddard's cross past David Seaman, to give the Rams a much needed 1-0 win. Derby lost their next two games 1-0 at home to Southampton and 1-0 away to Aston Villa. I just felt the squad needed freshening up, as Arthur Cox had very few options to make changes. They ended September in sixteenth place with eight points from eight games. They did, though, progress to the next round of the League Cup. A 5-0 home win against Cambridge United with Dean Saunders scoring a hat-trick gave them a 6-2 aggregate win. Saunders scored yet again, together with a brace from Paul Goddard in the 3-1 home win against Crystal Palace. Derby made it through to the fourth round of the League Cup with a 2-0 home win against Sheffield Wednesday. Wednesday, who wore very unfamiliar green and white shirts, took the lead with four minutes to go through a David Hirst penalty. Remarkably Derby then scored two, with that man Dean Saunders adding two more to add to his impressive season's tally, one of them from the penalty spot. Derby drew at Highbury in their next game at Champions Arsenal, with Paul Goddard scoring a late header to cancel out Alan Smith's opener for the Gunners.

The next day, Sunday 29 October, is another day I'll remember for the rest of my life. I was playing for Michigan Dynamo against Castle Gresley in the Derbyshire Sunday Cup. We lost the game 1-0 in a game that Gresley dominated, with the score line flattering us. With about five minutes to go, I chased a ball down the right-wing. I got barged by the Gresley left-back who was shorter than me but quite stocky. To be honest, the barge was quite fair, but I got my studs caught in the turf and I twisted my left knee. I felt something go but I wasn't sure what it was. I got some treatment but when I stood up, I couldn't put any weight on my left leg. After I got carried back to the changing rooms, I tried to put my jeans on, but my knee had swollen up so much I couldn't get them on! I couldn't drive, so someone had to drive my car home. The next day I couldn't walk when I got up and ended having the week off work. I managed to get to the Derbyshire Royal Infirmary for an X-Ray. The doctor told me there was nothing major wrong and I'd be playing again soon. I wasn't convinced and over the next few weeks when I tried the knee out, it kept giving way. I joined a private health care scheme through work which meant a trip to Manor House Hospital in Golders Green in North London to see an orthopaedic consultant. I travelled down to London on the Friday, with an arthroscopy in planned in for the Monday. On the Saturday, I made most of my trip by going to watch Barnet play Hereford United at Underhill, to get another ground in. In those days, Barnet were managed by Barry Fry and under the chairmanship of the late Stan Flashman which was quite a volatile relationship – in general, you either loved or loathed Fry. I always liked Fry, who like Neil Warnock, are two of the great characters of the modern game. They will be missed when they eventually call it a day, as there a very few characters left in the game nowadays. The only names I recognised from the match were ex-Luton Town striker Brian Stein and Carl Hoddle, brother of Glenn, for Barnet and ex-Coventry City and Norwich City left-back Greg Downs, who was Hereford player/manager. On the Monday, my fears were confirmed. I had ruptured my anterior cruciate ligament and it needed reconstructive surgery. The consultant told me they were reluctant to do an operation on a local footballer but they would do it if I wanted. In those days, the recovery and rehabilitation period took between twelve to fifteen months. What did put me off was that around the same time England under 21 international Paul Lake of Manchester City had the same injury. He had two or three operations that proved to be unsuccessful and his career ended after only playing a further four games in five years. I've read Lake's autobiography *I'm Not Really Here*, which is a very sad, powerful and moving read. I decided not to go ahead with the operation as I was concerned how long I would be off work, with a relatively new mortgage and young daughter. I was twenty-five and in fourteen years of playing I'd probably played over 350 games for school teams and local teams; now my playing days were over. It was very hard to take especially at such a young age, with potentially another ten seasons at least left in me. I was hardly ever injured. I'd never had a pulled muscle, just the occasional twisted ankle or dead leg. The good news now for ACL injuries, medical science nowadays is so far advanced, most players with this type of injury are back playing within nine months. Mentally this affected me quite badly, but I just had to get over it and move on.

The next Saturday, I went to Kenilworth Road for the away

game at mid-table Luton Town. This was my first away game of the season. Away fans were banned from Luton, but my friend Chris Stevenson, who was a milkman, knew Ted McMinn, who managed to get tickets for us. It was quite a surreal experience at Kenilworth Road. The entrance though the turnstiles to the ground at the Oak Road End was through some terraced houses, which was quite strange. Luton, like Queen's Park Rangers and Oldham Athletic had an artificial pitch. This was the first time also I'd seen Derby live in their new away kit. Iain Dowie with a header, scored his first goal for Luton, the only goal of the game. The following week, Manchester City visited the Baseball Ground. Mark Wright and Trevor Hebbard gave Derby a two-goal half time lead, before two penalties from Dean Saunders with his ninth and tenth goals of the season made it 4-0. Further goals by Paul Goddard and Gary Micklewhite completed the 6-0 rout, as Derby recorded their biggest win for five years since beating Lincoln City 7-0 in November 1985. The Saunders and Goddard partnership were at it again the following week, as they both scored in a 2-0 win against Sheffield Wednesday. Derby were now ready for the big home League Cup fourth round tie against West Bromwich Albion. Derby had never really made much progress in this competition in my time as a supporter, so this was a great opportunity to make further progress. A goal in each half from Ted McMinn gave the Rams a 2-0 win as their impressive run continued. The impressive League run continued at White Hart Lane against a Tottenham Hotspur line-up that included Gary Mabbutt, Paul Gascoigne and Gary Lineker. Yet again Dean Saunders and Paul Goddard added to their impressive goal tallies in a 2-1 win, after Paul Stewart had given the home side an early lead. The game though was marred to a serious knee ligament injury to Ted McMinn, following a challenge by Pat Van den Hauwe. Sadly, McMinn was to be out of action for fourteen months. Derby's good run had lifted them up to ninth place in the table, with twenty-one points from fifteen games, with the Goddard and Saunders combination the key to the good run.

Derby's good run continued with a 2-0 home win against Charlton Athletic, with nineteen-year-old Craig Ramage making his debut. Arthur Cox was making a lot of noises about Ramage's potential referring to him as a 'rough diamond'. My immediate impression of Ramage, was a good one as I'd never seen him play before. He replaced the injured Paul Goddard and partnered Dean Saunders. His close control with his back to goal was fine with good link up play, bringing the midfielders into the game. He wasn't very quick but had a good football brain and was a perfect foil for Dean Saunders. Nick Pickering came into the side for the injured Ted McMinn. Paul Goddard returned and scored in the 1-1 draw at Wimbledon, before Derby lost two games on the bounce, 1-0 at Norwich City and 2-1 at home to Everton on Boxing Day. The Everton game saw the final appearance in a Derby shirt for Paul Goddard. Arthur Cox kept his promise and he informed Goddard that Derby had received and accepted an offer from a club in the south. Millwall offered £800,000 for Goddard, who had scored eleven goals in the season to date. Fans weren't happy when the news about his pending departure broke in the media. Colin Gibson, BBC Radio Derby's sports presenter urged fans to phone in with their views on Goddard's imminent sale. The fans obviously weren't happy, as the club looked to be moving in the right direction. The Goddard sale triggered the start of Sportscene Talk-In on BBC Radio Derby, a program that has now been running on Monday evenings for thirty-one years and was the brainchild of Alex Trelinski. BBC Radio Derby have covered Derby County superbly over the years, with presenters like Colin Gibson, Mark Shardlow, Owen Bradley and Chris Coles. Graham Richards was a tough act to follow, but Ross Fletcher, the late Colin Bloomfield and Ed Dawes have done a fine job. Derby's last game of the calendar year was the home game against Coventry City, with Nick Pickering's header putting Derby in front against his former club. Trevor Hebbard's fine goalscoring contribution from midfield continued, adding two more to his tally, before Craig Ramage bundled the ball over the line late on, as Derby ran out 4-1 winners. Derby travelled to the Den on New Year's Day, in what was ironically Paul Goddard's debut for the Lions. Nick Pickering scored again to give Derby a first half lead, only for Ian Dawes to level, with the game finishing 1-1. Derby were tenth in the table with twenty-nine points from twenty-one games, as the season progressed past the halfway point.

In the FA Cup, Derby were drawn away at Division Two Port Vale who had been promoted the previous season, so a tough game lay ahead. I went to the game with Chris Stevenson, with the game played on the Sunday at Vale Park in front of a crowd of over 17,000. On a quagmire of a pitch the game finished 1-1, with Trevor Hebbard scoring yet again for Derby with Darren Beckford earning Vale a replay. Kevin Francis, at six feet seven inches tall, made his debut after moving from Mile Oak Rovers eleven months earlier, when he came on as second half substitute. Francis was something 'different' in the threat he offered. On the same day this was arguably the turning point in Alex Ferguson's Manchester United career. The vital 1-0 win at Nottingham Forest in the live BBCTV Sunday afternoon game with Mark Robins scoring the winner, probably saved Ferguson his job. Talking of Manchester United, I was due for my first visit to Old Trafford to watch Derby the following Saturday, but before that it was the Port Vale replay. Port Vale took the lead though a bizarre own-goal by Rob Hindmarch. His back pass looped over the advancing Peter Shilton. Craig Ramage equalised, but goals from Ray Walker and Nicky Cross put Vale 3-1 ahead. Kevin Francis reduced the arrears but it was all in vain, Derby were knocked out at home to lower League opposition. To make matters worse, I was on nights at work. There was nothing worse than going to work after losing a game. To be honest, it's not much better even when Derby win! On to Old Trafford, I went with my brother-in-law Pete Birks, and my nephew Matt. We stood on the terracing at the East end of the ground, opposite the Stretford End. Ten minutes into the game Steve Bruce was sent off for scything down Dean Saunders. Mark Wright gave Derby a half time lead with a header. Gary Pallister scrambled an equaliser before Nick Pickering swept in a left foot shot past Jim Leighton, following a left-wing cross from Michael Forsyth. Mark Wright, who'd earlier picked up a booking, got his marching order for bringing down Mark Hughes. But Derby held on and completed the 'double' over United and moved up to seventh in the table with thirty-two points from twenty-two games. In the midweek, I went to Upton Park for the League Cup quarter-final game, which I considered the biggest of the season against West Ham United. It was a feisty game with the game finishing 1-1. Dean Saunders was brought down in the box by Steve Potts, but the referee waved play on. Steve Cross was stretchered off following a reckless challenge by George Parris. Martin Allen known as 'Mad Dog' wasn't so lucky as he received a red card for a two-footed lunge on Mark Patterson. Ironically, Allen nearly signed for Derby the night before he signed for West Ham six months earlier, after he'd met Arthur Cox for talks. The game finished 1-1, with Julian Dicks scoring for West Ham and Dean Saunders scoring for Derby. Derby then signed experienced ex-England and Luton Town striker Mick Harford in a deal worth £450,000. Harford made his debut in the home match against Nottingham Forest. Derby played fairly well, but Forest, with goals from Steve Hodge and Nigel Jemson, won 2-0. Derby, no matter how hard they tried, just couldn't break Forest's dominance in this fixture.

In the League Cup replay against West Ham United, Derby gave a debut to reserve goalkeeper Martin Taylor, who replaced the injured Peter Shilton. Young left-back Robbie Briscoe also made his debut, coming on as a second half substitute, as Derby's light squad was being stretched to the limit. The scrappy game ended goalless and went to a second replay at Upton Park, which is unheard of in modern day football. In the second replay, Jonathan Davidson made his debut in central defence, as Mark Wright and Rob Hindmarch were ruled out injured. Derby lost 2-1, despite a fine volley from Dean Saunders, so success in the League Cup again had to wait for at least another season. Derby then had two home wins, 2-0 against Queen's Park Rangers, with Dean Saunders scoring his nineteenth of the season with a fine shot after running clear of Paul Parker from the halfway line, and 2-1 against Tottenham Hotspur, with Mick Harford scoring his first goal for the club. But then they lost three on the trot at the start of March, 1-0 away at Sheffield Wednesday, 2-1 at away at Southampton and 1-0 at home to Aston Villa. Paul Williams made his debut in the next game at Crystal Palace, as Derby halted the run of defeats with a 1-1 draw. I got on the Roadrider bus on a bright sunny day for the trip to Chelsea on the last day of March. The bus, though, broke down on the M1. We were promised a replacement bus, but by the time it arrived it was too late to get to London for the game! To be fair, that's the only time I've set out for a game and never got there. I know friends who have been stuck in motorway traffic jams before, so I've been quite lucky. With six games of the season left Derby were thirteenth in the table on forty points from thirty-one games. Derby won two and lost four of them, in a disappointing end to the season. In the final match Luton Town had to win away at Derby to stop up, but also needed Sheffield Wednesday to lose at home to Nottingham Forest. Luton won 3-2 and Sheffield Wednesday lost 3-0 so Luton survived on goal difference. Derby finished in sixteenth place, one place ahead of Luton, after a disappointing second half of the season. Before Christmas, the season was full of hope and promise with Derby in the top ten and in the quarter-finals of the League Cup, but the sale of Paul Goddard seemed to disrupt the side even though Craig Ramage and Mick Harford played very well. Rob Hindmarch made his last appearance for Derby against Luton before moving to Wolverhampton Wanderers, after a fantastic six seasons at the club, making 164 appearances. Sadly, Rob died in 2002 at the age of forty-one after a long battle with Motor Neurone Disease. Arthur Cox called him a man's man and how right he was.

In the summer, it was World Cup year, with Italia 90, which I think Mark Jarrett went to. Peter Shilton and Mark Wright played significant roles as England reached the semi-finals, before their usual defeat to West Germany in a penalty shoot-out. After the first group game against the Republic of Ireland, which finished 1-1, England manager Bobby Robson decided to change formation and play with three central defenders, which opened the door for Mark Wright to play as sweeper. In a very tight group together with the Netherlands and Egypt, England won the only group game against Egypt, with Wright scoring the only goal of the game. It was a fantastic tournament, with Paul Gascoigne arguably the player of the tournament.

1990/91

Paul Blades, who had come through the ranks as an apprentice, also left the club before the start of the new season, moving to Norwich City for a fee of £700,000. Blades made 166 appearances in his eight seasons at Derby and had shown good versatility, playing at right-back or his preferred position of centre-back. Surprisingly and to the annoyance of the supporters, there was no investment from chairman Robert Maxwell for Arthur Cox to improve the squad, especially with the departure of Hindmarch and Blades for a combined fee in excess of a million pounds. Derby started the new season away at Stamford Bridge against Chelsea. Dean Saunders scored but the Rams fell to a 2-1 defeat. Derby, following the Hillsborough disaster and subsequent enquiry, had now installed seats in the Osmaston and Normanton End lower tiers and removed the fences, which enhanced the view considerably. Their first two home games yielded 1-1 draws against both Sheffield United and Wimbledon. They then lost five League games in a row. A Paul Gascoigne hat-trick gave Tottenham a 3-0 win at White Hart Lane. Aston Villa won 2-0 at the Baseball Ground with Tony Daley and David Platt goals. They lost 2-1 at Norwich City, 2-0 at home to Crystal Palace, with Nigel Callaghan rejoining the club on a month's loan from Aston Villa. A 2-0 defeat at Liverpool sent Derby to the bottom of the League, with two points from the first eight games. Derby's only respite was a two-legged victory over Carlisle United in the second round of the League Cup.

Derby's first win of the season came at the end of October, with a 1-0 win at Southampton with a Mick Harford goal. Then, out of the blue, the Rams beat Sunderland 6-0 at home in the third round of the League Cup, with a Mick Harford hat-trick and a brace from Craig Ramage. Derby's improvement continued in the next two home games, with a 2-1 win against Luton Town and a goalless draw with Manchester United as Derby were replaced at the bottom of the League by Sheffield United. Their good run of form was short lived though, as they were beaten the following week 3-0 at Leeds United. Derby then met Nottingham Forest at home. At last, Derby ended their poor record against Forest with a 2-1 win. Steve Chettle gave the Reds a lead before Craig Ramage latched onto a Gary Micklewhite through ball and clipped it over Mark Crossley to equalise. A second half Dean Saunders header gave Derby victory with another piece of classic commentary by BBC Radio Derby's commentator Graham Richards, "Goal, Goal, Goal, 2-1 Derby, what a header, Forest are behind, dig that one

out of the net, Mark Crossley, not a chance, in the back, 2-1."
In the midweek, Derby earned a replay in the fourth round of the League Cup, following their 1-1 draw at Sheffield Wednesday. On the first day of December, I made the trip up to Roker Park for the away game at Sunderland with my nephew Matt Birks. It was a freezing cold day. I didn't realise there was a beach at Roker, with the ground quite close to the North Sea, until we made our way from the coach park. It was an important game, as Derby looked to move away from the relegation zone. We stood on the Clock Stand terrace opposite the Main Stand, with the open Roker terrace to our right with the covered Fulwell End terrace housing the Sunderland masses to our left.

Derby survived an early Sunderland onslaught, and took the lead with a fine run and shot from the edge of the area by Dean Saunders, with his tenth goal of the season. Mick Harford doubled Derby's lead with a superb diving header from Saunders' cross from the right. Gordon Armstrong pulled one back in the dying seconds but Derby held firm for a vital win. Derby's next match was the fourth round League Cup replay at home to Sheffield Wednesday. The game was dominated by Wednesday, who thoroughly deserved their 2-0 win, with John Harkes scoring a wonder goal with a thirty-yard drive that flew past Peter Shilton into the top corner. The following Saturday, Chelsea visited the Baseball Ground in one of the craziest games I've ever witnessed. Gordon Durie gave Chelsea the lead with Dean Saunders levelling with a close-range header. Kerry Dixon restored Chelsea's lead with Durie adding his second to give the visitors a 3-1 lead at the break. Derby remarkably fought back with Trevor Hebbard's first goal of the season with Saunders, equalising with another header to make it 3-3. Derby took the lead through Gary Micklewhite. But Chelsea scored three in the final quarter of an hour. Dennis Wise headed in at the far post, a fine solo run and shot by Gordon Durie completed his hat-trick, with Graeme Le Saux adding the sixth. Wow, what a game! Derby's last game before Christmas, against Queen's Park Rangers, was played on Sunday 23 December, with a morning kick-off. Dean Saunders with his thirteenth goal of the season salvaged Derby a point with a last-minute goal, after Roy Wegerle had given the R's a first half lead. The draw left Derby fourteenth in the table with seventeen points from seventeen games.

Derby then went on one of their worst runs of their history in the games post-Christmas. They lost fourteen and drew four of their next eighteen games, which included a club record of twenty League games without a win and a third round FA Cup defeat at Newcastle United. One good piece of news for Derby was the return of Ted McMinn, for the first time since he suffered his knee injury against Tottenham Hotspur in November 1989, for the Sheffield United game at the end of January. In late March, Derby suffered an embarrassing 7-1 home defeat against Liverpool. My memory of the game was a midfield masterclass by Jan Molby. He hardly broke sweat and only moved ten yards either side of the halfway line. The final nail in the coffin came in the away game at Manchester City. City took the lead through Niall Quinn. Dean Saunders then beat the offside trap, but was hauled down by Tony Coton, who despite his protests received a red card. Quinn went in goal and saved Saunders' spot kick with a fine save down to his left. City, with ten men, went further ahead, with David White extending the lead before Mick Harford pulled one back. It was a thoroughly wretched end to the season and the game just about summed up the second half of the season. In the final game of the season at Luton Town, three of Derby's best players all played their final games for the club.

The underrated Trevor Hebberd moved to Chesterfield after a month's loan at Portsmouth. Captain Mark Wright moved to Liverpool for £2.2 million, and fan's favourite and goal machine Dean Saunders also moved to Anfield, for a club record £2.9 million. Saunders had scored forty-two League goals in one hundred and six games for Derby. I would have to say I really enjoyed watching Saunders. Whole hearted, great pace, brave, two good feet and good in the air for his size. If I had to name my side of all-time, it would be close call between Saunders and Kevin Hector. It was sad to see him go but he wasn't going to hang around in Division Two, he was too good for that. The fans were in uproar with the lack of investment from Robert Maxwell. In the televised ITV live game against Tottenham Hotspur in January, Maxwell revealed he had turned down a £3 million pound bid for the club from local businessman Lionel Pickering, who was also promptly banned from attending the ground! Cries of 'Maxwell Out' rang around the ground, in a really toxic atmosphere. BBC Radio Derby's Graham Richards was also sued and also banned from the ground as he vented his anger at Maxwell. Chants of "There's only one Graham Richards", bellowed from the stands and terraces. After all the hard work, Derby were back in the Division Two after three seasons in Division One. I just felt we'd missed a golden opportunity to establish the club in the top flight. Boardroom wrangles and lack of investment when in the top flight had blighted Derby yet again, and they had paid for it.

CHAPTER 6

THE DREAM TEAM, LIONEL PICKERING, THE END OF THE COX ERA AND PLAY OFF PAIN

1991/92

Derby had made two summer signings ahead of the new season. Simon Coleman joined from Middlesbrough for £300,000, together with fellow central defender Andy Comyn from Aston Villa for £200,000. Derby kicked off the new season at Sunderland, in the opening game of the season at Roker Park. Coleman and Comyn made their debuts, with Gordon Armstrong giving Sunderland the lead with Mick Harford equalising. Harford scored again in the next game with a clever side foot volley after Andy Comyn stabbed home from close range, as Derby won their first home match against Bryan Robson's Middlesbrough on a very warm, early season evening. Derby had a setback in their next home match against Southend United. A Peter Shilton fumble from an Andy Sussex free kick put the Shrimpers 1-0 up, with former Ram Brett Angell doubling their lead before half time. Paul Williams headed one back but Derby slipped to their first defeat of the season. Williams scored again in the next game, a Sunday fixture against Charlton Athletic at their new temporary home of Upton Park. Derby won 2-0, with Mick Harford scoring what was his last goal for the club before he re-joined Luton Town. My memory of this game was Arthur Cox giving rookie goalkeeper Martin Taylor, who was deputising for Peter Shilton, a roasting for leaning against the advertising hoarding talking to fans during a break in proceedings instead of concentrating on the game. The first away game I went to was the midweek away game at the Manor Ground against Oxford United. Derby were very poor and lost 2-0. Derby only now had Phil Gee as a recognised striker on their books, and were in desperate need of reinforcements. Sixteen-year-old Mark Stallard made his debut coming on as a second half substitute for Gee. Following the defeat, Derby were fifteenth in the table with nine points from eight games, in a stuttering start to the season.

Fortunately, reinforcements arrived before the next game at home to Brighton and Hove Albion. Ian Ormondroyd, known as 'Sticks' due to his height and lanky appearance, signed on a two-month loan before a permanent deal from Aston Villa for £300,000 was completed. Also, thirty-two-year-old Bobby Davison re-joined the club on loan from Leeds United, in a popular move with the supporters. Davison was an instant success, as his right foot drive gave Derby the lead just before half time. Mark Patterson and Paul Williams, from the penalty spot, increased the lead to 3-0 before the Seagulls pulled on back through Raphael Meade. The following Saturday, I took my twelve-year-old nephew Richard Wilson up to St. James' Park for the game against Newcastle United. For some reason, Richard's a Newcastle fan who lives in Derby. I can't understand people who don't support their home town club, it's always baffled me! We stopped for brunch in Scotch Corner on the way up the A1 and bought tickets when we arrived at the ground, sitting in the Main Stand with the open terraced Gallowgate End to the right and the open terraced Leazes End to our left. Derby kicked towards the Leazes End in the first half. After some early pressure, that man Bobby Davison headed in Ted McMinn's free kick to give Derby a half time lead. Derby doubled their lead early in the second half when McMinn's cross was converted by Ian Ormondroyd, who beat the late Pavel Srnicek from close range. Newcastle though came back and scored two late goals, through Andy Hunt and Mick Quinn, with the game finishing 2-2.

Derby's and Bobby Davison's good run continued in the next game, at home to Bristol City. Davison scored two as the Rams ran out 4-1 winners and moved up to eighth in the table, with sixteen points from eleven games. Davison was cup tied for the League Cup second round second leg at Ipswich Town, with Derby winning 2-0 after the first leg ended goalless. Phil Gee and Paul Williams, who continued his good goal scoring run from midfield, netted Derby's goals. I went to the next away game at the County Ground for the match against Glenn Hoddle's high-flying Swindon, who were fourth in the table with Matt Birks. Paul Williams scored again with a deflected long range speculative effort. A dubious penalty converted by Micky Hazard saw Swindon level, before Phil Gee nutmegged Frazer Digby to give Derby maximum points, sending them into the top six. Derby then beat Portsmouth at home with two second half goals from Ted McMinn and Paul Williams. Williams was becoming a real powerhouse in midfield. He picked the ball up in his own half before bursting into the

Pompey box and firing past Alan Knight. The good run continued at the Den the following Saturday, with Bobby Davison and a last-minute header from Ian Ormondroyd scoring the goals, as Derby consolidated their place in the top six. It had been a fine run and a good six weeks from Derby, as my thoughts went back to the poor defeat at Oxford mid-September.

On Tuesday 5 November, the world woke up to the shocking news that sixty-eight-year-old Robert Maxwell fell to his death from his £15m yacht, Lady Ghislaine in the Canary Islands. This turned to anger within a few weeks when a £460 million shortfall was discovered in the pension funds of his companies. A borrower of unimaginable scale, he had illegally raided the funds to prop up his empire, which was on the brink of collapse. Just before this local businessman self-made millionaire Lionel Pickering became the majority shareholder of the club, putting up £13 million. This was welcomed by the supporters, who liked idea of the owner being a lifelong fan. The move would allow Arthur Cox to significantly improve the quality of the playing staff.

Derby then suffered three defeats on the trot. Oldham Athletic won 2-1 in a third round League Cup tie at Boundary Park. John King's Tranmere Rovers won 1-0 at the Baseball Ground, with John Aldridge, who would turn out to be a scourge of Derby throughout his whole career, scoring with a far post header. I was always a fan of John Morrissey who played wide right, a very neat player with good control and a fine crosser of the ball. I always hoped Derby would sign him but it never happened. He had a fine time at Tranmere, scoring fifty goals in a fifteen-year career. The other defeat came 1-0 at Port Vale, with Nico Jalink beating Peter Shilton with a curling free kick. Derby were back to their winning ways at Molineux against Wolverhampton Wanderers. Bobby Davison gave Derby the lead, with only two sides of the ground being used due to the re-development. A Simon Coleman own goal brought the home side back into the game. Coleman was then sent off by referee David Ellerey for bringing down Steve Bull, with Paul Cook scoring from the twice-taken penalty. Ian Ormondroyd levelled for Derby, scooping in a Mel Sage cross. In the final minute Gary Micklewhite's left wing cross was turned into his own net by Tom Bennett, in a remarkable finish. Derby then beat Ipswich Town 1-0, with Bobby Davison scoring. This game though will be more remembered for Mel Sage sustaining a knee injury which ended his career. He had been a very popular player, a fine servant for the club, making one hundred and forty appearances scoring four goals. The following Saturday, I drove to Twerton Park in Bath with Matt Birks for the away game at Bristol Rovers. We stood on the open terrace behind the goals on a late sunny November afternoon. Mark Patterson, who replaced Mel Sage, headed Derby into the lead before ex-Ram Steve Cross levelled for 'The Gas'. David Mehew put the home side ahead, before Paul Williams levelled from the spot. Bobby Davison pounced on a back pass to round 'keeper Brian Parkin to score a dramatic last-minute winner, with his ninth goal in as many games. Derby were now up into the top three with thirty-four points from nineteen games, three points behind leaders Middlesbrough and second place Cambridge United.

Derby lost 2-1 at home to Leicester City with Bobby Davison

playing his final game on loan before returning to Leeds United, with the big question being who would replace him. Derby's really good away form continued with their sixth away win of the season at Watford. Ian Ormondroyd headed Derby in front before a late Luther Blissett goal looked like it would earn the Hornets a point. But Ormondroyd popped up in the box to beat David James from close range to give the Rams a fine 2-1 win. Martyn Chalk made his debut in the home, goalless draw against Grimsby Town on Boxing Day, nearly two years after his move from non-League Louth United. Chalk came on as a second half substitute for Phil Gee. Derby then lost 2-1 in their last game of the year, in a disappointing display against Charlton Athletic.

On New Year's Day, I made the trip up to Ayresome Park with Matt Birks for the away game at third-placed Middlesbrough. We stood on the opened terraced south-east corner, with the Middlesbrough fans massed behind the goal at the opposite end of the ground on the Holgate End. Martyn Chalk and Mark Stallard both started for Derby. Nicky Mohan gave the home side a first half lead, but Chalk levelled in the second half with his first goal for the club, with the game ending 1-1. Three days later, it was FA Cup third round day. Matt and I were on our travels again, for the game at Turf Moor against Division Four Burnley. We'd made it a bit of a habit of calling at a Little Chef for a midday brunch on match days. At Turf Moor, we stood on the covered Longside terrace opposite the Bob Lord Stand with the Bee Hole End terrace to our left. It was a cracking atmosphere in the ground, with a 18,000 plus crowd. Martyn Chalk gave Derby the lead with a far post of header, following a fine run and cross down the left by Mark Stallard. Burnley levelled before half time through Steve Harper. Andy Comyn bundled the ball home to restore Derby's advantage. With six minutes remaining though, Roger Eli headed home to earn the Clarets a replay at the Baseball Ground. It had been a really good old-fashioned cup-tie. On our way home, we heard ex-Ram loanee Micky Thomas had scored a fantastic free kick for Wrexham, which knocked the mighty Arsenal out of the FA Cup. Derby lost their next two games, 1-0 at Southend to an Andy Ansah goal and 2-1 at home to Sunderland. The Black Cats dominated the first half and could have been three up before Don Goodman headed in John Byrne's cross. Byrne then scored himself to double the lead. Geraint Williams pulled one back, but Derby were struggling the recapture their autumn form and had slipped down to tenth in the table with thirty-nine points from twenty-six games. Blackburn were the League leaders, with Derby nine points behind them.

Derby progressed to the fourth round of the FA Cup, with a 2-0 victory in the Burnley replay that was actually played on the fourth-round day. The original replay in the midweek following the game at Turf Moor had to be abandoned as heavy fog descended on the Baseball Ground with Derby leading 2-0. Arthur Cox had been searching for players to boost his squad, with money to spend following the arrival of Lionel Pickering. The first player to arrive was Marco Gabbiadini for £1 million from Crystal Palace. Gabbiadini had struggled to make an impact at Selhurst Park following his £1.8 million move from Sunderland, where he had scored seventy-four League goals in one hundred and fifty-seven appearances and had earned the nickname 'Marco Goalo'. Gabbiadini made his debut at Portsmouth in the next game and scored in Derby's 1-

0 win, with a right foot drive that beat Alan Knight at the near post. Gabbiadini was cup-tied, but he was paraded before the home crowd before the fourth round FA Cup tie against Ron Atkinson's Aston Villa. In a rip-roaring first half, Phil Gee headed Derby into an early lead. Villa then stunned Derby with Dwight Yorke scoring twice, both with close range efforts. Garry Parker, a player I'd always admired, scored with a rasping drive from the edge of the box to increase Villa's lead, but Gee scored again to reduce the arrears. Just before the break Yorke completed his hat-trick, following up after Peter Shilton had saved his penalty. Remarkably, Shilton saved another Yorke penalty after Simon Coleman had handled. Derby pulled one back with one of the finest goals I've seen at the Baseball Ground. Paul Williams scored with an acrobatic falling right-foot volley from Martyn Chalk's cross to make it 4-3 to Villa. It had been a great game and a fantastic advert for the FA Cup, with Derby unlucky to go out.

Derby lost the next two games 2-0, at home to Millwall and away at League leaders Blackburn Rovers. This was then followed by two wins, 1-0 at home to Bristol Rovers and then 2-1 at Leicester City, with Paul Simpson scoring on his debut following his £500,000 move from Oxford United. Phil Gee was then sold to Leicester City together with Ian Ormondroyd as part of the deal that saw England under-21 striker Paul Kitson join Derby for a club record £1.3 million, made up of £800,000 plus Gee and Ormondroyd. Gee had certainly played his part during his seven years at the club, but I, like a lot of other supporters felt this was the best decision for all parties. This started a frenzy of transfer activity with ins and outs at the club. Peter Shilton made his final appearance in the

Watford home game, in a game Derby won 3-1 with a Paul Williams hat-trick. Shilton moved to Plymouth Argyle as player-manager and ironically his first game in charge was the 1-1 draw with Derby the following week at Home Park. The agreement between the clubs though was that Shilton couldn't play in the game. Martin Taylor replaced Shilton for the home win 3-1 win against Port Vale. Derby made a further signing, with Tommy Johnson joining the Rams from Notts County for £1.3 million as Arthur Cox continued to splash Lionel Pickering's cash. It certainly was an exciting time at the club, as Matt Birks and I made our way up to Birkenhead for the away game against Tranmere Rovers at Prenton Park. It was a crazy afternoon, with Johnson making his debut. Paul Kitson headed Derby into an early lead with John Aldridge levelling. Simon Coleman and Paul Simpson put Derby 3-1 up and in total control. Martin Taylor then made a howler, allowing a Kenny Irons free kick slip through his hands. John Aldridge, the scourge of Derby, then slotted home a penalty and a far post header to send the Rams crashing to a 4-3 defeat, as the supporters looked on in utter disbelief to what they had just witnessed.

I made the long trip with Matt Birks to Suffolk for the away game at Ipswich Town on the last Saturday in March. Jason Dozzell put the home side 2-0 up, before Paul Simpson pulled one back as Ipswich went to top of the table. With eight games to go Derby were eighth in the table with fifty-eight points from thirty-eight games, just one point outside of the play-off places. Third-placed Cambridge United were the next visitors to the Baseball Ground. They were managed by John Beck, who loved the long ball playing style, and despite their success the media were very critical of this and it didn't endear him to supporters of other clubs. To support his long ball tactics, he ordered the groundsman to keep the grass long in the corners to slow the ball up. He also of threw buckets of cold water over players before a match. It was all very weird. The game finished in an uneventful goalless draw. Derby then went on a tremendous run, winning six and drawing one of their remaining seven games. They won four successive away games 3-0 at Barnsley, 1-0 at Grimsby Town, 2-1 at Brighton and Hove Albion and 2-1 at Bristol City. The weather at Bristol City was absolutely appalling. Matt and I got absolutely drenched during the game as we stood on the open terrace. A late Gary Micklewhite goal gave the Rams the win and then the heavens opened. As we left the ground, the road was ankle deep in water as we headed back to the car.

Derby moved up to third place in the table with seventy-five points from forty-five games, a point ahead of Middlesbrough, who were on seventy-four points but had a game in hand. All eyes were on Ayresome Park for their midweek match at home to Grimsby Town, who still needed a point to be certain of avoiding relegation. Boro won 2-0, and moved up to second place on seventy-seven points, together with Leicester City, who were now down to third place, also on seventy-seven points from forty-five games. A tense final Saturday was now guaranteed. Middlesbrough's goal difference was plus sixteen, Leicester's was plus eight and Derby's was plus seventeen. Middlesbrough's final game was away at mid-table Wolverhampton Wanderers, with Leicester at home to Newcastle United and Derby at home to Swindon Town. Derby needed to beat Swindon and hope Middlesbrough and

Leicester didn't win their games. Who would join Ipswich Town as the other automatically promoted club? Leicester lost at home to Newcastle, so they were out of the equation. Middlesbrough were down to ten men after Jamie Pollock was sent off, so hope was rising at the Baseball Ground. With fifteen minutes remaining, Derby were leading, and ten-man Middlesbrough drawing, so Derby were in the automatic promotion place. But a Paul Wilkinson header at Molineux put Boro ahead. They held on to win and were promoted. It was the play-offs for the Rams, but they had good momentum following a fine run of results in during April and May. The result of this was that third place Derby would play Blackburn Rovers in the play-off semi-finals with the first leg at Ewood Park. Blackburn, who were bank rolled by the late Jack Walker, had suffered a poor run of form during late March and April, which saw them lose five games on the bounce and scuppered their chances of automatic promotion. Only a late rally in their last five games saw them sneak into six place and a crack at the play-offs. Walker had really backed manager Kenny Dalglish in their pursuit of reaching the top flight. I really rated Tim Sherwood, who had chosen to join Blackburn instead of Derby when he moved from Norwich City. In the first leg at Ewood Park, Derby had a fantastic start to the game, in front of a packed house and cracking atmosphere. Marco Gabbiadini headed Derby in front and Tommy Johnson nutmegged Bobby Mimms to increase the lead with less than fifteen minutes gone. But Blackburn roared back before half time, with Scott Sellars and Mike Newell scoring to level up before the half-time break. Blackburn's fine comeback was complete when David Speedie scored two second half goals to give them a 4-2 advantage going into the second leg. Derby really had thrown away a golden chance of having one foot in the play-off final door.

Derby had it all to do then in the second leg. Surely an early goal for Blackburn would put the nail in Derby's coffin? The Baseball Ground was bouncing as Andy Comyn headed in from close range to give Derby an early 1-0 lead. Kevin Moran equalised with a header through a ruck of players, and with it, Derby's hopes were fading. Ted McMinn gave Derby the lead again on the night, as Derby searched for another goal to level the overall score. Paul Williams, who had scored sixteen goals from midfield, fired narrowly wide twice, and Michael Forsyth headed against the bar as Derby applied constant pressure but couldn't find that elusive goal. Derby could take great heart from a really good end to the season following Lionel Pickering's massive investment, and things were looking good for a promotion push. Blackburn made it to the top flight, winning the play-off final against Leicester City.

1992/93

The start of the new season saw the end of Division One as everybody knew it, with the start of the new FA Premier League. The twenty-two Division One clubs broke away from the Football League, with Rupert Murdoch's Sky television merging with satellite competitor BSB to form a new company BSkyB and agreeing a five-year deal worth an eye watering £304 million to have exclusive rights to televise live games. The Premier League also at times has been called the Premiership. For simplicity in this book, I'll refer to it as Premier League! The Football League now consisted of three divisions, with Derby in the First Division.

Lionel Pickering gave Arthur Cox further funds to boost his squad, with the aim of joining the new 'elite' of English football. Cox signed Welsh international midfielder Mark Pembridge from Luton Town for £1.25 million. Central defender Darren Wassall joined Derby from Nottingham Forest for £600,000, after apparently having a fallout with manager Brian Clough. Derby recouped some of their outlay with the sale of Geraint Williams to Premier League Ipswich Town for £650,000. Williams had been the rock in the midfield for seven seasons and a crucial cog in the double promotion. What a good signing he had been for £40,000 from Bristol Rovers. Derby's first game of the season was away to promoted Peterborough United at London Road on a very warm August afternoon. I drove to the match with Matt Birks to witness a very limp performance from the Rams, as we stood on the covered terrace at the Moy's End with the Main Stand to our right. Ken Charlery's second half scuffed shot gave the Posh a 1-0 win. The poor start to the season continued with two more successive defeats, 2-1 at home to Newcastle United and 3-2 away at Leicester City, with ex-Ram Phil Gee bagging a pair of goals. Matt and I went to the next away match at Vicarage Road, Watford. It was a very poor spectacle, with the game finishing 0-0, with very few chances either end. Derby's next home game was on the first Sunday afternoon in September against Bristol City. It was Derby's first game shown live on ITV, as part of a new deal showing live football League games on terrestrial TV. Paul Simpson gave Derby an early advantage with two neat left foot finishes, before Steve Sutton was sent off for inexplicably pulling down Gary

Shelton on the goal line. Paul Williams took over as keeper and was beaten by Martin Scott's penalty. Junior Bent made it 2-2. Andy Comyn came on as a substitute for Tommy Johnson, and immediately headed into his own net seconds after coming on, to give City a 3-2 lead. Paul Simpson completed a fine hat-trick, taking his tally for the season to five, but the Rams couldn't hang on and Wayne Allison headed in City's winner. Derby, the bookmakers pre-season favourites for promotion were bottom of the League with one point from five games.

After the 1-1 draw at Barnsley, Arthur Cox broke Derby's transfer record with the purchase of centre-half Craig Short from Notts County for £2.4 million. It was widely expected that Short would join Blackburn Rovers in the Premier League, but he opted to join Derby instead and made his debut in the away 1-1 draw at West Ham United. The astonishing spending spree continued, as Portsmouth captain Martin Kuhl signed for Derby for £650,000 and made his debut on the last Saturday in September in the 2-0 home win against Southend United, which was Derby's first win of the season in their eighth match. Derby's first away win came the following week in the 3-1 defeat of Cambridge United. Paul Simpson scored twice, making it seven for the season, and he made it nine for the season in a crushing 7-0 win in the League Cup second round second leg against Southend United after Derby had lost the first leg 1-0. Derby lost their next League match 1-0 to Oxford United, with John Durnin scoring late on. Derby then put a run of four successive League wins together, three of them coming away from home. They won 3-1 at Luton Town, 2-0 at Wolverhampton Wanderers and 2-0 at Notts County. I went to the midweek game at Meadow Lane along with 9,000 other Derby fans, in a crowd just in excess of 14,000. Derby also beat Charlton Athletic 4-3 as they moved up to eighth place in the table, with twenty-one points from fourteen games. Derby's frustrating inconsistency continued through November though. Despite a 2-1 away win at Bristol Rovers, they lost three homes games. Millwall and Tranmere Rovers both won 2-1, with it being no surprise that John Aldridge scored two. Sunderland also won, 1-0, on a rain-soaked afternoon on a waterlogged pitch. I have to admit, John Aldridge, is one of the best finishers I've ever seen. His tally of 330 League goals is the sixth highest in the history of English football. He made a total of 673 appearances and basically scored a goal every two games – absolutely phenomenal.

Derby who had held Arsenal to a 1-1 draw at home in the League Cup third round, and were beaten 2-1 in the replay at Arsenal. The Gunners first two goals came from poor defending from Derby, and from long David Seaman clearances in which Ian Wright and Kevin Campbell scored, with Mark Pembridge replying from the spot. In the three next League games running up to Christmas, Derby won all three, 4-2 at Swindon Town, 2-1 at home to Birmingham City and 2-0 away to Grimsby Town. Derby were now in the top six after their really poor start to the season, but seventeen points behind runaway leaders Newcastle United and seven points behind second place Tranmere Rovers. Derby suffered a poor Christmas, losing 2-1 at Brentford and 4-2 at home to Portsmouth.

The third round of the FA Cup paired Derby at home to

Stockport County on the first Saturday of January at a misty Baseball Ground. Craig Short powered in a header from a Tommy Johnson cross. Stockport came back strong, with ex-Ram Brian McCord, heading the visitors level. A late David Miller own goal gave Derby an underserved victory. Derby looked to get back to winning ways in the League, but suffered a 2-0 home defeat against a strong West Ham United outfit. The Hammers played really well, with first half goals by Stewart Robson and Trevor Morley, giving them a 2-0 victory as they moved up to second place in the table. Derby slipped down to eleventh place. A 0-0 draw at Roots Hall against Southend United halted Derby's run of three defeats on the trot. It was back to the FA Cup the following week, with an away tie at Kenilworth Road against Luton Town. Matt Birks and I went to the game, in what was only my third away game of the season. The away fans ban at Luton had been lifted, so Derby took a good contingent of fans housed in the Oak Road Stand behind the goal. Fortunately, the artificial pitch had also gone too. Paul Telfer put the Hatters ahead, but Derby came back strong, with Craig Short stabbing home from close range. Mark Pembridge then scored twice before half-time against his former club, to give the Rams a 3-1 half time lead. Pembridge completed his first ever hat-trick with Marco Gabbiadini completing the rout in a 5-1 away win.

Next up for Derby was a trip to leaders Newcastle United, who were fourteen points clear at the top of the League on the last day of January, in a game shown live on ITV Sport. Derby made a dream start, when Newcastle fan Tommy Johnson slotted home, following a strong run and cross from ex-Mackem Marco Gabbiadini. Derby held on until the final minute, when Liam O'Brien volleyed in at the far post to send the home crowd away happy. It was heart-breaking for Derby, who'd defended heroically throughout the game. Derby's inconsistency continued to frustrate supporters when Peterborough United completed a double over Derby with a 3-2 win at the Baseball Ground, despite two goals from Paul Kitson.

Pressure was mounting on Arthur Cox, with the team failing to play to their potential. The 'dream team' as they were known had slipped to sixteenth in the table ahead of the midweek game against Barnsley. Outside the Baseball Ground, supporters were asked to sign a petition to remove Cox. The players responded to the growing unrest as goals from Marco Gabbiadini, Paul Kitson and Paul Williams saw off Barnsley. The fifth round of the FA Cup Derby were pitched against third tier Bolton Wanderers, so there was a massive opportunity for progress. Tommy Johnson, who had been dropped for the Barnsley game, returned to the bench as one of the two substitutes. Craig Short gave Derby the lead, with a brave header from Mark Pembridge's cross, with Andy Walker levelling for the Trotters. Short scored again to restore Derby's advantage, with Paul Williams sealing the tie, scoring from close range. For the first time in nine years since the infamous games against Plymouth Argyle, Derby were through to the sixth round and supporters were dreaming of Wembley. The inconsistency in the League continued, with Watford winning 2-1 at the Baseball Ground and Derby winning at home 2-0 to Leicester City. Shane Nicholson made his first League appearance in the Leicester game, after joining the club for £60,000 from Lincoln City during the previous summer. It was very strange to see ex-Ram Bobby Davison playing for the Foxes. A fine away win at Oxford United followed, with a Paul Williams goal. The three League wins in four games propelled Derby to eighth, just on the edge of the play-offs.

Derby had a tough draw in the FA Cup sixth round, after they were paired at home to Premier League Sheffield Wednesday. The Owls took the lead with John Sheridan netting from the spot, but Shane Nicholson hit a fabulous thirty-yard left foot strike that hit the bar, hit England goalkeeper Chris Woods and bounced over the line, with the Baseball Ground erupting. Defender turned striker Paul Warhurst restored Wednesday's lead, steering home from just inside the box. With Wednesday 2-1 up at the break, Marco Gabbiadini used his strength to hold off a challenge from Carlton Palmer, before hitting his drive into the roof of the net to make it 2-2. The crowd went wild, when, with thirteen minutes to go, Paul Kitson headed in from Nicholson's cross, to give Derby the lead for the first time in the tie. Could Derby hold on and reach the semi-finals since 1976? Wednesday turned on the gas and their incessant pressure paid off, with Warhurst sweeping home from Nigel Jemson's cross to earn a replay. It had been a fantastic end to end match, arguably the best game I'd seen in years. Two nights later, it was like after the 'Lord Mayor's show', as Derby beat Bristol Rovers 3-1 in what felt like a really low-key encounter. It was though, three very important points in the Rams' quest to reach the play-offs. I went to Hillsborough, more in hope than expectation, for the FA Cup replay with Wednesday. Paul Warhurst was again the Owls scorer, as the home side made it through to the semi-final to play their city rivals Sheffield United at Wembley with a 1-0 win. It was a brave effort by Derby but they could have no complaints on the night. I don't know how many times I'd been to Hillsborough but I'd never seen Derby draw there, let alone win! Throughout the season Derby competed in Anglo Italian Cup, which was a tournament for tier two sides from the two countries. I've absolutely no interest in these types of tournaments; together with domestic tournaments like the Simod Cup and the Zenith Data Systems Cup, as they just give top tiers clubs more fixtures that don't really benefit anyone. I feel a bit hypocritical because Derby got to the final to play Cremonese, and I went after not going to any of the other games leading up to the final. I think Graham Richards and Colin Gibson from BBC Radio Derby enjoyed it though, as it gave them some nice jollies out in Italy commentating and reporting on the games! I didn't enjoy the day one bit though. It was a very strange experience, as there were about 35,000 Derby fans at one end of the stadium and about 2,000 Cremonese at the other end. The Italians won 3-1, but I can hardly remember anything about the game. The tournament ran for another couple of seasons, but having very poor support in both countries, never to returned again.

Going into April and with ten games remaining, Derby had a mountain to climb to reach the play-offs, as they were ten points behind sixth-placed Leicester City. The run in didn't start well, as Derby lost 2-1 at Tranmere Rovers. I went to St. Andrews with Matt Birks, my first ever visit there, for the midweek away game with Birmingham City that finished in a 1-1 draw. We stood at the Tilton Road End with the Main Stand to our right and the big Spion Kop to our left. Nineteen-year-old Dean Sturridge made his debut when he came on as a second half substitute. He looked very raw, but also looked like he had pace to burn. On Easter Monday, Derby beat Brentford 3-2 and then travelled to promotion chasing Portsmouth managed by Jim Smith, who were second in the table for the Easter Monday fixture. Derby put in a real abject performance and lost 3-0. I can remember listening to the game on BBC Radio Derby with Graham Richards being scathing about Arthur Cox and the team. The play-offs were a distant dream, with Derby now eleventh in the table, thirteen points behind sixth place with six games to go. Matt Birks and I went to the final away game of the season at the Valley for the game against Charlton Athletic. The Valley, one of English football's most iconic and largest stadiums, had not been used, as the club was unable to finance the improvements needed to make the ground meet new safety requirements after they had financial troubles in the mid-1980s. Between 1985 and 1992, Charlton played their home games at Selhurst Park and Upton Park. The ground re-opened in December 1992. We sat in the West Stand towards the Jimmy Seed Stand, opposite the vast East Stand. The game had a real feel of being an end of the season encounter, and ended in a Charlton 2-1 win. The game saw the final appearance of Gary Micklewhite in a Derby shirt before he moved to Gillingham as player-coach. He was a real team player; an unsung hero and I'll never forget the role he played in the double promotion winning squad. It had been a season to forget for Derby, who, following the massive investment from Lionel Pickering, finished eighth in the table. To say the 'dream team' had under achieved was a vast understatement. The pressure was certainly mounting on Arthur Cox ahead of the new campaign.

1993/94

Arthur Cox made one signing in pre-season, with the arrival of England right-back Gary Charles from Nottingham Forest for £750,000. Surely this was the last of Lionel Pickering's unbelievable financial backing for the club? Derby opened their season with a home game against Sunderland. The Rams produced a fine display, winning 5-0, with Charles making his debut. Mark Pembridge scored twice, once from the spot and the other a fine left foot curling drive from the edge of the box. Marco Gabbiadini, Paul Kitson and Craig Short completed the rout. Derby then made yet another signing, with United States international John Harkes joining the Rams from Sheffield Wednesday. He made his debut in the first away game, a midweek game at relegated Nottingham Forest on a warm August evening. A very rare Michael Forsyth goal with his right foot following a poor punch from Mark Crossley gave the Rams the lead, but Ian Woan's left foot strike earned the Reds a point. Derby put in two really poor performances in their next two away games, losing both 3-0 at Middlesbrough and Birmingham City. After five games, the Rams were ninth in the table with seven points. There was an improvement in the next two games, with a 2-0 win at home to Peterborough United and a dogged 0-0 draw at Millwall.

The next opponents were Exeter City in the League Cup second round first leg, at St. James Park. This was Derby's first ever competitive match against the Devon side. I drove the two hundred plus miles down the M5 to the midweek game with Matt Birks and Carl Smith. We sat in the Main Stand just behind the dugout, with the Derby fans away to our right on a very shallow open terrace, and the Exeter fans away to our left on the large covered terrace. Arthur Cox missed the game, as he was suffering from a severe bad back. Exeter took the lead, with Stuart Storer running eighty yards and evading a defensive slip by Darren Wassall, before sliding the ball past Martin Taylor. Paul Kitson equalised before half-time with a low shot from the edge of the box. Second half goals by Paul Simpson and Marco Gabbiadini gave the Rams a comfortable 3-1 victory.

Derby then travelled to Meadow Lane for the away game at Notts County. It was a disastrous afternoon for the Rams, as they were thrashed 4-1 by their near neighbours, with Gary McSwegan bagging a hat-trick. Derby were now eleventh in the table with eleven points from eight games. Arthur Cox then resigned due to his on-going back problem. He had been Derby's second longest serving manager, being at the helm for just over nine years with his biggest achievement being the successive promotions in 1986 and 1987. I think it was time for a change, because the multi-million-pound investment in assembling the 'dream team' hadn't worked out. For some reason, although the players were very good individuals, they didn't gel or achieve a consistent run of form. Supporters though will remember him with great fondness for what he achieved. I believe his biggest error was to sell Paul Goddard back in 1989, even though he kept his promise to allow Goddard to move back down south if the opportunity came along. It broke up his partnership with Dean Saunders, which was as good as any strike force in the country at the time. Who know what the club would have achieved if that pair had stayed together?

Assistant manager Roy McFarland took over from Cox, but I wasn't a fan of this decision. McFarland, although he was of the club's all-time great players, had been with Cox for the whole time he was manager, and I just think a fresh face was needed, with new ideas to take the club forward. McFarland's first match in charge was the incredible home live ITV game against West Bromwich Albion. There was a cracking atmosphere for the game. Derby took a 2-0 lead with goals from Paul Kitson and Paul Simpson. Bob Taylor immediately pulled one back, but a Mark Pembridge penalty restored the two-goal advantage. Paul Simpson made it 4-1 as Derby played some great high tempo football. The incredible first half scoring continued, with Andy Hunt scoring twice, one with a spectacular overhead kick. Craig Short then jabbed one home to make it 5-3. This was the only match in the years I'd followed football with a 5-3 score line at half time. Strangely there were no further goals in the second half. Derby duly beat Exeter City in the second leg and won their next two home games against Luton Town 2-1 and Crystal Palace 3-1, before meeting Tottenham Hotspur in the third round of the League Cup. Tottenham won the game 1-0, with a Nick Barmby goal with nineteen-year-old Sol Campbell having an outstanding game. I thought what a prospect and was proved right! Derby then recorded their first and second away wins of the season against Bolton Wanderers and leaders Charlton Athletic, as they moved up to fifth with twenty-six points from fourteen games, as they gathered momentum. Derby at this stage had a hundred percent home record with six wins going into the home game with Wolverhampton Wanderers. The record came to a shuddering halt with a crushing 4-0 defeat, with Steve Bull scoring a hat-trick. They lost their next game by 2-0 at Oxford United. In the run up to Christmas, the inconsistency continued with a win, a draw and two defeats, with the last game before Christmas a 1-0 defeat at Sunderland. Derby had slipped to tenth place with thirty points from twenty games. In their Christmas games on consecutive days, Derby won 1-0 at Barnsley and 3-2 against Leicester City. Derby lost their New Year's Day game 2-1 at Stoke City, after leading through Marco Gabbiadini's tenth goal of the season. Gabbiadini's fine scoring run continued, as he helped himself to a hat-trick in the 4-0 thrashing of Tranmere Rovers two days later.

The FA Cup third round draw had given Derby a tough draw at Premier League strugglers Oldham Athletic. I loved a good cup run, but priority was promotion to the Premier League and the new found riches that was creating. Tommy Johnson gave Derby a half-time lead at Boundary Park. Darren Beckford equalised for the Latics, and Rich Holden scored from close range to send Derby crashing out. Back to the League, Derby beat Portsmouth 1-0 at home and then lost 2-1 at Luton Town, with the Hatters winning with a wonder goal from Scott Oakes who picked the ball up in his own half and shrugged off four challenges before beating Martin Taylor with a drive into the roof of the net. Derby signed thirty-five-year-old Gordons 'Sid' Cowans from Aston Villa for £200,000 to add much needed experience to a young side. It was very sad to hear recently that 'Sid' was suffering from the early stages of Alzheimer's disease. He made his debut in the 1-1 draw at Crystal Palace. With a strange quirk of fate on the fixture list, Derby played Watford twice in three weeks. Watford won 2-1 at the Baseball Ground and Derby won 4-3 at Vicarage Road, with Marco Gabbiadini scoring the winner with four minutes to go. Derby were now fifth in the League with forty-nine points from thirty games, six points behind leaders Crystal Palace. The top seven teams were only separated by one point each, so it looked like a tense battle ahead to finish in the top two automatic promotion and four play-off places. The next five games though saw Derby lose 1-0 at home to Middlesbrough, and then record four successive draws. Thirty-three-year-old former Welsh international defender Kevin Ratcliffe made his debut in one of the four draws at Bristol City. Derby fortunately only slipped dropped down one place to sixth. Derby won their next match at struggling West Bromwich Albion 2-1, with Tommy Johnson and Paul Simpson scoring. There were no fans behind the Smethwick End, as this was being redeveloped. Derby were then thrashed 4-0 away at fellow promotion hopefuls Tranmere Rovers at Prenton Park. That man John Aldridge scored two, with Ged Brannan and Liam O'Brien completing the scoring to complete the misery. Derby then had a decent run of three home wins 2-0 against Barnsley, 4-2 against Stoke City and 2-0 against Charlton Athletic. This was backed up with three away draws, 3-3 at Leicester City and 1-1 at both Grimsby Town and Notts County. This catapulted Derby to fifth in the League with sixty-eight points from forty-three games ahead of the big game against second place Nottingham Forest, who were four points ahead of Derby but had two games in hand. In one of the biggest East Midlands clashes in years, Forest took the lead with Colin Cooper's speculative free kick which Martin Taylor should have saved. A bizarre own-goal by ex-Red Gary Charles, much to the delight of the travelling support, sealed the win for Forest and more importantly for them a return to the Premier League at the first time of asking. Derby's 2-1 win against Oxford United virtually sealed their play-off spot with one game to go. Even though they lost 4-3 at Southend United on the final day of the season, Derby secured their play-off place and would play Millwall at home in the first leg. Derby dominated the first leg and lead through a Gordon Cowans goal, his first for the club, halfway through the first half. Tommy Johnson added the second with a rising drive past Kasey Keller, to give Derby a 2-0 first leg advantage.

Derby then just needed to be professional in the second leg, in what no doubt would be a very hostile and intimidating atmosphere at the New Den, which had opened in the previous year. Marco Gabbiadini gave Derby a fine start, steering in a Tommy Johnson cross. Johnson doubled the lead with a fine run and cross just before half time. It was now 4-0 on aggregate and surely no way back for the Lions. During the first half, the Millwall fans invaded the pitch, with referee Brian Hill taking the players off as the mounted police tried to restore order. When the game restarted Derby increased their lead through a comical Pat Van den Hauwe own-goal after a complete mix up with Kasey Keller. During the second half Millwall pulled one back through Greg Berry. There was a second pitch invasion with hundreds of Millwall fans on the pitch in some confusion, as they were awarded a penalty which was then rescinded. As the players left the pitch, Martin Taylor was assaulted by Millwall fans as it turned ugly and violent. The pitch was cleared and the game restarted after a twelve-minute stoppage. There was no further scoring and Derby made it to Wembley for their first ever play-off final, with

Leicester City their opponents. After the game around a thousand Millwall fans went on the rampage in the car park outside the main West Stand, attacking cars including the BBC Radio Derby car which was overturned. Fortunately, the mounted police gained controlled of the situation and broke the crowd up. It was all very unsavoury, but not unexpected with the Millwall notoriety.

On Monday 30 May, the day of the play-off final, I went on a bus ran by the Wilmot Arms in Borrowash, with Pete and Matt Birks. It was a very warm day and I was confident the Rams were going to reach the promised land by beating Brian Little's Leicester City. Derby had a young team with a sprinkling of experience, but were inconsistent. If Derby turned up, they would win. Leicester, a workmanlike team with defender turned striker Steve Walsh their main threat mainly from set pieces, had no real star quality. In front of a crowd in excess of 73,000, Tommy Johnson had a great chance to give Derby an early lead, but a lack of composure saw his scuffed shot drift wide from a Marco Gabbiadini cross. Johnson did make amends and gave Derby the lead latching on to a fine through ball from Paul Simpson. Steve Walsh equalised, just before half time, after his goal bound header from a long Gary Coatsworth cross should have been headed clear by Paul Williams, who for some reason managed to duck under it. Martin Taylor appeared to be fouled by Iwan Roberts from the cross, but referee Roger Milford allowed the play to continue. John Harkes had a golden opportunity to restore Derby's lead but screwed his shot horribly wide with only Gavin Ward to beat. Leicester then scored with four minutes to go to break Derby hearts. A fantastic cross from Simon Grayson was met by ex-Ram Ian Ormondroyd whose header was brilliantly saved by Martin Taylor, only for the ball to drop to Walsh who drove the ball in from close range. I just wanted the ground to open up and swallow us up. In footballing terms, it's the worst feeling in the world to lose in the play-off final, even worse than an FA Cup semi-final. We quickly got back on the bus and back up the M1. The bus was very quiet on the way back as I think everyone was stunned on what they had just witnessed. Leicester fans decked the bridges on the M1 as we approached the East Midlands. To be honest, I'm just glad we hadn't been beaten by Nottingham Forest, that would have been even more unbearable. The season was over and another season in the second tier loomed. The 'dream team' had failed to deliver for the second successive season.

CHAPTER 7

McFARLAND GONE, JIM SMITH IN, THE CROATIAN INFLUENCE AND GOODBYE TO THE BASEBALL GROUND

1994/95

So how quickly could Derby bounce back from the nightmare at Wembley? I just hoped there wouldn't be a hangover from that fateful day on the last Monday in May. The season opened in warm sunshine with a trip to Oakwell for the opening game with Barnsley. Matt Birks and I went to the game and sat in the West Stand, with the Derby masses to our left. Andy Rammell scored twice to give the Tykes a 2-0 lead, with Mark Pembridge pulling one back, but Barnsley held on to secure the three points. Derby didn't have a great start to the season. Their only point in August was a home goalless draw with Luton Town, with two defeats; 4-1 at Millwall, with Dean Sturridge scoring his first goal for the club, and by 1-0 at home to Middlesbrough. Ex-Nottingham Forest star Steve Hodge joined the Rams on a month's loan from Leeds United and made his debut in the Middlesbrough game. September was a much better month though, and Derby were unbeaten with four wins and a draw. The wins came in the home games against Grimsby Town 2-1, Oldham Athletic 2-1 and Stoke City 3-0.

The Oldham game was Paul Kitson's final game in a Derby shirt before he left to join Newcastle United for £2.25 million. Kitson was obviously a talented player, but I got the impression he was a bit moody and didn't always see eye to eye with his strike partner, Marco Gabbiadini. The away success was a 2-0 win at Bristol City. Twenty-year-old Lee Carsley made his League debut in the 1-1 draw at Swindon Town. This good run moved Derby up to sixth in the table, with fourteen points from nine games, six points behind leaders Middlesbrough.

On Saturday 1 October for something completely different, I went to the Ibrox Stadium with Pete and Matt Birks for the Glasgow Rangers home League game against Dundee United. It was a ground I'd always wanted to go to. Pete and I shared the driving on the five-hundred and eighty-mile round trip. Ibrox was fantastic, with a great atmosphere and great view from where we were seated in the Broomloan Stand, with the Main Stand to our right. Rangers, managed by Walter Smith, were a top side and included Andy Goram, Richard Gough, Basil Boli, Stuart McCall, Mark Hateley and Brian Laudrup in their side. Hateley and Laudrup scored as the Gers won 2-0 in front of a 43,000 plus crowd. In hindsight I wished we'd stopped in Glasgow for the night, and travelled back the next day. Derby travelled to Southend United in mid-October for a game that was shown live on ITV. With the score at 0-0 after fifty minutes, Southend striker Dave Regis chased a ball that was threaded through into the Derby box. Martin Taylor came out and collided with Regis, which resulted in Taylor suffering a double fracture of his left leg. The injury was so bad that Taylor, the current Derby Player of the Year, would not play again for twenty-nine months. He was never the same keeper at Derby, but went on to have a successful career at Wycombe Wanderers. It was so disappointing for him as Everton were touting after him when he was in his prime at Derby. Dave Regis, who escaped injury from the collision, scored the winning goal for Southend with three minutes to go in their 1-0 win. Derby drew 0-0 at Notts County and then won 1-0 at Portsmouth in the third round of the League Cup, after overcoming Reading over the two legs in the second round. Paul Simpson scored with a right foot curling shot from outside the box. This was the only goal I can recall 'Simmo' scoring with his right foot in his time at Derby. Derby then drew at home 2-2 with Charlton Athletic and lost at home 2-1 to Reading, before returning to Portsmouth for the League game. This resulted in a 1-0 win with Marco Gabbiadini scoring the winner, following up Martin Kuhl's header that was superbly saved by Alan Knight in the Pompey goal. Tommy Johnson was back on the scoresheet, as his brace saw off Port Vale 2-0 at home. He then scored in the 2-0 away win at Wolverhampton Wanderers as Derby ended November in eleventh place, with twenty-six points from nineteen matches, only three points away from the final play-off place. Derby's run in the League Cup came to an end when they lost 2-1 at Swindon Town. In the League, Derby played out two goalless draws at home to Notts County and away to Luton Town. Paul Trollope made his debut in the 1-0 win against Barnsley in their last home game before Christmas. Trollope joined on loan from Torquay United, before making his move permanent. On Boxing Day, Derby made the trip to Tranmere Rovers. Prenton Park had not been a happy hunting ground for the Rams and they usually were on the end of a good hiding.

This unhappy trend continued, as Tranmere won 3-1. This game saw two of Derby's players playing their last game for the club. Gary Charles moved to Aston Villa in a £1.4 million deal, and captain Martin Kuhl had a very brief loan at Notts County before signing for Bristol City. Kuhl was described by Arthur Cox as being the 'final piece of the jigsaw' of the 'dream team', but I thought he was very disappointing for the Rams and he never really reproduced the form that persuaded Derby to pay £650,000 for his services from Portsmouth. Derby's last game of the year resulted in a 1-1 draw at Sunderland. Roy McFarland continued to break up the 'dream team' with Tommy Johnson following Gary Charles to Villa Park for a fee of £1.45 million. I always liked Johnson. Great speed, good work rate and a good finisher with his record of thirty goals in ninety-eight League games backing that up. I was sad to see him go. Derby finished the year in fifteenth place with thirty-two points from twenty-four games, eight points away from the final play-off spot. I felt the pressure was starting to mount on Roy McFarland. It would be interesting to see how he'd reshape his squad with the recent departures.

In the FA Cup third round Derby were drawn away at Everton. This was my only second Derby away game of the season. Pete Birks drove up to Merseyside with Matt Birks and myself. We sat in the lower tier of the Bullens Road Stand with the Main Stand opposite, the Park End Stand to our left and the Gwladys Street End to our right. Andy Hinchcliffe's late goal gave Everton a 1-0 win. It was quite cruel on Derby who played well on the day and Craig Short put in a tremendous performance. In a remarkable game at Charlton Athletic the following week, Derby were 3-1 down at half time only to comeback in the second half with Marco Gabbiadini scoring twice. Mark Stallard added the other to record a 4-3 win. Derby then beat Portsmouth 3-0 at home with a fine second half Paul Simpson hat-trick. Derby then lost three games in a row. The 3-2 home defeat against Sheffield United was Michael Forsyth's last appearance in a Derby shirt in his nine-year association with the club. He was Mr. Dependable and a very solid performer, and played his part in the rise of the club under Arthur Cox. He moved onto Notts County for £200,000. Coming the opposite way was Dean Yates in a £300,000 deal. Yates had made over 300 appearances for the Magpies, but had suffered a cruciate ligament injury in 1992 that had cost him two years of his career. A very elegant defender, who I always held in high regard, he was touted for a move to Liverpool as a replacement for Alan Hansen. But his knee injury had put paid to that. Yates' first two games in a Rams shirt didn't go too well, as they lost both 1-0 to Reading and Port Vale. Derby's squad continued to be overhauled by McFarland, and this continued with the arrival of striker Lee Mills in a £300,000 deal from Wolverhampton Wanderers and goalkeeper Russell Hoult, who came in on loan from Leicester City. Mills and Hoult made their debuts in the home live ITV game against Bolton Wanderers. Jason McAteer gave the Trotters the lead with a goal in the first minute after Hoult failed to hold onto a low drive by Richard Sneekers. Dean Yates equalised with his first goal for the club, his first for four years, on his home debut. Lee Mills hit a stunning twenty-five-yard drive with five minutes to go, to give the Rams their first win for over a month. Derby then went on a tremendous run of results. After a goalless draw at Stoke City, they won five games in a row. Mark Pembridge's goal gave the Rams a 1-0 win at Grimsby Town. Millwall and Burnley were beaten 3-2 and 4-0 respectively, at the Baseball Ground. Lee Mills scored twice in a rare, but great win, at leaders Middlesbrough, and he scored again in the 3-1 home win against Swindon Town, with Mark Pembridge scoring his fourth goal in five games. Derby surged up to seventh in the League with fifty-eight points from thirty-seven games, two points behind sixth place Wolverhampton Wanderers. The new signings had made a really good impact and Craig Short was now showing the type of form to justify his £2.4 million fee. Derby then had a setback losing two of their next three games with 1-0 defeats at Oldham and at home to Sunderland. Just prior to Easter, Derby had a must win game at home to Wolverhampton Wanderers. Don Goodman gave the visitors an early lead with Paul Simpson levelling from the spot just before half time. Marco Gabbiadini put the Rams ahead with a shot Mike Stowell should have saved and Paul Simpson increased the lead to 3-1. Dean Richards pulled one back with fifteen minutes to go and cruelly for Derby, he scored again in injury time to level the score at 3-3. On Easter Saturday Derby fell to a 3-1 defeat at relegation threatened Burnley. But on Easter Monday, Derby recorded their biggest win of the season with a thumping 5-0 win against Tranmere Rovers at a rain-soaked Baseball Ground. Left-back Chris Boden made his debut following his move from Aston Villa. With three games to go, Derby were two points behind sixth place Barnsley. Derby though failed to win any of their last three games. A 0-0 draw against West Bromwich Albion was followed by a woeful performance in a 2-1 defeat in the must win home game with Southend United. This defeat put paid to Derby's play-off aspirations, as the pressure was mounting on manager Roy

McFarland. Lionel Pickering ran out of patience and sacked McFarland before the final game of the season at Watford. Assistant the late Billy McEwan took charge of the team, with Derby slipping a 2-1 defeat. It had been a really disappointing end to the season after it promised so much with the fine run of results in March.

1995/96

Lionel Pickering sprung a surprise, by appointing Chief Executive of the League Manager's Association and former Portsmouth manager, the late Jim Smith as their new manager. Smith appointed former player Steve McClaren as first-team coach. Smith started wheeling and dealing, assembling his squad for the new season. There were four major departures. Record signing Craig Short was sold to Everton for £2.4 million, with Gary Rowett joining Derby as part of the deal. Paul Williams left the Rams to join Coventry City in a deal worth £750,000, and Mark Pembridge joined Sheffield Wednesday for £900,000. Surprisingly, Smith sold Lee Mills to Port Vale, after he had made a good impact with six goals in fifteen games since his move from Wolverhampton Wanderers. I liked Mills, he was very honest and a willing worker. Smith bought in Robin van der Laan from Port Vale as part of the Mills deal. Other new arrivals included Sean Flynn from Coventry City for £250,000. Midfielder Daryll Powell, who was with Smith at Portsmouth, signed for £750,000. Fellow midfielder David Preece joined on a free transfer from Luton Town after spending eleven years at Kenilworth Road. Derby then signed goalkeeper Russell Hoult from Leicester City, who had done well in his loan spell in the previous season. All five outfield players made their debuts on the opening weekend of the season at home to Port Vale in a game that was chosen for live ITV coverage.

I bought a season ticket in the Normanton End upper tier with Carl Smith, a friend of mine who I worked with at Rolls-Royce. Derby announced that they were planning a ten-million-pound redevelopment of the Baseball Ground. The Ley Stand would remain with the Main Stand, with the Osmaston and Normanton Ends being replaced, increasing the capacity to 26,000. Smith adopted a 3-5-2 formation with three central defenders and two wing-backs and he made Robin van der Laan his captain. This was the first time I'd seen Derby play with this type of formation. The game was fairly dull and ended goalless. That evening after the game Julie, Sarah and I travelled up to Manchester Airport for a ten-p.m. flight to Zante for a two-week holiday. Whilst we were away, Derby lost their second match away at Reading 3-2. I had to phone home to find out the score from my dad as there were no mobile phones in those days. He also told me they had signed a Dutchman but he couldn't remember his name! I found out later it was striker Ron Willems, who had been playing for Grasshoppers in Switzerland. Willems cost Derby £370,000 and he made his debut at Reading. The day before we travelled back home, Derby drew 1-1 at home to Grimsby Town. The Rams signed central defender Simon Webster on a month's loan from West Ham United as cover for the injured Dean Yates. Webster made his debut in the midweek match at Wolverhampton Wanderers, on a warm August evening. Matt Birks and I went to the match and we sat behind the goal on the South Bank. Molineux is a fantastic stadium together with its great city centre location. Derby put in a dreadful performance, littered with defensive errors, and lost 3-0 with all goals scored in the first half by Tony Daley, Don Goodman and John de Wolf. It was only the end of August, but I said to Matt I was concerned already. The only player to come out of the game with any credit was striker Dean Sturridge, who looked very lively with his pace but he had very little support. To back this up, Sturridge scored twice as Derby won their first game of the season, with a 2-1 win at Luton Town on the following Saturday. Derby lost their next home game, yet another Sunday live ITV game, against 10-man Leicester City, who won 1-0 with a first half Julian Joachim goal. Early days, but after six games Derby were fourth-from-bottom of the table, with six points from five games.

Fortunately, Dean Yates was fit again and he made his first appearance of the season in Derby's first home win of the season. They won 1-0 in the midweek game against Southend United with Dean Sturridge again scoring, his fifth of the season. In their last game of September, Derby lost 2-0 at Barnsley and there was a bit of disquiet amongst the travelling fans with one or two shouts of 'Smith out'. It was far too premature for me, but things needed to improve – and quickly. Derby were fifth-from-bottom of the League with nine points from as many games. Ron Willems scored his first goal for the club in the home 2-2 draw with Millwall, and he then scored again in the 2-0 win at Sheffield United. Russell Hoult replaced Steve Sutton in goal for the home 1-1 draw with Ipswich Town, a game in which Geraint Williams received a superb reception on his first return to the Baseball Ground since he left in 1992. Derby were steadily improving and beat

Oldham Athletic 2-1 at home in their final game of October. The win lifted Derby up to thirteenth in the table with eighteen points from thirteen games. Jim Smith then pulled off a major coup, by signing twenty-eight-year-old Croatian international central defender Igor Stimac from Hadjuk Split for £1.57 million. Stimac went straight into the team, partnering Dean Yates and Gary Rowett in the back three for the visit to Prenton Park, Tranmere. Derby got their usual stuffing on Birkenhead. Although Stimac scored, Derby lost 5-1. Not surprisingly, John Aldridge scored twice as the Rams suffered their biggest defeat of the season.

Out of nowhere, Derby then went on an unbelievable club record of twenty League games without defeat that ran from mid-November until early March. In the twenty games, thirteen were won and seven drawn. The first two wins came in home games, beating West Bromwich Albion 3-0 and winning 2-0 against Charlton Athletic. The next game, in my opinion, was the best of the unbeaten run. The Rams hammered Birmingham City 4-1 at St. Andrews, with a magnificent performance. The team was starting to pick itself. Russell Hoult was in goal behind the solid back three of Gary Rowett, Igor Stimac and Dean Yates. Lee Carsley and Chis Boden were the wing backs, with Robin van der Laan and Daryll Powell adding the power in midfield. Ron Williams played in the hole just behind Marco Gabbiadini, who added strength, and Dean Sturridge, who had electric pace. Birmingham had no answer that night as Derby moved up to eighth place with twenty-seven points from eighteen games. After a 0-0 draw at Crystal Palace, which was Chris Boden's last game before returning to Aston Villa, Derby had two home wins, scoring four in both games against Sheffield United and Barnsley. Shane Nicholson came into the side, replacing the departed Boden. Dean Sturridge then scored the winner in the tough away game at Millwall as Derby surged up the table to third place, three points behind League leaders Sunderland who were due at the Baseball Ground in the last game before Christmas. In that game, Michael Gray gave the Black Cats the lead, with Marco Gabbiadini levelling before half time. A Ron Willems penalty and Dean Sturridge made it 3-1 in a great atmosphere that sent Derby top of the League. It had been a truly remarkable turnaround especially after the debacle at Molineux at the end of August. Wow!! Two further wins over the Christmas period, 1-0 on Boxing Day at Huddersfield Town with Ron Willems scoring, and a 2-1 win over Norwich City at home, gave Derby a seven-point lead at the top of the League.

Derby were at home to Leeds United in the FA Cup third round in a game that was selected by Sky Sports for live TV coverage. Leeds had already beaten Derby in the League Cup and were lying mid-table in the Premier League. I was very relaxed going into the game. Usually, I was desperate for a good cup run but I didn't want anything to get in the way of the promotion push. Derby were reduced to ten men after half an hour, when Gary Rowett pulled down Brian Deane, denying him a goal scoring opportunity even though he was fifty yards from goal. The ten men of Derby took the lead just after half-time, through Marco Gabbiadini with his twelfth goal of the campaign. Paul Simpson incredibly doubled, the lead capitalising on a mix up between Carlton Palmer and Mark Beeney in the Leeds goal. Leeds, playing in an unfamiliar green and blue stripped shirts and blue shorts, pulled one back through the late Gary Speed, and Deane equalised as the pressure mounted. In injury time, Leeds scored twice through Gary McAllister and Tony Yeboah. It was harsh on Derby, but I was relieved there was no replay and they'd put up a fantastic performance in a really good cup tie. After beating Reading 3-0 at home which was their seventh win in a row, Derby had three successive draws, the first two at Port Vale and Grimsby Town, with both games finishing 1-1. Left-back Chris Powell joined Derby from Southend United for £750,000, with Shane Nicholson moving to West Bromwich Albion for £150,000. The third was the goalless draw at home to Wolverhampton Wanderers. Derby were still top with fifty-two points from twenty-nine games, seven points ahead of third-place Huddersfield Town. The sequence of draws was broken with a 2-1 win at Southend United with Ron Willems scoring a late winner. Jim Smith added experienced thirty-two-year-old midfielder Glyn Hodges to his squad from Sheffield United, who made his debut as a substitute in the 1-1 home draw with Luton Town. Prior to the Luton game, Chairman Lionel Pickering made the very exciting announcement that Derby were going to build a new 30,000 plus stadium on the Pride Park area of the city, rather than following the original plan to rebuild the Baseball Ground as a 26,000-seat stadium. The new stadium was due to open for the start of the 1997-98 season.

On a very heavy pitch at the Baseball Ground, Derby fell behind an hour in, to a Paul Hall goal for Portsmouth. A rare Dean Yates goal ten minutes later brought Derby back into it. Dean Sturridge gave Derby the lead and a Marco Gabbiadini header increased the lead to 3-1. A penalty from the late Alan McLoughlin decreased the deficit but Derby held on, to make it seventeen games unbeaten. I went to the next away game with Matt Birks, which was the midweek game on the last day of February at Filbert Street, Leicester. On the way to the game, we saw Sean Flynn at the Leicester Forest East Services on the M1, presumably waiting for the team bus to pick him up. We stood on the East Stand terrace, just like twenty-one years earlier for Derby's penultimate match of the 1974-5 winning Championship season. The new impressive Carling Stand had replaced the old Main Stand. Otherwise, the rest of the ground was no different. It was a hard-fought game that Derby got a good point, in a 0-0 draw. In the next home game at home to Huddersfield Town, on a pitch devoid of most of the grass, Andy Booth scored after two minutes to give the visitors the lead. Paul Simpson levelled and Robin van der Laan put the Rams ahead with a low left foot drive going into half time. Simpson scored his second of the game and sixth of the season with a fine left foot shot from the corner of the box. It was now nineteen games unbeaten, with Derby top with sixty-four points from thirty-five games, one point ahead of Sunderland and nine ahead of third-placed Ipswich Town. Following the 0-0 draw at Watford, it was a trip to Sunderland for the top of the table clash on the second Saturday in March. Derby, playing in an unfamiliar yellow/gold shirts and black shorts, were very much second best on the day and lost 3-0 to two goals by Craig Russell and another from Steve Agnew. Sunderland took over at top of the League, but it had been an incredible twenty-game unbeaten run by Derby, that will probably stand as a club record for years to come. With ten games to go Derby just had to hold their nerve. In their next game at home to second-bottom Watford, a late Paul Simpson penalty rescued a point for Derby in a 1-1 draw. Jim Smith then strengthened his squad on transfer deadline day with the arrival of Norwich City striker Ashley Ward for £1 million. Two days later, Ward was back at Carrow Road making his debut in the 1-0 defeat, with Jeremy Goss scoring the Canaries winner. After two defeats in three games Derby had a vital 3-1 win at home to Stoke City. Mike Sheron gave the visitors a half-time lead. Dean Sturridge, who came on as a second half substitute, scored twice, with a rare Daryll Powell goal completing the scoring. With seven games to go, Derby were seven points behind leaders Sunderland but only three points ahead of third place Crystal Palace, who had been on a fine run of seven wins and two draws, which had shot them up the table. Derby lost 1-0 at Ipswich Town. Steve Sedgeley fired wide a controversial penalty, but a Tony Vaughan header sealed the points for the home side. Two vital wins over Easter though, were just what Derby needed. A Paul Simpson penalty earned Derby the points on their Easter Saturday visit to Oldham Athletic. Derby recorded their biggest win of the season in the Easter Monday home game against Tranmere Rovers. Paul Cook gave Tranmere the lead with a thirty-yard free kick that deceived Russell Hoult. Daryll Powell equalised before half time. Derby ran riot in the second half scoring five times through Dean Yates, a Paul Simpson hat-trick and Dean Sturridge. John Aldridge pulled one back with his usual goal from the spot, but the game finished 6-2 and gave Derby a much-needed confidence boost going into the final four games. It was also good to put one over Tranmere, for all the drubbings Derby received at Prenton Park. Derby were now five points ahead of third-placed Crystal Palace and three points behind Sunderland, who had a game in hand. Derby drew 0-0 in their next game away at Charlton Athletic, a game which was live on ITV. Derby drew 1-1 in their next game with Birmingham City. Crystal Palace were closing in on Derby, after winning 2-0 at Wolverhampton Wanderers and narrowing the gap to one point with the two sides due to meet at the Baseball Ground the following Sunday. The equation was straight forward, if Derby won, they'd be back in the big time.

The following Saturday, my eleven-year-old daughter, Sarah, was complaining of stomach pains and was confined to the settee. The big game against Crystal Palace the following day, in front of a capacity 17,000 crowd with a tremendous but tense atmosphere, started well for Derby who took the lead through Dean Sturridge, who scored his twentieth goal of the season, with a lovely finish following Marco Gabbiadini's flick on. Kenny Brown levelled for the Eagles with a fine left foot shot from fifteen yards. Robin van der Laan's free header at the far post from Paul Simpson's header midway through the second half restored Derby lead. Derby held for a famous victory to a crescendo of noise at the final whistle, with the jubilant fans invading the pitch. I had other things on my mind though. I raced home and that evening around seven p.m., we took Sarah to the children's hospital in North Street. She was admitted, with the medics trying to diagnose her problem. On the Tuesday morning she was doubled up in pain, so we agreed for her to have exploratory surgery. It was found that she was suffering from a burst appendix, so she had surgery to remove it. It could had been fatal if it had been left any longer. Whilst in hospital, Sarah also contacted pneumonia and could hardly walk down the ward. She was in hospital for a fortnight. When she returned home, she missed school for the rest of the school term and didn't go back until the September. It had been a traumatic time, with the football quite irrelevant. In the final game of the season Derby lost 3-2 at West Bromwich Albion in what was a 'dead rubber'. Derby were in the Premier League for the first time. The team just gelled with a solid base and hard-working midfielders. The strikers all made good contributions, with Dean Sturridge, in my opinion, the main man. The impact of Igor Stimac on the club was immense, with the twenty-match unbeaten coinciding with his arrival. How different this team was to the 'dream team', with fine individuals but the wrong blend.

1996/97

In the summer of 1996, England hosted Euro '96. There was a massive feel-good factor sweeping the country as 'Football's Coming Home' by the Lightning Seeds was the sound of the summer. This was the first time a major football tournament had been staged in the country for thirty years, since the 1966 World Cup. Houses were decked with the St. George's flag as football fever gripped the nation. England reached the semi-finals overcoming Switzerland, Scotland and the Netherlands in the group stages, and rather fortunately Spain, following a penalty shoot-out in the quarter-final. In the semi-final though it was old adversaries Germany who knocked England out, following another penalty shoot-out after England had played so well in normal and extra time.

Derby were preparing for the new exciting season ahead, in what would be their last ever season at the Baseball Ground.

Jim Smith pulled off a masterstroke before Euro 96, by signing Croatia international midfielder Aljosa Asanovic from Hadjuk Split, even though he had been on loan in Spain at Real Valladolid. The fee for Asanovic was £950,000. He had a brilliant Euro 96 as Croatia lost in the quarter-final to Germany, but they had a team full of talent with the likes of Davor Suker, Robert Jarni, Igor Stimac, Slaven Bilic, Robert Prosinecki and Zvonimir Boban in their squad. Three other additions to Derby's squad were Danish international defender Jacob Laursen from Silkeborg IF for £500,000, Scottish under 21 international Christian Dailly, signed from Dundee United for an initial fee of £500,000 and ex-England defender Paul Parker joined from Manchester United on a free transfer. Darren Wassall left Derby to join Birmingham City for £150,000 after not really fulfilling his potential, and he had struggled with niggling injuries.

Julie, Sarah and I travelled to Gran Canaria for our summer holiday. Much to our relief, Sarah was on the mend following the events in April. We were away as Derby kicked off the new season. Fortunately for me but may be not for Julie, most bars had TVs with Sky Sports with their comprehensive coverage of the Premier League, so I was in my element! Derby were at home to Leeds United in their first game with all four summer signings making their debuts. One change in the Premier League was that players wore squad numbers and had their name on the back of their shirts. In what looked a very entertaining game, a Jacob Laursen own goal gave Leeds a first half lead. There were five goals in the last eighteen minutes. Ian Harte doubled Leeds advantage before a superb left foot volley from Dean Sturridge gave Derby hope. Paul

Simpson seized on a poor back pass to equalise. Lee Bowyer restored the lead for Leeds before Dean Sturridge earned Derby their first Premier League point in a 3-3 draw. The first away game was at Tottenham Hotspur. The Rams wore their new maroon away kit, which Graham Richards referred to as their 'Heart of Midlothian' kit. Derby got a very creditable draw in North London. Teddy Sheringham, one of the stars for England in Euro 96, fired Tottenham ahead, but a last-minute Christian Dailly header salvaged Derby a draw. Derby lost 2-0 at Aston Villa, before I went to my first game of the season, a midweek game at home to Premier League Champions Manchester United. Jacob Laursen gave Derby the lead with a stunning free kick that flew past Peter Schmeichel. United levelled with a great strike from David Beckham. Derby were searching for their first win but were competing well. That first win came in their next match, which was live on Sky Sports Monday Night Football at Blackburn Rovers. This Monday night game was a new experience for Derby and their supporters. Derby made a sensational start, with Ron Willems stabbing the ball across the line to give Derby a forty second lead. Chris Sutton equalised for Rovers. Sean Flynn restored Derby's lead with a lovely side foot finish following good work by Marco Gabbiadini. Derby held on for a great win at Ewood Park, which had never been a happy hunting ground. Derby followed this up with their first home win of the season, with a 1-0 win over ten-man Sunderland. Aljosa Asanovic, who was on a different level from everyone else, scored the winning goal from the spot. Derby then lost two successive home games, 2-0 against Wimbledon and 1-0 against Newcastle United. Republic of Ireland international Paul McGrath made his debut for Derby in the Newcastle match following his £200,000 move from Aston Villa. Alan Shearer scored the Magpies' winner. Coming away from the ground, I felt this was going to be a tough winter for Derby. Derby travelled to the City Ground for the first ever Premier League East Midlands derby. Dean Saunders, who was now at Forest, gave the Reds a first half lead with Christian Dailly's first goal for the club earning Derby a point.

Derby were mid-table with eleven points from ten games which was a decent start to the campaign. Two Robbie Fowler goals gave Liverpool a 2-1 victory at Anfield, before Derby started November with two wins on the trot at home, beating Leicester City 2-0 and Middlesbrough 2-1. November finished well, as Derby drew 1-1 at West Ham United and they beat Coventry City 2-1 at home. Derby visited Highbury on the first Saturday in December, in what turned out a thrilling match against top-of-the-table Arsenal. A fine strike by Ashley Ward crashed against the bar before a Tony Adams far post diving header gave the Gunners a 1-0 half time lead. Dean Sturridge then cut in from the left before unleashing an unstoppable drive off the underside of the bar and in past David Seaman, in what was Derby's best goal of the season so far, to level the score at 1-1. Daryll Powell volleyed Derby in front with a close-range effort, but Patrick Vieira equalised to deny Derby victory. This was the afternoon, though, which supporters felt that Derby belonged in the Premier League. The Rams were very unlucky not to win.

Derby then had their worst run of the season losing five and drawing three of their next eight games. The only respite was in the FA Cup, beating Gillingham away in the third round after the original game was abandoned due to a frozen pitch after an hour. Derby then beat Aston Villa with a fine display in the fourth round by 3-1, at the Baseball Ground. Derby had slipped to fifth-from-bottom of the League, with the next match a massive game against third-from-bottom West Ham United at the Baseball Ground.

Derby were only three points ahead of the Hammers so this was a real six-pointer even though it was only mid-February. Ex-Ram Paul Kitson made his West Ham debut following his move from Newcastle United with nineteen-year-old Rio Ferdinand in their back four. In a tense encounter, Aljosa Asanovic was magnificent for Derby and he scored the second half penalty, which gave Derby the three points after he was brought down in the box by Ferdinand. It was Derby's first win since the end of November and very much needed. The FA Cup fifth round draw gave Derby a good chance to progress as they were drawn at home to Coventry City, who were below them in the Premier League table. It didn't start well though, as Coventry raced into a two-goal lead through Darren Huckerby and Noel Whelan. A close-range effort by Ashley Ward and a Robin van der Laan header brought the Rams level by half time. A fantastic through ball by Paul Trollope that split the defence was coolly finished by Dean Sturridge and the comeback was complete. The Rams were into the sixth round for the first time since 1993 and the memories of Sheffield Wednesday came flooding back! Derby had another 3-2 victory following their cup success, when Chelsea visited the Baseball Ground in the next game. Scott Minto gave Chelsea the lead on a dry bobbly pitch, but then scored in his own net to level for Derby. Frank Leboeuf restored Chelsea's lead but was then sent off for handling on the line. Aljosa Asanovic slotted away the resulting penalty and Ashley Ward continued his good scoring with a close-range winner. It was a big win for Derby who were now seven points clear of the drop zone.

The next two games were against Middlesbrough, away in the League and at home in the sixth round of the FA Cup. Derby had an unacceptable evening on their first ever trip to the Riverside Stadium and were thrashed 6-1, with Fabrizio Ravanelli bagging a hat-trick for Boro on an evening to forget. I just hoped psychologically that wouldn't damage Derby too much, with the FA cup tie only a couple of days away. I was dreaming of Wembley again as I headed to the Baseball Ground, for what was, in my opinion, the biggest game of the season. I was so desperate to see Derby in a FA Cup Final. Jim Smith made a big call by dropping Russell Hoult and playing Martin Taylor. Derby just didn't turn up on the day and slipped to a 2-0 defeat, with Juniniho and Fabrizio Ravanelli scoring again to send the Rams crashing out. To make matters worse, Middlesbrough drew third tier Chesterfield in the semi-final. Derby would never have had a better chance of getting to the FA Cup Final. Remarkably Chesterfield, who had current Burnley manager Sean Dyche skippering their side, should have won the game at Old Trafford. Boro's Vladimir Kinder was sent off for two bookable offences in the first half. Andy Morris put the Spirites ahead at the start of the second half with Dyche doubling the lead from the spot. Ravanelli pulled one back for Boro. Then the major controversy of the game.

Jonathan Howard's close-range shot appeared to cross the line after hitting the bar. It would have given Chesterfield a 3-1 lead but referee David Elleray and the linesman didn't give the goal. A Craig Hignett penalty made it 2-2 with Gianluca Festa scoring making it 3-2. In an extraordinary game Jamie Hewitt's header made it 3-3 in one of the most dramatic FA Cup games of all time. Middlesbrough won the replay which was played at Hillsborough.

Derby lost 1-0 away at Everton, but then had a fine 4-2 win at home against Tottenham Hotspur. Ahead of the trip to Old Trafford for the Manchester United game, Jim Smith made three signings before the transfer deadline day. He signed twenty-five-year-old Estonian international goalkeeper Mart Poom from Flora Tallinn for £595,000. Poom had been with Smith at Portsmouth. I'd seen Poom play in one of his four appearances for Pompey but I thought he was a bit shaky, so I wasn't convinced about his signing. He'd returned to Flora Tallinn following his time at Fratton Park. Derby also signed two unknown Costa Rican internationals; striker Paulo Wanchope and midfielder Mauricio Solis from CS Herediano, for £600,000 each. Poom and Wanchope made their debuts in the daunting trip to face the League leaders at Old Trafford. Derby got off to a great start, with Ashley Ward's deflected looping effort giving Derby the lead. Derby's second goal was a fantastic solo wonder goal by debutant Paulo Wanchope described by more classic Graham Richards commentary. "Wanchope comes into the Manchester United half, dribbles on, finds some space, goes into the box, shoots, and it's in, what a run, Wanchope took them on down the middle and as Schmeichel came out he picked his spot and United look absolutely second rate. Wanchope took them on down the middle, he beat four players, they just couldn't take the ball off him and Schmeichel looked mesmerised, as he came towards him, he gave up, he just flicked it in the net. And Wanchope treated Manchester United's defence with absolute contempt. Manchester United nil Derby two." Brilliant by Wanchope, and even better by Richards! After Derby went in 2 nil up at half time, the great Eric Cantona, who probably was at his peak then pulled one back. Dean Sturridge then restored Derby's two-goal advantage. Ole Gunnar Solskjaer reduced the lead, but Derby held on for a famous victory that virtually confirmed their Premier League status. With six games remaining, Derby still had to play Nottingham Forest at home in their penultimate home game. It would be the final time they would ever play at the Baseball Ground. Forest, deep in relegation trouble, were four points from safety, so for me it was important for Derby not to lose. In a dour game it finished 0-0 and Forest were as good as down. Forest's fate was sealed when they failed to beat Wimbledon. Derby on the same day beat Coventry City, who were also having their annual fight against relegation.

The final ever match at the Baseball Ground on Sunday 11 May. It was an emotional day. For me, it was twenty-six years of watching football there. The highs of the Championships, promotions, European nights and the lows of relegations. I consider myself very lucky and privileged to have been to every single European Cup and UEFA Cup home game that the Rams have ever played in. The European Cup was very special. For me, you can keep the Champions League. It's just a money-making exercise with a lot of pointless group games. In the end, the cream always rises to the top and it's pretty easy to predict who the semi-finalists will be. As I've previously said, don't get me started on the Europa League. More pointless group games, there was nothing wrong with the UEFA Cup format. Thursday night has never been and never will be a football night. The problem with this arrangement is that all the clubs end up playing their League games on a Sunday. I'm a traditionalist, football for me is for three p.m. on Saturdays. The greatest goal I've seen at the ground was Charlie George's against Real Madrid. The technique to hit a ball like that is special. I also liked his goal against Newcastle United in the 1976 FA Cup following his combination with Kevin Hector. Memories that will last forever. The Rams and Arsenal played out the final game at the great ground in front of a sell-out crowd of 18,287. It was hard to imagine that the record attendance was over 41,000. Tony Adams was sent off early but they went on to win 3-1. It would have been nice to go out with a win but it didn't really matter. Paul McGrath, who'd been magnificent for Derby, and had a major role in their survival, played his last game for the club and received a standing ovation when he was substituted after an hour. He was one of the greatest players of his generation and would be sadly missed. Derby finished twelfth in the table, ensuring top flight football for their new home. The curtain came down on one hundred and two years of football at Baseball Ground with the start of a new chapter in Derby's history at the new 33,500 all seater stadium on Pride Park.

CHAPTER 8

PRIDE PARK STADIUM, THE ITALIAN JOB AND McCLAREN DEPARTURE

1997/98

Her Majesty the Queen officially opened Pride Park Stadium on Friday 18 July. I was really pleased my dad went to witness this historic occasion, even though he didn't go to any games nowadays, in his advancing years.

Utility player Sean Flynn joined West Bromwich Albion for £260,000. Marco Gabbiadini left to join Greek side Panionios on a free transfer. The major signing was the arrival of Italian international midfielder Stefano Eranio from AC Milan on a free transfer. He had won three Serie A titles and played in two Champions League finals. Portsmouth striker Deon Burton joined Derby for a fee of £1 million and midfielder Jonathan Hunt cost Derby £500,000 from Birmingham City. Derby opened the season away at Blackburn Rovers and fell to a 1-0 defeat, with both Stefano Eranio and Jonathan Hunt making their debuts. We were away on holiday in Majorca for the first ever home game at Pride Park which took place on Wednesday 13 August. Wimbledon were the visitors for the midweek game. Unexpectedly the floodlights failed at the start of the second half with Derby leading 2-1 and the game was abandoned! Derby lost their second game at Tottenham Hotspur also 1-0 with Deon Burton making his debut. Derby strengthened their attacking options with the arrival of a second Italian, the diminutive Fiorentina striker Francesco Baiano for a fee of £650,000. I was back from holiday to take my place for the first time at Pride Park for the home game against promoted Barnsley, with Baiano making his debut. Carl Smith and I had bought season tickets in the West Stand lower tier about eight rows from the front, level with the eighteen-yard box at the North Stand of the ground. It was just great to have no posts or obstructions in the way of the view. Derby won 1-0 with a twice-taken penalty. Baiano's effort was saved and Eranio followed up to score, but referee Paul Durkin ordered it to be re-taken, which Eranio duly converted. During the international break, Jim Smith sold Ashley Ward to Barnsley for £1.3 million. Derby beat Everton 3-1 with Jonathan Hunt and Chris Powell scoring their first goals for the club with Dean Sturridge also netting on his first appearance of the season. After a 2-1 setback at Aston Villa, Derby scored nine goals in their next two games putting Sheffield Wednesday to the sword in a 5-2 victory, their first win at Hillsborough since 1936. The goals were shared by Jacob Laursen, Paulo Wanchope, Francesco Baiano with two and Deon Burton. Southampton were hammered 4-0 at home with all the goals coming in the last fifteen minutes. Lee Carsley, who was now playing in his much-preferred central midfield role, scored the last goal much to the amusement coach Steve McClaren in the dug out!

Derby's good start to the season continued. After completing a

6-0 aggregate win over Southend United in the second round of the League Cup, with young central defender Steve Elliott making his debut in the game at Roots Hall, Derby had a fine 2-1 win at Leicester City in a game that was shown live on Sky Sports Monday Night Football on the first Monday evening of October. Francesco Baiano gave Derby the lead with his fifth goal of the season, and he made it six following a mix up between Leicester keeper Kasey Keller and Robbie Savage. Matt Elliott pulled one back for the Foxes, but Derby held firm to move up to sixth in the table with fifteen points from eight games. Paul Simpson, the last remaining link of the 'dream team', left Derby to join Wolverhampton Wanderers initially on a month's loan which was made permanent for a fee of £75,000. Further success followed in the League Cup, with Derby winning 2-1 at Tottenham Hotspur. Derby's good record against Manchester United continued, even though they let a two-goal lead slip. Francesco Baiano scored yet again to give Derby the lead. Mart Poom saved a Teddy Sheringham penalty before Paulo Wanchope doubled the lead. United though came back strongly in the second half, with Sheringham and Andy Cole salvaging a point. The Rams suffered their heaviest defeat of the season, losing 4-0 at Liverpool, but then produced their best display of the season on a very wet day at home to second-placed Arsenal. Derby ran Arsenal ragged and ran out worthy 3-0 winners after Ian Wright had hit the bar with his penalty. Paulo Wanchope scored twice, and Dean Sturridge, who arguably had his best game in a Derby shirt, completed the scoring with a fine solo effort. In a crazy game the following week at Elland Road, Leeds, Derby stormed into a three goal first half lead with two from Dean Sturridge and a Aljosa Asanovic penalty. Leeds though came roaring back in the second half scoring four through Rod Wallace, Harry Kewell, Jimmy Floyd Hasslebaink, and in the last minute, Lee Bowyer, to complete a stunning comeback, with Derby looking shellshocked after the final whistle. Derby were becoming the 'great entertainers' with a glut of goals in their games since the end of September.

Derby lost their unbeaten record at Pride Park, losing 1-0 to a Jon Dahl Tomasson goal for Newcastle United in the fourth round of the League Cup. The goal glut continued in the League as Derby beat Coventry City 3-1 at home, but then lost heavily at Chelsea going down 4-0. Two bad errors from West Ham United goalkeeper Ludek Miklosko gifted Derby the points in a 2-0 victory. Derby then recorded three draws in a row in the run up to Christmas. Derby drew 3-3 at Bolton Wanderers in a game covered live on Sky Sports Monday Night Football after letting a 3-1 lead slip. Two goalless draws followed away at Newcastle United and at home to Crystal Palace. Derby ended the year beating Newcastle 1-0 at home on Boxing Day, but then lost 1-0 away at rock bottom Barnsley with ex-Ram Ashley Ward scoring. How often does that happen – ex-players scoring against you?! Aljosa Asanovic, who did as much as anyone to keep Derby in the Premier League in the previous season, left the club to join Napoli in Serie A. He was a wonderfully gifted footballer, one of the best I've seen in a Derby shirt and I was sad to see him go. I got the impression Jim Smith thought he was a bit a luxury player and hard to fit into a team system. If I had to name an all-time Derby XI, he would be in my side and I would build the team around him. The New Year started well for Derby, with a 2-0 win over Southampton in the third round of the FA Cup, followed by a fine 3-1 win at home to Blackburn Rovers, a game shown live on Sky Sports Super Sunday. Derby's front three had been a constant menace to defences all season. Paulo Wanchope was unorthodox and powerful, and Dean Sturridge had strength and pace to burn, with the clever Francesco Baiano playing just behind them. Derby followed this up with a well-earned point against Wimbledon, who were now playing at their adopted home Selhurst Park. Derby's FA Cup dreams came to an end with a fourth round 2-0 defeat at Coventry City, with Dion Dublin scoring twice. Derby ended January beating Tottenham Hotspur 2-1. The win-maintained Derby's position in the top six, with thirty-nine points from twenty-four games, ten points behind leaders Manchester United.

Derby signed young full-back Rory Delap from Carlisle United for £200,000, who made his debut in the 2-1 win at Everton. Duncan Ferguson was sent off for elbowing Paulo Wanchope. Igor Stimac headed Derby into the lead before a lovely eight-man passing move was finished off by Wanchope, which sealed the points for Derby. I went to Old Trafford the following week, which was my first away match for ages, with Matt and Pete Birks. We sat in the South East corner. Derby were never at the races and lost 2-0, with Ryan Giggs and a Denis Irwin penalty scoring their goals. I always felt Old Trafford was very quiet, with no atmosphere for their 'run of the mill games' against teams like Derby. Their big games were against the likes of Liverpool and Manchester City. After beating Sheffield Wednesday 3-0 at home, Derby had an afternoon no-one saw coming when they played Leeds United, another game shown live on Sky Sports Super Sunday. Derby lost 5-0 in what was their biggest home defeat since Liverpool won 7-1 in March 1991. Derby also lost their next two games, 1-0 at Coventry City and 1-0 at Chelsea. Deadline day signing Lars Bohinen, who joined Derby for £1.45 million from Blackburn Rovers, made his debut in the Coventry game. These three defeats seriously dented Derby's hopes of qualifying for the Europe for the first time since 1976-77. They slipped to eighth in the table with forty-five points from thirty-one games, with seven games of the season remaining. Derby halted the run of defeats with a goalless draw at West Ham United, before getting a much-needed confidence boosting 4-0 win at home to Bolton Wanderers with Deon Burton, who'd struggled to hold down a regular starting place, scoring twice. The inconsistent form continued and Derby lost their next three games. They lost 3-1 at Crystal Palace and 4-0 at home to Leicester City, in a remarkable start to the live game on Sky Sports Super Sunday. The Foxes were 4-0 up in fifteen minutes. All the goals were headers, from Muzzy Izzet and Ian Marshall, with two from Emile Heskey. Jim Smith looked a worried man as boos rang around the ground and some fans left the stadium early. Arsenal completed the trio of defeats winning 1-0 at Highbury. Derby did though win their last two games, 2-0 at Southampton and 1-0 at home to Liverpool. It had been a great season though, with Derby playing some of their most entertaining football for years, with the Italians Stefano Eranio and Francesco Baiano having a major impact. Ninth place was a fair reflection on the first season at the impressive Pride Park Stadium. The heavy home defeats against Leeds United and Leicester City were a bit worrying though.

1998/99

Jim Smith sprang a surprise by selling left-back Chris Powell to Charlton Athletic for £825,000. I couldn't understand the move as Powell had been a model of consistency since his move from Southend United. Gary Rowett also departed, joining Birmingham City for £1 million. Also, ahead of the new season, Dean Yates left the club to join Watford on a free transfer. What a fine acquisition and model professional he had been, who played a vital role in the club gaining promotion. He couldn't play every week due to his knee problems, but when he played, he hardly put a foot wrong. Robin van der Laan, captain of the 1995/96 promotion winning team also left the club, joining Barnsley for a fee of £325,000. There were three incoming defenders to Pride Park. Argentine defender Horacio Carbonari joined Derby in a £3 million pound deal from Rosario Central. German left-back Stefan Schnoor arrived on a free transfer from SV Hamburg as a replacement for Chris Powell. Spencer Prior also signed from Leicester City for £1 million. Smith was certainly ringing the changes. Schnoor and Carbonari both made their debut on the opening day of the season at Blackburn Rovers, which strangely was a repeat of the opening day fixture in the previous season. The game finished goalless, as did Derby's first home game against Wimbledon with Spencer Prior making his first start in a Rams shirt. In the week after the Blackburn game, Christian Dailly joined Rovers for a club record £5.35 million. It was an astonishing fee for a player who'd only played less than seventy League games for Derby. Dailly couldn't possibly turn it down either, with the lucrative personal terms on offer.

Carl Smith and I renewed our season ticket but we moved to

the North Stand behind the goal. The next game at promoted Middlesbrough also ended in a draw, this time 1-1, with Paulo Wanchope scoring. On the first Saturday in September, I went to Lord's with Carl for the NatWest Trophy final between Derbyshire and Lancashire. On a rain affected day, play didn't start until mid-afternoon. Derbyshire collapsed from 70-0 to 108 all out, and ended up losing on the following day in what was a total anti-climax and disappointment. Back to the football, Derby's first win of the season was a 1-0 success against Sheffield Wednesday with a goal from Dean Sturridge. One thing that was becoming apparent was that Rory Delap's long throw was a great weapon to have, both in the attacking and defensive sense. Derby followed this up this win with two more, 2-1 at Charlton Athletic and 2-0 at home to Leicester City, a result which partly erased the memory of the 4-0 home defeat at the end of the previous season. Stefan Schnoor scored his first goal for the club, with Paulo Wanchope adding the second. Derby though lost three games on the spin at the end of September and beginning of October. They went down 2-1 at Aston Villa, 1-0 at home to Tottenham Hotspur and 2-1 at Newcastle United.

Former England full-back, the experienced Tony Dorigo joined Derby from Italian side Torino, as Jim Smith continued to ring the changes. I was hoping the changes wouldn't disrupt the progress of the club. Dorigo came on a substitute in the 1-1 home draw against Manchester United. Deon Burton put Derby ahead, with Jordi Cruyff levelling as Derby's impressive run against United continued. Jim Smith then signed non-League striker nineteen-year-old Malcolm Christie from Nuneaton Borough. Derby were in mid-table as October came to an end with a 2-2 draw with Leeds United. In this game Kevin Harper, who was a £300,000 acquisition from Scottish Premier League side Hibernian during September, made his debut. In the next game away at Liverpool, Harper started and scored, with a far post header at the Kop end, which Derby won 2-1. It was their first win at Anfield since 1970. The East Midlands derby at the City Ground was selected for the Monday Night Football, covered live on Sky Sports. The game came to life after a goalless first half, with Tony Dorigo giving Derby the lead from the penalty spot. Forest, who had been promoted as Division One Champions, stormed back though and scored twice in five minutes through Dougie Freedman and Pierre van Hooijdonk. Horacio Carbonari levelled to share the points, which in all honesty was a fair result. At the end of November, Derby lost 2-0 at home to West Ham United, and won 1-0 at Southampton before drawing four successive games up to and including the goalless draw at Everton on Boxing Day. Derby beat Middlesbrough in a feisty encounter in the final game of the calendar year. Dean Sturridge gave Derby the lead, lifting the ball over the advancing Mark Schwarzer. Paulo Wanchope was sent off right on half time following an altercation with Andy Townsend, who appeared to stamp on Wanchope, but was only booked. After the break, Mikkel Beck headed Boro level but a late Jonathon Hunt goal gave Derby a very unlikely 2-1 victory.

In the FA Cup third round, Derby were drawn away to Plymouth Argyle. Derby were much too strong for their lower League opponents. A brace from Deon Burton and a Stefano Eranio penalty gave Derby a comfortable passage through to the next round. Burton scored again in a 1-0 home League win against Blackburn Rovers. Derby ended January with another

FA Cup away win, this time 1-0 at rain-soaked Swansea City with a Kevin Harper goal. Memories of the mascot 'Cyril the Swan' came flooding back! Derby's good form continued with a Spencer Prior goal giving them victory at Sheffield Wednesday. Derby moved up to eighth in the table with thirty-four points from twenty-three games. The good run came to an end at Old Trafford, as Derby fell to a 1-0 defeat to Dwight Yorke goal. Steve McClaren, who'd made a massive impression at Derby, was approached by Manchester United to replace Brian Kidd as assistant manager to Sir Alex Ferguson. Kidd had left United to become manager of Blackburn Rovers. When United come knocking, it was hard to stand in anyone's way. McClaren though, outside of Derby, was probably unknown to a lot of people. This probably included United chairman Marin Edwards, who when introducing McClaren to the media called him Steve McClaridge! Billy McEwan replaced McClaren as assistant manager. By a strange coincidence I saw McClaren's first game with United at Nottingham Forest. Pete Birks had managed to get some tickets for the game on the day of the game and asked me if I wanted to go. As Derby were playing on the Sunday I said yes, so we made the short journey to the City Ground. We sat in the Peter Taylor Main Stand, level with the penalty area towards the Trent End. In an astonishing game United won 8-1, with Ole Gunnar Solskjaer scoring four times in the last ten minutes, after he'd come on as a seventieth minute substitute. It was the largest away win in Premier League history.

    I went with Carl Smith to the next away game, which was the FA Cup fifth round tie against Huddersfield Town for my first visit to the Alfred McAlpine Stadium. We sat in the away end behind the goal, with the 4,000 other Derby fans. There was a really good atmosphere in the ground. Derby fell behind to a Chris Beech goal just before the break, but two quick goals from Deon Burton and a Tony Dorigo penalty looked like sending Derby through. Marcus Stewart though, a prolific scorer in the lower Leagues, earned the Terriers a replay. Derby won that replay 3-1 and yet again I was dreaming of Wembley. Surely this year! In the FA Cup sixth round, Derby drew Arsenal away and I was so disappointed. The draw was about as tough as it could get. Before the game at Highbury, Deon Burton continued his fine run of scoring as Derby earned a 1-1 draw at Arsenal's North London rivals Tottenham Hotspur. In the game at Arsenal, Derby fought really hard but were under the cosh for most of the game. They suffered a cruel blow, as a late Nwankwo Kanu goal sent Arsenal through to the semi-final. Much to the surprise of the supporters, Lee Carsley made his final appearance in this game before he was transferred to Blackburn Rovers in a £3.4 million deal.

The Rams put their FA Cup disappointment behind them with two fine home wins, 2-1 against Aston Villa, with two fine finishes from Francesco Baiano and Deon Burton. This was followed up with a 3-2 win against Liverpool, which completed the League double against the Reds, with Paulo Wanchope scoring twice. Greek full-back Vassilis Borbokis then joined Derby from Sheffield United for £500,000. Jim Smith tried to sign midfielder Seth Johnson from Crewe Alexandra before the transfer deadline day, but he decided to stay with Crewe to help them in their First Division relegation battle. The two wins moved Derby into the top six, with forty-four points and nine games of the season left. Derby suffered two defeats, 4-1 at Leeds United and 4-3 at home to Newcastle United. New signing Mikkel Beck, who joined the Rams from

Middlesbrough for £500,000, made his debut in the Newcastle game. Derby also signed young defender Paul Boertien from Carlisle United for £250,000. It was then time for bottom of the table Nottingham Forest, with only four wins all season, to play at Pride Park for the first time ever. They were eleven points from safety so it was a must win for them. A great piece of skill and a fine finish from Horacio Carbonari five minutes from the end secured the points for Derby, with Forest now right in the mire, with relegation looking inevitable. As we left the ground and headed back into town for some celebratory beers, the only sound to be heard was Carbonari's name ringing out from the Rams faithful. Derby came back down to earth in the next game, suffering a 5-1 defeat at West Ham United, with young midfielder seventeen-year-old Adam Murray making his debut. Derby only won one of their last five games, a 2-1 victory at Leicester City, with Mikkel Beck scoring the winner with his first goal for the club. Derby finished eighth in the table, which was very respectable due to quite a few changes of personnel. Deon Burton, who I got the impression wasn't well liked by the majority of the supporters, was top scorer with twelve goals from twenty starts. I always liked Burton. Any player who can control a ball with his back to goal will always impress me. He wasn't as eye catching as Dean Sturridge, Francesco Baiano or Paulo Wanchope, but was certainly a good back up. Defender Jacob Laursen was Player of the Year. Very consistent, he was a top clubman and unsung hero. He'd turned out to be an excellent signing by Jim Smith.

CHAPTER 9

THE FUERTES FIASCO, THE £3 MILLION MEN AND TARIBO WEST

1999/00

Jim Smith finally got his man when Seth Johnson completed his £3 million move from Crewe Alexandra. Smith also dipped into the transfer market to strengthen his striking options with the arrival of Argentine striker Esteban Fuertes from Colón de Santa Fe for £2.3 million, following the departure of Paulo Wanchope who joined West Ham United for £3.5 million. Goalkeeper Andy Oakes joined Derby from Hull City for £465,000, as back up to Mart Poom and Russell Hoult. Johnson made his debut in the opening game at Elland Road, Leeds, in a game that ended goalless. The Rams then lost three games in a row, with two at home. Arsenal won 2-1 and Middlesbrough won 3-1, both at Pride Park. Derby then lost to two Robbie Keane goals at Coventry City, in what was a slow start to the season. Derby then won two games, 2-0 away at Sheffield Wednesday and 1-0 at home to Everton, with Fuertes heading in the winner as the season at last got going. Derby then sold popular Croatian defender Igor Stimac, also to West Ham United for £600,000. Stimac had been a major player in Derby's rise in the four years he had been at the club. Derby drew 2-2 at Wimbledon, but then suffered a very poor 5-0 home defeat at the hands of Sunderland. Kevin Phillips helped himself to a hat-trick for the Black Cats in what was a demoralising afternoon for the Rams. Derby completed an aggregate second round League Cup win against Swansea City, but suffered a second successive home League defeat with newly promoted Bradford City winning 1-0. Derby's next away game was an entertaining 3-3 draw at Southampton in a game shown on Monday Night Football covered live on Sky Sports. Rory Delap gave Derby the lead with his first goal of the season. Marians Pahars scored a stunning equaliser for the Saints with a long-range drive. Matt Oakley put Southampton ahead, with Stuart Ripley increasing the lead with his first goal for the club. Derby fought back though, through a Jacob Laursen free kick and a last minute Mikkel Beck header that earned the Rams a point.

Derby then went on a really poor run, with only one win and seven defeats from their next eight games, which saw them quickly drop down the League to third-from-bottom by the start of December. Bolton Wanderers also knocked Derby out of the third round of the League Cup. Following the defeat at Newcastle United at the end of October, Francesco Baiano left the club. The fans loved the little Italian who scored sixteen goals in sixty-four appearances. His biggest problem though, was his inability to play ninety minutes. He was though a joy to watch and played a massive part in Derby establishing themselves in the top flight. After the Liverpool defeat at the start of November though, there was then a bombshell to hit Derby's season. Esteban Fuertes, following a trip back from the international break training camp in Portugal, was refused entry back into Britain when immigration officials discovered that his Italian passport was forged, meaning he would require a work permit. Derby were able to sell him on to Lens France for £2.8m. His Derby career was over before it had started. Jim Smith during this time added more new players to his squad. Winger Lee Morris joined from Sheffield United for £3 million. Israeli international Avi Nimni joined on loan from Maccabi Tel Aviv. Craig Burley joined from Celtic for £3 million and Georgi Kinkladze joined on loan from Ajax. There was far too much change too soon to the squad from the first season at Pride Park. Mikkel Beck, who failed to make an impact following his move from Middlesbrough, joined Nottingham Forest on loan.

The FA Cup third round took place in mid-December in a change to the traditional first weekend in January. Apparently, the decision was made to help British teams competing in Europe, especially those in the expanded Champions League. It had also been announced that holders Manchester United wouldn't compete in the FA Cup, as they were competing in January's World Club Championship in South America. I wasn't impressed by their decision. I think these World Club tournaments are absolutely pointless and are yet another money-making exercise. It also left the FA Cup with an odd number of teams, so one team from among those lower-division teams defeated in the second round would be re-instated to progress to the third round as a 'lucky loser'. This was absolutely farcical. In my opinion, the FA Cup since then has lost most of its credibility, as well as teams playing weakened teams in favour of the Premier League riches. Third tier Burnley were the visitors to Derby in the third round. Their support was fanatical and they filled the South Stand. They also deservedly won with an Andy Cooke goal in the second half, as Derby's slump continued. They did though get a much-needed win in their last game before Christmas with a 1-0 win at Leicester City with a strange goal from Daryll Powell, who lobbed the ball back into the box from a cleared corner which Tim Flowers in the Leicester goal completely misjudged. The Rams signed Croatian-born Belgian international striker Branko Strupar for yet another £3 million from FC Genk, as Jim Smith continued his spending spree. He made his debut in the home 2-0 defeat against Aston Villa. Strupar had good pedigree, finishing top scorer in the Belgian top tier in the previous season. The year ended with the Rams drawing 1-1 at West Ham United but they were still third-from-bottom, a point from safety, with a lot of work needed in the new Millennium to preserve their Premier League status. In the first game of 2000, Derby played Watford, who were below them in the table. Branko Strupar gave Derby an early lead and then he made it two with a fine free kick to give Derby a much-needed win. Goalkeeper Russell Hoult moved to Portsmouth initially on loan, making the move permanent two months later, for £300,000.

I went to the next away game, my first of the season at Middlesbrough with the late Paul Church, who was a good friend of mine from work. We both shared similar sporting interests in Derby County and Derbyshire County Cricket Club. It was our first visit to the Riverside Stadium, which was a bit of a replica of Pride Park Stadium. We sat in the North Stand behind the goal, right at the back of the stand. Striker Malcolm Christie made his debut, replacing Branko Strupar who was injured. Christie made a dream start, heading in from Seth Johnson's corner. Deon Burton doubled the lead at the start of the second half with Christie scoring his second following indecision from Boro keeper Mark Schwarzer. The locals weren't happy, as a chorus of boos rang around the ground. Mart Poom then saved a Hamilton Ricard penalty before Andy Campbell pulled one back. Craig Burley scored his first goal for the club to complete a fine 4-1 victory. The two wins in the New Year moved Derby up to fifth-from-bottom, four points ahead of the drop zone. Derby were involved in an astonishing finish to their home game with second-from-bottom Sheffield Wednesday at the start of February, in a game that flowed from end to end from start to finish with chances galore. Gilles de Bilde headed in from a corner to give the Owls the lead halfway through the first half. Mart Poom made some fine saves to keep his side from going further behind. Gerald Sibon doubled the lead with a fantastic volley from outside the box, much to the delight of the Wednesday masses behind the goal in the South Stand. Branko Strupar reduced the arrears with a close-range header. Against the run of play, Wednesday extended their lead in the eighty-ninth minute through Simon Donnelly. Almost immediately Craig Burley pulled one back and Malcom Christie bundled the ball over the line deep into added on time to earn the Rams a unexpected point. What a game! It was then back up to the north-east for my next away trip. I went to Sunderland with Paul Church and Carl Smith for our first visit to the Stadium of Light. We parked up and as we approached the ground, it was just a sea of red and white in all the pubs. We sat in the lower tier of the North Stand opposite the Roker End, in a crowd of over 41,000. The teams came out to the deafening sound of Prokofiev's Dance of the Knights from Romeo and Juliet. Derby played very well and took the lead after the break through Malcolm Christie, but Alex Rae levelled two minutes later and the game finished 1-1.

Derby recorded their biggest win of the season scoring four times in the second half against Wimbledon at Pride Park. Derby dominated from start to finish, with goals from Georgi Kinkladze, Malcolm Christie, Deon Burton and Dean Sturridge. Kinkladze played in the hole just behind Christie, who, with his youthful exuberance, was really making an impact – but Derby were only just above the drop zone, two points ahead of Bradford City with twenty-eight points from twenty-seven games. Youngster Adam Bolder joined Derby from Hull City. Their position didn't immediately improve though, with defeats by 3-1 at Old Trafford, 2-0 at home to Liverpool and by 2-1 at Villa Park. Central defender Spencer Prior's short spell at the club ended, as he moved on to Manchester City for £500,000. The home game against Leicester City at the start of April was the game shown on Sky Sports Super Sunday. Craig Burley gave Derby the lead before Stan Collymore suffered a horrendous broken leg after he played the ball out to the wing unchallenged. Collymore wasn't the most popular man in Derby due to his Nottingham Forest connections, but you wouldn't wish that on anyone. The Rams added two further goals through Rory Delap and Dean Sturridge headers just before half time to give them a 3-0 win. Delap was proving to be a very useful acquisition, popping up with his fair share of goals. With seven games to go Derby moved five points clear of the drop zone. Fortunately, the teams below them, Bradford City, Sheffield Wednesday and

Watford weren't making much of a fist it. Derby played bottom of the League Watford the following week. In a game of few chances, it ended goalless. Derby lost their next game at home to West Ham United, but then travelled up to Valley Parade for a must not lose game at Bradford City on Good Friday afternoon. I thought it would be a cagey, typical relegation battle but how wrong was I! Rory Delap put Derby ahead after twenty-three seconds with Branko Strupar's free kick doubling the lead after six minutes. Two great strikes from Dean Windass put the Bamtams level and then Rory Delap was sent off by Alan Wilkie for pulling back Robbie Blake before the striker had put the ball in the net. The goal didn't stand, but the resultant Peter Beagrie penalty put the home side ahead. Malcolm Christie was felled in the area with Craig Burley hammering home the spot kick to make it 3-3 in thirty-five minutes. Bradford amazingly took the lead before half time, with Dean Windass completing a fine hat trick. Craig Burley converted his second penalty, the third of the match, early in the second half, as the topsy-turvy game finished 4-4. More importantly, with four games remaining, Derby were six points ahead of the drop zone. Derby fears were eased further with a 2-0 home win against Southampton and a great 1-1 draw at Tottenham Hotspur, who denied Derby the win with a last-minute Stephen Clemence goal. A goalless draw though, in the final home game of the season against Newcastle United secured Derby's place in the Premier League for another season. Richard Jackson, a full-back who looked very young for a nineteen-year-old, made his debut as substitute. He had joined Derby from Scarborough in a £30,000 deal. Paul Church and I went to Stamford Bridge for the last game of the season against Chelsea. We had a replica view of the TV cameras, as we sat behind the dug out in the lower tier of the West Stand. Derby put in a disappointing performance and were well beaten 4-0, with all the goals scored in the second half. Bradford City who had been in the bottom three most of the season, beat Liverpool at home on the final day of the season which sent Wimbledon down into the First Division. Derby finished sixteenth after a poor season. Much improvement was needed in the next campaign.

2000/01

Jim Smith wasn't holding back in wheeling and dealing as he continued to reshape his squad. Manchester United left sided defender Danny Higginbotham signed for £2 million, and Norwegian international defender Bjorn Otto Bragstaad for £1.5 million from Rosenborg. Derby also completed the signing of twenty-one-year-old French defender Youl Mawene for £500,000 from Lens. Australian defender Con Blatsis joined from South Melbourne and Finnish international Simo Valakari moved from Scottish Premier League outfit Motherwell on a free transfer. Georgi Kinkladze completed his permanent move to Derby, joining Seth Johnson, Lee Morris, Craig Burley and Branko Strupar all as £3 million signings in the previous twelve months. Jacob Laursen moved back to Denmark to join FC Copenhagen on a free transfer. Tony Dorigo was released and left the club to join Stoke City.

There were goals galore in Derby's first six games of the new season as they drew two and lost four of their first six games. Julie, Sarah and I were on holiday in Ibiza, so I missed the first game of the season. Derby came back from two goals down to draw 2-2 at home to Southampton with Danny Higginbotham, Con Blatsis, Bjorn Otto Bragstaad and Simo Valakari all making their debuts. This was followed with a 3-2 defeat at Newcastle United. Derby were also two goals down at Everton before a bullet header from Dean Sturridge and curling free kick from Branko Strupar salvaged a draw. Carl Smith and I continued with our season ticket in the North Stand, with the midweek game at home to Middlesbrough at the start of September being the first game I went to. Middlesbrough were 3-0 up with twenty minutes to go, before Derby staged a stunning fightback with goals from Branko Strupar and two from Malcolm Christie. Strupar, who had scored in each of the first four games and who I rated very highly, missed Derby's next home game against Charlton Athletic, which was shown live on Sky Sports Super Sunday. The reverse happened to that in the Middlesbrough game, with Derby taking a 2-0 lead, but the Addicks rallied in the second half, scoring twice to earn a point. Their fourth defeat in six games was at Sunderland, who won 2-1. Derby dropped to second-from-bottom with only West Ham United below them. Derby then lost in their second round League Cup first leg tie by 2-1 at home to West Bromwich Albion, but won their first game of the season in the second leg, winning 4-2 at the Hawthorns. Derby born centre-back Chris Riggott made his debut and scored, with Bjorn Otto Bragstaad scoring twice also.

The Rams then lost another four League games on the spin. The run started with a heavy defeat 4-1 at Aston Villa. The 4-0 defeat at home to Liverpool, with Emile Heskey scoring a hat-trick was shown live on Sky Sports Super Sunday. This was followed by two away defeats by 3-1 at Tottenham

Hotspur and 2-1 at Leicester City. Colin Todd joined the club as assistant manager, replacing Billy McEwan who stayed with the club in a coaching capacity. It was as poor a start to a season I can remember, as the Rams hit rock bottom at the end of October with five points from eleven games. The League Cup though gave Derby some relief, as they beat First Division Norwich City 3-0 to progress to the fourth round. Derby arrested the run of defeats with two goalless draws at home to West Ham United and at high flying Arsenal with French defender Lilian Martin playing in both games following his free transfer from Marseille. Seth Johnson became the first Derby player since the days of Peter Shilton and Mark Wright to play for England, when he came on as a substitute in the friendly with Italy in Turin. Johnson had certainly deserved his chance, following some consistent displays in a poor performing team. Jim Smith then signed Nigerian international Taribo West on an initial three-month loan from AC Milan. West had only played a handful of games since his move from city rivals Internazionale. I couldn't quite weigh West up when I had seen him on television, so I was looking forward to see how he would fit in at Derby. He made his debut in a home game, a bottom of the table clash with Bradford City, in his black and white gloves, playing on the left side of the back three with Horacio Carbonari in the middle and Chris Riggott on the right. Derby finally won a League game at their fourteenth attempt much to the relief of the home support, who continued to come in their numbers, with over 31,000 at this game. Rory Delap and Malcolm Christie scored the second half goals in the 2-0 win. Derby lost at Fulham in the League Cup fourth round, but won their first away game of the season with a 1-0 win at Ipswich Town at the beginning of December with Rory Delap again the scorer. After a poor performance in a 4-1 defeat at Chelsea, Derby won back-to-back home games in the run up to Christmas without conceding, beating Coventry City 1-0 and Newcastle United 2-0. The Riggott/Carbonari/West combination was bearing fruit together with the impressive Mart Poom, who just seemed to be getting better and better. I certainly didn't have any doubts about him now as I did when I saw him briefly at Portsmouth. Dean Sturridge, who'd been a massive part of last five years, was sold to Leicester City for £375,000. In the next two away games, the Rams got a battling point in a goalless draw against Manchester City but lost 1-0 at Southampton with Youl Mawene making his first start, with Taribo West missing due to an unexplained absence. Derby ended the year fifth-from-bottom, only a point above the drop zone. I got the feeling the home form would be the key to survival in the second half of the season. The New Year started well, as Derby beat Everton 1-0 with another gritty performance, with Deon Burton scoring the winner and Taribo West returning to the side. Mart Poom was in fine form again with a string of fine saves. Derby followed this up with a third round FA Cup victory over West Bromwich Albion. Young Malcolm Christie was really making a name for himself, as he celebrated his first year as a regular starter by scoring twice in the 3-2 victory. Derby's away form was still a concern, and this was confirmed by a 4-0 defeat at Middlesbrough who were below Derby in the table, so it was a bad game to lose.

Paul Church and I went to the next game, which was a midweek away game at Charlton Athletic at the end of January. Paul drove on a freezing cold day with a dusting of snow covering the fields, as we headed towards London on the M1. Pre-match, we went for a beer in Charlton Village, which was situated in a lovely area not far from the ground. When we got inside the ground, the players were out practicing. I couldn't see Taribo West which concerned me, as he was having a massive influence on the side. I was very impressed with the Valley, as now it was fully redeveloped. We sat in the Jimmy Seed Stand behind the goal, with the massive East Stand to our right. I have to say it is one of my favourite away grounds. Youl Mawene's own goal gave Charlton an early lead but Craig Burley deceived Dean Kiely in the Charlton goal with a twenty-five-yard-curling free kick. Kiely was very lucky to stay on the pitch after a 'kung-fu' style kick felled Malcolm Christie, which resulted in a penalty. Referee Mike Dean only booked the Charlton keeper. To add salt into the wound, Kiely saved Craig Burley's spot kick. Scott Parker scored Charlton's winner on the hour, but I felt Derby had been hard done by. After the game Jim Smith confirmed that Taribo West had gone back to Milan to visit his church. The things football managers have to deal with! Who'd be one?

The Rams crashed out of the FA Cup in the fourth round. After drawing 0-0 at Ewood Park, in a game Brian O'Neil made his debut following his arrival from German side Wolfsburg. This involved full-back Stefan Schnoor moving in the opposite direction. Schnoor was the replacement for Chris Powell, but I thought Jim Smith had made a mistake with this, as Powell was far more accomplished than Schnoor. Blackburn won the replay at Pride Park by 5-2. I wasn't too concerned, as Premier League survival was of paramount importance. Derby then had a decent little mini-run, picking up a point in a 1-1 draw at

Leeds United with Branko Strupar returning to the side after his long lay-off. They then secured back-to-back vital home wins 1-0 against Aston Villa with a Deon Burton penalty, and 2-1 against Tottenham Hotspur, with Strupar bagging both. This was followed with a 1-1 draw at Liverpool, with Deon Burton scoring with his knee to give Derby the lead, with Michael Owen replying.

Derby were now eight points clear of the bottom three in fifteenth place. When things seemed to be going in the right direction, Derby lost three games on the bounce. They lost 2-0 at Coventry City, 4-0 at home to Chelsea and 3-1 at West Ham United. Icelandic international midfielder, Thordur Gudjonsson, on loan from Spanish side Las Palmas, made his debut at Highfield Road. The three defeats had put Derby back in trouble, dropping to fourth-from-bottom, five points clear of safety.

The Easter Monday home game against Leicester City took on greater significance now. Paul Boertien, who made his debut against Chelsea, put the Rams ahead in the first half with Stefano Eranio sealing the 2-0 win in the last minute. The Leicester game was the last time we saw Taribo West in a Derby shirt. I thought he'd been an absolute colossus and as strong as an ox since his arrival and did as much as anyone in a Derby shirt in their climb away from the bottom of the table. He was an enigma and he didn't play too many games, but he's up there with the following pack behind McFarland and Todd as one of the best central defenders I've seen at the club. Derby lost their next two games, 2-0 at Bradford City and 2-1 at home to Arsenal. Derby were four points ahead of third bottom

Manchester City, with two games left, away to Champions Manchester United, who were fourteen points ahead of second placed Arsenal, and at home to Ipswich Town. The Rams inflicted only the second home defeat of United's season with a left foot drive from Malcolm Christie into the top corner after turning sharply in the box. It was a totally unexpected win which secured Derby's survival. From the horrific start to the season without a win since mid-November, Derby did well to finish fourth-from-bottom. There were plusses with the emergence of Malcolm Christie and telling contributions from Seth Johnson and Rory Delap. Branko Strupar's injury problems didn't help. I felt the club needed stability in terms of less player turnover. There had been far too much of that.

CHAPTER 10

SMITH OUT, TODD IN AND OUT, GREGORY AND THE DREADED DROP

2001/02

I felt Jim Smith was under quite a bit of pressure going into the new season, considering how much money he'd spent, and Derby narrowly missing relegation. Lionel Pickering offered Smith the post of Director of Football but he flatly refused. He did make a major signing though, with the arrival of former Italian international thirty-three-year-old Fabrizio Ravanelli from Lazio, on a free transfer. He signed a two-year deal that reputedly made him the highest earner in Derby's history. There was also a major departure, with Rory Delap making a £4 million move to fellow Premier League side Southampton. Ravanelli's fellow countryman, Daniele Daino, joined Derby on loan from AC Milan. Both made their debuts in the opening game of the season, with Derby beating Blackburn Rovers 2-1, with Ravanelli scoring Derby's first goal. Ravanelli scored again in the 3-1 midweek defeat at Ipswich Town. Derby then drew 0-0 away at with newly promoted Fulham, who were playing in the top flight for the first time since 1968. Another goalless draw followed at home to West Ham United.

Derby beat Hull City 3-0 in the League Cup second round on the day after the United States 11 September terror attacks, with Deon Burton scoring twice. Derby then had one of their poor runs, which seemed to become a common theme in recent seasons. They lost four League games on the spin. After the defeat in the third of these games at home to Arsenal, Jim Smith resigned, after just over six years in the hot seat, with Colin Todd taking over the reins. It didn't start well for Todd as Derby were beaten 5-2 in the League Cup third round game at Fulham. They also lost 3-1 at Tottenham Hotspur in the League, with American goalkeeper Ian Feuer on loan from Wimbledon, making his debut as Mart Poom was injured. Derby were in the bottom three with five points from eight games, in another poor start to the season. Todd's first major act was to sell Seth Johnson for a club record £7 million to Leeds United. Todd, who was still searching for his first win as manager, then made three signings. Argentine left-back Luciano Zavagno joined Derby from French side Troyes, French midfielder Pierre Ducrocq joined on loan with view to a permanent deal from Paris Saint Germain, and Benito Carbone also arrived on loan from Bradford City. All three players made their debut in the 1-1 draw at home to Charlton Athletic.

The following week, I travelled to Dublin with the late Paul Disney to take part in the Dublin Marathon on the last Monday in October, which is always a bank holiday in the Republic of Ireland. Paul was a good friend of mine who I'd worked with for fifteen years and he loved travel, but was definitely not a runner! I'd not ran a marathon for quite a while following my knee problems, but had got back into running with Dave Thompson, a good work mate of mine. We became good training partners and subsequently ran miles together. I'd booked the accommodation in Dublin for Paul and myself online, which in those days was in its infancy. When we got to the hotel, they had no recollection of the booking even though I'd got the paperwork to prove it. Somehow, they had double booked! So, Paul and I had to traipse around Dublin on the Saturday afternoon looking for an alternative. Virtually everywhere was booked up. We had just about given up when we found a place. What a nightmare beginning to the weekend! I finished the race in 3.37, which was a personal best. We had a great night in Dublin on the Monday evening, as I had my first real taste of Irish Guinness. Back to the football, things didn't get any better, as Derby were hammered 5-1 at Middlesbrough. The Riverside Stadium was becoming a very unhappy hunting ground, with all six goals scored in the second half. Todd signed another Frenchman with the acquisition of right-back Francois Grenet, for a reported £3 million from Bordeaux. He made his debut in the game in which the Rams finally got a win, beating Southampton 1-0 at Pride Park, with Youl Mawene scoring his first goal for the club. The following week, I went with Paul Church and Carl Smith to St James' Park for the game against Newcastle United. It was my first visit since 1992 and the ground had changed remarkably, especially the Leaves End terrace where I had stood in 1984. We actually sat in the Leazes End upper tier right up in the gods. It is reached by climbing fourteen flights of stairs, with a warning sign for anyone with a heart condition! I have never sat so high in a ground, but we had a fantastic view of the Newcastle skyline. In front of a crowd of just over 50,000, Derby lost 1-0 to Alan Shearer's first half penalty but played very well on the day, with the home keeper

Shay Given making a string of fine saves. It was though like watching ants, being so far away from the pitch. It was an experience, but I wouldn't recommend it and I wouldn't go there again! A Michael Owen goal earned Liverpool the points in a 1-0 win at Pride Park on the first weekend of December. Derby then won their third game of the season at home, against Sam Allardyce's Bolton Wanderers with Malcolm Christie scoring the all-important goal in the 1-0 win. Derby then suffered two away defeats. Manchester United completely dominated the game in front of over crowd of 67,000, as they beat Derby 5-0. Everton then beat Derby 1-0 at Goodison Park, with a goal from substitute Joe-Max Moore. Derby did though go into the Christmas break with a 3-1 win against Aston Villa. Fabrizio Ravanelli, Malcolm Christie and Benito Carbone, with his first goal for the club, gave Derby a much-needed win. It had been a tough baptism of fire for Colin Todd, as Derby ended the first half of the season in the relegation zone. The away form was a major concern, with seven defeats and a draw in their eight games. This became eight defeats on Boxing Day, as Derby were beaten 4-0 at West Ham United. Trevor Sinclair scored one of the goals of the season for the Hammers with a spectacular overhead kick. Derby though did win at Blackburn Rovers in their final game of 2001, with Malcolm Christie scoring the only goal. It was absolutely freezing for the first game of the New Year against Fulham at Pride Park. The Rams put in a sloppy performance and lost 1-0, with Horacio Carbonari's own goal sending the Cottagers home happy and Derby remained entrenched in the bottom three.

The third round of the FA Cup paired Derby with fourth tier Bristol Rovers, in a game which was played on the first

Sunday in January. It turned out to be a totally humiliating afternoon for the Rams, who lost 3-1 with Nathan Ellington scoring a hat-trick for the 'Gas'. They filled the South Stand with their travelling support from the south-west. Derby's defending was dire and they got what they deserved. With confidence at a low ebb, the Rams lost three League games in a row. Aston Villa then beat Derby 2-1 at Villa Park with this being the final straw for Lionel Pickering. He pulled the trigger and sacked Colin Todd only three months into his tenure. Todd's three signings Luciano Zavagno, Pierre Ducrocq and Francois Grenet were struggling and although you couldn't fault their effort, they didn't look like Premier League players. Billy McEwan took over before Derby suffered two home defeats, 3-1 against Ipswich Town who were one of two teams below Derby, and 1-0 against Charlton Athletic. Derby continued their policy of appointing ex-players as their manager with John Gregory, who'd just resigned as manager of Aston Villa, being appointed at the end of January. Gregory signed ex-England international Warren Barton for £200,000 from Newcastle United and he went straight into the team as Derby beat Tottenham Hotspur 1-0 in Gregory's first game. Lee Morris, who'd had an injury ravaged start to his Derby career scored the only goal. Gregory returned to Newcastle to sign thirty-six-year-old midfielder Rob Lee for £250,000. Lee made his debut in the 1-0 home defeat to Sunderland before Derby recorded their biggest away win of the season, defeating bottom of the table Leicester City 3-0 at Filbert Street. The goals came from Georgi Kinkladze, who didn't feature under Todd, Branko Strupar and Lee Morris. Goalkeeper Andy Oakes, who was deputising for Mart Poom, was injured in the first half. He was replaced by on loan signing Swiss keeper

Patrick Foletti, who had joined Derby from FC Luzern as Derby suffered a goalkeeping injury crisis. Gregory had instilled new optimism and belief into the supporters. Derby though were still in the drop zone, four points away from safety. Oakes was back in the side as Derby got a very creditable 2-2 draw in their home game with Manchester United, with Malcolm Christie scoring twice at the start of March. Derby lost 1-0 at Highbury against Arsenal, before facing at crunch game at Bolton Wanderers.

I went with Paul Church and Carl Smith to the game at the Reebok Stadium. The Rams were second-from-bottom in the table, four points behind fourth-from-bottom Bolton with both clubs having played the same number of games. The first thing we realised was that was that the ground was nowhere near Bolton and nearer to Horwich. It was also in the middle of a retail park, next to the likes of Marks and Spencer and KFC. We sat in the lower tier of the South Stand behind the goals. The pitch looked very bare, bumpy and devoid of grass. Malcolm Christie gave Derby the lead halfway through the first half after he pounced on a mistake by Paul Warhurst. Ricardo Gardner levelled for the Trotters, but then Derby dominated with Fabrizio Ravanelli heading in at the far post. In the closing stages of the game, Lee Morris was brought down by Jussi Jaaskelainen, who was sent off by David Elleray. Danny Higginbotham converted the penalty to give Derby a 3-1 win. After this game, Horacio Carbonari went on loan to First Division Coventry City. Bolton, in that game, looked very poor. As we left the stadium, we all agreed Bolton looked certainties for relegation, with Derby looking a good bet to avoid the drop. How wrong we were. Derby couldn't have picked a worse time to have a poor run of defeats. They lost seven games on the bounce. The next away game I went to was the game at Southampton at St. Mary's Stadium on the first Saturday in April. Carl Smith and I went to the game. I remember it vividly. It was a sunny day but with a freezing cold wind. Derby were still second-from-bottom, six points from safety with five games remaining. It really was a must win. We sat in the North Stand as Derby put in a totally inept performance with no passion, as they looked totally devoid of ideas and confidence. Matt Oakley and Marian Pahars scored as Derby started staring into the abyss. All the confidence gained from the game at Bolton had quickly evaporated. Derby let a two-goal lead slip at home to Newcastle in the next game with Trésor Lomana Tresor LuaLua scoring a last-minute winner for the Magpies, with Ian Evatt making his debut after coming on as a substitute. Derby were seven points adrift with three games remaining, with a daunting trip to title chasing Liverpool the next game. Liverpool put Derby out of their misery with a comfortable 2-0 win, with goals from Michael Owen. Derby were relegated together with Ipswich Town and Leicester City. Back in March I was convinced Bolton Wanderers would go down, but somehow, they survived. Derby's five-year spell in the top flight was over; it was time for the inquest. Derby had a great first season at Pride Park, but I felt that team wasn't given more time to grow together. Chris Powell and Gary Rowett moved on and the likes of Stefan Schnoor and Spencer Prior came in. I'm certainly not blaming Schnoor and Prior, I just don't think there was any need for change. This was just the start of a big turnover of players in a short period of time.

The following week after relegation, it was marathon time for me again. Dave Thompson and myself entered the Lochaber Marathon up in Fort William. On the Friday we flew up to Edinburgh with Paul Disney and Mark Elliott, who was also a good friend of mine from work. We picked a car up in Edinburgh and Paul volunteered to drive the scenic route through Glencoe up to our hotel in Fort William. On the Saturday, we had a trip up to the beautiful Isle of Skye via the Bridge over Loch Alsh. Derby were playing Leeds United in their last game of the season and lost 1-0. Dave and I completed the race on the Sunday. I finished in 3.35, another personal best, so I was quite happy. We had a good evening in Fort William with the beers flowing, travelling back to Derby on the Monday. It was a welcome change to football!

2002/03

Derby's spending during the Premier League years saw the club enter a serious financial crisis and there was a massive feeling of gloom hanging over the club, due to the way the previous season ended. John Gregory was tracking nineteen-year-old Nigerian Maccabi Haifa frontman Yakubu Ayegbeni, who ended up spending six weeks on trial as Gregory was impressed by his pace and power. A deal around £200,000 with the Israeli club was agreed but there were complications in obtaining a work permit for Yakabu, as he'd not played in seventy-five percent of Nigeria's recent internationals and much to Gregory's frustration the deal fell through. Pierre Ducroq's unsuccessful loan spell came to an end and he returned to Paris Saint Germain. Deon Burton went on loan to Portsmouth, but returned to Derby following injury. Derby kicked off their season in League Division One at home to Reading. Carl Smith and I continued with our season ticket in the North Stand. On a warm sunny August afternoon, Derby won 3-0 in front of 33,000 fans with Rob Lee, Fabrizio Ravanelli and Malcolm Christie on the scoresheet. If anyone thought the League was going to be a cakewalk, they were in for a surprise, as they lost three of their next four games. Derby lost 1-0 at Gillingham with young striker Marcus Tudgay, who had progressed through Derby's youth system, making his debut. They also suffered a disturbing 4-1 defeat at home to Wolverhampton Wanderers and 2-1 at Rotherham United. The Rotherham defeat was the end of the road for Francois Grenet. The Frenchman, to put it kindly, never got to grips with the English game and supporters couldn't quite see how Colin Todd was justified in paying £3million for the full-back. Derby's only win was 2-1 at Grimsby Town with Adam Bolder scoring twice. The Rams ended August beating Stoke City 2-0, with two Malcolm Christie goals, but the crowd had dropped by 12,000 from the Reading game and Derby lay in mid-table with nine points from six games. Derby lost their next two games, 2-1 at home to Burnley with nineteen-year-old Lee Grant making his debut in goal, and by 3-1 at Leicester City, which was sandwiched in by a comfortable first round League Cup 3-1 win at Field Mill against Mansfield Town. Georgi Kinkladze scored a late winner in the 1-0 win at Crystal Palace, with young full-back Lewis Hunt making his debut. But the inconsistency continued, with Preston North End winning 2-0 at Pride Park. Derby then won 1-0 at Ipswich Town, with seventeen-year-old striker Izale McLeod making his debut. Horacio Carbonari, who had returned from his loan spell at Coventry, made his first start of the season and scored in the 1-0 win. Derby were beaten 2-1 at home to Oldham Athletic in the second round of the League Cup. Carbonari then played in the 2-2 home draw with Walsall, the first time Derby had played the Saddlers since 1986. Surprisingly, this also turned out to be Carbonari's final appearance in a Rams shirt. John Gregory didn't really fancy him and he returned to his homeland and to Rosario Central.

A crowd of over 30,000 saw Derby and Nottingham Forest play out a goalless draw at Pride Park in what was a very cagey game. Millwall overturned Derby 3-0 the following week, with Neil Harris scoring twice. Derby's really disappointing start to the season saw them lying in fifteenth place in the table, amassing eighteen points from fifteen games. At the start of November, Mart Poom made his final appearance for the club away at Sheffield Wednesday. Derby won 3-1 in that game, through a Lee Morris double and Izale McLeod. Poom joined Sunderland initially on loan, which was made permanent in a deal worth £3.2 million. Poom had become one of the fans favourites in his six years at Pride Park. I rate him as the third best keeper I've seen watching Derby, behind Colin Boulton and Peter Shilton. Lee Grant was picked ahead of Andy Oakes to press his claim for the number one shirt. Grant's first two games ended in defeat, 2-1 at home to Portsmouth and 1-0 away to Brighton and Hove Albion. Derby beat Wimbledon 3-2 at Pride Park on the last Monday in November in front of a 25,000 plus crowd. The significance of this was that I cannot remember seeing a Wimbledon supporter in the stadium. Wimbledon had been ground sharing with Crystal Palace since they left Plough Lane in 1991. In 2001 Wimbledon announced their intention to move the fifty or so miles north to Milton

Keynes after rejecting a variety of possible sites in the London area. In May 2002, despite opposition from the majority of Wimbledon fans, the FA and Football League approved the move with the club being renamed Milton Keynes Dons. Crowds plummeted and their away followings were largely boycotted. This was quite a remarkable story, one which I believe will never be repeated. A new football club, AFC Wimbledon, was born, and they entered the Premier Division of the Combined Counties League, the ninth tier of English football.

Derby won their next two home games, 3-0 against Watford and 1-0 at home to Brighton at the start of December, now lying mid-table with thirty-three points from twenty-two games. Deon Burton returned to Portsmouth again, this time permanently, for £250,000. Julie and I then went to York for the weekend for her birthday and our wedding anniversary. On the Saturday, there was freezing fog all day and it was pretty cold. Derby's game at Coventry City was chosen for live TV on Sky Sports on the Saturday teatime. We watched the game in The Hole in the Wall pub. Derby put in a really poor performance, losing 3-0. I think we were the only ones in the pub watching, or just me as Julie wasn't that bothered about it! On Boxing Day, Derby played Grimsby Town, who were hovering just above the relegation zone. John Gregory handed a debut to Lee Holmes, who was the youngest player to play for Derby aged fifteen years and 268 days, when he came on as a second half substitute. Derby were poor again and lost 3-1, with John Oster scoring twice for the Mariners. I drove to Reading for the last game of the year with Carl Smith. We stopped at a pub in Didcot for a pint and a bite to eat before making our way to the Madejski Stadium. We sat in the South Stand with the travelling support. Like Bolton the ground was in the middle of a retail centre, a soulless ground with not much atmosphere. Defender Pablo Mills made his first appearance in a Derby shirt. Nathan Tyson gave Reading the lead inside five minutes, with Craig Burley levelling three minutes later. Reading dominated with Jamie Cureton's last-minute winner giving the Royals a deserved 2-1 win. The pressure was mounting on John Gregory with the poor run of results and the side had no real identity. 2002 finished with Derby seventeenth in the table with thirty-three points from twenty-six games. Derby put in another abject performance against third tier Brentford at Griffin Park in the third round of the FA Cup. Stephen Hunt's first half strike was the only goal of the game. Following a draw at home to Gillingham, Derby had two good wins, 3-1 at Stoke City and 3-0 at home to Rotherham United.

Derby sold defender Chris Riggott and Malcolm Christie to Premier League Middlesbrough for a combined fee of £3 million to relieve the financial pressure on the club. Danny Higginbotham also left, joining Southampton in a £1.5 million deal. Derby had lost three of their best players. The Premier League spending had hit the club hard, with reports of £20 million debts. Derby then lost 6-2 in their biggest defeat of the season at Fratton Park, Portsmouth. Rampant Pompey were top of the League and heading for the Premier League. Svetoslav Todorov scored twice and to add salt into the wound Yakabu, who Derby had tried to sign, also scored twice. His work permit had been granted as he married a European girl and now allegedly had played the correct quota of games for his country. Adam Bolder scored twice in the 2-2 home draw with Sheffield Wednesday. Fabrizio Ravanelli made his first start since August in the 2-0 defeat at Burnley, following surgery on his Achilles tendon. After a 1-1 draw at home to Leicester City at the start of March, Derby went on one of their losing streaks that had become all too common in recent seasons. They lost four games on the bounce. It was announced that BBC Radio Derby commentator Graham Richards was retiring from his role as the voice of Derby County at the end of the season, with Ross Fletcher taking over. Nick Chadwick on loan from Everton made his debut in the home defeat to Crystal Palace, and Derby were then beaten by Bradford City. This was followed by away defeats at Preston North End and 3-0 at play-off chasing Nottingham Forest, which saw Tommy Mooney, on loan from Birmingham City, make his debut at the City Ground. It was also the end of John Gregory's fourteen-month spell as manager. Gregory was suspended, with the club citing serious misconduct as the reason. Mark Lillis, who was part of the coaching staff, took over for the Sheffield United away game, which Derby lost 2-0. The season was going from bad to worse. Derby had slumped to fifth-from-bottom and in serious danger of relegation, only six points above the drop zone, with seven games to go. That weekend, we spent the weekend in Windsor for our good friend Steve Hallam's fortieth birthday, with him and his wife, Dawn. On the afternoon of the Sheffield United match, we went to Kempton Park races. Steve can always remember, when we reminisce about this particular weekend, that Stoke City played Watford. He's as bad as me!

CHAPTER 11

THE GEORGE BURLEY YEARS, LIONEL PICKERING'S SAD END AND THE 'THREE AMIGOS'

Lionel Pickering appointed George Burley as Interim Manager. I always liked Burley as a player and manager. His playing career spanned over six hundred games and he was part of the great Ipswich Town side of the late 1970's and early 1980's managed by the late Sir Bobby Robson. He had also taken Ipswich to four play-off finals before achieving promotion. Burley won his first game in charge at home to Norwich City on the first Saturday in April. Burley had signed Paul Ritchie on loan from Manchester City, and he made his debut. Norwich took the lead through Paul McVeigh but Burley's nephew Craig levelled. With the score at 1-1, Darren Kenton passed the ball back to goalkeeper Rob Green who inexplicably missed his kick and the ball trickled over the line to give Derby a much-needed victory. This was followed up with a 2-0 away win against Wimbledon at Selhurst Park, as Derby moved nine points clear of the drop zone. The crowd at Selhurst Park was just 1,934. This is the lowest crowd I can ever remember for a Derby League game. I remember this weekend fairly well, as I was in the capital for the London Marathon. Julie and I travelled down on the day of the match because I had to collect my race number. I was toying with the idea of going to the match but decided against it as I didn't want to race around London and save my energy for the big day. The race went well and I finished in 3.34. This was the day Paula Ratcliffe broke the women's world record in 2.15, so it was quite a historic occasion that I was involved in the same race! Derby then lost 2-1 at home to Millwall, but the 1-0 victory at home to Coventry City, with Fabrizio Ravanelli scoring only his fourth goal of his injury hit season, preserved Derby's First Division status.

I went with Carl Smith to only our second away game of the season, the last away game against Walsall at the Bescot Stadium. We stood behind the goal with covered terracing with the Main Stand on our left. Derby lost 3-2, with Brazilian striker Junior bagging a hat-trick. Fabrizio Ravanelli scored one of Derby's goals but my abiding memory of the afternoon was him blasting over from a yard. How he missed, I'll never know. I wasn't impressed by Ravanelli in his spell at Derby if I'm honest. He always looked a bit laboured to me. He certainly didn't make the impact of fellow Italians Stefano Eranio or Francesco Baiano. Ravanelli's final appearance in a Derby shirt was in the final game, a 4-1 home defeat against Ipswich Town. He moved on to Dundee after his two-year-deal expired.

2003/04

George Burley faced a tough time ahead, with very little money to spend on new players with Lionel Pickering looking to sell the club. New faces who appeared in the summer included experienced midfielder Ian Taylor, who had been released by Aston Villa. Centre-back Dave Walton who had rejected a new deal at Crewe Alexandra joined on a two-year contract. Fellow centre-back Gary Caldwell also joined on loan from Newcastle United. Another loan signing was Portuguese winger Candido Costa from Porto. Walton was injured in pre-season, but the other three players all made their debuts in the opening game at home to Stoke City, together with sixteen-year-old Tom Huddlestone. There were high hopes for Huddlestone who had come through the ranks at Derby and he'd represented England at junior levels. Julie and I were on holiday in Santorini but we couldn't find a bar with Sky Sports! I had a text from Steve Hallam who went to the game. He told me Stoke City won 3-0 and that Derby had been very poor. Carl Smith and I decided against having a season ticket for the first time in many years. George Burley after the game spoke of this being a tough season ahead and he urgently needed to add experience to his young squad. The Rams were knocked out of the League Cup, losing 2-1 at Huddersfield Town, before George Burley added experienced defender Michael Johnson on a free transfer from Birmingham City. Striker Lee Bradbury also joined on loan from Portsmouth. Both players made their debuts at Gillingham, in a game that ended 0-0. Burley then signed striker Junior from Walsall, who must have impressed him by scoring a hat-trick at the back end of last season. Striker Mathias Svensonn joined on loan from Charlton Athletic. Both Junior and Svensonn made their debuts in the 3-2 home defeat at home to Reading. The August Bank Holiday fixture away to Cardiff City was shown live on Sky Sports with a teatime kick-off. Svensonn scored and looked impressive, but Derby crashed to a 4-1 defeat. August ended with a 1-0 defeat at home to West Bromwich Albion, with Derby rock bottom of the League table. September was a far better month though, as Derby won 1-0 at Walsall with Junior scoring the late winner and this was followed up with a 3-2 win at home to Watford. Junior scored again, as did Mathias Svensonn, as their partnership started to blossom. Two draws followed, 1-1 at home to Sunderland with ex-Derby 'keeper Mart Poom amazingly scoring a last-minute stunning far post bullet header, and a 1-1 draw at Nottingham Forest. Junior put Derby ahead before Andy Reid equalised minutes later. Derby suffered a major blow though, as Junior suffered a knee ligament injury late on in the game. The month ended with a fine 2-1 win at Bradford City, with Lee Morris scoring twice. The League table was looking a lot healthier, with Derby climbing to sixteenth in the table with twelve points from ten games. Derby started October with a home game against West Ham United, who had Sir Trevor Brooking in charge as caretaker manager. The game was shown live on Sky Sports, with the Hammers winning 1-0 with a very late Don Hutchinson goal. Crucially for Derby, Mathias Svensonn limped off injured before half time.

The following week, Derby's parent company, Derby Limited, briefly went into liquidation. Lionel Pickering, the majority shareholder, gave way to a new board with John Sleightholme becoming Chairman, Jeremy Keith became Chief Executive and Steve Harding, who bought the club for £3. Sleightholme owned two thirds of the club and Keith one third. Murdo Mackay was appointed by Sleightholme as Director of Football. The money the three used to support their takeover was a £15 million loan from Panama registered company ABC

Corporation, at a cost of ten percent interest per annum. Why would they need a loan to support the takeover? The only way they could make this work was by selling their major assets on the pitch or reaching the Premier League. It was a worrying time for supporters. They would become known to the supporters as the 'Three Amigos'. I had great sympathy for Lionel Pickering, a man who I really liked, who pumped millions into the club and was heavily influential in the move to Pride Park.

The Rams fell to three more defeats on the trot and it looked like a long hard winter ahead to try and avoid a second relegation in three seasons. The three defeats were 2-1 at Norwich City, with Dave Walton making his long-awaited debut, 3-1 at home to Coventry City with Walton suffering a re-occurrence of his injury and 2-1 at Preston North End. This resulted in Derby slipping to just a point above the bottom three. Derby born sixteen-year-old Nathan Doyle and left-back Peter Kennedy, on loan from Wigan Athletic, made their debuts in the Preston defeat. Mathias Svensonn made his last appearance in the Coventry game before returning to Charlton Athletic, his parent club. I really liked Svensonn, he was quick, strong and had good movement. I would have loved to have signed him, but it was totally out of the question given the dire financial position of the club. On the weekend of the Coventry match, it was marathon time for me again, this time the Snowdonia Marathon. Julie and I travelled to North Wales on the Friday to make a bit of a weekend of it. The race at the title suggests was quite a tough one, but I was well prepared, as this was my third marathon of the year following London and the White Peak Marathon at the end of May. The first four miles of the run were uphill from the start in Llanberis. The next nine miles were fairly downhill. It then flattened out for seven or eight miles before we turned right and had to run up a one-in-four hill! It was hardly a run, as everybody had to walk this stretch. The view though at the top of the hill was absolutely stunning, as it was a bright sunny day without a cloud in the sky. It was then steep downhill for the rest of the race and I finished in 3.51.

I was pretty pleased with that on a very tough course.

Derby drew at home to Ipswich Town and beat Burnley 2-0, before Carl and I made the trip to the New Den for the Millwall away game. We went on the Ashbourne supporters club bus. On the way down when we stopped at Toddington services on the M1, and we watched most of the second half of the Rugby World Cup final between England and Australia in Sydney. I'm not a great rugby fan to be honest, but it was great to watch the match unfold, with Johnny Wilkinson's last gasp drop kick giving England victory. We headed on to London, stopped at pub near London Bridge for a couple of beers, before continuing to South Bermondsey. It was a bit of an eye-opener, as we approached the ground with the high raised flats and verbal abuse we were receiving from the streets, even by women in their sixties! We parked in a 'caged' area right outside the turnstiles before taking our seats in the upper tier of the North Stand, opposite the Cold Blow Lane end. The game finished goalless, with Derby hardly creating a chance, and were thankful to goalkeeper Lee Grant, who made a string of fine saves. Derby then had a 3-1 win against bottom of the table Wimbledon in a must win game, to end November fifth-from-bottom but only two points above the drop zone. Derby lost 2-1 at play-off chasing Ipswich Town at the start of December. The following day, I travelled down to Luton to take part in my fourth and final marathon of the year with the sole aim of running sub-3.30. Fortunately, the course was flat, but consisted of three soul destroying laps around a Luton housing estate! It was mission accomplished though as I achieved my personal best finishing in 3.27. Derby drew their next two games, starting with a goalless draw at Rotherham United and then on Boxing Day, 1-1 at West Bromwich Albion with Candido Costa scoring, which turned out to be his only goal for Derby. That morning we'd taken Sarah to Manchester Airport, as she was flying to Australia to meet her then boyfriend, as he was on there on a backpacking holiday. We were travelling back down the M6, after spending the day in the Arndale shopping centre, when news of Costa's goal filtered through on the radio. Derby ended the year with a crushing 4-0 home defeat against Norwich City, with all the goals being scored in the second half. George Burley strengthened his striking options by signing Manel Martinez Ferdandez, who joined Derby on a deal to the end of the season following his release from Sporting Gijon. Manel, as he was known, made his debut in the 3-0 defeat at Ipswich Town in the FA Cup third round. Burley then signed full-back Rob Edwards on loan from Aston Villa in another deal, to the end of the season. He made his debut in the away 2-1 defeat at Stoke City. Lee Morris, who scored the goal at Stoke, was sold to Leicester City for £120,000. Morris never realised his full potential after costing the Rams £3 million when they signed him, but he was continually plagued by injury. The team was very unsettled as Burley was trying to find the winning formula, but then another couple of players arrived. Former

German international winger Marco Reich joined from Werder Bremen on a free transfer, and left-back the late Jamie Vincent joined from Portsmouth. Both players made their debuts in the home game with Gillingham. Both players made an immediate impact, with Vincent scoring and Reich having a storming match on the left wing, which left supporters scratching their heads thinking, "What's he doing here?" This was followed by another home win with Marcus Tudgay and Izale McLeod scoring in the 2-0 win against Sheffield United.

George Burley then signed twenty-two-year-old relatively unknown Everton midfielder Leon Osman and experienced Millwall striker Noel Whelan. Both made their debuts at the start of February in the 2-2 home draw against Cardiff City, with the team was totally unrecognisable from the team that started the season. The results continued to be mixed during the rest of February with a 2-0 defeat at Wigan Athletic, a 2-1 home win against Crystal Palace and a 2-0 defeat at Coventry City.

Carl and I missed the 2-1 win against Crystal Palace as we went with our wives (Julie and Carl's wife Christine) to London for the weekend. We stopped in South Kensington taking in Madame Tussauds, a debut trip to Harrods and the highlight of the weekend at a London Show watching the amazing Chitty Chitty Bang Bang at the London Palladium which starred Russ Abbot as Caractacus Potts and Wayne Sleep as the Child Catcher.

The month ended with Derby in the bottom three, one point away from safety. It was certainly going to be a tense end to the season. March continued with mixed results, starting with a 0-0 home draw with Crewe Alexandra. George Burley then signed experienced striker Paul Peschisolido from Sheffield United with young Izale McLeod moving in the opposite direction, on loan until the end of the season. Peschisolido scored the winner on his debut in the 1-0 home win against Rotherham United. Another debutant in the Rotherham match was experienced Republic of Ireland defender thirty-three-year-old Jeff Kenna. He joined on a free transfer from Birmingham City. Saturday 20 March was the date for the East Midlands derby, as third-from-bottom Derby met Nottingham Forest who were four places and three points above the Rams in the table, so the game was really crucial. There was a real frenzied atmosphere in the sell-out crowd at the start of the game, with litter strewn all over the pitch on a very windy day. Captain Ian Taylor gave Derby an early lead with a cool finish, slotting past keeper Barry Roche. Paul Peschisolido then doubled the lead with one of the most outrageous goals you'll ever see. As the ball was passed back to Roche in the Forest goal it hit a plastic coffee up which caused Roche to miskick the ball to Peschisolido who calmly volleyed into the empty net. I've never witnessed that ever in a football match, either professionally or on the local park. 'Pesch' made it 3-0 following a good interchange with Marcus Tudgay, with the Derby fans in raptures. Gareth Taylor pulled one back right on half-time to give Forest a glimmer of hope. Gareth Williams pulled one back halfway through the second half after he followed up Taylor's header, which hit the bar. The tension was unbearable. Marcus Tudgay settled the nerves though, with a strike from just inside the box with ten minutes remaining, to give Derby a vital win.

Derby then earned an excellent point at promotion chasing Sheffield United, before they lost 2-1 at Sunderland and 1-0 at home to fellow strugglers Walsall. The two defeats left Derby still in the bottom three two points from safety. On the weekend of the Sunderland game, I went to Galway on the west coast of the Republic of Ireland for the Connemarra Marathon with Dave Thompson, Paul Disney, Mark Elliot and Carl Smith. Dave and I had entered the race, with the other three coming along for the craic. We had entered the race before Christmas, sorting the flights and accommodation out. Unfortunately, I came down with bronchitis in January, so I had to pull out of the run as the illness stopped me running for eight weeks. Galway and the Connemarra coastline are stunning and comes well recommended. The River Corrib in Galway has a frightening current and if you fell in you wouldn't stand much chance. Well, I wouldn't anyway! I can only swim about a length and have a massive fear if my feet don't touch the floor. In contrast, Julie is a fine swimmer. She wanted to swim the English Channel as a teenager and spent most mornings before school swimming lengths at Queen Street baths. It's embarrassing when we go on holiday. Julie can do all the strokes and tumble turns. I just cling on to the rail at the edge of the pool! A creditable 0-0 draw at West Ham United on Easter Saturday set Derby up for the Easter Monday showdown with second to bottom Bradford City. This was an absolutely must win game, and one of the most important in Derby's history. Leon Osman, who was becoming a massive influence on the team, gave Derby a first half lead. Ian Taylor doubled the lead halfway through the second half, but Peter Atherton and then a Rob Wooleaston effort silenced the crowd.

But a late own goal from the Bantams keeper Alan Combe sealed three very vital points for Derby. Mid-table Preston North End were the next visitors to Pride Park. In an astonishing first half, Derby driven on again by Leon Osman led 4-0, with Manel and Marcus Tudgay both scoring twice. Youl Mawene's own goal pulled one back, but Junior, who had recently returned from his six-month lay off, made it five for Derby, and they moved up to nineteenth in the table, two points above the drop zone. The following Saturday, the Rams made the trip to Turf Moor to play third-from-bottom Burnley, which in all honesty, was a must not lose match. A Graham Branch goal though just before half time was enough to give the home side victory. With two games to go, Derby had slipped to fourth-from-bottom, only one point ahead of Walsall, who were third-from-bottom. Walsall were the only side who could overtake Derby. On Saturday 1 May, Walsall were playing in a three-p.m. game at Crystal Palace, and Derby's home game against Millwall was selected for live coverage on Sky Sports with a 5.35 p.m. kick off. In my opinion both games should have kicked off simultaneously, to be fair to both Walsall and Derby. Walsall lost 1-0 at Crystal Palace which meant Derby needed a win to survive. The tension again was unbearable! Derby won 2-0 with goals from Adam Bolder and Marco Reich, to guarantee another season in the First Division. The final game of the season, against the already relegated Wimbledon was at the National Hockey Stadium in Milton Keynes. It was on the Sunday afternoon. I was desperate to go just to get a new ground in, but my mum and dad were having their wedding anniversary do on the same afternoon. My dad said he wouldn't be very happy if I'd missed it and gone to watch football. I couldn't complain really, as my mum and dad never really stopped me doing anything. I would never ever go to the National Hockey Stadium! Derby had endured a really tough season. I really liked George Burley; he gave me hope for the future. This was a major achievement in keeping Derby up, thanks to the likes of Ian Taylor who'd scored twelve goals from midfield, Youl Mawene, an up-and-coming centre-back and the experience later in the season of Paul Peschisolido and Jeff Kenna. It was just a pity the partnership of Junior and Mathias Svensoon wasn't able to flourish. The top man though was Leon Osman. I still believe to this day Derby would have been relegated without him. He has been the best loan signing I have seen supporting this club.

At the start of June, I went to the City of Manchester Stadium to watch England beat Iceland 6-1 with Carl Smith and Paul Disney, just four hours after getting off the plane from a work trip to Hong Kong. Wayne Rooney and Darius Vassell both scored twice, and England's preparations were going well ahead of Euro 2004.

2004/05

The First Division was now re-named as the Football League Championship, or the Championship as it's widely known nowadays. George Burley continued to rejig his squad. Danish Midfielder Morten Bisgaard arrived from FC Copenhagen, Spanish midfielder Inigo Idiakez from Rayo Vallecano, Tommy Smith from Sunderland and Mo Konjic from Coventry, all arrived on free transfers. Youl Mawene left to join Preston North End, Andy Oakes joined Walsall, Dave Walton joined Shrewsbury Town, Izale McLeod joined MK

Dons and Simo Valakari joined FC Dallas. Leon Osman went back to Everton now that his loan deal had expired. Derby played away at relegated Leeds United in their opening fixture played in thirty-degree heat, in a game picked for live TV coverage on Sky Sports with a lunchtime kick-off. George Burley gave debuts to Bisgaard, Idiakez and Smith. He also made a tough call by giving nineteen-year-old goalkeeper Lee Camp his debut ahead of Lee Grant. Derby lost 1-0 to a second half Fraser Richardson goal.

Carl Smith and I decided to become turnstile operators in the North Stand at Pride Park. Looking back, I'm still not sure why we went down this route, but we did. Our usual routine of going for a couple of pre-match beers at the Station Inn would now have to stop, as we needed to be at the ground two hours before kick-off, with the turnstiles opening ninety minutes before kick-off. I'm not sure why fans need to be in the ground that early in this era of all seater stadiums? Derby's first home game ended in a 2-1 defeat against Leicester City, but they then won two games on the trot, the first a 3-2 at home to Ipswich Town coming back from 2-1 down with a superb bending free-kick from Inigo Idiakez. The other win came away with a 2-0 victory at Queen's Park Rangers. Idiakez scored another great free kick at Lincoln City in the first round of the League Cup, but the Rams fell to a 3-1 defeat. On August Bank Holiday Monday, Crewe Alexandra capitalised on some very poor defending by the Rams, running out 4-2 winners at Pride Park. The Rams ended August with another defeat 1-0 at Stoke City, sitting fifteenth in the table with six points from six games. Julie and I then travelled to Protaras in Cyprus for our summer holiday over the international break. We did manage, though, to watch two England games whilst away. They drew 2-2 in Austria in a 2006 World Cup qualifier. England were cruising, when keeper David James inexplicably let a long shot slip through his body. They did win their next game 2-1 in Poland a few days later. It was great being in a bar abroad full of England fans, having a few beers, watching the game. Even Julie enjoyed it – probably the drink, not the football! Whilst we on holiday, we were in the process of moving house to Littleover, and we exchanged contracts with the moving day agreed to be on the Saturday, the day after we returned home. As usual I couldn't let anything get in the way of football and I listened to the Derby 2-0 win at Cardiff City, with Marco Reich and Ian Taylor scoring either side of half-time. Mo Konjic who George Burley was always bulling up, made his debut.

George Burley made two signings before the next home game against League leaders Wigan Athletic, managed by Paul Jewell. Left-back Jason Talbot joined on loan from Bolton Wanderers, and more significantly, Polish international striker Grzegorz Rasiak on a free transfer, after he had left Dyskobolia Grodzisk where he had scored thirty-four goals in sixty-six games. He was due to join Italian side AC Siena but there was an issue with his registration, so Derby moved quickly to secure his services. The Rams earned a very creditable 1-1 draw against a strong Wigan side, including Leighton Baines, Jimmy Bullard, Jason Roberts, Lee McCulloch and Nathan Ellington. Three more draws followed 1-1 at home to West Ham United, 0-0 at Sunderland and 2-2 at home to Watford, with Rasiak scoring his first goal. Derby's game at Burnley was chosen for live TV coverage on Sky Sports and switched to a Friday night. On a wet and windy night at Turf Moor, Derby won 2-0, with Marcus Tudgay and Marco Reich scoring in their first win at Burnley since April 1985. Derby ended October coming from 2-0 down to beat Rotherham United 3-2 at home, finishing the month in tenth place, with twenty-two points form sixteen games. I felt something good was around the corner, with a decent team developing with a good blend of youth and experience with a European influence. November started well, with a 3-0 home win against Brighton and Hove Albion, a 2-2 draw at Watford and 2-0 win at Gillingham. Grzegorz Rasiak was becoming a major factor, not only because of his goalscoring, but he was also a big physical presence and wouldn't let defenders settle. The month ended with two defeats though, 1-0 at home to Sheffield United and 3-0 at Preston North End. In the Preston game, George Burley gave a debut to Nigerian international midfielder Blessing Kaku, the most exotic footballer's name I've come across, who had joined on loan from Bolton Wanderers. The first East Midlands derby of the season was at Pride Park in mid-December, against third-from-bottom Nottingham Forest, now managed by Joe Kinnear. In the usual cracking atmosphere, Tommy Smith gave Derby the lead, sweeping in at the far post following great work from Morten Bisgaard down the right. Ian Taylor blazed over a penalty following Andy Impey's handball as the Rams went in 1-0 up at half-time. Grzegorz Rasiak bravely headed in at the far post to increase Derby's lead from a Smith cross. Rasiak scored again to complete a thoroughly deserved 3-0 win. Rasiak had given Wes Morgan a torrid afternoon. I've never rated Morgan and I would never have believed he would later go and lift the Premier Trophy as captain of Leicester City and get an FA Cup winners medal.

Fair play to him though, and to Leicester City for winning the Premier League in 2016/17, which was a fantastic achievement. Derby then recorded two fine away wins. They won 2-0 at Plymouth Argyle and then on Boxing Day they came from behind to beat League leaders Wigan Athletic at the JJB Stadium 2-1 with goals from Grzegorz Rasiak and Tommy Smith. In the last game of the year though, a Barry Hayles hat-trick sent Derby crashing to a 3-0 home defeat at the hands of Millwall. Nevertheless, it had been a good first half of the season for George Burley, as Derby ended 2004 in eighth place with thirty-nine points from twenty-six games. There were though, rumours, of Burley having a strained relationship with the Director of Football, Murdo Mackay.

The FA Cup third round paired Derby with fellow Championship side Wigan Athletic. In the third meeting of the clubs in the current season, Alan Mahon gave the Latics a first half lead with a fine left foot drive. For the second time in a fortnight Derby came from behind to beat Paul Jewell's side. Inigo Idiakez pulled one back with what was becoming his trademark free-kick from outside the box, with Junior firing in from close range for what was his first goal of the season. Derby then agreed a fee with of £2.5 million with Tottenham Hotspur for nineteen-year-old Tom Huddlestone, who was becoming an integral part of Derby's team. The deal would allow Huddlestone to remain at Derby until the end of the season. It was believed the board agreed the deal without consulting George Burley. Back in the League, Derby lost 2-0 against promotion chasing Sunderland the following week in a Sunday lunchtime kick off game shown live on Sky Sports. Derby ended January well though, with a very rare 2-1 win at

West Ham United in yet another Sunday lunchtime game shown live on Sky Sports. Grzegorz Rasiak headed Derby in front inside ten minutes with Carl Fletcher levelling ten minutes later. Rasiak volleyed home from close range to give Derby, who survived a late onslaught, a fine win. Derby won their midweek game 2-0 with a dominant performance against Leeds United. Even though the Rams had a relatively small squad, I was really enjoying watching this team play as they pushed up the table into fifth place with forty-eight points from thirty-one games. There was definitely a whiff of the play-offs in the air!

Premier League Fulham were the visitors to Pride Park in the FA Cup fourth round. This would be good for Derby to gauge their progress that had been made under George Burley. Substitute Marcus Tudgay gave the Rams the lead ten minutes into the second half steering the ball past Edwin van der Sar from Jeff Kenna's right-wing cross. Collins John equalised for the Cottagers to take the tie to a replay. The following Saturday, I drove to the south coast with Carl Smith for the game at Brighton and Hove Albion. The trip to the Withdean Stadium was our first away day of the season. On the way down, we stopped for a drink and a bite to eat at a pub in Hurstpierpoint. We made our way into Brighton and picked up a park 'n ride service to the ground. The Withdean Stadium was Brighton's temporary home, an athletics stadium with the pitch encircled by a running track. The ground was in a very affluent area, amid some expensive looking properties. We sat in the away section with the view overlooking the edge of the eighteen-yard box. It was very low down and we seemed miles away from the pitch. Derby, playing in all black, took the lead with Morten Bisgaard's first goal for the club. Mark McCammon equalised a minute later, but Marcus Tudgay restored the lead right on half time following a mistake from David Yelldell in the Brighton goal. McCammon levelled again on the hour, but then Ian Taylor was given a straight red card for raising his hand against Leon Knight. A great left foot finish though by Marcus Tudgay gave Derby the lead again to send the travelling fans wild and to give ten-men Derby a famous win, making it a happy long journey home. Derby travelled down to the capital for the FA Cup fourth round replay with Fulham. As Derby had consolidated their place in the Championship play-off places, I wasn't too concerned about FA Cup progress, as I didn't want any interference in the run-in to the end of the season. Derby gave a good account of themselves though, taking the game into extra time. The score at ninety minutes was 2-2, but Fulham proved too strong, with goals from Collins John and Claus Jensen knocking Derby out. Chris Makin joined the Rams on loan from Leicester City, and he went straight into the side for the away game at Rotherham United. Derby again showed their resilience, winning 3-1 after going a goal down, with goals from Grzegorz Rasiak, Marcus Tudgay and Inigo Idiakez's penalty.

Three successive draws followed, 1-1 at home to Barnsley, 2-2 at Nottingham Forest and 3-3 at home to Wolverhampton Wanderers. The Wolves game was an eventful night for Inigo Idiakez. He gave Derby an early lead with his trademark free kick. Wolves, playing in a very unfamiliar blue shirts, white shorts and light blue socks, took the lead with goals from Kenny Miller and Joleon Lescott. Idiakez then scored with a penalty that was retaken three times, something I've never seen before, to level the score at 2-2. Carl Cort regained the lead for Wolves in the last minute, before Marco Reich earned Derby a point with a last gasp header. Idiakez was at it again in the home game with Plymouth, Argyle scoring with another sublime free kick. I have to say Idiakez is up there with David Beckham as the best free kick specialist I've seen. He always hit the target with plenty of bend and pace on the ball. It was great to watch. Derby beat Plymouth 1-0, but the visitors missed a great opportunity to equalise when Paul Wooton's penalty was that bad it that ended up in the upper tier of the North Stand. The Rams went into the international break fourth in the table, with sixty-one points from thirty-eight games following a 0-0 home draw with Queen's Park Rangers. With eight games to go, an exciting end to the season lay ahead. Derby started April with a 3-2 defeat at third-place Ipswich Town, but were back to winning ways with four wins on the bounce, starting with a vital 2-1 win at Gresty Road against Crewe Alexandra. Stoke City were beaten 3-1 at Pride Park. The game at Sheffield United was switched to Friday night for live TV coverage on Sky Sports. United were two points behind Derby so this was a real 'six-pointer.' Carl and I went to the White Swan in Littleover to watch the game. The pub was absolutely rammed and to be honest we didn't see much of the game. Derby won 1-0 with a second half Morten Bisgaard goal, that gave Derby their twelfth away win of the season. Worryingly for Derby though, Inigo Idiakez limped off injured just before half-time. Gillingham were beaten 2-0 at Pride Park in the last of the four wins.

Carl and I then went to Leicester City for the midweek game at the Walkers Stadium. We were joined by Paddy Haughey, who worked with us on the turnstiles. It was my first visit to Leicester's new ground, that had been open for three years. We sat in the away section in the North East corner of the ground. Derby put in a poor performance and were deservedly beaten by a David Connolly second half strike. Derby picked up another injury with Grzegorz Rasiak going off at half time. With two games left Derby were in fifth place, three points ahead of seventh-placed Reading. A win against Coventry City in the last ever game at Highfield Road would clinch a play-off place. Carl and I went to Pride Park to watch the 'beam back' of the match. The 'beam back' was unwatchable, with poor camera angles of the game which didn't go well with the watching fans. To make matters worse, the Rams were hammered 6-2. I don't think anyone saw that coming. Fortunately, West Ham United and Reading, the two clubs chasing Derby, also both lost that weekend. A point in their final game at home to Billy Davies' Preston North End, who'd already booked their play-off place, would be enough for Derby. The Rams took a gamble by playing Inigo Idiakez, even though he was nowhere near being fully fit. He gave Derby the lead which Tommy Smith doubled. Patrick Agyemang pulled one back, with Idiakez going off again, but Paul Peschisoliso sealed the win the final minute. Derby had sealed their play-off place, and ironically would play Preston with the first leg at Deepdale. It was fully deserved and all credit to George Burley and the players. At Deepdale, Grzegorz Rasiak and Inigo Idiakez were missing, which was a big blow to Derby's hopes. The pair had played a major part in Derby's fine season. Derby were never at the races and fell behind to David Nugent's goal seven minutes before half time. The killer blow, though, was a goal a minute from time. The ball hit Kevin

Cresswell from a clearance and sneaked under Lee Camp's body to give North End a 2-0 win, with a right uphill struggle for Derby looming in the second leg. George Burley took a massive gamble in the second leg playing Rasiak and Idiakez. To be fair he had no choice, but he had to go for it. Derby huffed and puffed but didn't look like scoring as Youl Mawene and Claude Davis held firm in the North End back four. Rasiak hit the post with a late penalty and was in tears when he left the pitch, but over the two legs Preston thoroughly deserved to win.

Rumours were starting to circulate about Burley's future a couple of weeks after the Preston defeat. Burley had major differences with Murdo Mackay and his relationship with the board deteriorated following Tom Huddlestone's sale. The debts alarmingly increased in excess of £30 million and in an attempt to reduce the debts, the board put in place a refinancing scheme which involved Pride Park stadium being sold to the Panama-based ABC Corporation, and the club paying rent of £1 million a year to play at the ground. There was speculation about Burley's behaviour. I prefer to act on facts and I don't like to get involved with tittle tattle, so it was difficult to get the true story. Burley resigned on 7 June and was appointed manager of Heart of Midlothian before the end of the month. I was totally gutted. I have never been so disappointed to lose a manager. With Brain Clough and Dave Mackay, I was too young to fully understand. Arthur Cox and Jim Smith had achieved great success, but when they left it was naturally the correct time for their departure. For me, it was a very sad day. What would the future hold?

CHAPTER 12

PHIL BROWN, THE END OF THE 'THREE AMIGOS', PETER GADSBY, BILLY DAVIES AND PLAY-OFF SUCCESS AT LAST

2005/06

The Derby board appointed Bolton Wanderers assistant manager Phil Brown as the new manager in late June. I was very surprised, as Brown had no previous experience in a top job. My initial thoughts were would he be another Colin Addison. I was hoping to be wrong and that he would succeed. I always liked Brown when I saw him as a player in the lower Leagues as a right-back. He appointed Dean Holdsworth as player-assistant manager, who was playing at non-League Havant and Waterlooville after having a good career at the likes of Wimbledon and Bolton Wanderers. I found this to be a strange move and thought Brown should have appointed a more experienced assistant, someone who had 'seen and done it'. Brown signed three players in the pre-season and they all made their debuts in the opening game of the season in the 1-1 draw against Brighton and Hove Albion. Experienced defender Marc Edworthy joined on a free transfer from Crystal Palace, midfielder Paul Thirlwell joined from Sheffield United and centre-back Andrew Davies came on loan from

Middlesbrough. Ian Taylor was released and he joined Northampton Town and Jamie Vincent went on loan to Millwall.

Carl and I carried on with turnstile duties and we were joined by Dave Thompson, Graham Perry and Steve Gascoyne. Graham, who I met at work in the mid-1980s is a good friend of ours, along with his wife, Carol. I knew Steve from work too, and he's Graham's brother-in-law. Following the 1-1 draw at Preston North End, Derby had two good wins, 2-0 at Plymouth Argyle and 2-1 at home to Cardiff City. Seth Johnson re-joined Derby from Leeds United and came on as a substitute in the Cardiff game. Derby crashed out of the League Cup first round, 1-0 at home to Grimsby Town, just after Julie and I had travelled to Skiathos on holiday. In Skiathos, we met Pete Freeman and Sue Latty, who live just fifteen minutes away from us in Burton-on-Trent. Pete's a Leicester City fan and we had a few nights in the Christakis Sports Bar in Troulos, one night taking in the England v Wales game.

Graham told me a good story regarding Phil Brown early on in his tenure. Graham, who is a self-employed gardener, was once cutting a hedge at a house on Codnor-Denby Lane.
The owner of the house had recently rented the house out to a tenant. A tanned guy in a tracksuit and gold watch appeared said, "Good Morning," to him and offered Graham a cup of tea. Graham asked him how he was, and he said, "It would have been better if we'd got three points last night." Graham replied, "Did you go?" The guy replied, "I'm the manager." Graham's football knowledge is pretty good, but didn't

recognise him!

Derby were struggling financially and sold their prize asset Grzegorz Rasiak to Premier League Tottenham Hotspur in deal worth up to £3 million. Derby drew three games in a row following the international break. The 1-1 draw at Crewe Alexandra was shown live on Sky Sports, with youngster Giles Barnes making his debut from the bench. Khalilou Fadiga, on loan from Bolton Wanderers and the first Senegalese player to represent Derby, made his debut in the 1-1 draw at home to Coventry City. The 2-2 home to Southampton was also shown live on Sky Sports, with the late Peter Whittingham, on loan from Aston Villa, making his debut. The Rams ended September losing away games at Sheffield United 2-1, and 3-1 at Leeds United, with Rob Hulse scoring a first half hat-trick for the Elland Road club, and with Trinidad and Tobago striker Stern John, on loan from Coventry City making his Derby debut. Derby were sixteenth in the table with twelve points from eleven games, with only two wins. Another loan signing, Mounir El Hamdaoui, who joined from Tottenham Hotspur, made his debut and scored a late equaliser in the 1-1 home draw against Leicester City at the start of October. Also making his debut was forty-two-year-old goalkeeper Kevin Poole, who was Derby's goalkeeping coach. Derby beat Stoke City 2-1 at home with seventeen-year-old Lewin Nyatanga making his debut, together with another Tottenham Hotspur loanee, midfielder Johnnie Jackson. Derby drew 1-1 at Wolverhampton Wanderers, with El Hamdaoui scoring but then dislocating his shoulder. This was so frustrating because he showed real promise in his short time at the club.

Carl and I went to the KC Stadium for the away game with Hull City. Paddy Haughey came too. It was a wet, gloomy day. We went for a drink around the delights of Hull pre-match, before heading up to the ground. We sat in the North Stand with the Main Stand to our right. Derby played really well and Stern John, who'd had a difficult start to his Derby career, had an outstanding game. He just couldn't convert his chances and the Rams lost 2-1, when a 6-2 win would have been more realistic. Andrew Davies was sent off for two yellows for dissent after his goal was ruled out. Derby ended the month with another defeat 2-1 at home to Queen's Park Rangers. The loans kept on coming in, as Phil Brown just couldn't keep a settled side. Central defender Emerson Thome joined from Wigan Athletic, and striker Dexter Blackstock from Southampton. Blackstock scored twice as Derby started November with a 3-3 draw at home to Ipswich Town.

Derby were totally outplayed by Glenn Hoddle's Wolverhampton Wanderers, in a game moved to Friday night and shown live on Sky Sports in mid-November. To add salt into the wound, Tom Huddlestone on loan at Wolves from Tottenham Hotspur scored one on the goals. Derby recorded only their second away win of the season with a 2-1 win at Stoke City, and finished November with a goalless draw at Brighton and Hove Albion, with yet another loanee, Danny Graham, making his debut following his move from Middlesbrough. Stern John's unhappy loan spell came to an end and he returned to his parent club Coventry City. Graham worked tirelessly during the fourteen games whilst he was at Derby. He did everything right, but he just couldn't score. Derby started December with a 2-0 win over Norwich City with two Andrew Davies goals, but they were then winless for the rest of the month. There were three successive draws, 1-1 at home to Preston North End, 0-0 at Cardiff City and 1-1 at home to Luton Town on Boxing Day. Crystal Palace beat Derby 2-0 at Selhurst Park, and on New Year's Eve in the 5.15 p.m. kick off against Reading drew 2-2 at Pride Park. The advantage of working on the turnstile on New Year's Eve was receiving treble time pay! The League table was looking a bit worrying, with Derby finishing the year in seventeenth place, with twenty-nine points from twenty-seven games.

The FA Cup third round provided Derby with a bit of respite from their troubles in the League, seeing off fellow Championship side Burnley with two Paul Peschisolido goals, who for some unknown reason, together with Jeff Kenna, had been banished by Phil Brown to the train with the youngsters. The confidence from that win was apparent the following week, as Derby recorded their biggest win of the season, with bottom-of-the-table Crewe Alexandra being soundly beaten 5-1 at Pride Park. Carl, Paddy and I went to Coventry City for Derby's first ever visit to the Ricoh Arena. On a freezing cold late January day, we sat behind the goal in the South Stand in the impressive 32,000 all seater stadium. Derby got off to a great start with Paul Peschisolido giving the Rams a second minute lead. Stern John, who didn't score during his time at Derby, equalised minutes later. At half time with the score at 1-1, I didn't see the Derby capitulation coming in the second half. John scored again, with further goals from Dennis Wise, Dele Adebola and two from Gerry McSheffrey, who once scored a hat-trick against Derby for Notts County, completing the 6-1 rout. It was a truly embarrassing afternoon for Phil

Brown and his team. Brown then sold Marcus Tudgay to Sheffield Wednesday for an undisclosed fee, which enabled him to sign experienced centre-half Darren Moore from Premier League West Bromwich Albion for £300,000. Polish international Tomasz Hajto also joined the Rams from Southampton on an eighteen-month deal. It was so disappointing to see twenty-two-year-old Tudgay leave, who I believe had loads to offer – it was a bad decision. Hajto made his debut in the fourth round of the FA Cup against third tier Colchester United at Layer Road. In another forgettable afternoon, Derby crashed to a 3-1 defeat. Colchester were flying, with remarkably their seventeenth win in nineteen games. The board acted swiftly by sacking Phil Brown after only seven months in charge. He was replaced by Academy manager Terry Westley, whose only previous managerial experience was a very brief spell as Luton Town manager, as caretaker manager. It didn't start well for Westley as Derby fell to a 1-0 home defeat to Sheffield United, with Darren Moore making his debut and Giles Barnes given his first start. I remember this day very well, as it was the funeral of my good friend and work colleague Colin Potter, who had sadly passed away due to cancer. Dave Thompson, Jonathan Kinder and I agreed to organise an annual 10K race in his memory, which carried on until the final event in 2022. Three successive draws followed. There were two goalless draws, at home to Southampton and away at Leeds United, with Mounir El Hamdaoui making a welcome return to the side. They also drew 2-2 at home to Leicester City, as Westley tried to make the team hard to beat. He was then appointed manager until the end of the season. Westley finally got his first win with Adam Bolder's goal at home to Plymouth Argyle at the end of

February, with striker Kevin Lisbie on loan from Charlton Athletic making his debut. It was an important win as it lifted the Rams up to nineteenth, nine points above the relegation trap door. Experienced left-back Alan Wright made his debut in the 2-2 draw at Watford, following his loan move from Sheffield United. Westley recorded his biggest win as goals from Tommy Smith, Inigo Idiakez and a first goal for Darren Moore saw Burnley off 3-0, with Michael McIndoe making his debut following his loan move from Doncaster Rovers.

At this stage, the 'Three Amigos' came under closer scrutiny and fire from the two supporters' groups, the Rams Trust and The Rams Protest Group. The club was eventually sold to a local consortium led by local businessman Peter Gadsby, with Pride Park Stadium again owned by the club. Jeremy Keith, Murdo Mackay and Andrew MacKenzie, the finance director, were sentenced to seven and half year's imprisonment after being charged with taking a secret commission worth in excess of £440,000 from the club. Neither John Sleightholme (who resigned as Chairman) nor Steve Harding were involved in the fraud and were not charged with any offence. Hopefully the club could now move forward with the new consortium now in place.

The following weekend, Julie and I spent the weekend in Norwich as I was competing in the Bungay Marathon on the Norfolk/Suffolk border on the Sunday. We had a nice evening in the Norwich pubs on the Friday night and a trip to Great Yarmouth greyhounds on the Saturday. Derby were beaten 5-0 away, by runaway leaders Reading, who were on course to win the League with over hundred points. I'd targeted the race to run a personal best, and had trained really well for it, especially after missing out in Connemarra two years earlier. I passed halfway in 1.32 with things going perfectly to plan, running at seven-minute mile pace. I got to twenty-four miles in 2.50, and on course for 3.08. The last two-and a-bit miles though were a disaster as I hit the dreaded 'wall'. After running most of the race at seven-minute mile pace, the last two miles took me twenty-four minutes! I finished in 3.14, and even though it was a personal best I was totally gutted. I'd finished seventeenth out of 156 but felt I'd failed big time! The remaining five games of the season started well for Derby as they beat Millwall 1-0 at home with a Tommy Smith goal. Derby confirmed their survival with a 1-1 draw at Queen's Park Rangers the following Saturday, with Smith scoring again.

2006/07

In early June, Terry Westley was relieved of his duties as new chairman Peter Gadsby appointed Preston North End manager Billy Davies as the new manager of Derby. Davies immediately got to work bringing in new players, with the arrival of Luton Town striker Steve Howard for £1 million, experienced midfielder Matt Oakley on a free transfer from Southampton and Arsenal winger Ryan Smith on a three-year deal. Carl and I continued with turnstile duty. The season didn't start too well. After the opening weekend's 2-2 draw against George Burley's Southampton, which was shown live on Sky Sports, Derby were defeated 2-0 at Stoke City. Derby's first win came at Hull City on the following Saturday teatime in another game shown on Sky Sports. The Rams won 2-1, with goals from Oakley and a Tommy Smith penalty. Two more new signings made their debuts. They were central defender Dean Leacock who signed from Fulham for £375,000 and goalkeeper Stephen Bywater, who arrived from West Ham United initially on loan, which became a permanent deal for £225,000. There were further arrivals, with left-back Mo Camera signing on a free transfer from Celtic and Arsenal youngster nineteen-year-old Arturo Lupoli. He only looked about fifteen and joined on a season long loan! Lupoli scored twice in the 4-3 defeat at Colchester United before the international break. Billy Davies sold Inigo Idiakez to Southampton for £250,000, reuniting him with George Burley. I loved watching Idiakez, and I have to say he is one of my all-time favourite players. It was sad to see him leave. Also very sad was the passing of former owner Lionel Pickering at the start of September. He had been a massive part of a successful part of the Derby County story. He will be remembered with great affection by the supporters.

Julie and I travelled to Spain for a two-week holiday at Dave Thompson's apartment, in La Mata near Torrevieja on the Costa Blanca. We watched England beat Andorra 5-0 in a Euro 2008 qualifier in a bar near Dave's place, with Peter Crouch and Jermaine Defoe scoring twice. Derby only played once whilst we were away, losing 2-1 at home to Roy Keane's Sunderland, who were bottom of the table. The day after we arrived home, a Steve Howard goal gave Derby a 1-0 win at Wolverhampton Wanderers. Defensive midfielder Bob Malcolm made an outstanding debut at Molineux following his move from Glasgow Rangers. Derby finished September on the front foot with a 2-1 win at Sheffield United and a 3-0 home win against Southend United, with Arturo Lupoli scoring twice. Derby were ninth in the table with fifteen points from ten games. Derby were knocked out of the League Cup in an extraordinary game at Belle Vue, Doncaster. Derby came back from 3-0 down to draw 3-3 before losing 8-7 on penalties.

Much travelled striker Jonathan Stead joined Derby on loan from Sunderland and he made his debut in the 3-1 defeat at Plymouth Argyle, in another game shown live on Sky Sports. Derby's results continued to be mixed as the new signings were trying to get together. Derby won 2-1 at Queen's Park Rangers, lost 1-0 at home to Birmingham City and drew 2-2 at Cardiff City. The Rams then went on a tremendous run, winning six games in a row during November. It started with two home wins against Barnsley and West Bromwich Albion, with Matt Oakley scoring an absolute twenty-five-yard screamer to give Derby a 2-1 win. I remember this day clearly. I'd cut my knee on chicken wire whilst out running about ten days earlier which required about ten stitches. It became infected and I was in so much pain I couldn't get up to celebrate Oakley's goal! Two fine away wins followed, beginning with a 2-1 win at Coventry City, which was a relief having been hit for six in their two previous visits, and 2-0 at Luton Town. David Jones, on loan from Manchester United made his debut at Kenilworth Road. Jon Stead scored the winning goal in the 1-0 win against Leicester City, with Pete Freeman joining Carl and myself to watch the match. Derby then came from behind to beat Ipswich Town 2-1. The six-game winning run catapulted Derby up to fourth in the table, only one point behind leaders Preston North End. It was quite strange, as the performances weren't too good with not much flowing football. It was not great to watch, with supporters scratching their heads trying to understand how Derby were actually winning all of these games. They were though, very organised and disciplined, typical of a Billy Davies side. December started with the winning streak coming to an end, as Derby lost to a late John Hartson goal at West Bromwich Albion. The following week a Giles Barnes header gave Derby a rare 1-0 win at Leeds United. It was Derby's first win at Elland Road since November 1974. The win moved Derby up to second, three points behind leaders Birmingham City. David Jones scored his first goal for Derby in the next game, a 1-0 home win at home to Crystal Palace. This was backed up in the last game before Christmas, with a goalless draw at Burnley. Derby lost 2-0 at home to Wolverhampton Wanderers on Boxing Day, but ended the year with a 1-0 home win at home to Plymouth Argyle with a late Morten Bisgaard goal. It had been a fine start to the Billy Davies era, with a solid base to build on in the New Year. The New Year's Day Preston North End game, Billy Davies' first return to Deepdale since his departure in the summer, was really hostile. Preston and Derby were second and third in the table respectively, just to add a bit of spice to the occasion. Two goals from Steve Howard, one from the penalty spot, just after half time gave Derby a 2-1 victory with David Nugent replying. The win ended Preston's unbeaten home record and Derby leapfrogged them in the table, three points behind leaders Birmingham City.

A hat trick from Arturo Lupoli saw off fourth tier Wrexham in the third round of the FA Cup, before Billy Davies delved into the January transfer window with three signings. Wigan

Athletic's Gary Teale signed for £600,000. Craig Fagan left Hull City for Derby in a £750,000 deal, and Scottish international Stephen Pearson also joined for £750,000 from Celtic. Teale started with Fagan and Pearson coming off the bench as the Rams beat Sheffield Wednesday with a last-minute David Jones free kick from out wide on the right wing. It had also been a pretty ordinary performance but Derby were finding a way to win. Derby recorded their ninth away from the season at Roots Hall against Southend United, with Steve Howard scoring the winning goal. The win took Derby to the top of the Championship.

The fourth-round draw was kind to Derby, who were paired with another fourth-tier side in Bristol Rovers. I sound like a broken record, but the Rams were unconvincing again, but still won with a late Paul Peschisolido goal. It did, though, slightly erase the memory of the 2001 defeat and *that* Nathan Ellington hat-trick. Derby ended January with another 1-0 win with an early Steve Howard goal at home to Burnley. Remarkably Derby went six points clear at the top of the Championship. There were another three more arrivals to the already large squad. Tyrone Mears joined on loan in a deal to the end of the season from West Ham United. Jay McEveley signed from Blackburn Rovers for a reported £600,000 and Jonathan Macken arrived on a free transfer from Crystal Palace. It was all rather surreal, what was going both on and off the pitch. February also began well, with Steve Howard again on the scoresheet, with a late winner at Southampton being the only goal of the game. Phil Brown returned to Pride Park the following week, as his Hull City side snatched a late equaliser though David Livermore in a 2-2 draw, much to Brown's delight on the touchline. Derby were drawn away to fellow Championship side Plymouth Argyle in the fifth round of the FA Cup. It was a poor afternoon for Derby who were beaten 2-0, and had Darren Moore sent off in the second half. Two League defeats followed, with Stoke City winning 2-0 at Pride Park. Derby were so poor and Steve Hallam asked me how were Derby top of the League. To be honest I couldn't answer him, as I was unconvinced as he was. Sunderland then completed the double over Derby with a 2-1 win, with last minute winner from Liam Miller. February ended with Derby dropping to second in the table on goal difference to new leaders West Bromwich Albion. March started a lot better for Derby, as they won their first game of the month on a Friday night against mid-table Colchester United, managed by Geraint Williams, in a game selected for Sky Sports live coverage. Derby won 5-1, with arguably their best performance of the season. This was followed by a fine confidence boosting win 2-1 midweek win at Norwich City. Young Chris Martin put the Canaries ahead, but two fine strikes from David Jones sealed the points as Derby returned to the top of the table. Derby then travelled to St. Andrews for the bid top-of-the-table clash with Birmingham City. The game was switched to Friday night for Sky Sports live coverage. A Rowan Vine goal right on half time was the winning goal for the Blues, who were reduced to ten men with Gary McSheffrey sent off. Billy Davies made another signing with the arrival of the highly experienced Darren Currie on loan from Ipswich Town. Currie came off the bench for the 3-1 home win against Cardiff City.

The following weekend, Julie and I went with Steve and Dawn

Hallam for a weekend in Dublin. It was international break weekend and I tried desperately to try and get hold of tickets for the Republic of Ireland's game against Wales in a Euro 2008 qualifier. It was being held at Croke Park as Lansdowne Road was being redeveloped, but I had no chance as it was a complete sell out. On the last day of March, I went to my first away game of the season at Barnsley. I went with Carl and Dave Thompson, who was making his 'away day' debut. We bumped into Gavin Chadwick, or 'G' as we know him. Gavin's a good friend of mine from work, and before the game he looked rather the worst for wear with drink. We sat with the 7,800-travelling support in the North Stand. Derby won 2-1, with goals from David Jones and Matt Oakley, as Derby moved back to the top of the League three points ahead of second place Sunderland. With six games to go, the Rams just had to hold their nerve and a place in the Premier League was theirs. The next two Easter games though only yielded two points. Derby recorded two 1-1 draws, in the Good Friday game at Leicester City shown live TV Sky Sports with an afternoon kick-off, and at home to Coventry City on Easter Monday. In the game with the Sky Blues, Matt Oakley scored an unbelievable acrobatic back heel to salvage a point. Lewin Nyatanga bundled the ball over the line to give Derby a crucial Friday night win 1-0 against Luton Town. With two games left, Derby were second in the table, a point behind leaders Sunderland and a point ahead of third-placed Birmingham City, who had a game in hand.

The game in hand for Birmingham was on the Sunday away at play-off chasing Wolverhampton Wanderers. Cruelly for Derby, Cameron Jerome's last gasp goal gave the Blues a 3-2 win. It was now out of Derby's hands to finish in the top two. Sunderland played on the Friday night, beating Burnley to move onto eighty-five points from forty-five games. Birmingham played the following day on the Saturday with Derby playing at Crystal Palace on the Sunday. Birmingham beat Sheffield Wednesday and went top with eighty-six points from forty-five games. Derby had to win at Palace. They produced a really poor performance, losing 2-0, so it was the play-offs for Derby and a two-legged game against Southampton. To be fair to Derby, they had exceeded expectations and it had been a good season, even if the performances were not quite of a promotion chasing team. I just felt all the additions in the January transfer window had actually given Billy Davies too many options and there were too many changes game to game.

The first leg of the play-off semi-final against Southampton was at St Mary's. The other game was between black country rivals West Bromwich Albion and Wolverhampton Wanderers. Seth Johnson, much to the delight of the fans, forced his way back into the team as Billy Davies seemed reluctant to pick him. Andrew Surman gave the Saints an early lead with a fine curling shot from outside the box. It was the last thing Derby needed, with confidence fragile following the poor end to the season. Steve Howard equalised with a looping header before half time. Just before the hour mark, Stephen Pearson was pulled back in the box. Howard converted the penalty with his nineteenth goal of the season and wheeled away to the Derby fans behind the goal with his trademark 'Alan Shearer' goal celebration. Derby hung on for a fantastic 2-1 win. In the second leg the following Tuesday evening, Grzegorz Rasiak and Inigo Idiakez, who had both done so much to propel the Rams to the play-offs two years earlier, were on the Southampton bench. With Pride Park buzzing in anticipation, Derby had a dream start, with Darren Moore heading in from a corner. Jhon Viafara equalised immediately, when he volleyed in following a poor headed clearance from Stephen Bywater. The ground fell silent, apart from the travelling fans in the South Stand, as Viafara scored again ten minutes into the second half as he finished off a fine flowing move. An own goal from Leon Best levelled the score on the night, with Derby holding the one goal aggregate lead. With a minute to go Grzegorz Rasiak, of all people, pounced on a loose ball in the box to send the tie into extra time. There were no further goals as the game ebbed and flowed during extra half hour, so it was down to a penalty shoot out to decide who would go to Wembley. Billy Davies could barely watch from the bench. It was pissing it down with rain as Leon Best missed the first penalty, missing the target. David Jones, Steve Howard, Giles Barnes Jay McEverley scored for Derby as did Andrew Surman, Rudi Scakel and Grzegorz Rasiak for the Saints. Up stepped Inigo Idiakez, who had to score to keep Southampton in it. He fired over and Pride Park erupted and we were on the pitch celebrating. What an evening it had been.

A week before the play-off final on Monday 21 May, I had one of the saddest days of my life. My mum, who had been suffering from broncho-pneumonia, died. My dad told my three sisters and I to expect the worst a few days earlier. She had beaten oesophageal cancer in 1995, but her quality of life was never the same in the next twelve years. I can remember going to the hospital after her operation, and it was frightening to see how many tubes she was connected to. As our daily visits continued, the tubes gradually came out, but it must have been two weeks before she was discharged. I was under no illusions; this would change her life forever. I knew when I got to this stage of the book it would be very emotional, and tears are streaming down my face as I'm writing this. I wasn't in the frame of mind to go to the play-off final, but my dad insisted I go, as mum would have wanted me to. I drove to Wembley on May Bank Holiday Monday for the game with West Bromwich Albion, with Carl, Graham Perry and Steve Gascoyne. This was the first Championship play-off final to be played at the newly rebuilt Wembley Stadium. I wasn't particularly bothered about drinking that day, so I volunteered to drive. We parked up at Cockfosters Underground station and made our way to Covent Garden for pre-match with the thousands of other Derby fans. We headed up Wembley Way with the weather wet and windy, more akin to November than the end of May. We sat up in the gods in the North Stand at the East End of the stadium, level with the six-yard box. The ground was truly magnificent with the towering arch across the skyline. Billy Davies sprang a surprise, playing Paul Peschisolido up front with Steve Howard. 'Pesch' had hardly featured recently but I was pleased, as I always rated 'Pesch', with his tireless running and an eye for a goal. He had a great chance early on after being played in by Howard but scuffed his shot. West Brom dominated to game, but Derby held on. Kevin Phillips shaved the bar and Matt Oakley had a fine shot tipped over by Dean Kiely. Derby took the lead on the hour when Stephen Pearson scored his first goal for the club, steering in Giles Barnes' right wing cross after he'd just come on a substitute. Derby hung on for the remainder of the game to seal their place in the promised land. Seth Johnson was injured during the game which turned out to be his last ever professional game, which was very sad for such a talented player. My thoughts though were with my mum; football was certainly not in the forefront of my mind.

CHAPTER 13

GSE, 11 POINTS AND 'WORST TEAM IN HISTORY'

2007/08

Billy Davies after the play-off final refused to confirm whether he'd still be at the club for the new season, which I found quite strange. I don't know him but from the outside, he appears quite an intense character. There were rumours of him having a strained relationship with the board, but it wasn't clear what his issues were. Ahead of the new season, it was obvious Derby needed to strengthen their squad. As far as I could see we didn't have too many players of Premier League quality, and it was key to get the recruitment right. Davies decided to stay and additions started to arrive. The major signings were Claude Davis from Sheffield United for £3 million on a four-year-deal, and the Rams broke their transfer record to sign striker Robert Earnshaw for £3.5 million from Norwich City, with Davies calling him his 'fox in the box'. Andy Todd, son of Colin, arrived from Blackburn Rovers for £750,000 and full-back Andy Griffin signed from Portsmouth on a three-year deal, after spending the previous season on loan at Stoke City. USA international midfielder Benny Feilhaber joined from SV Hamburg. Goalkeeper Lewis Price joined from Ipswich Town, as back up for Stephen Bywater. The new signings apart from Feilhaber and Price made their debuts in the opening day 2-2 draw with Portsmouth. Todd salvaged a point for the Rams with an equaliser five minutes from time. Derby then lost four games on the bounce before the end of August; 1-0 away at Manchester City, 4-0 at Tottenham Hotspur and 2-1 at home to Birmingham City, with USA international Eddie Lewis making his debut following his move from Leeds United. Blackpool, who'd just been promoted to the Championship knocked the Rams out of the League Cup also via a penalty shoot-out at Pride Park, with Billy Davies giving a debut to right-back Jason Beardsley.

Julie and I went then on holiday to the Greek Island of Paros, which involved flying to Mykonos and then picking up a ferry to Paros. On the Saturday evening, a week into the holiday in the resort of Parikia, with its lovely cobbled streets, I was trying to find out the score of Derby's trip to Liverpool. I managed to get onto the BBC website to search for the score in an Internet cafe. I found out Derby had lost 6-0! Not surprisingly, following their start to the season, Derby were rock bottom of the able with a solitary point from five games. Kenny Miller then arrived from Celtic on a three-year contract for £2.2 million, as Billy Davies looked to boost his striking options. I was back home in time for Derby's next game at home to Newcastle United that was shown live on Sky Sports' Monday Night Football. As a bit of a treat, I'd been invited into the Trac executive box for the first time at Pride Park. Trac did sub-contract work for Rolls-Royce. Gavin Chadwick asked me if I'd like to go in the box for a pre-match meal and drinks. I was very fortunate to be invited into the box on a regular basis during the next few seasons. Kenny Miller made his debut and scored the winning goal in the 1-0 win, which I missed as I needed the toilet! The following weekend, I went to my first away game of the season. Pete Birks, who worked at Pride Park, managed to get some tickets for the game at Arsenal at the Emirates Stadium, with Matt Birks coming as well. We parked up and made our way to the ground, stopping at a pub near the ground. The streets were full of men selling scarfs, banners, programmes, burgers and hot dogs. It was a real throwback to the time when I first went to the Baseball Ground. We sat in the away end in the corner of the South Stand in the lower tier in a crowd in excess of 60,000. A first for me was sitting on a padded seat. The ground was magnificent and certainly had a 'wow' factor. Derby were hammered on the day. Arsenal took the lead with a screamer from the rangy Abou Diaby, with Emmanuel Adebayor doubling the lead halfway through the first half. Adebayor got his second, with Cesc Fabregas hitting another screamer to make it four. Adebayor completed his hat-trick. Arsenal were a joy to watch and were on a different planet to Derby. It was only the end of September, but it had the feel already of being a very long hard winter. Derby drew 0-0 at Craven Cottage in mid-October, but then lost seven games in a row. The first of these defeats was 2-0 at home to Everton, with Leon Osman receiving a fantastic ovation on his first return to the ground since his loan spell in 2004. The following day, Adam Pearson was named as the new executive chairman of the club after buying the majority shareholding from Peter Gadsby. The next two defeats were 2-0 at Aston Villa and a worrying 5-0 defeat at home to West Ham United. The fourth defeat was the end of the road for Billy Davies, following the 2-0 home defeat Saturday evening game against Chelsea, shown live on Sky

Sports, the week after the November international break. Adam Pearson was quick to act as he wanted to give the new manager as much time as possible to save the season. Paul Jewell, two days after the Chelsea game, was the man appointed to replace Davies. I quite liked Jewell who'd done a fantastic job with Wigan Athletic, but he faced a mammoth task at Pride Park. Three more defeats to complete the seven followed, 1-0 at Sunderland, 4-1 at Manchester United in front of a 75,000 crowd, and 1-0 at home to Middlesbrough. Derby then picked up only their seventh point of the season, in a 2-2 draw at Newcastle United, just before Christmas. Derby were winning 2-1 with three minutes to go, when Mark Viduka equalised to deny Jewell a first win. The Rams were bottom of the table, seven points away from safety. In the Boxing Day game at home to Liverpool, Derby played pretty well, but cruelly lost to a last-minute goal from Steven Gerrard. The last game of the year at home to Blackburn Rovers, shown live on Sky Sports Super Sunday, was also a missed opportunity. Matt Oakley gave Derby the lead, but then Brad Friedal saved Steve Howard's penalty. Before half time, Roque Santa Cruz and David Bentley scored, and Rovers went home 2-1 winners. This was Steve Howard's last act a Derby shirt, before he was sold to Leicester City for £1.5 million two days later. I always liked Howard, he was big, strong, could hold the ball and was brave. The biggest compliment I can pay him is that he would have been a great partner for Bobby Davison in the 1980s or Dean Sturridge in the 1990s. He had played a major part in the 2006/07 promotion. Paul Jewell signed Argentine striker Emanuel Villa from Mexican side Tecos UAG as a replacement for Howard. Stephen Pearson went to Championship-promotion-chasing Stoke City on loan.

The FA Cup paired Derby at home to Sheffield Wednesday. The Rams came from 2-0 down to draw 2-2 and earn a replay at Hillsborough, with goalkeeper Lewis Price and Danny Mills, on loan from Manchester City making their debuts. Matt Oakley was then also sold to Leicester City in a £500,000 deal, as Paul Jewell was looking to re-jig his squad. Before the next game at home to Wigan Athletic, there were three more arrivals. Robbie Savage signed from Blackburn Rovers for £1.5 million after rejecting a move to Sunderland. Egyptian international Hossam Ghaly joined on loan until the end of the season from Tottenham Hotspur, and Laurent Robert signed a contract until the end of the season following his release from Levante. The new signings didn't make an immediate impact, as Wigan won 1-0. The visit to Portsmouth the following week wasn't fruitful either, as Benjani's hat-trick sealed the three points for Pompey. Jewell then signed goalkeeper Roy Carroll on a three-year deal from Glasgow Rangers. The delayed FA Cup replay at Sheffield Wednesday, though, saw Derby clinch only their second win of the season. The game finished 1-1 with Derby going through on penalties to earn a home tie with Preston North End. That proved to be a damaging afternoon for Paul Jewell and his side, as they were 3-0 down at half time and eventually losing 4-1. Bob Malcolm left the club with his contract paid up.

The club then confirmed that United States based General Sports and Entertainment (GSE) were the club's new owners. Adam Pearson was to remain as Chairman, Tom Glick as President Chief Executive, Tim Hinchey as Vice President, Andy Appleby joined the board, with Don Amott and Peter Gadsby remaining as non-executive Directors. GSE's plan was to establish the club as a Premier League Force and make

Derby County a worldwide brand. I was sceptical about their intentions, but would stay curious. The natives though, were already getting restless with Paul Jewell. Another new signing arrived with the purchase of Australian international Mile Sterjovski from Turkish side Hacettepe. Derby drew 1-1 at home with Manchester City, before defender Alan Stubbs signed from Everton on an eighteen-month deal. Stubbs and Roy Carroll made their debuts in the 1-1 draw at Birmingham City. That point moved Derby on to nine points, thirteen points from safety. Two more defeats at the end of February followed, 3-0 at home to Tottenham Hotspur and 2-0 at Wigan Athletic. Quite remarkably, Derby were still maintaining 30,000 plus crowds for their home games. Michael Johnson moved to Notts County on loan for the remainder of the season, in a move that became permanent. March began with a goalless draw at home to Sunderland. The following week, Craig Fagan returned to Hull City on loan, with a view to a permanent deal. But three defeats followed, starting with a 6-1 defeat at Chelsea with Frank Lampard scoring four goals. A Cristiano Ronaldo goal gave Manchester United a 1-0 win at Pride Park, and there was also a 1-0 defeat at Middlesbrough with Tuncay scoring. March ended with a 2-2 home draw with Fulham. Emanuel Villa scored Derby's two goals. Derby's record after thirty-two games was one win, eight draws, twenty-three defeats, amassing eleven points.

On Saturday 12 April, Julie and I travelled down to London to take part in my fourth London Marathon, with Dave Thompson and some of his family. What a traumatic day it was. Around dinnertime, I left my running kit, including my running shoes, at the digs where Dave was stopping. Dave and I went across London to collect our running numbers. When we returned to the digs about three p.m., I couldn't find my bag amongst the hundreds of other bags at the digs. To make matters worse, the fire alarm went off at the gym next to the digs with both buildings having to be evacuated, so I couldn't search for my bag. I began to panic as time was moving on, and I'd potentially have to buy some new running shoes, which is the last thing you want to wear for a marathon! Derby, meanwhile, were playing Aston Villa at home that day. Carl kept texting me: 1-0 down, 2-0 down, 3-0 down, Carroll's having a mare, 4-0 down, 5-0 down, 6-0 lost. What an embarrassment! Much to my relief I found my bag in the digs about 4.45 p.m. avoiding the need to buy some new shoes! The run went well the following day. Passing Gordon Ramsey on the way, I finished in 3.22, which was a personal best, and Dave finished in a brilliant time of 3.10.

The following Saturday, Julie and I travelled to India. We drove down to Heathrow very early in the morning to catch the dinnertime Gulf Air flight to Bahrain, and then the connecting flight to Trivandrum in Kerala on the southern tip of India. A good friend of mine, David Denton, who I knew from the running scene, had a five-bedroom house in Kovalam. The house was situated a five-minute walk through a wood to the beach on the Indian Ocean. We were there for eight nights and he only charged us £8 a night. It was a wonderful experience, the colour, the mad drivers, the sacred cows roaming freely everywhere. We had a trip to the Kerala Backwaters which included an overnight stop on a houseboat. Everywhere was very green, something we didn't expect. My favourite place was Varkala, set on a cliff top with the beach below. There were bars galore along the cliff, playing reggae music. It was stunning and well worth checking out on google! David had a

TV in the house. I wanted to get away from football for a bit, but he had Sky Sports and I found out that Derby had lost again at West Ham United by 2-1. We travelled back on the Monday. We arrived back at Heathrow about three p.m. The Rams were playing Arsenal at home that night, so it was touch and go whether we'd get back in time to see it in person. We were delayed on the M25 so didn't get back in time. We pulled up outside our house at 7.30 p.m, so I watched the game live on Sky Sports Monday Night Football. For the second home game in a row, the Rams conceded six with Emmanuel Adebayor helping himself to another hat-trick. The worst season I have ever witnessed as a Derby County supporter finished with two more defeats at Blackburn Rovers, with Miles Addison making his debut, and 4-0 at home to Reading. Derby finished on eleven points; a record I believe will never be broken. It was totally humiliating being the 'Worst team in history.' We are constantly reminded about it, even now, every time that lot from down the A52 visit us. Where did it all go wrong? For me there were numerous reasons. George Burley was building the club nicely and left. Phil Brown was, in all honesty, at the club at the wrong time. Billy Davies' promotion workmanlike team lacked quality. Poor recruitment by Davies before the start of the campaign was the major factor. In his defence, he probably wasn't given the enough funding to bring in more quality. Paul Jewell's signings didn't work. Jewell in hindsight would have preferred to come in during March, and not December. An interesting summer was ahead trying to sort the mess out. The turnover of players in the past couple of seasons was totally alarming.

CHAPTER 14

JEWELL OUT AND THE NIGEL CLOUGH YEARS

2008/09

Paul Jewell had a monumental task on his hands. Mentally the club were shot. His main objective was to stop the rot, steady the ship and avoid another relegation. The major signing was the arrival of striker Rob Hulse for £1.75 million from Sheffield United, who was one of the successes of the Crewe Alexandra production line. Another big money arrival was striker Liam Dickinson for £750,000 from Stockport County. Steve Davies signed from Tranmere Rovers for £275,000, a fee that would rise to £725,000 if Derby won promotion. A raft of players on free transfers arrived. Defender Martin Albrechsten arrived from West Bromwich Albion on a two-year deal and Doncaster Rovers midfielder Paul Green on a three-year deal. Right-back Paul Connolly joined from Plymouth Argyle, and Jordan Stewart joined from Watford. The most controversial signing was Kris Commons from Nottingham Forest, a move that didn't go down well down the A52. There were also three loan signings. Nathan Ellington from Watford, Latvian winger Andrei Pereplotkins from Skonto Riga, and Polish international Przemyslaw

Kazmierczak from Porto.

The list of outgoings was endless too. Players who demanded fees were Robert Earnshaw, who moved to Nottingham Forest for £2.65 million. I appreciate he's had a good career, but I've never really rated Earnshaw, even before he came to Derby. Kenny Miller joined Glasgow Rangers for £2 million. David Jones joined Wolverhampton Wanderers for £1.25 million. Other departures included Darren Moore to Barnsley, Eddie Lewis to LA Galaxy, Benny Feilhaber to Aarhus and Mo Camara on loan to Blackpool. The turnover of players in recent seasons was nothing short of startling. In my opinion, stability in the only way to achieve success. Carl, Graham, Steve and I continued with turnstile duties as Derby started the season with a 1-0 defeat against promoted Doncaster Rovers in front of a 33,000 crowd, which was quite staggering considering the previous season. Nathan Ellington's hat-trick saw Derby through to the second round of the League Cup as they beat Lincoln City 3-1 after extra time. The first League win was still elusive though. Derby drew 1-1 at Bristol City in a game shown live on Sky Sports on Saturday teatime, and were then beaten 1-0 at home to Southampton, with Nacer Barazite on loan from Arsenal making his debut as a second half substitute. Derby made further progress in the League Cup though beating Preston North End 1-0 at Deepdale with Paul Green scoring. Another League defeat followed though, 2-0 at Barnsley as August came to an end.

Controversially, Tyrone Mears flew to France for a trial with Marseille without the knowledge of Paul Jewell, who was outraged at the move. He was fined six weeks wages, and

Jewell vowed that Mears would never play for the club again whilst he was manager. The Rams then won their first League game in four days short of a calendar year, when they beat Sheffield United at Pride Park. The win triggered an unbeaten League run of a further three wins and three draws. The wins were 2-0 at Queen's Park Rangers, 2-1 at Norwich City, with Ruben Zadkovich making his debut, and 2-1 at home to Plymouth Argyle. The day after the Plymouth victory I completed the Leicester Marathon in 3.14 which finished in Victoria Park. My mile split times were more disciplined following my bad experience in the last two miles in the Bungay Marathon, finishing this race far more comfortably. Blackpool halted Derby's unbeaten run at Bloomfield Road towards the end of November. At least Derby had become competitive and were fourteenth in the table with sixteen points from twelve games, five points clear of the relegation zone. The first East Midlands derby of the season was at Pride Park at the start of November, and shown live on Sky Sports on the Sunday lunchtime in what turned out to be a crazy afternoon. Second-from-bottom Nottingham Forest took the lead through an Emanuel Villa own goal ten minutes into the second half. Villa redeemed himself by equalising ten minutes later. Lewis McGugan was sent off with fifteen minutes to go. Two minutes into injury time, Miles Addison headed the ball in past Lee Camp, but referee Stuart Attwell ruled the goal out, giving a penalty for an earlier infringement. Nacer Barazite stepped up but Camp saved the spot kick, diving to his right. More drama was to follow. Four minutes later Addison headed in again from a corner only for Attwell to rule out again, with all the players on both sides looking absolutely stunned. Emanuel Villa's good scoring run continued, as he bagged a hat-trick in the 4-1 win in the League Cup third round against Brighton and Hove Albion at the Withdean Stadium, with Nathan Ellington scoring the other goal. Villa and Ellington scored again as Derby's success in the tournament continued, with a fourth round 2-1 win at home against Leeds United, setting up a quarter-final tie at Stoke City. The next three games in the League ended with mixed results. Derby beat Sheffield Wednesday 3-0 at home, lost 2-0 at Ipswich Town with Darren Powell making his debut following his release from Southampton, and drew 2-2 at home to Preston North End.

The following week, on the last Saturday in November which was a dark gloomy day, I travelled to Cheddleton in Staffordshire to take part in their 10K race, with Gavin Chadwick, Dave Thompson, Lee Griffiths and Joe Rees. The race started at two-p.m., and I said to the lads I wanted to get back to the car as quick as possible, to listen to Derby's game at Burnley. We did the run and by the time we'd all got back to the car it was 3.25 p.m. We turned the radio on and Burnley had just scored their third goal, and Derby were already 3-0 down! We found out that James Tomkins, on loan from West Ham United, made his debut along with Luke Varney, who was also on loan from Charlton Athletic. Incidentally, the game finished 3-0…

To the Britannia Stadium for the League Cup quarter-final against Stoke City. It's one of my bugbears in modern football, grounds with the name of the sponsor. I can understand the obvious financial rewards but what's wrong with Maine Road or Victoria Ground? I suppose I'm just a traditionalist. Kris

Commons headed against the bar and Miles Addison hit the post before Derby were awarded a last-minute penalty that Nathan Ellington coolly converted. Derby were through to the League Cup semi-finals for the first time since the 1967/68 season. Following the win at Stoke City, Derby lost 2-1 at home to Crystal Palace and 3-0 at Wolverhampton Wanderers. In the two games prior to Christmas, Derby drew 2-2 at Charlton Athletic and beat Watford by 1-0 at home, with Rob Hulse scoring the late winner. Derby had a poor Christmas, losing 2-0 at Preston North End and 1-0 at home to Ipswich Town. The Ipswich game was the final straw for Adam Pearson, who relieved Paul Jewell of his duties, with Derby eighteenth in the League with twenty-nine points from twenty-six games. Assistant manager Chris Hutchings took over for the FA Cup third round tie away to Conference outfit Forest Green Rovers. I went to the game with Carl Smith, Gavin and Nick Chadwick. I'd heard of Forest Green Rovers, but I hadn't got a clue where it was. We found out it was in Gloucestershire, so we made our way down the M5. We stopped at a pub on the way down for a pint and a game of darts. The New Lawn Ground was in Nailsworth, which from the main road was up a steep hill in a what appeared to be a small village. It was the coldest I've ever been at a Derby away match. Carl and I stood behind the goal in the South Stand. Gavin and Nick stood on the West Terrace, on the same side where the TV cameras were positioned. The pitch was rock hard and I believe the only reason the game was played was because the highlights were on BBC's Match of the Day. There was an unbelievable start to the game with Derby going 2-0 down in twenty minutes. Fortunately, Derby levelled before half time with goals from Rob Hulse and Martin Albrechsten.

Rovers restored their lead with twenty minutes to go, but Derby's superior fitness came to the fore with Paul Green equalising, and Steve Davies converting a penalty three minutes from time to spare Derby's blushes. Chris Hutchings' very short reign was over, as he was replaced by Academy head coach David Lowe for the League Cup semi-final first leg with Manchester United. Adam Pearson announced on the day of the semi-final that Burton Albion manager Nigel Clough would take over from Paul Jewell as permanent manager. Clough left Burton thirteen points clear at the top of the Conference, following eleven straight wins. Andy Garner, Gary Crosby and Martin Taylor followed Clough to Derby from Burton also.

Clough took his place in the stands as the Rams took on United, who started with regulars Nemanja Vidic, Paul Scholes and Carlos Tevez, with Cristiano Ronaldo, Wayne Rooney and Ryan Giggs on the bench. Derby played well on the night and won 1-0, with a fabulous left foot strike from Kris Commons. Commons is a very gifted player, technically Derby's best player, but it was difficult to fit him into a system. Clough's first game in charge was due to be the away game at Cardiff City, but was postponed. In his first game, Queen's Park Rangers won 2-0 at Pride Park. Manchester United comfortably won the second leg of the League Cup semi-final at Old Trafford 4-2. Giles Barnes scored twice late on to give United a bit of a scare. Derby then cancelled the contract of Mo Camara and released Darren Powell. The FA Cup fourth round draw paired Derby against Billy Davies' Nottingham Forest. Davies had recently replaced Colin Calderwood in the Forest hot seat. In the usual deafening noise when these two sides meet, Rob Hulse gave Derby a first half lead with Robert Earnshaw equalising, with Nigel Clough still waiting for his first win as the new boss. That win came on the last day of January as Derby beat Coventry City 2-1. Derby were struggling though to get out of the bottom half, sitting in eighteenth place with thirty-two points from twenty-nine games. Nigel Clough made his first major signing, with the arrival of Motherwell striker Chris Porter for £400,000, on a two-and-a-half-year contract. In the FA Cup fourth round replay against Nottingham Forest at the City Ground, the home side were off to a flyer with an early goal from Chris Cohen. That lead was doubled with a Nathan Tyson penalty ten minutes later, but Rob Hulse pulled one back heading in Gary Teale's cross. On the hour, Paul Green headed in from another Teale cross as Derby clawed their way back into the tie. Kris Commons' low drive struck a post as the game flowed end to end. Derby's comeback was complete, with fifteen minutes to go, as Commons' shot from the edge of the box deflected past Lee Camp to send the away fans in the Bridgford End delirious. Robbie Savage, who'd been frozen out by Paul Jewell loved it. At the end of the game, he was twirling his black and white scarf above his head in front of the Derby fans. Derby had a good 3-0 away win at Plymouth Argyle, before Manchester United knocked Derby out of the FA Cup with a 4-1 win at Pride Park.

The Rams then had two good wins. 4-1 at home to Blackpool. With the score 1-1, Derby scored three goals in the last fifteen minutes through Kris Commons, Paul Green and Nacer Barazite. That night I was very impressed with Blackpool's centre-back who had bleached blonde hair and was absolutely everywhere. I'd never heard of him, but his name was Shaun Barker. Carl and I both agreed he was one to watch. Derby were back at the City Ground for the League game. In a game Derby dominated, Lewin Nyatanga fired Derby into an early lead. Rob Hulse and a Steve Davies penalty increased the lead in the second half before Rob Earnshaw scored a consolation goal minutes from time. It was Derby's first League win at the City Ground since 1971. The following Friday night, Carl and I made the trip to Doncaster Rovers for Derby's first ever visit to the Keepmoat Stadium. We sat in the North Stand with the sell-out Derby away support. Robbie Savage gave Derby the lead with a curling free kick from the edge of the box just after half time. Derby fell apart though, and an error by Stephen Bywater gifted Rovers their second goal as they came from behind to win 2-1. February ended with Derby in sixteenth place with forty-one points from thirty-three games. Derby won their next home game 2-1 against Bristol City with a late Rob Hulse goal. Another late goal the following week by Steve Davies salvaged a point at relegation-threatened Southampton, with experienced midfielder John Eustace making his debut following his loan move from Watford. Nigel Clough signed another midfielder on loan, with youngster Barry Bannan joining from Aston Villa. Bannan made his debut at Sheffield United and scored, but Derby slipped to a 4-2 defeat. Derby ended March with a goalless draw at home to Barnsley, as they still hovered six points above the relegation trap door. Derby's crowds were still incredible with over 33,000 in attendance for the home 1-1 draw with promotion chasing Burnley. A last-minute Paul Connolly goal earned Derby a point. Derby got a 4-1 drubbing on their trip to South Wales to play Cardiff City at Ninian Park. A 1-0 win at Hillsborough though, with a Rob

Hulse goal on half-time, his seventeenth goal of the season, saw Derby break the fifty-point barrier and close to safety. Four defeats from their last five games though didn't fill the supporters will much optimism for the following season. Rob Hulse was named Player of the Year, with the average League attendance a staggering 29,500. I got the impression a few tough years were ahead, with Nigel Clough's main remit from the board was to reduce the playing staff, cut the wage bill and maintain Championship status. Clough then appointed Johnny Metgod as first-team coach.

2009/10

Ahead of the new season, Nigel Clough strengthened his squad with three major signings. The most expensive was Blackpool centre-back Shaun Barker from Blackpool for £900,000 on a three-year-deal. Apparently, Clough, who had been pursuing Barker for some time, had beaten Nottingham Forest for his signature. I was really pleased, especially after seeing Barker in action for Blackpool the previous season. Exeter City left-back Dean Moxey signed for £300,000 after six years at the Devon club. Midfielder Lee Croft also joined on a free transfer from Norwich City. Other signings included goalkeeper Saul Deeney and defender Jake Buxton from Burton Albion, both on one-year deals. Young midfielder Ben Pringle also signed on a one-year deal from non-League Ilkeston Town. There were plenty of departures during pre-season and into the first month of the season, including Liam Dickinson, who cost £750,000 and never made a senior appearance for the club. Roy Carroll, Martin Albrechsten, Przemyslaw Kazmierczak, Andy Todd, Mile Sterjovski, Tyrone Mears, Emanuel Villa,

Jordan Stewart, Claude Davis and Lewin Nyatanga all left. Season long loanees Nathan Ellington and Nacer Barazite returned to their parent clubs Watford and Arsenal respectively.

Derby went on a pre-season tour of Devon at the end of July to play Yeovil Town, Torquay United and Exeter City. Carl and I saw this as an opportunity to go to some new grounds. On the Tuesday afternoon we travelled down to Yeovil for the game at Huish Park. We sat in the East Stand with the Main Stand opposite, and the large open terrace to our right. There were around five hundred Derby supporters there, who probably had the same idea as Carl and myself. To be honest I can't even remember the score but it was another ground ticked off! After the game we drove the seventy miles down to Torquay. We arrived in Torquay about eleven p.m. and checked into the B&B we had booked. We had a relaxing couple of days, having a few beers and playing golf in Paignton and Torquay. The next game was on the Thursday night against Torquay at Plainmoor. We stood on the shallow Warbro Road covered terrace, again with around five hundred Derby supporters, with the Main Stand to our right. My only memory was a game of poor quality that finished 0-0. We travelled home after the game, but in hindsight we should have stopped another night and gone home the next morning!

Derby got off to a winning start with an opening day 2-1 at home to Peterborough United with Dean Moxey, Jake Buxton and Lee Croft all in the starting line-up. Ben Pringle made his debut coming on from the bench with Gary Teale scoring the winning goal three minutes from time. Carl, Graham, Steve and I continued with turnstile duty. The big difference on the turnstiles was that Derby went to an electronic ticket system, so we would stand outside the ground to address any issues with fans trying to enter the ground and not inside the ground collecting actual tickets. Julie and I travelled to Halkadiki for our summer holiday. It was poor planning on my behalf, as I missed the opportunity of going to a new ground when Derby drew Rotherham United away in the League Cup! The Millers were now playing their home games at the Don Valley Stadium, which was used for athletics. Despite taking the lead through another Gary Teale goal, Derby lost 2-1. Derby lost their next match at Glanford Park against promoted Scunthorpe United 3-2. I followed the game on Sky Sports Soccer Saturday in a bar in Hanioti's main square. The Rams next win was in the home game with Plymouth Argyle, with Tottenham Hotspur young midfielder Jake Livermore making his debut. Another player to join Derby was Paul Dickov on a three- month loan from Leicester City, and he was named on the bench for the trip to Nottingham Forest. Derby were looking for their third successive win at the City Ground, but the game started badly. Derby were 3-0 down by half time, with Radi Majewski, Dextor Blackstock and Nathan Tyson scoring. Derby rallied and replied with a Wes Morgan own goal and Livermore's first goal for the club, but Forest hung on to win. There was controversy at the end, when Nathan Tyson started goading the Derby fans by waving the corner flag above his head in front of them. This incensed the Derby players, who confronted Tyson. If Tyson had celebrated in front of the Forest supporters, then fair enough, but he stepped across the line. Billy Davies didn't endear himself to the Derby fans by saying Tyson did 'nothing wrong'. Derby had a poor

September, losing three games on the spin. They lost 1-0 at home to Sheffield United, 3-2 at home to Barnsley and 2-1 at Crystal Palace, with Nigel Clough giving a debut to James Vaughan, who was on a three-month loan from Everton. Their only win came in a 1-0 win at home to Bristol City with a late Gary Teale goal, with Lee Hendrie on loan from Sheffield United making his debut from the bench. Disaster struck in Derby's first ever visit to the Cardiff City Stadium, as they were thrashed 6-1. Michael Chopra scored four for the Bluebirds, with Fredrik Storr on loan from Fulham making an unhappy debut. It had been a poor start to the season with Derby lying fifth-from-bottom, only three points above the drop zone. October wasn't much better. It started with a 3-0 home win against Sheffield Wednesday, with Academy player Arnaud Mendy making his debut as a last-minute substitute. Three further defeats followed. Derby lost 2-0 at Middlesbrough and 4-2 at home to Queen's Park Rangers, before a 1-0 defeat at bottom of the table Ipswich Town. Bryan Hughes, on loan from Hull City, made his debut in the Queen's Park Rangers game. Adam Pearson's short reign as chairman ended by mutual consent, with Andy Appleby taking over. Two Rob Hulse goals gave Derby a much-needed win at home to Coventry City, before the November international break. Another win, 2-1 at home to Reading, gave Derby some breathing space and lifted them up to sixteenth in the table, five points above the drop zone.

The West Bromwich Albion game at the start of December was the last time Graham Perry and myself were on turnstile duty. Due to the introduction of the electronic ticketing system, we didn't really have a job anymore. Graham and I were given roles in the Director's Box, assisting the VIPs to their seats. The only problem was that one of us had to 'patrol the stairs' inside the ground, to ensure no-one got into the Director's Box by mistake. Graham and I alternated every ten minutes, but the problem was when 'patrolling the stairs', it was away from the view of the pitch and we couldn't watch the game! When we were on the turnstiles, five minutes after the start of the game, you were free to watch the game. This new 'arrangement' was no good to Graham and I, we wanted to watch the majority the game! We had a supervisor who told us we also had to stop for half an hour after the game to ensure the VIPs were directed into the right areas of the ground for post-match refreshments. Graham and I were having none of that. At the end of the game, we headed off, never to return! Our five-year stint was over, we had to revert to being paying customers, as clubs call the fans nowadays. The West Brom game finished 2-2, with DJ Campbell on loan from parent club Leicester City scoring a last-minute equaliser. Campbell had made quite an impression on loan at Blackpool. Derby only won one more game before the end of the year, 1-0 away at Watford. It was followed by two really poor home performances, losing 2-0 to both Doncaster Rovers and Blackpool on Boxing Day.

The New Year didn't start much better. Despite a 1-1 draw at Millwall in the third round of the FA Cup, with Lee Johnson on loan from Bristol City making his debut, Derby crashed to a 4-1 home defeat at the hands of Scunthorpe United. I was really impressed with twenty-one-year-old Gary Hooper, who played up front for the Iron and looked like a player to keep tabs on. Derby then unexpectedly won three games in a row. Millwall were beaten on penalties in the FA Cup third round replay. DJ Campbell impressed and scored twice in the 3-0 win at Peterborough United, with Nicky Hunt on loan from Bolton Wanderers making his first start, as did Russell Anderson following his release from Sunderland. Derby also progressed to the fifth round of the FA Cup after seeing off Doncaster Rovers with a very late Jay McEveley goal. Derby got revenge for their defeat earlier in the season at the City Ground, by beating promotion chasing Nottingham Forest at the end of the month with Rob Hulse's bullet header from Kris Common's free kick. Derby had thoroughly deserved their win, which ended Forest's nineteen game unbeaten run after dominating the game. In injury time there were some shenanigans involving players and both dugouts, with Billy Davies refusing to shake Nigel Clough's hand at the end of the game. The important win lifted Derby six points clear of the drop zone. Clough signed Michael Tonge on loan until the end of the season, and he made his debut as the Rams drew 1-1 at Sheffield United. This was followed up with a great 3-0 home win over leaders Newcastle United, with Dave Martin, on loan from Millwall, making his debut from the bench. Derby were knocked out of the FA Cup at Birmingham City, but their good run of form in the League continued with 5-3 win over mid-table Preston North End. Derby were beaten in a feisty encounter at home to high flying Swansea City. Jay McEveley was sent off ten minutes into the second half, with Shefki Kuqi a minute later heading the visitors in front. The Swans substitute Gorka Pintado was also sent off five minute later for a wild tackle on Robbie Savage near the corner flag, which triggered a mass brawl between the players. Derby then had a run of three defeats in four games. Gilles Sunu, on loan from Arsenal, made his first start in the 3-1 defeat at West

Bromwich Albion. A 2-0 home win over Watford was followed up with two away defeats, 4-1 at Reading and 2-1 at Doncaster Rovers. The inconsistency continued, as Derby went five games undefeated with three successive draws and two wins. The 1-0 home win against Leicester City was the result of bizarre own goal by Andy King. His back pass slipped under Chris Weale's foot and into the net. Shaun Barker scored the winner in the Easter Saturday 1-0 win at Coventry City, as Derby all but secured their Championship status. Tomasz Cywka made his debut, following his loan move from Wigan Athletic, in the Easter Monday 3-1 home defeat by Ipswich Town. Derby won their final game of the season, beating Cardiff City, who had qualified for the end of seasons play-offs. Academy players Callum Ball and Ryan Connolly made their debuts from the bench. Derby finished fifteenth in the table in what had been a tough season. Nigel Clough was under no illusions this was a going to be a long job, but the club needed stability. GSE were running a very tight ship, with little money for Clough to spend. There was a lot of inconsistency in the results, like beating leaders Newcastle United but losing to Scunthorpe United. Derby becoming a worldwide brand and in the Premier League, as GSE had suggested, seemed a very long way away.

2010/11

Nigel Clough signed four players ahead of the new season. Midfielder James Bailey and defender John Brayford arrived from Crewe Alexandra for a combined fee of £1 million, both on three-year deals. Experienced left-back Gareth Roberts joined from Doncaster Rovers on a two-year deal, after turning down a new deal at the Keepmoat Stadium. Conor Doyle, an American youth player, signed a two-year deal after impressing during a trial. Clough was very keen on Gary Hooper from Scunthorpe United, but they were priced out of the deal. There were three permanent departures, Jay McEveley left to join Barnsley, Gary Teale moved to Sheffield Wednesday and Paul Connolly signed for Leeds United. Luke Varney moved to Blackpool on a season long loan. Derby got off to a fine start to the season, with an opening day 2-1 win at Leeds United with all three close season signings making their debuts. Strangely, prior to the game, Clough stopped the team coach and made the players walk the two hundred yards to the ground through the Leeds supporters. Rob Hulse and Kris Commons scored for Derby from the spot. This was the last time we saw Rob Hulse in a Derby shirt after the club accepted a £500,000 bid from Queen's Park Rangers. I was baffled by the decision, as Hulse had scored twenty-eight League goals in his two seasons in a struggling team.

James Bailey and John Brayford made a quick return to Gresty Road in the League Cup first round, in a game in which Derby slipped to a 1-0 defeat. Derby then lost four out their next five League games. The only point Derby gained was in the draw at home to Queen's Park Rangers. Derby were 2-0 up when Rangers scored twice in injury time through Patrick Agyemang and Jamie Mackie to grab a very unlikely point. In the last of the four defeats at Hull City, Nigel Clough gave starts to two loan players. Spanish under-twenty-one international Alberto Bueno from Valladolid, and Swansea City's Finnish international striker Shefki Kuqi who arrived to fill the void left by Rob Hulse. Derby then went on a fine unbeaten run of six games with two draws and four wins. The two draws came in away games at Barnsley and Swansea City. The wins were 5-0 at home against Crystal Palace with Alberto Bueno netting twice, 3-1 at home to Middlesbrough, 3-0 at home to Preston North End and 3-2 away at Doncaster Rovers. On loan Blackburn Rovers goalkeeper Frank Fielding made his debut at Preston, and another loan signing Luke Moore from West Bromwich Albion made his debut at Doncaster. The unbeaten run hoisted Derby up to seventh place in the table with eighteen points from twelve games. Derby fell to a 2-0 defeat at Millwall, but were back to winning ways defeating Watford 4-1 at home, with a Tomasz Cywka brace, Portsmouth 2-0 at home, and a great 2-0 win away at Ipswich Town, with Kris Commons scoring twice. Derby moved up to fourth place in the table, as confidence started to ooze through the side.

The following weekend, Julie and I went with Graham Perry, Carol Perry, Steve Gascoyne and Jackie Gascoyne, to Cork for a long weekend, to celebrate Graham's fiftieth birthday. We were really impressed with Cork with its fantastic 'oldie worldie' pubs, and we met some fascinating characters. On the Saturday we did a bit of a tour around County Cork and County Kerry. We also heard Derby lost 2-0 at Leicester City, with ex-Ram Steve Howard scoring a penalty for the Foxes. On the Sunday, we went to Cork Races, which is twenty-four miles north of Cork, so I'm not sure why it's called Cork Races? It was absolutely freezing. I'm no expert on horse racing, but we like to go once a year for a bit of a social, but I'm never going in the winter again! Derby beat Scunthorpe United 3-2 to consolidate their position in the top four, but then went on a poor run of five defeats. After Derby took the lead at Burnley through Luke Moore, the home side scored twice late on to take the points. Norwich City took an early two goal lead at Pride Park, with Chris Martin scoring one of the goals and eventually won 2-1. A pair of Brett Pitman goals resigned Derby to a 2-0 defeat at Bristol City, and Shane Long scored twice as Reading won 2-0 at Pride Park.

On Christmas Eve, Julie and I travelled to Australia for a once in a lifetime three-week holiday. The Cathay Pacific flight left Heathrow for Hong Kong at ten p.m. From Hong Kong, we got the connecting flight to Sydney arriving on Boxing Day morning. Derby didn't have a game on Boxing Day, but England were playing Australia in the fourth Ashes test match in Melbourne. We went for a spot of lunch in Circular Quay overlooking the Harbour Bridge. England had a fantastic day bowling the Aussies out for 98, and then reaching hundred for no loss at the end of day one. We spent the next few days relaxing in Darling Harbour, on Bondi beach and Manly beach. Derby were away at Nottingham Forest in the period before the New Year. Steve Hallam phoned me to let me know Derby had lost 5-2, with ex-Derby players Marcus Tudgay and Robert Earnshaw both scoring twice. We had a fantastic New Year's Eve on a boat on Sydney Harbour. It cost £250 each for six hours, which included free food and drink, but we just had to do it as we'd may never have another opportunity in the future to do it. We boarded the boat at seven p.m. with an outdoor temperature of twenty-seven degrees. It was a fabulous experience watching the firework display and something to cross off the bucket list. On New Year's Day we left for a couple of days in the Blue Mountains, before returning to Sydney to visit Taronga Zoo. The next day was another tick on the bucket list, for the second day of the Sydney Test match at the SCG. England, who had won the previous test in Melbourne, had Australia 134-4 at the close on day one. We saw Australia being bowled out for 280, with England's Alistair Cook and Andrew Strauss then setting off like a train and closing on 167-3. England eventually won the game, winning the Ashes for the first time in Australia for twenty-four years. We left Sydney to fly to Cairns to spend the second half of the holiday in Northern Queensland in Port Douglas. We had great time travelling on the Kuranda Scenic Railway in the rainforest, with visits to Mossman Gorge and Cape Tribulation. We also had a fantastic day snorkelling the Great Barrier Reef, with the Pacific Ocean like a sheet of glass in perfect conditions. Whilst snorkelling, I was desperately holding onto Julie! Whilst we were in Port Douglas, the unthinkable happened to Derby. My nephew Richard Wilson text me to tell me Derby had been knocked out of the FA Cup third round at Conference side Crawley Town, who scored with a last-minute goal. We left Australia on 18 January, after three fantastic weeks. On our way home, we arrived at Hong Kong airport for the connecting flight back to Heathrow. I received a text from Joe Rees to inform me that Derby had lost 3-0 at Watford. My body clock was all over the place and I hadn't got a clue what day or what time it was!

When I got home, I tried to catch up with what was happening, Derby-wise. Ben Davies had joined the Rams from Notts County for £350,000 on a two-and-a-half-year deal. Derby had slumped to fourteenth in the League after such a promising autumn. In the next game, Nottingham Forest completed the double over Derby, with a Robert Earnshaw goal ten minutes from time. Earnshaw had a nasty habit of scoring against Derby! It appeared that Kris Commons was going to sign a new deal for Derby after months of negotiations, but he signed to Celtic for £300,000 just before the end of the January transfer window. It was a bitter blow, losing both Commons and Hulse. Derby also accepted a bid of £400,000 for Dean Moxey from Crystal Palace. February started poorly, with Ipswich Town winning 2-1 at Pride Park. Derby stopped the run of defeats with a 1-1 draw at Portsmouth, with David Nugent scoring the equaliser for the home side in the last minute. Nigel Clough publicly criticised Tomasz Cywka after the game for losing the ball before Nugent scored. The PFA weren't too happy with Clough following this incident. Clough added two more loan players to his squad, both made their debuts in the goalless draw at Scunthorpe United. Jamie Ward joined from Sheffield United with a view to a permanent deal, and Daniel Ayala arrived from Liverpool. Derby only won one game in February, which was 1-0 at Sheffield United at the end of the month, with another loan signing, Theo Robinson, scoring on his first start following his move from Millwall. March wasn't much better for Derby, with only one win. The 2-1 win came against Swansea City, who were second in the table, chasing automatic promotion. Attendances, although still very good, were dropping to around 25,000. March ended with Derby in seventeenth place, nine points clear of the drop zone with eight games remaining.

April started with Derby suffering another heavy defeat at the Cardiff City Stadium. The Bluebirds won 4-1, with Australian goalkeeper Brad Jones making an unhappy debut following his loan move from Liverpool. Derby came back from 2-0 down to draw 2-2 at home to Coventry, before beating Leeds United 2-1 in what turned out to be Derby's last win of the season. Derby lost their last four games, in a worrying end to the season. Burnley won 4-2 at Pride Park on Easter Saturday. Simeon Jackson's hat-trick gave Norwich City a crucial 3-2 win in their quest for promotion at Carrow Road. Academy product Jeff Hendrick, who Nigel Clough had high hopes for, made his debut from the bench. Bristol City won 2-0 at Pride Park and the season ended with a 2-1 defeat at Reading. Robbie Savage made his final appearance in a Derby shirt, in a career spanning seventeen years. It had been a really strange season. The poor start followed by the unbeaten autumn run that saw the Rams climb to fourth in the League, and then the alarming slump with only four wins in the calendar year.

2011/12

Derby's major signing before the start of the season was the arrival of Barnsley defender Jason Shackell for £750,000. There were two arrivals from the Scottish Premier League. Craig Bryson from Kilmarnock and Chris Maguire from Aberdeen. Both players cost £400,000 and both signed three-year contracts. Nathan Tyson joined on a free transfer from Nottingham Forest on a three-year deal. Goalkeeper Frank Fielding turned his loan deal into a permanent one for £400,000 from Blackburn Rovers. Burton Albion's goalkeeper Adam Legzdins also signed as back up to Fielding, with both keepers on three-year deals. Chris Riggott joined Derby on a one-year deal following his release from Cardiff City. Jamie Ward and Theo Robinson made their loan moves permanent, and Kevin Kilbane moved on a six-month loan from Hull City.

Miles Addison joined Barnsley on a six-month loan deal. Luke Varney, who'd spent the previous season at Blackpool on loan moved to Portsmouth for £750,000. Chris Porter and Ben Pringle also left the club, joining Sheffield United and Rotherham United respectively.

The Rams opened their season with a 2-1 home victory over Birmingham City, with new signings Jason Shackell, Kevin Kilbane and Craig Bryson all making their debuts. Academy player Mark O'Brien was also a debutant, coming on from the bench. Curtis Davies gave the Blues the lead, but Shackell and Steve Davies ensured Derby got off to a winning start in front of a 27,000 crowd. Despite losing at home to Shrewsbury Town in the first round of the League Cup, Derby won their next three League games. Steve Davies scored again in the 1-0 win at Watford, and Craig Bryson scored his first Rams goal in the 1-0 away win at Blackpool, with Jeff Hendrick making his first start. Derby made it four League wins in a row, seeing off Doncaster Rovers with a 3-0 win. It was Derby's best start to a season since 1905-6 and were lying second to Southampton in the League table. The winning run though was ended, with Burnley winning 2-0 at Pride Park with two Charlie Austin goals and a 2-0 defeat at Coventry City. The following week Derby travelled down the A52 to meet Steve McClaren's Nottingham Forest. The Rams had the worst possible start. Frank Fielding was sent off for hauling down Ishmael Miller. Adam Legzdins replaced Fielding, with Tomasz Cywka being sacrificed. Andy Reid converted the resulting penalty. Controversy followed on the half hour. Chris Cohen went down, injured, as he attempted a tackle on Jeff Hendrick. Derby carried on playing, with boos ringing around the ground. The ball ended up with Jamie Ward out on the left wing. He evaded a couple of tackles along the by-line before firing past Lee Camp at the near post. Jeff Hendrick missed a golden chance to give Derby the lead when he headed wide from a Ben Davies cross, but the ten men went ahead with twenty minutes remaining, when Hendrick redeemed himself with his first goal for the club, with a fine side foot finish when the ball dropped to him on the edge of the box, sending the Derby masses wild behind the goal. I loved Colin Bloomfield's commentary on BBC Radio Derby. "Jeff Hendrick, you little beauty." The Forest v Derby games are always dramatic, but this one had everything. Derby ended September with a 3-0 home win against Millwall and 1-1 draw at Barnsley, as Derby remained in second spot in the table, level on points with Southampton. Derby then slumped to their heaviest defeat of the season, losing 4-0 at Leicester City. This was followed with a 1-1 draw with leaders Southampton in front of 33,000 at Pride Park and a 2-2 draw at Reading.

The following week, Julie and I travelled to Olu Deniz in Turkey for a ten-day holiday with Pete Freeman and Sue Latty. It was warm in the day with temperatures of twenty-five degrees, but in the evenings, it turned cold, with the bars having open log fires to keep warm. On the Saturday, Derby lost 2-0 at Middlesbrough, with Nigel Clough giving fifteen-year-old Mason Bennett his debut, becoming Derby's youngest ever player to make a League appearance. The following day, Pete and I watched the Manchester derby, with City remarkably winning 6-1 at Old Trafford. Julie and I decided to go paragliding as Olu Deniz was cited as one of the best destinations in the world for this. We travelled up the scary winding roads to the top of Mount Babadag, a 2000-

metre-high mountain to start the tandem jump. The guy who accompanied me was a former goalkeeper for Borrusia Monchengladbach in the German Bundesliga, and a member of the 1974 West Germany World Cup squad! He did tell me his name but I couldn't remember. When I got home, I found out his name was Wolfgang Kleff. What a wonderful experience it was. We both loved it but I don't think I'd do it again! On the way back to the airport for our return journey home, I found out that Derby had beaten Portsmouth. Derby signed Tom Naylor from Mansfield Town on loan with a view to a permanent deal. The Rams lost all five games in November. Over the past season and a half, it was quite strange how they could go on long unbeaten runs, or alternatively have runs of defeats. Cardiff City, who Derby always seemed to struggle against, won 3-0 at Pride Park. Peterborough United won 3-2 despite two Theo Robinson goals. Hull City won 2-0 at Pride Park. Tamas Priskin, making his debut on loan from Ipswich Town, gave Derby the lead at Upton Park, but West Ham United came back to win 3-1. Craig Mackail-Smith's goal gave Brighton a 1-0 away win. The five defeats saw Derby fall to sixteenth in the table as the alarm bells started to ring, not for the first time in the club's recent history. The next game Derby won was 2-1 at home to Bristol City in mid-December.

Around this time, my sisters, with a little help from myself, were caring for my dad at home, who was suffering from bowel cancer. He had been diagnosed about fifteen months earlier and had been coping as well as expected, but he'd had a fall and started to deteriorate. He was receiving twenty four-hour care from my sisters and visits from care workers who were doing a fantastic job. Football again was taking a back seat from my point of view. A week before Christmas, Derby lost 1-0 at Ipswich Town. We spent a lot of quality time together as a family, reminiscing about the good times. We didn't know whether dad would make it to Christmas, but we were so relieved when he did. Sadly, he died on Thursday 29 December with all the family around him. At least now he was pain free. I thought he coped very well since my mum died, but it's strange even now to know they're not around and we all miss them dearly. If my dad hadn't been a big football and cricket fan, my life could have been so much different.

Derby terminated the contract of Stephen Bywater and released Chris Riggott from his contract as he failed to overcome his injury problems. The Rams were on a roll again, winning five games on the bounce including the FA Cup third round tie at home to Crystal Palace. The games around this time were a bit of a blur following my dad's passing. For a change of scenery, we went on a bus trip to Scotland with the Perry's and Gascoyne's. We were the youngest six on the bus, on the twelve-hour journey up to Loch Awe for the four-night trip. It was just what I needed and I thought it was quite poignant that we were there for Robert Burns' night, which was my dad's birthday. Glencoe was stunning with snow on the mountains, as we made our way up to Fort William on the Saturday. That day, Derby were knocked out of the FA Cup at home to Tony Pulis' Stoke City. On the last day of January, which was the last day of the transfer window, Derby lost 3-2 at Barnsley, with Tom Carroll, on loan from Tottenham Hotspur, and Ryan Noble, on loan from Sunderland, making their debuts. Paul Green was left out of the side, after being linked with a move to the Premier League, but it didn't materialise. Derby were twelfth in the table, with forty-one points from twenty-eight games. Tomasz Cywka left the club and joined Reading on a free transfer. Derby's Jekyll and Hyde results continued in February. Following a goalless draw at Millwall, Derby lost three games on the trot. They lost 1-0 at home to Reading, 4-0 at promotion chasing Southampton and another 1-0 home defeat, this time to Leicester City. The inconsistent results were quite hard to fathom. The team was fairly settled with very few changes. The Rams' next win was 2-1 at home to high flying Blackpool. Steve Davies scored a brace after Tom Ince had given the Seasiders an early lead. The crowds were still very respectable with over 26,000 in attendance. In mid-March, Nottingham Forest were in town trying to avenge their defeat by ten-man Derby in September. Forest lay fourth-from-bottom in the table only a point above the drop zone. It was a night that changed Shaun Barker's life forever. With the game at 0-0 with fifteen minutes to go, Barker was involved in an innocuous looking collision with Frank Fielding. Barker suffered the most horrendous knee injury possible. He ruptured every ligament and tendon in his right knee, the anterior and posterior cruciate ligaments, lateral and medial collateral ligaments and patella tendon. It was four and half years later before Barker returned to a professional football pitch. Derby won 1-0 with a last-minute Jake Buxton goal, but the whole night was overshadowed by Barker's injury. Derby won 2-1 at Doncaster Rovers with Tom Naylor, who had completed his move from Mansfield Town, making his first start. Derby lost 2-0 on their first visit to the Amex Stadium, the new home of play-off chasing Brighton and Hove Albion. Derby beat Crystal Palace 3-2 at home as the games started to have an end of season feel, as they were safe in mid-table. Derby won their next away game on Easter Monday at Leeds United 2-0. Craig Bryson, who was settling in very nicely, scored the first goal, with Steve Davies scoring the second, his eleventh of the campaign. Derby won one of their last four games of the season 2-1 away at Portsmouth, with Jake Buxton scoring again. Academy product sixteen-year-old Will Hughes made his debut, coming off the bench for the last twenty minutes. Progress was slowly being made, with Derby finishing eleventh in the table up eight places from the previous season. The club announced Chief Executive Tom Glick was leaving the club taking up a new position at Manchester City at the start of the new season.

2012/13

With Shaun Baker's injury, Nigel Clough's priority was a centre-back to replace him. He signed Richard Keogh from Coventry City for £1 million on a three-year-deal. Keogh was named captain after the departure of Jason Shackell, who was a man in demand, to Burnley for £1.1 million. Other arrivals before the season started included winger Michael Jacobs from Northampton Town, midfielder Paul Coutts for £150,000 from Preston North End and defender James O'Connor from Doncaster Rovers. Young Albanian defender Valentin Gjokaj signed a two-year deal after impressing in a trial. Chris Maguire, who had failed to establish himself moved on to Sheffield Wednesday for £200,000. Paul Green rejected a new deal and signed for Leeds United and Miles Addison joined AFC Bournemouth.

Julie and I travelled to Lanzarote for our summer holiday before the season started. For the first time I can remember the season started with the first round of the League Cup. Derby were drawn at home to Scunthorpe United. In a crazy game, the final score was 5-5. I cannot recall ever Derby being involved in a 5-5 draw. Derby were 5-3 up when Scunthorpe scored twice in injury time, to take the tie extra time and penalties. With no more goals in extra time, Scunthorpe won 7-6 on penalties! The League campaign started with a home game against Sheffield Wednesday with Richard Keogh and Paul Coutts in the starting line-up. I was in a bar in Playa Blanca following the game on Sky Sport's Soccer Saturday. I was gutted when, with Derby 2-1 up, the Owls equalised in injury time through Reda Johnson. Derby then sold Steve Davies, who had been top scorer the previous season, to Bristol City for £750,000, with Conor Sammon joining Derby from Wigan Athletic for £1.2 million on the same day. Nigel Clough had finally got his man after an 18-month pursuit of the Irishman. Full-back Kieron Freeman also joined Derby on a two-year deal from Nottingham Forest. Derby visited Bolton Wanderers who had been relegated in the midweek. I remember this day clearly. We'd just gone out for the evening in Puerto Del Carmen. As we were walking along the seafront it was blowing a gale, but the air was unbelievably hot, just like a hairdryer. Bolton scored two late goals, one from Kevin Davies, a player I'd always admired, with Chris Eagles adding a second, winning 2-0. Derby's first win came at the start of September with a 5-1 win against Watford, with Richard Keogh, Will Hughes and Conor Sammon all scoring their first League goals for the club. Two goals from Jamie Ward helped Derby to a 3-2 win at home to Charlton Athletic, but they lost their next home game 2-1 to Burnley, with Charlie Austin scoring twice, just as he did in the corresponding game during the previous season. Derby travelled to the City Ground for the first East Midlands derby of the season at the end of September. After a goalless first half, Dexter Blackstock was given a red card for an elbow on Richard Keogh. I thought it was a harsh decision to be honest. Craig Bryson's close-range finish from a great cross from Paul Coutts gave Derby their first away win of the season. Derby were twelfth in the table with eleven points from eight games. Derby's inconsistency continued in October with three draws, a win and a defeat. A 2-2 draw at Middlesbrough was followed with two home draws, 0-0 against Brighton and Hove Albion and 1-1 against Blackburn Rovers. Following a fine 2-1 at Ipswich Town with a last-minute winner from Nathan Tyson, Derby put in a poor performance at Peterborough United and lost 3-0.

Worryingly for Derby, the attendances were tailing off. Even though respectable for Championship standards, only 22,000 were present for the 4-1 win at home to Blackpool at the start of November, with Theo Robinson scoring twice and Kieron Freeman making his debut from the bench. Crystal Palace were top of the table when Derby visited Selhurst Park. Glenn Murray scored twice, as the home side eased to a 3-0 with Nigel Clough having no complaints. Conor Sammon scored twice in the 3-2 home win against Birmingham City, as Derby ended the month with a 1-1 draw with Cardiff City. Inconsistency continued during December, as Derby won two and lost two in their games running up to Christmas. A 4-1 defeat at Leicester City, with David Nugent, continuing his good scoring run against Derby, scoring twice. Derby followed this up with beating Leeds United 3-1 at home and winning 2-0 away at Bristol City. Hull City though, won 2-1 at Pride Park. After Christmas, Derby lost 2-0 at Burnley on Boxing Day and then Jamie Ward's penalty salvaged Derby a point in the last game of the year at Charlton Athletic.

GSE appointed Sam Rush as Chief Executive following the departure of Tom Glick to Manchester City. Rush was Head of Football Operations at Wasserman Media Group, a global sports and entertainment agency. Derby were mid-table in eleventh place, with thirty-four points from fifteen games. Derby had a crushing 5-0 win over Tranmere in the FA Cup third round, with Mason Bennett's scoring his first competitive goal for the club. The following week I drove to Brighton and Hove Albion with Gavin Chadwick, for our first trip to the Amex Stadium. It was the first away game I'd been to for quite a while. Steady rain fell as we made our way down the various motorways to the South Coast. We parked up at Lewes Football Club and caught the train to take us to Falmer, which is quite a distance from Brighton. We sat in the South Stand, with the fantastic semi-circular roofs on the stands running down both sides of the ground. The Amex Stadium is a stunning ground, with superb acoustics and one of my favourites of the new grounds that have sprouted up in recent years. As with all Brighton home games, the teams come out to 'Sussex by the sea'. After travelling all that way, the Rams were 2-0 down in twenty-five minutes. Jeff Hendrick pulled one back with twenty minutes to go, but for all their pressure Derby couldn't find a way through.

It was time for the return match in the East Midlands derby the following week. Alex McLeish was Forest's new manager, having recently replaced Sean O'Driscoll. They took the lead through Chris Cohen on the half hour, with Jamie Ward levelling following good work by Conor Sammon. This game was quite tame really, compared to some fiery encounters in recent seasons. Derby were knocked out of the FA Cup at the fourth-round stage by Blackburn Rovers, who won 3-0 at Pride Park, with Colin Kazim-Richards scoring their first goal. The only activity in the January transfer window was Lee Croft leaving the club after his contract was terminated. Derby began February with a fine 3-0 home win over Huddersfield Town. This should have been followed up with an away win at Sheffield Wednesday but Derby let a two-goal lead slip to draw 2-2. Gareth Roberts was sent off in the 2-1 defeat at Hull City, as the inconsistency continued to frustrate Nigel Clough, who believed the side should be closer to the top six. Derby signed Norwich City striker Chris Martin on loan. He had spent the earlier part of the season on loan at League One Swindon Town. Martin made his debut the next day, coming off the bench in the 2-1 defeat at Watford. Derby were still stuck in mid-table, with forty-four points from thirty-four games. March began with two defeats and a draw. Crystal Palace won 1-0 in a game switched to Friday night, in a game Derby should have drawn as Conor Sammon missed a late penalty. Derby avoided their usual pummelling at the Cardiff City Stadium, drawing 1-1 after taking the lead with fifteen minutes to go through Conor Sammon, with on loan signing Craig Forsyth from Watford making his debut. They also took the lead through Ben Davies at Birmingham City, but fell to a 3-1 defeat. Chris Martin scored his first goal for the club in the 2-1 win at home to Leicester City, which was followed up with a 3-0 home win at home to Bristol City on Easter Saturday.

On Easter Monday morning, Julie and I went with Steve and Dawn Hallam to Exeter to celebrate Steve's fiftieth birthday for three nights. Derby were playing at Leeds United in a teatime kick, so obviously we found a pub to watch, as the game was live on Sky Sports! Derby's recent good record at Elland Road continued. Ross McCormack gave Leeds the lead with Paul Coutts equalising, with Jake Buxton popping up with the winner two minutes from time. With six games to go Derby were ninth in the table six points below the final play-off place. I believed Derby would need to win five out of their last six games to make the play-offs. It didn't happen as Derby only won two of those games and finished tenth, seven points shy of sixth place. Progress had been made. Richard Keogh proved to be a good acquisition, there was good quality in midfield with Paul Coutts, Craig Bryson, Jeff Hendrick and Will Hughes all having good seasons. Jamie Ward was top scorer with twelve goals. Nigel Clough was doing a good job reducing the wage bill, cutting the squad numbers down and improving the League position, albeit slowly. I wasn't their biggest fan, but to be fair to GSE they had brought much needed stability to the club.

CHAPTER 15

McCLAREN, PLAY-OFF HEARTACHE (WITH A CAPITAL H), MEL MORRIS AND THE CRAZY END TO 2014/15

2013/14

Nigel Clough continued to wheel and deal to try and improve the squad. The main arrival was Scottish striker Johnny Russell from Dundee United for £750,000 on a four-year-deal. The other player to cost a fee was Craig Forsyth, who signed from Watford for £150,000 on a three-year-contract. Goalkeeper Lee Grant returned to the club on a three-year-deal when his contract at Burnley expired. Chris Martin also arrived on a free from Norwich City on a two-year-contract. Thirty-three-year-old John Eustace completed the arrivals, also on a free, from Watford on a one-year-deal. Eustace had previously been on loan at Derby in 2009. Right-back Adam Smith joined on a season long loan from Tottenham Hotspur. The main departure was right-back John Brayford, who joined Premier League new boys Cardiff City in a £1.5 million deal. Goalkeeper Frank Fielding moved to Bristol City for £200,000. Theo Robinson joined Doncaster Rovers for £150,000 and veteran Gareth Roberts joined Bury on a free transfer. There were several players loaned out. Conor Doyle to DC United, Callum Ball to Torquay United and Tom Naylor to Newport County.

The season opener was at Pride Park against Blackburn Rovers. Johnny Russell, on his debut, gave Derby the lead right on half-time. Derby sat back in the second half trying to preserve their lead, but Leon Best levelled in the dying moments to deny Derby a winning start. A Michael Jacobs goal gave Derby victory in the second round of the League Cup at Oldham Athletic. Derby recorded their first League win away at Brighton and Hove Albion, with two really good finishes from Chris Martin. Leicester City won 1-0 at Pride Park, with a Lee Grant own goal resigning Derby to their first defeat of the season. The Rams then produced a fine performance at Yeovil Town, who were playing in the second tier of English football for the first time in their history. Johnny Russell gave the Rams the lead three minutes from half time. Craig Bryson doubled the lead, finishing off a fine passing move right on half time. Chris Martin added a third in the second half to give Derby an emphatic 3-0 win. Brentford were put to the sword in the second round of the League Cup. Chris Martin and Conor Sammon both scored twice in a 5-0 win. Derby ended August being brought back to earth by Burnley, who won 3-0 at Pride Park. Burnley were proving to be a real bogey side to Derby during this era.

During the September international break, Nathan Tyson moved to Blackpool on a free transfer. Derby then won 5-1 at Millwall, which was their biggest away win since beating Swansea City by the same score in December 1984. Craig Bryson scored the best hat-trick I've ever seen, with three stunning strikes. Two goals by Johnny Russell earned Derby a point at Bolton Wanderers, but Derby then lost at home for the third time of the season 3-1 to fifth-placed Reading. Leicester knocked Derby out of the League Cup at the King Power Stadium. The first East Midlands derby of the season was on the last Saturday of September at the City Ground. Billy Davies was seven months into his second spell as Nottingham Forest manager. A Jack Hobbs header just before half time gave Forest the lead. Richard Keogh was sent off for two bookable offences as Derby struggled to get back into the game and eventually lost 1-0. That evening it emerged that Nigel Clough, who was the fourth longest serving manager in the country, had been sacked by Sam Rush. I was surprised to be honest. Despite the three home defeats, I thought the performances were pretty good. Clough was very upset about it, claiming Rush hadn't understood the remit he had to cut the wage bill, reduce the squad numbers and maintain Championship status. The squad Clough had put together was now very much his own, with the recruitment team lead by his brother Simon. The man to replace Nigel Clough was Steve McClaren, who'd previously been England manager and first team coach under Jim Smith. McClaren appointed ex-players Paul Simpson and Eric Steele as his number two and goalkeeping coach, respectively.

The first game in the post-Nigel Clough era was at home to Ipswich Town, with Academy manager Darren Wassall put in charge, with Steve McClaren sat in the stands. Zak Whitbread joined Derby on loan from Leicester City and went straight into the side, replacing the suspended Richard Keogh. The game against Ipswich was one of the most astonishing Derby games I've been to. Derby suffered a massive hangover from the events of the previous few days. The Rams were 2-0 down in ten minutes, with some shambolic defending, before Whitbread pulled one back. Ipswich continued to press and added to their lead going in 4-1 at time. McClaren and Simpson went into the dressing room at half time, with Simpson apparently going ballistic. Mason Bennett came on to add some pace in the wide areas. Craig Bryson pulled one back at the start with of the second half with Jamie Ward making it 4-3 on the hour. Derby pressed and pressed for the equaliser and were rewarded with Bryson's second two minutes from time. It had been the most remarkable comeback.

Steve McClaren's first official game was the home game with Leeds United. Derby put on a superb display running out 3-1 winners. The following morning, I received some devasting news from Cath Disney, Paul's wife. She told me Paul had been diagnosed with a brain tumour. They had been on holiday in Greece but had to come home due to Paul's illness. This really affected me badly. I started suffering from anxiety, and having bad headaches myself. I couldn't concentrate at work and really was in a bad place. The only person who knew about it was Julie. I'm not sure whether Sarah picked up on it as well. Derby won their next match 3-2 in a great game at Watford, with a late Conor Sammon goal, who latched onto a great through ball from Will Hughes. Derby gave a debut to Simon Dawkins who was had joined on loan from Tottenham Hotspur. The Rams ended October with a 1-1 draw at home to Birmingham City, with Andre Wisdom on loan from Liverpool making his debut. Julie made her one and only visit to Pride Park, as we sat in the corner of the North and West Stand. Pre-match we went to The Harvester for a drink, and she enjoyed that more that the game. Derby were on the up and moved into eighth place, with nineteen points from thirteen games. Following the defeat at promotion chasing at Queen's Park Rangers at the start of November, Derby went on a tremendous run, starting with a 3-0 win against Sheffield Wednesday. Mali international Kalifa Cisse who joined the club as a free agent, made an impressive debut in place of the suspended John Eustace. Following the international break, On Friday 22 November, Julie and I travelled down to Heathrow for a two-week holiday in Thailand. I still wasn't feeling great at the time and was a bit daunted at the prospect of going, which was totally unlike me. On the way down to Heathrow we stopped at the services on the M40. I went to the toilet and to my surprise, I saw a lot of guys in purple tracksuits. It was the Derby players, who were travelling down to the weekend game at AFC Bournemouth. I wished Will Hughes good luck. I think he was surprised that I recognised him! We arrived at Heathrow for the evening flight. When we were in the queue to board the aeroplane, we received some terrible news. Our fourteen-year-old Yorkshire Terrier Joey, who Sarah was looking after, had died. He had been in poor health for a couple of years but we knew he was struggling, but this was devastating. I think all pet owners will understand!

We arrived in Bangkok after the twelve-hour flight and headed to our hotel from the airport. On the journey, all we could see was at the side of the road was billboards of footballers like John Terry and Wayne Rooney. We headed out into Bangkok and ended up at the Black Swan Pub. I couldn't quite get my head around the time difference but the Merseyside derby was on in the pub! We found out that a Jamie Ward goal had given Derby the three points at the Vitality Stadium. We spent a couple of nights in Bangkok, which in all honesty was a concrete jungle, but we had a lovely trip to see the floating markets and temples. The humidity at times was unbearable. After leaving Bangkok, we went to the stunning idyllic Phi Island for four nights via a flight to Krabi, a ferry to Phi and then a long tail boat to the other side of the island. It was like paradise. Derby didn't play until the following week. Manchester United Michael Keane joined Derby on a month's loan. We had moved on to Ao Nang when Derby won 3-1 away at Wigan Athletic, scoring three goals in the first half hour. I continued to struggle with anxiety and headaches, but I wasn't sure how I could get out of it. A last-minute goal from Conor Sammon, that barely crossed the line, saw Derby home against Middlesbrough. We arrived home for Derby's next game, that I watched live on Sky Sports, at home to Blackpool, with Pride Park now renamed as the iPro Stadium. Derby blew the Seasiders away, winning 5-1 with a Chris Martin hat-trick. Derby were playing their best football since the Jim Smith days. They surged up the table to fourth place, five points behind leaders Burnley. Two more wins followed before Christmas, 2-0 at Charlton Athletic and 3-1 at home to Doncaster Rovers. The winning run of seven games on the trot ended with a 1-1 draw at Huddersfield Town on Boxing Day, with Michael Keane making debut in place of the injured Richard Keogh. Derby were back to winning ways at Barnsley in the final game of the year, with Chris Martin scoring twice in the 2-1 win. Derby moved up to second place, four points behind leaders Leicester City. Some sad news that emerged was the death of Gerald Mortimer at the age of seventy-seven.

The New Year started with two home defeats. Wigan Athletic won 1-0 and Chelsea won 2-0 in the FA Cup third round, with John Obi Mikel and Oscar scoring the second half goals. Steve McClaren strengthened his squad with the on-loan arrival of Patrick Bamford from Chelsea, and Simon Dawkins made his move from Tottenham Hotspur permanent for a fee of £500,000. A third defeat followed, a heavy 4-1 loss at Leicester City. David Nugent, like John Aldridge previously, was the scourge of Derby, scoring twice. Derby though, went on another unbeaten run. Bamford scored in the 1-0 win at home to Brighton and Hove Albion and then again at Blackburn Rovers the following week, with a late equaliser in the 1-1 draw. The Rams signed Dutch goalkeeper Kelle Roos for £30,000 from Nuneaton Borough. At this time, I was starting to feel much better, but still had Paul and Cath very firmly in my thoughts. I had increased my running mileage and this was really helping. I decided to enter the Blackpool Marathon at the start of April. Derby came from 2-0 down at home to Yeovil Town, scoring twice in the last three minutes through Craig Bryson and Chris Martin, to win 3-2. I went to the next away game at Birmingham City with Gavin Chadwick. We sat behind the goal in the Gil Merrick End. After a scrappy first half with Craig Bryson missing a penalty, the game burst into life. Birmingham took the lead through Brian Howard, but Derby hit back with three quick goals through Patrick Bamford, Chris Martin and Craig Forsyth. Chris Burke pulled on back with twelve minutes to go with, Federico Macheda, on loan from Manchester United, scoring a last-minute equaliser. The unbeaten run continued, with John Eustace heading in a rare goal in the 1-0 win at home to Queen's Park

Rangers in a game shown live on Sky Sports. I went to the next away game at Hillsborough with Gavin Chadwick. Patrick Bamford scored a late winner at the Leppings Lane End, with a fantastic strike from the corner of the box. The following week, the final Saturday in February, I took part in the National Cross-Country Championships at Wollaton Park in Nottingham with Lee Griffiths, Joe Rees, Gavin Chadwick and Nick Chadwick, with 1650 people running the two laps of 10K distance. The course was tough, going with shin deep mud in places. Nick, who had only just started running, was lapped by Olympian Jonathan Brownlee, who finished in the top ten. Nick finished with a Jurgen Klinsmann style dive. What a great lad he is! I got back to the car and put the radio on. Derby were playing AFC Bournemouth at home. With ten minutes to go Derby were awarded a free kick on the edge of the box. I thought "Chris Martin, Chris Martin". Up he stepped and scored with fine effort. This was a vital win, with Derby now in third place, two points behind second place Burnley and ten points behind runaway leaders Leicester City. The win over AFC Bournemouth set up nicely Derby's trip to Burnley the following week the start of March. Ex-Ram David Jones gave Burnley the lead on the hour. The Rams suffered a major blow on half time as Chris Martin was sent off on half time for two bookable offences. Derby were right up against it when Dean Marney doubled the lead, as Derby's poor form against Burnley continued. This result was a massive blow for the Rams' automatic promotion hopes. Millwall won 1-0 at the iPro Stadium the following week, with Steve Morison scoring on the hour. Derby's scoring drought extended to four games following goalless draws at home to Bolton Wanderers and away to Reading, as the gap to Burnley extended to six points.

The following week fifth-placed Nottingham Forest visited the iPro Stadium. Derby gave a debut to George Thorne, who had joined on loan from West Bromwich Albion at the end of January but couldn't force his way into the side, due to the impressive form they had shown. Derby got off to a fantastic start in the usual electric atmosphere. Craig Bryson fired the Rams in front on six minutes and swept in his second on the half hour. Jeff Hendrick broke away to add the third before half time. The fans were in dreamland! Johnny Russell added the fourth with a fantastic rising left foot drive from the edge of the box. Craig Bryson completed his second hat-trick of the season from the spot, after Patrick Bamford was brought down by goalkeeper Karl Darlow. The result was too much for Forest owner Fawaz Al-Hasawi, who sacked Billy Davies two days later. Derby ended March with a 3-0 home win over Charlton Athletic, but were ten points behind second place Burnley, with seven games remaining. It was looking like Derby would have to settle for a place with the play-offs.

Immediately following the 1-0 defeat at Middlesbrough at the start of April, I travelled up to the north west to take part in the Blackpool Marathon. I went up on my own and stopped overnight in a B&B in Lytham St. Annes. The weather was quite calm by Blackpool standards, as I lined up for the run. Mentally I was fine now but I wouldn't wish that on anybody what I went through in the autumn and early winter. Nowadays most people open up about their problems, but I didn't, when in hindsight I should've done. My aim in the run was to finish in under 3.15, to guarantee me a good for age time to enter the London Marathon. My race plan went perfectly and I finished in 3.14.26. I finished in thirty-eighth place out of the 400 runners. Ironically, Derby were in Blackpool for their next game, two days after the run. Derby won 3-1, which was the start of five successive wins. Huddersfield Town were beaten 3-0 at the iPro. On Good Friday, the Rams won 2-0 at Doncaster Rovers in a game shown live on Sky Sports, with George Thorne scoring his first goal for the club, which conformed Derby's place in the play-offs. Two back-to-back home wins followed, 2-1 against Barnsley on Easter Monday, and 4-2 against Watford.

Derby finished in third place with meant they would play Brighton and Hove Albion in the play-off semi-final, with the first leg at the Amex Stadium. Brighton put Derby under a lot of early pressure and it was no surprise when Jesse Lingaard gave the Seagulls the lead on twenty minutes. Chris Martin levelled from the spot ten minutes later, after Craig Forsyth was brought down by Matthew Upson. On half-time, Chris Martin struck the bar with a fierce drive, which hit Tomasz Kuszczak on the back and the ball rolled into the net. Lee Grant made some fine saves in the second half, as Derby hung on to take a priceless lead back to the iPro Stadium. Derby were ninety minutes away from Wembley. Will Hughes replaced the injured Craig Bryson for the second leg and he put the Rams in front with a sublime back-heeled finish ten minutes before half time that calmed the crowd's nerves. Chris Martin doubled the lead ten minutes into the second half to increase the aggregate lead to 3-0. George Thorne's volley made it 3-0 twenty minutes later, with Jeff Hendrick putting the icing on the cake three minutes from time. Kazenga Lua Lua pulled one back, but Derby were on the way to Wembley.

The crowd were on the pitch, this team certainly had a different feel to the 2006/07 team. Derby would meet Queen's Park Rangers in the Championship play-off Final on Saturday 24th May.

I went to Wembley with Joe Rees and Nick Chadwick. We bought £76 tickets for the South Stand, towards the halfway line at the West Stand of the ground, with the managers opposite us. Joe was stopping in Hazelmere near Wycombe overnight at his in-laws so I picked him up. We drove to Beaconsfield train stain, parked the car got the train into London. We went for a couple of drinks near Wembley. We met Nick, who'd travelled down from Derby with his brother, Gavin. We got to our seats but were disappointed with the view, as we were sat under the overhang of the upper tier with no mention of that on the ticket. Steve McClaren's biggest decision was in midfield, on whether he would play Will Hughes or sixteen-goal Craig Bryson. McClaren opted for Hughes, following his display in the second leg of the Brighton game. The first half was quite cagey, with no real clear-cut chances at either end. Derby started to get the upper hand in the second half, but Richard Dunne was outstanding at the heart of the Rangers defence. The game changed on the hour, when Gary O'Neil was sent off by Lee Mason for bringing Johnny Russell down when he was clean through. Derby huffed and puffed but couldn't break through. In my opinion they strived too hard to win the game in normal time. They should have worn Rangers down in extra-time. This led to Bobby Zamora seizing on a Richard Keogh mistake, scoring a last-minute winner. What a cruel way to lose and it was an absolutely crushing blow. I couldn't get out of the ground quick enough, and back on the train to Beaconsfield, so I could then drive home. It had though been a brilliant season, with Derby playing some of the best football since the Jim Smith days. Could they go one better in 2014-15? In a major development, it was announced local business man Mel Morris bought a twenty-two percent stake of the club. Morris had been involved with the club back in 2006, as a Director under the Chairmanship of Peter Gadsby.

Four weeks after the play-off final, we had some great news, when our first grandson, Austen Harry, was born on Saturday 21 June. Julie and Sarah suggested to me that I have a fiftieth birthday party, as my birthday was three days after Austen's. I'd never really had done this before and was a bit reluctant but decided to go ahead with it. Julie said it would be a nice idea to invite my old school mates who I'd played with at Michigan Dynamo. All of the players had lost contact since the mid-90s when the club disbanded. Most of the players still lived in and around Derby, but a few had moved away, but still remained close enough to Derby. I managed to get hold of most of the lads and they all came, most of them with their partners. It was one of the best things that has happened. We're all back in contact and go out on a regular basis. It was also great that Paul Disney, although very poorly, came for an hour. Most of my other friends and family I've mentioned in this book came too, and it was a really good night.

2014/15

The biggest concern going into the new season was whether Derby would suffer a play-off defeat hangover, as quite of few other clubs have. The major signing of pre-season was George Thorne, in a £2 million deal from West Bromwich Albion, much to the delight of the fan base, as he had played a significant role in the run in to the end of the season and play-offs. Full-back Cyrus Christie signed from Coventry City on a three-year deal. Zak Whitbread signed a one-year deal, following his release from Leicester City. Two players arrived on loan, Omar Mascarrell from Real Madrid and Leon Best from Blackburn Rovers. Craig Bryson signed a new five-year-deal, after turning down the opportunity to join Premier League new boys Burnley. The departure list included James O'Connor to Walsall, Callum Ball to St. Mirren, Adam Lezdgins to Leyton Orient, James Bailey to Barnsley and Ben Davies to Sheffield United. Derby went on a pre-season tour of Austria and suffered a major setback. George Thorne, five days after he signed, suffered a torn cruciate ligament injury that would rule him out for up to nine months. This was a crushing blow for Thorne and the club.

I decided to have a season ticket in the South Stand with Gavin Chadwick and Joe Rees. Carl wanted to join us, but unfortunately, his weekend work commitments prevented this. Derby kicked off the season with a 1-0 win at home to Rotherham United, with Jeff Hendrick scoring the late winner and Omar Mascarrell coming on for his debut. On the Monday afternoon, I made the long drive up to Carlisle United, for my first ever visit to Brunton Park in the first round of the League Cup. The game was shown live on Sky Sports, as I sat with about another five hundred diehard Derby fans in the East Stand, towards the Petterill End open end terrace. Derby, although not at their best, won 2-0, with goals from Jeff

Hendrick and Chris Martin. Derby lost their first League game 3-2 away at Charlton Athletic, before beating a poor Fulham side 5-1, four of the goals coming in the second half. The following day, Julie and I went for a week's holiday in Dubrovnik, Croatia with Steve and Dawn Hallam. We had a great week in a beautiful city. Mentioning Derby County went down quite well with the barmen and waiters. They all knew about Derby with the Igor Stimac and Aljosa Asanovic connection, with Split only a couple of hours drive north of Dubrovnik. Whilst we were away, Derby beat Charlton Athletic in the League Cup and drew 1-1 at home to Ipswich Town. Much to Steve's delight, Stoke City won 1-0 away at Manchester City. Derby strengthened their squad with the two players on loan. Ryan Shotton arrived from Stoke City with a view to a permanent deal, and nineteen-year-old Jordan Ibe joined on a three-month loan from Liverpool. Shotton made an immediate impact, scoring the equaliser in the 1-1 draw at Nottingham Forest. Four players went out on loan; Conor Sammon to Ipswich Town, Mason Bennett to Bradford City, Mark O'Brien to Motherwell and Tom Naylor to Cambridge United.

In the midweek following the Forest game, I went to Blackburn Rovers with Howard Williams, a workmate of mine. We got to the game late, missing Richard Keogh's own goal that gave Rovers the lead. Derby produced a fantastic performance to win 3-2, despite a late onslaught from Rovers. The Rams beat Reading 2-0 in the League Cup third round, with Kelle Roos making his debut in goal. This was followed up by two 2-0 wins, away at Bolton Wanderers and at home to AFC Bournemouth. Derby ended September in fifth place in the table, only a point behind leaders Norwich City. Kieron Freeman joined Mansfield Town on a three-month loan. Following a goalless home draw against Millwall, Derby won 3-0 at Reading and 1-0 at Blackpool, with England under-21 goalkeeper Jack Butland making his debut following his loan move from Stoke City. Derby though lost 2-1 at home to Wigan Athletic, despite taking the lead through John Eustace. I missed this game, as Julie and I were away for the weekend in Suffolk. Derby progressed through to the fifth round of the League Cup, following a fine 5-2 win at Fulham, coming back from two goals down. Derby were really playing some great football, a joy to watch, with the goals distributed around the team. November began with a 2-1 defeat at Brentford, with Stuart Dallas scoring a last-minute winner. Two home wins followed, 3-2 against Huddersfield, and with Derby producing a five-star display against Wolverhampton Wanderers. Derby won 5-0, with Jeff Hendrick and Johnny Russell both scoring twice, a win that took Derby to the top of the League. Following the international break, we had the first Michigan Dynamo 'Old Boys' away day at Watford. We decided to do two away days a season at grounds where you could get a decent ticket allocation, as some of the lads didn't have season tickets. We travelled in a minibus, got there at midday, and went to the Southern Cross pub for a few pre-match beers and a bite to eat before walking down to the ground. We sat in the Vicarage Road Stand right at back in the corner, but with a great view. I'd been to Watford about three times, but the ground now at least looked like a football ground and not a speedway stadium. It was a fantastic game between two good sides. Jordan Ibe, who was having a great impact playing wide left, gave Derby the lead before half time with a fine strike from the corner of the box. Derby were on top and really should have been three up before Gianni Munari pulled one back. With ten minutes to go Craig Bryson, who had come on from the bench, struck an unstoppable right foot drive that we were right in line with, to give Derby a fine 2-1 win. The Rams ended November losing 2-0 at Leeds United, but were still League leaders. December started with a 3-0 win against Brighton and Hove Albion, but then put in a poor performance losing 2-0 at Middlesbrough, with ex-Ram loanee Patrick Bamford scoring Boro's opening goal. I watched this game in a pub in Chester on the Saturday lunchtime, as Julie and I were away for the weekend. Julie, for some reason, preferred to go around the Christmas market. To be honest, Derby were so poor that I should have done the same! Chelsea knocked Derby out the League Cup 3-1, with a massive gulf between the sides. Jake Buxton was sent off with the score at 2-1. In the final game before Christmas, Derby drew 2-2 at home to Norwich City. Derby visited a freezing and snowy St. Andrews on Boxing Day, and came away with a very comprehensive 4-0 win. The year ended with a 2-0 home win at home to Leeds United, with Derby third in the table, three points behind leaders Ipswich Town. Steve McClaren signed ex-England striker Darren Bent on loan from Aston Villa. Bent had been on loan at Brighton and Hove Albion and I thought this was an astute piece of business. Ryan Shotton turned his loan into a permanent deal. The FA Cup third round paired Derby at home to non-League Southport, who had lost their League status in 1978. It proved to be a real struggle and only a last-minute Chris Martin penalty saw the Rams progress. McClaren added two new faces to his squad, with the arrival of Stephen Warnock, and the much-heralded arrival of Raul Albentosa from Spanish side Eibar.

The following week, Derby travelled to Portman Road for the top of the table lunchtime clash with Ipswich Town shown live on Sky Sports. Chris Martin was again Derby's match winner in the 1-0 win, with John Eustace being sent off in the last minute. Prior to Nottingham Forest visiting the iPro Stadium, Liverpool manager Brendan Rodgers recalled Jordan Ibe from his loan. This was so frustrating, as Ibe was playing a major role in Derby's surge up the League. Forest, in the bottom half of the League, won 1-0, with a last-minute goal from Derby-born Ben Osborn. Derby were drawn against Derbyshire rivals Chesterfield in the fourth round of the FA Cup. It was the first time the sides had met since 1986. Steve McClaren adopted a 'back three' which looked like it needed further work on. In a carnival type atmosphere, Chesterfield, backed by a large travelling support, gave a good account of themselves, and I was impressed by Sam Morsy in their midfield. Darren Bent, who scored Derby's first goal, and Raul Albentosa both made their first starts, as the Rams progressed winning 2-0. On the last day of January, I made my first visit to the Cardiff City Stadium and sat with the away following in the Grange Stand corner, as Derby were pretty dominant and went in at half time winning 2-0, with no further goals in the second half. The win maintained Derby's position in the top two, level on points with AFC Bournemouth. Steve McClaren strengthened his squad further, with the loan signings of Tom Ince from Hull City and Jesse Lingaard from Manchester United. Ince made his debut in the next game at home to Bolton Wanderers and scored twice, as did Jeff Hendrick, as Derby ran out 4-1 winners. I watched the big top of the table clash away to AFC

Bournemouth on a beam back at the iPro Stadium. Derby twice came from behind to draw 2-2, with goals from Tom Ince and Darren Bent, but suffered an injury to key man Chris Martin, who limped off after fifteen minutes. Jesse Lingaard made his debut in the FA Cup fifth round tie at home to Reading. A late Yakubu goal for Reading knocked Derby out, but I wasn't too concerned as the League was the main priority.

I went to the next game, the midweek trip for Derby's first ever trip to Rotherham United's New York Stadium, with Gavin Chadwick and Joe Rees. We stopped for a pre-match pint on the outskirts of the town before parking up near the ground. It was a crazy evening, as we watched from the South Stand with the Main Stand to our left. Ex-Ram Paul Green gave the Millers the lead, with Tom Ince levelling a minute later with a fine strike. A bad mistake by Lee Grant, when he tried to punch clear a Richie Smallwood free kick, which flew straight in. Matt Derbyshire made it 3-1, as he pounced on errors by Omar Maskerell and Richard Keogh. Tom Ince pulled one back as Derby piled on the pressure. Darren Bent equalised with seven minutes to go with a neat finish to earn Derby a point. But it was a definitely a missed opportunity and two points lost. Two Jake Buxton goals helped Derby to a big 3-2 victory at home to Sheffield Wednesday. George Thorne made his return following his pre-season injury, lasting an hour, but he didn't look fit to me. This was followed up with a 2-0 victory over Charlton Athletic with two early goals, one a debut goal for Jesse Lingaard. I thought Derby were going to give Charlton a hiding but it never materialised. The win moved Derby three points clear at the top of the table. There were rumours since the turn of the year of Newcastle United interest in Steve

McClaren, but he never dismissed these rumours. The next Michigan Dynamo 'Old Boys' away day way the trip to Craven Cottage to meet Fulham. In my opinion, this is the best away trip in the country. We got there quite early and went to the Boathouse pub on Putney Bridge. We sat in the Putney End, but unfortunately, we were on the second row from the front, so had a poor view. Blame me as I bought the tickets! Derby, put in a really poor performance and lost 2-0. We had a great day apart from the watching the match! When we arrived back in Derby, a few of us met up with Martin Fisher, who we'd not seen for years, at the Brewery Tap. Like all the other lads, Martin is back in regular contact now.

Another defeat followed at Brighton and Hove Albion in the midweek, with the home side winning 2-0, with supporters starting to worry with two poor performances. Another crazy game followed when Birmingham City visited the iPro Stadium, with Derby 2-0 up and cruising. In the final minute Tom Ince gave the ball away out on the right, and brought the attacker down in the box, with Paul Caddis scoring the resultant penalty. Unbelievably, the Blues scored again deep into added on time, when Clayton Donaldson forced the ball home from corner. Talk about 'snatching defeat from the jaws of victory!" The crowd went home dumbstruck. With seven games to go Derby were in second place on goal difference to AFC Bournemouth, and a point ahead of Norwich City, who Derby were meeting at Carrow Road the following week. Steve McClaren sprung a surprise, giving a debut to Academy product defensive midfielder Jamie Hanson. Cameron Jerome fired the Canaries ahead on the half hour, with Hanson scoring direct from a corner following an error by John Ruddy to earn

Derby a point in a game in which it was important not to lose. Two more defeats followed, 1-0 at home to Middlesbrough. McClaren played Johnny Russell in the Chris Martin 'role' but it didn't bear fruit. This was followed with 2-0 defeat at Wolverhampton Wanderers. Supporters were questioning whether McClaren had a 'plan B' as an alternative to his preferred 4-3-3 system. After the defeat at Molineux, Derby went into the international break in sixth place, six points behind second place AFC Bournemouth, who had two games in hand.

On Good Friday evening, Derby were at home to Watford, with sixth position against fourth, for Derby, it was an absolute must win. There was a really electric atmosphere for the game that was shown live on Sky Sports. Matej Vydra gave the Hornets the lead halfway through the first half, but a Darren Bent penalty right on half time levelled the scores after Marco Motta was sent off for a foul on Johnny Russell. Tom Ince gave Derby the lead ten minutes in the second period. Against the odds, Odion Ighalo levelled with fifteen to go, so more heartbreak for the Rams as the game ended 2-2. Steve McClaren rung the changes for the away game on Easter Monday at Wigan Athletic. Richard Keogh moved to right-back, Craig Forsyth moved to centre-back and Stephen Warnock came in at left-back as McClaren tried to find the winning formula. Derby had a much needed, but unconvincing 2-0 win, with Chris Martin scoring on his return following two months out injured. Derby were unconvincing again in a 1-1 draw at home to Brentford, but followed that up with a 4-0 win at home to already relegated Blackpool. With three games to go Derby were in fifth place with seventy-five points, seven points behind second-placed Norwich City. Automatic promotion was now out of the question, it was all about qualifying for the play-offs. Derby then travelled to Huddersfield Town, with Chris Martin left out of the side as he still wasn't right since his return. Tom Ince gave Derby the lead on fifteen minutes, but the Terriers hit back, scoring three times in the seven minutes leading up to half time. Derby recovered and equalised through Simon Dawkins and Jesse Lingaard. Nakhi Wells restored the home side's lead before Tom Ince scored again to earn Derby a point with the game finishing 4-4. Yet another crazy game followed in the penultimate game at Millwall. Lee Gregory scored twice to give Millwall a two-goal lead, with Tom Ince pulling one back. Gregory completed his hat-trick from the spot, but a Chris Martin penalty and a spectacular Jeff Hendrick volley secured Derby an unlikely 3-3 draw. With one game to go, Derby needed a point from their final game of the season to reach the play-offs. Reading, who were in the bottom six, were the visitors. Derby, again playing with a back three with two wing-backs, fell behind in the second minute to a Kwesi Appiah goal following a catalogue of errors. Darren Bent had a penalty saved by Adam Federici, with boos ringing around the ground. Michael Hector doubled the lead, with the Derby players looking like they wanted the ground to open up beneath them. A Garath McCleary penalty made it 3-0. The Rams failed to make the play-offs. It had been the most astonishing run of games, probably the craziest in all my years watching the club. It's something I'll never quite understand how it happened. With twelve games to go, Derby were three points clear and finished eighth. Inexplicable, even by Derby standards!

CHAPTER 16

McCLAREN OUT, CLEMENT IN AND OUT AND WASSALL IN

2015/16

Three weeks after the Reading debacle, Mel Morris sacked Steve McClaren, who, not surprisingly, ended up as the new manager of Newcastle United. McClaren's replacement was Paul Clement, who had been assistant to Carlos Ancelotti. I'd never heard of Clement, who had made his name on the Chelsea coaching staff, and with Ancelotti at Paris St Germain, but he had never been a manager, which I thought was a bit risky. Clement got to work reshaping the squad. There were seven new arrivals. The major deals were Tom Ince, who made his loan from Hull City permanent for £4.75 million, Jason Shackell returned to the club from Burnley for £3 million, Andreas Weimann joined from Aston Villa for £2.75 million. Scott Carson arrived from Wigan Athletic for an undisclosed fee. I hate how 'undisclosed fees' are allowed and the fee should be made public, after all football is supposed to be entertainment industry and without supporters, the game is nothing. Three players arrived on free transfers, Chris Baird from West Bromwich Albion, Darren Bent from Aston Villa and Alex Pearce from Reading. The lengthy list of outgoing players included Shaun Barker, John Eustace, Tom Naylor, Mark O'Brien, Zak Whitbread and Jamie Ward. Kelle Roos, Raul Albentosa and Conor Sammon all went out on loan to Rotherham United, Malaga and Sheffield United respectively.

The Rams opened the season away with a goalless draw at Bolton Wanderers. It proved to be an eventful afternoon, as both Will Hughes and Craig Bryson suffered long term knee injuries to give Paul Clement a major headache. Derby were knocked out of the first round of the League Cup at Portsmouth. On the evening of the Portsmouth game, Julie and I travelled to Birmingham to stop overnight before an early morning flight to Venice, to pick up a Mediterranean cruise ship. Derby were playing at home to Charlton Athletic on the Saturday. I had left my phone charger in the Birmingham hotel the night before the flight, so I had no phone to find out Derby's score! We got to Mykonos on the cruise, I managed to find an English newspaper with the Derby score, and more importantly, a charger for my iPhone. What a relief! The cruise was fantastic, as we took in Athens, Kusadasi in Turkey, Istanbul, Pisa, Rome, the Amalfi coast, St.Tropez and Barcelona. Derby then recorded two further draws 1-1, home to Middlesbrough and away at Birmingham City, whilst we were away.

The first game of the season I went to was the last game in August against Leeds United at the iPro. The winless start to the season continued, with the visitors winning 2-1, with a tremendous Chris Wood strike two minutes from time. My first impression of the Paul Clement style of football was a bit 'pedestrian'. On the last day of the transfer window, Derby announced two major signings. Bradley Johnson arrived from

Norwich City for £6 million and Jacob Butterfield from Huddersfield Town for £4 million, as replacements for the injured Hughes and Bryson, respectively. In an interview discussing his move, Johnson called the club Derby City! Derby were finally off to winning ways after the international break, with away wins at Preston North End and Reading. Bradley Johnson and Jacob Butterfield made their debuts at Deepdale, as two fine Chris Martin goals saw the Rams home to victory. In my opinion, his first goal was the best of his Derby career, as he deftly controlled a fine forty-yard ball by Johnny Russell before coolly finishing past Jordan Pickford. His second was an edge of box free kick which arrowed past Pickford. A second half Tom Ince goal gave Derby the edge at Reading. At the end of September, I made my first visit to Stadium MK for the game with MK Dons, with Howard Williams and John Wayne, another work mate. Stadium MK was very impressive, but far too big for a club with MK Dons meagre fan base. We sat in the North Stand with the vast following support for the lunchtime kick-off, with the game being shown live on Sky Sports. The Rams didn't play very well in all honesty. Only two late goals by Tom Ince and Darren Bent gave Derby victory, as they ended September up to eighth in the table, with fourteen points from nine games after their slow start to the season.

October carried on where September left off, as the Rams won four and drew one of their five League games. The standout performance came in a 4-2 win at home to Wolverhampton Wanderers, with Chris Martin again in fine form, scoring twice. The other wins were 2-0 at home to Brentford, 2-1 at Huddersfield Town and 2-1 at home to Rotherham United. The trip to Huddersfield was the first Michigan Dynamo 'Old

Boys' away day of the season. As usual, Mark Jarrett ensured we got there early. We spent most of the time pre-match in the Cherry Tree Pub in the town centre before the short walk to the ground. We sat in the sold out away end. It was a fine performance by Derby, who won 2-1, with George Thorne scoring a stunning second half volley that secured the three points. As a bonus when we left the ground, pies and sausage rolls were being sold off for a £1 each, so happy days! Derby suffered a major injury in their home 1-0 win against Queen's Park Rangers, when Craig Forsyth suffered anterior cruciate knee ligament damage. The first East Midlands derby at the start of November was held at the City Ground, with Derby cock-a-hoop following their unbeaten run since the end of August. Nottingham Forest were struggling in the bottom half of the League table. But as people say, form goes out of the window on derby day and it did on this occasion, with Nelson Oliveira's early strike giving the Reds a 1-0 victory. Derby though put this behind them and went on another unbeaten run until the end of the year. They recorded five wins and three draws in eight games, including a fine Friday night 2-0 win at leaders Hull City, shown live on Sky Sports, with Jacob Butterfield scoring twice. The other wins were 2-0 at home to Cardiff City, a 4-0 win at home to Bristol City in which Tom Ince scored a hat-trick, and he also scored the only goal at Ipswich Town. Julie and I were away in Birmingham during the Ipswich match for her birthday weekend, again taking in a Christmas market! The Rams beat Fulham on Boxing Day at the iPro, with Jacob Butterfield scoring again. Derby ended the year in second place a point behind leaders Middlesbrough. Paul Clement had certainly banished the memories of the previous season with a great first half of the season.

It was up to Middlesbrough for the first game of the New Year, for the clash of the top two. Just when it looked like Derby were going to escape with a goalless draw, Albert Adomah and George Friend scored within a minute, with seven minutes left. The Riverside Stadium has always been a bit of a graveyard for Derby, their only win there was on my only visit in 2000. Paul Clement signed two players, completing his January transfer business early in the month. Striker Nick Blackman signed from Reading for £2.5 million, and Guinean winger Abduol Camara joined from French club Angers for £1.5 million. Both players started when it was back up to the North East the following week for the FA Cup third round, at Hartlepool United. Derby fell behind, but goals from Jacob Butterfield and Darren Bent eased Derby through to round four. Paul Clement was publicly very critical of the team, following the midweek home 1-1 draw with Reading. I thought he was very harsh, especially as they were still sitting second in the League, even though they had played poorly. Another poor performance followed when Birmingham City won 3-0 at the iPro. My thoughts turned back to the previous season, was history about to repeat itself? Derby then lost 4-1 at Burnley, yet another side they couldn't seem to handle, as the wheels looked like they had truly come off again. Derby slipped down to fifth in the table. With Craig Forsyth injured, Clement signed Blackburn Rovers left-back Marcus Olsson for an undisclosed fee. Derby didn't fare much better in the FA Cup when Manchester United came to town. Wayne Rooney scored United's opener as they went on to record a comfortable 3-1 win. Derby then drew 0-0 at Preston North End and 1-1 at Fulham, with Craig Bryson scoring on his first start after returning from injury. Mel Morris pulled the trigger and sacked Paul Clement. Whether he panicked and didn't want a repeat of the previous season or whether he was concerned by the drop in quality of the performances and results, I don't know the reason for Clement's departure. Not many managers get sacked when they're fifth in the table. To the surprise of the fan base, Mel Morris appointed Academy Manager Darren Wassall as manager until the end of the season. It didn't start well for Wassall, as he lost his first game in charge 1-0 against MK Dons on their first ever visit to Derby for a competitive game. Derby had their first win since Boxing Day, when they played the next game away at Brentford. Three goals in the last ten minutes from Jeff Hendrick, Cyrus Christie and Chris Martin gave the Rams a much-needed win. A 1-0 win at home to Blackburn Rovers boosted confidence further, but they ended February losing 2-1 at Wolverhampton Wanderers to a late George Saville goal. Derby were fifth in the table, eight points adrift of leaders Middlesbrough.

For the second successive season, Derby were involved in an astonishing game at relegation-threatened Rotherham United. After a goalless first half, Derby scored three goals in ten minutes with Tom Ince scoring twice. With fifteen minutes to go, Darren Wassall replaced George Thorne and Chris Martin with Nick Blackman and Darren Bent respectively. Rotherham came back to score three times in the last seven minutes, with ex-Ram loanee Leon Best scoring twice. Best failed to score in his fifteen appearances for the Rams. Wassall received a lot of flak from the supporters for his substitutions but I don't buy that. In all my years playing or watching football, I've never known a team to lose a three-goal lead in the final seven minutes. The previous evening I'd gone out to the Balti International Indian restaurant, with Gavin Chadwick, Nick Chadwick, Dave Thompson, Joe Rees and Lee Griffiths. We had a great evening, which was made even better with us bumping into Roy McFarland. He posed for a photograph with us, which rounded off the evening nicely. Derby recovered the following week when they beat Nottingham Forest 1-0 at the iPro in a Sunday lunchtime game shown live on Sky Sports, with Marcus Olsson the hero, sweeping in a right foot from the inside left position. April began with Derby losing 2-1 at Cardiff City. Derby then won four games on the bounce. Fellow promotion chasers Hull City were beaten 4-0, as the Rams produced a fine performance. Derby also scored four at home to bottom-of-the-table Bolton Wanderers, with Will Hughes returning from his long injury lay off. Two good away wins followed 1-0 at Charlton Athletic and 3-2 at Bristol City. The Charlton game was a Michigan Dynamo 'Old Boys' away day. Unfortunately, I missed the game with a chest infection which also cost me my place in the London Marathon following my good for age time at Blackpool, although I could defer my place until the following year. Also missing from the Charlton away day was Dave Mortimer affectionally known as 'Mort'. Mort was on his way to meet the lads in Derby to pick up the minibus when his car got stuck in a ford. The lads also missed a treat, as Mort promised to bear his arse in Charlton Market Place (if it actually exists) in response to Leicester City winning the Premier League, as Mort thought it would never happen. Mort is a great lad, loves his football, cricket, horse racing, live music etc. He's also renowned for late night rants on our WhatsApp group after he's had a bottle of red or two or three! The lads also went to The Yacht pub in Greenwich, but apparently, they didn't have any beer! The four wins concreted Derby's place in the top six, now requiring just two points from three games to confirm their play-off play. Derby achieved the points they required in next two games, with a 1-1 draw at home to Sheffield Wednesday, and 1-1 away at automatic promotion chasing Brighton and Hove Albion. In the final game of the season, Derby played Ipswich Town which was effectively a dead rubber. Ipswich were winning 1-0 with ten minutes to go when George Thorne suffered an horrendous double fracture of his right leg following a collision with Jonathan Douglas. It was a really serious blow to their play-off hopes.

Derby played Hull City in the first leg on the play-off semi-final at the iPro stadium. It turned out to be an absolute disaster. Abel Hernandez gave the Tigers the lead on the half hour. A Moses Odubajo shot was deflected in by Jason Shackell to double their lead five minutes before the break. Andy Robertson made it three in the last minute as the ground quickly emptied. It had been a woeful performance by the Rams, and they had the preverbal mountain to climb now. Not only a mountain, but Everest! In the second leg at the KC Stadium, three days later, Derby were desperate for an early goal to unsettle Hull. Johnny Russell obliged when he stabbed home from close range on seven minutes, following a great run and cross from Cyrus Christie. Derby were right back in it when Andy Robertson put through his own goal from Marcus Ollsonn's cross, with the game was following a similar trend to the first leg. Craig Bryson missed a gilt-edged chance late on as Derby piled on the pressure. The damage had been done in the first game, with Robertson's late goal proving crucial. It was to be another season in the Championship for the Rams.

CHAPTER 17

FOUR MANAGERS IN ONE SEASON

2016/17

To fair to Darren Wassall, his record was quite good after being thrown into the deep end following Paul Clement's departure. But he was never going to be the long-term appointment. Ten days after the Hull City play-off defeat, Nigel Pearson was the man chosen by Mel Morris to move the club forward. The majority of the fan base were delighted with the appointment, following the fine job Pearson did in two spells at Leicester City and at Hull City. There were no incoming players during the pre-season, but Stephen Warnock was released, Raul Albentosa joined Deportivo La Coruna and Jake Buxton joined Wigan Athletic.

The day before the season, started Julie and I went with Steve and Dawn Hallam to Belfast for a long weekend. After we flew into the George Best International Airport, we spent the afternoon at the impressive Titanic Museum. On the Saturday it was a bus trip up to the Giant's Causeway and a walk across the Carrick-A-Reed rope bridge, before travelling back down the Antrim coast to Belfast. That afternoon, Derby were at home to Brighton and Hove Albion in their opening game of the season. I was quite surprised with Nigel Pearson's team selection with Chris Martin, Johnny Russell and Will Hughes on the bench with Nick Blackman, Darren Bent and Bradley Johnson starting. The game finished goalless; with the reports I heard that the performance was disjointed. The following day in Belfast, we spent the morning in a black cab, touring the Unionist Shankill Road and the Falls Road in the Republican area, with the stunning murals and the giant peace wall separating the two areas. We spent the afternoon at Downpatrick races, before heading home the following day.

Derby progressed to the second round of the League Cup with a 1-0 win over Grimsby Town. I went to the first away game of the season with Mark Jarrett, Nigel Lee, Matt Lee and Dave Hudson to Barnsley. We went to the Joseph Bramah pub in Barnsley town centre for pre-match beers before walking to Oakwell. Derby were extremely poor and deservedly lost 2-0. Nigel Pearson got a bit of verbal abuse from some of the fans as he left the pitch at the end of the game. Derby recorded their first win of the season with a late Craig Forsyth goal at Preston North End. James Wilson joined the Rams on a six-month loan from Manchester United. Derby progressed to the third round on the League Cup following a remarkable 14-13 win on penalties against Carlisle United. Derby made their first ever visit to the Pirelli Stadium for a competitive game on the Friday night of the August Bank Holiday weekend, for the game against Nigel Clough's Burton Albion, which was shown live on Sky Sports. Derby's poor run continued as they suffered an embarrassing defeat to a Jackson Irvine first half header. The following day, Pearson signed Matej Vydra from Watford for a club record £8 million. On the final day of the transfer window, Jeff Hendrick joined Burnley for a club record £10.5 million. There were two more incomings, with Ikechi Anya also arriving from Watford for £4 million, and goalkeeper Chris Weale, on a free transfer from Yeovil Town. Three players left on loan; Kelle Roos to Bristol Rovers on a five-month loan, Lee Grant on a similar arrangement to Stoke City, and most surprisingly, Chris Martin on a season long loan to Fulham. Two more League defeats followed, 2-0 at home to pre-season promotion favourites Newcastle United and 1-0 at home to Ipswich Town. It was a really unexpected and worrying start to the season, as Derby slipped to fourth-from-bottom in the table.

The following Saturday was the Michigan Dynamo 'Old Boys' first away day of the season. As usual, Mark Jarrett had us on the minibus early for the trip down the M5 to Bristol City on a warm, sunny mid-September Saturday. We spent pre-match in the Mardyke pub and then onto the Grain Barge pub on the harbour-side. Bristol is one of the finest cities in England, and they've made a fantastic job of developing the harbour-side area. We walked to the ground, passing the imposing Clifton suspension bridge. We sat in the Ateyo Stand with the impressive new Lansdown Stand to our right, but the top tier wasn't yet open. I'd been to Ashton Gate a couple of times but couldn't get my bearings, as I'd stood on the open terrace, but I wasn't sure which end that was now. Ikechi Anya scored his first goal for the club right on half time, to give Derby the lead as he lobbed the keeper. Matej Vydra missed a golden chance in the dying moments before Aaron Wilbraham levelled for City. Liverpool visited the iPro for the next round of the League Cup and totally dominated the game. The gulf in class between the sides was massive, as the Reds easily won 3-0 with goals from Ragnar Klavan, Phillipe Courtinho and Divock Origi. Derby ended September with another defeat at home to Blackburn Rovers. Ex-Ram Danny Graham grabbed the winning goal for Rovers. The League table wasn't good reading for Derby, who were still fourth-from-bottom.

On the day of the Cardiff City game with Nigel Pearson with the side in the Welsh capital, Mel Morris decided to suspend him, pending an internal investigation. Michigan Dynamo 'Old Boy' Gary Parkin, who worked for Derby County, had the dubious pleasure of having to go and pick Pearson up and bring him back to Derby. Morris put Chris Powell in caretaker charge. Powell started with a 2-0 win at Cardiff, with Academy product Max Lowe making his debut at left-back. Tom Ince and Nick Blackman, from the spot, were Derby's scorers. Powell was in charge for the next game, which ended in 1-1 draw at Reading before Morris sacked Pearson after only ten games in charge. Steve McClaren was re-appointed as manager, seven months after being sacked by Newcastle United. McClaren won his first game back, 1-0 at home to Leeds United with a Johnny Russell goal resulting in their first home win of the season. Julie and I travelled up to Manchester to catch a flight to Cuba for our two-week holiday. Derby lost at Huddersfield Town on our first day there. I made sure my phone was fully charged, and I had a spare charger! We really enjoyed Cuba, the lovely white sands and warm climate. We met Al and Jackie Green from Birmingham, and Sanju and Atul Patel from Wolverhampton, and spent most nights with them, and we met up when we arrived home. I think we were the only six from England in the hotel. We had an overnight trip to Havana. It's one of the great cities in the world, a fascinating place, but the buildings are crumbling. It's full of colour, vibrant with music playing from every street corner, with some great old cars, but you can chew the petrol fumes! Derby beat Sheffield Wednesday 2-0 at home, which was the start on seven League wins on the bounce.

We arrived home at the start of November. Derby were playing at Wolverhampton Wanderers at Molineux in a Saturday lunchtime kick-off, with the match yet again shown live on Sky Sports. The Rams won 3-2 with a stunning volley from Darren Bent as he latched on to a pass from Will Hughes, as the McClaren magic was beginning to work. Two home wins, 3-0 against Norwich City and 1-0 at home to Rotherham United, were followed by a 1-0 win away at Wigan Athletic. Derby produced a fine performance at home to Nottingham Forest, again live on Sky Sports, with Tom Ince scoring the second with a top finish following a sublime through ball that split the back four from Chris Baird. The seventh win came with Ince scoring again, four minutes from time at Queen's Park Rangers. In the three games up to the end of the year Derby drew 2-2 at Fulham, beat Birmingham City 1-0 at home and drew 0-0 at home to Wigan Athletic, extending the unbeaten run to ten games. Derby were just outside the play-offs in seventh place, a point behind Sheffield Wednesday in sixth. The New Year started with a 3-0 defeat at Norwich City, as the unbeaten run came to a crushing end. Lee Grant made his move to Stoke City permanent in a £1.3 million deal. Steve McClaren signed the relatively unknown Julian De Sart, on loan until the end of the season, from Middlesbrough. The FA Cup third round paired Derby with a trip to Premier League

West Bromwich Albion. Goals from Darren Bent and Tom Ince saw Derby come from behind to win 2-1, and through to the next round. McClaren strengthened Derby's squad further with the arrival of experienced striker David Nugent from Middlesbrough for a reported £2.5 million. Nugent, like John Aldridge, always seemed to score every time he played against the Rams. Chris Martin, who was at loan at Fulham, signed a new deal at Derby as McClaren urgently wanted him back. Martin angered Fulham manager Slavisa Jokanovic by refusing to play for them, but Fulham wouldn't let him return to Derby until his loan deal expired. What a mess this situation was!

Derby lost 1-0 at Leeds United and beat Reading 3-2, before meeting Leicester City at the iPro in the FA Cup fourth round shown live on Sky Sports on the Friday night. Derby gave a good account of themselves and were four minutes away from victory when Wes Morgan equalised for the Foxes with the game ending 2-2. Derby ended January with a fine 3-0 victory at Ipswich Town, as Derby moved into the top six. Derby lost 1-0 at leaders Newcastle United, and were then knocked out of the FA Cup in the replay 3-1 at Leicester City, with the game again live on Sky Sports. I then went down with another chest infection, with the London Marathon looming at the end of April. I was quite concerned, as they normally stop me running for six to eight weeks. Derby came back from three goals down to draw 3-3 at home to Bristol City. I was hoping this wasn't a start of the return to the crazy games at the back end of the 2014/15 season. My fears were confirmed with Cardiff City winning 4-3 at the iPro in the next game, with Joe Ralls' last minute penalty! Burton Albion made their first ever visit for a competitive game at Derby. They 'parked the bus', aiming for a draw, and succeeded with the game ending goalless. Derby ended February with two 1-0 defeats at Aston Villa and Blackburn Rovers. It had been a poor month, and Derby slipped to eleventh in the table, ten points away from the play-offs. March started better with a 2-1 home win over Barnsley and a 1-1 home draw with Preston North End. Derby then travelled to second in the table Brighton and Hove Albion for a Friday night fixture, again live on Sky Sports. Derby were ripped apart and lost 3-0 in a very poor performance. It was too much for Mel Morris, who sacked Steve McClaren two days later. I felt it was a strange decision. Stability was required, along with a bit of a rebuild in the summer. Derby were searching for their fourth manager of the season. That man was former player Gary Rowett, who had recently been sacked from Birmingham City. Rowett's first game in charge was a baptism of fire, a trip to the City Ground for the East Midlands derby. Derby drew 2-2, with Dani Pinnillos earning Forest a draw with a last-minute leveller. Derby then re-ignited their slim play-off hopes with three wins in a row, with home wins against Queen's Park Rangers and Fulham. This was followed with a 2-1 away win at Birmingham City, with Tom Ince's last minute winner. Derby, going into Easter, were eighth in the table, seven points shy of the play-offs with five games remaining. The Good Friday 4-0 defeat though, at Brentford, put an end to their play-off hopes after Derby put in an inept performance.

On Saturday 22 April, I travelled to London by train for the marathon weekend with Joe Rees. Julie came too, with Joe's mum and auntie. I'd had a real battle to get fit as the chest infection I had in February ruled me out of running for four weeks. I started training steadily on 6 March and gradually built my mileage up during the month, so I could run the Oakley 20 in Bedford, albeit slowly, on 2 April, just three weeks before the Marathon. Normally, I like to run three twenty mile runs before a marathon but I was running out of time – apologies for the pun! We stopped at the Citadines Barbican in Islington on the Saturday night, fuelling up with pasta before heading by train to the start in the morning. Joe and I were on different start lines. He was at Greenwich and I was at Maze Hill. Derby had lost 2-1 at Sheffield Wednesday on the day before. I bumped into BBC newsreader Sophie Raworth on the walk up to the start, and we had a nice chat and wished each other well. The run went very well, considering my lack of training. I had promised Julie this would be my last ever marathon as I was now fifty-two and this would be by my fifth London Marathon, so an apt place to finish. The London Marathon in my opinion is the greatest sporting event in the world. The constant din from the thousands in the crowd spurring the runners on from start to finish is deafening, creating a real party atmosphere. There's music playing everywhere and plenty of beer being drunk! I feel very privileged to have been involved in such an iconic event and have some great memories. It was quite emotional running down the Mall towards the finish, thinking about my mum and dad, with tears in my eyes, thinking of all the support they'd given me when I was running. I finished in 3.22. I was over the moon with that time, considering my lack of preparation. I went for a beer, bumping into Ben Hall, a fellow runner from work, in a pub near the finish. Joe came in at over four hours, and he met us with the girls at the pub. I was a bit surprised as I thought he would do better than that, but he said he wasn't feeling too good. To his credit, he ran the White Peak Marathon a few weeks later in 3.34, so fair play to him, as he's a very decent runner. We had another pint at St. Pancras before heading home. Derby only won one of their last four games of the season, finishing ninth in the table. I was a bit disturbed about Mel Morris' hire and fire policy.

2017/18

Gary Rowett made a big decision ahead of the season by selling both Tom Ince and Will Hughes. Ince moved to Premier League new boys Huddersfield Town for a reported record £11 million. Hughes moved south to Watford for a reported £8 million. After he burst onto the scene, it appeared Hughes was likely to end up at the likes of Liverpool. Although technically very gifted, I don't think he scores enough goals and he can't really drive a ball. Don't get me wrong, he's an excellent player who I'd have back at Derby anytime. Cyrus Christie also left to join Middlesbrough for £2.5 million. Abdoul Camara was also released. Rowett started to change his squad with the acquisition of Andre Wisdom in a £2 million deal from Liverpool, and experienced Hull City duo; Curtis Davies, for £500,000, and Tom Huddlestone for £2 million, who was back for his second spell at the club. Chris Martin returned from his loan spell at Fulham. Nick Blackman joined Israeli side Maccabi Tel Aviv on a season long loan.

Derby began the season with a 1-1 draw at Sunderland on the Friday night, after Bradley Johnson had given them an early lead. I was watching Derbyshire in the Twenty20 cricket at the

County Ground, and so didn't really follow the events at the Stadium of Light. The League Cup first round tie at Grimsby Town was abandoned after twenty minutes due to heavy rain, with the Rams leading 1-0. Derby eventually won the re-arranged game, with Matej Vydra's penalty the only goal. Derby's first home game was at home to Wolverhampton Wanderers, the away team's first season under new head coach Nuno Espírito Santo. Their intent was obvious, with the arrival of £15.8 million Ruben Neves from Porto. Wolves totally outplayed Derby and ran out 2-0 winners. Derby's first win was 1-0 at home to Preston North End, with a Matej Vydra penalty. The Rams followed this up with a 2-1 win at Bolton Wanderers, with striker Tom Lawrence making his debut from the bench following his £5 million move from Leicester City. On the last Saturday in August, I went to Sheffield United on the train with Mark Jarrett, Nigel Lee, Matt Lee, Gary Parkin, Bill Brown and Nick Stocks. Gavin Chadwick joined us later in the Sheaf Island pub. Derby put in a very worrying performance and lost 3-1. United took the lead through Billy Sharp after a poor Scott Carson clearance. Johnny Russell put through his own net to double the lead five minutes before half time. Craig Bryson pulled one back in the final minute, but Derby then conceded again, with Billy Sharp bagging his second. Derby signed Sheffield Wednesday striker Sam Winnall on a season long loan, with Jacob Butterfield moving the opposite way. Fans favourite Craig Bryson also left on a season's long loan joining Neil Warnock at Cardiff City.

Julie and I then went to Crete for a ten-day break to the resort of Agios Nikolaos. We met up with Colin Newcombe, an ex-workmate of mine, and his wife, Pat, who were staying nearby. He saw my Facebook post and we had a few beers and a catch up. Colin, known as captain due his time in the navy, is a lovely chap and looks very well for seventy-three. He's a Derby fan, but has given up on going nowadays. We travelled back on the Friday night that Derby were playing Hull City at home. Derby put in a fine performance by all accounts and won 5-0, which took them to fifth in the table, with ten points from six games. Derby lost 3-2 at Barnsley in the League Cup second round, with Academy product Max Bird making his debut. George Thorne made his first start since he suffered his double leg fracture in May 2016. Derby took the lead at Bristol City in the next game with a first half Matej Vydra penalty, but collapsed in the second half, conceding four goals. Gary Rowett signed the experienced Joe Ledley following his release from Crystal Palace. The Rams then went on a seven-game unbeaten run, with three successive draws and four successive wins. The draws were 1-1 at home to Birmingham City, 1-1 at Brentford and 0-0 at Cardiff City. Matej Vydra gave Derby a first minute lead in the live Sky Sports home game at home to Nottingham Forest, which David Nugent doubled. Sheffield Wednesday lost 2-0 at the iPro, with Vydra continuing his good run of scoring with an early penalty after Glenn Loovens was sent off. Two fine away wins followed, as Sam Winnall scored late goals in 2-1 wins at Norwich City and Leeds United. Scott Carson was having a fine season in goal, with many Rams fans calling for him to be on the plane for the Russia World Cup. The Rams ended October in fifth place, with twenty-six points from fifteen games, six points behind leaders Wolverhampton Wanderers.

The unbeaten run came to an abrupt halt on the first Saturday in November, with Reading winning 4-2 at the iPro. Derby were outplayed in the first half the following week in the live Sky Sports TV game at Fulham, going in at half-time 1-0, but performed better in the second half, earning a point through Matej Vydra. Derby recorded their first win at the Riverside Stadium for seventeen years, beating Middlesbrough 3-0 with Vydra, who was becoming a goal machine, scoring a hat-trick. Derby hoping to build on this, lost the next game 1-0 to Ipswich Town. The Rams ended November in sixth place, with thirty-three points from twenty games. December was a really good month for Derby. Burton Albion lost at the iPro to a late Johnny Russell goal. We had a Michigan Dynamo 'Old Boys' Christmas jumper away day at a freezing cold Barnsley. We spent pre-match in the Joseph Bramah pub again, before Mark Jarrett insisted that we go for the customary pre-match fish and chips before heading to Oakwell. Derby put in a commanding performance, winning 3-0. In the run up to Christmas, the Rams beat fellow play-off hopefuls Aston Villa 2-0, and Millwall 3-0 a week later, with David Nugent scoring twice. The Boxing Day visit to Hull City was a scrappy, goalless draw. The year ended with a 2-1 victory at Ipswich Town, with Sam Winnall, who was having a big impact, scoring the winning goal with a fine twenty-five-yard drive into the top corner. The League table was looking good, with Derby up to second, nine points behind leaders Wolverhampton Wanderers.

On New Year's Day, Derby drew 1-1 at home to Sheffield United. The FA Cup, which was a distraction Derby didn't want, ended in a 2-0 defeat at Old Trafford, with two late Manchester United goals. Back to League matters, the Rams won 3-0 at Birmingham City. Gary Rowett signed experienced striker Cameron Jerome, for £1.5 million from Norwich City on an eighteen-month deal. The win at Birmingham was followed by two goalless home draws with Bristol City and Millwall. Before the end of the January transfer window, Kasey Palmer joined on loan from Chelsea, until the end of the season. Five players left the Rams on loans until the end of the season. Chris Martin joined Reading, Jason Shackell joined Millwall, Darren Bent joined Burton Albion, Mason Bennett joined Notts County, and Max Lowe joined Shrewsbury Town.

Cameron Jerome scored his first Derby goal in the 3-0 win at home to Brentford at the start of February. Lucas Joao scored twice as Derby lost 2-0 at Sheffield Wednesday. The next Michigan Dynamo 'Old Boys' away day was the trip to Reading at the end of February, just before the country experienced freezing conditions with the 'beast from the east'. As usual, we arrived early on the minibus and spent pre-match in the Worlds End pub on the outskirts of Reading. The game was poor, even though it finished 3-3, with Kasey Palmer scoring his first goal for the club, as Derby slipped to fourth in the table, three points behind second place Cardiff City.

The Rams lost 2-1 at home in a six-pointer against promotion chasing Fulham, who in my opinion were the best side in the League with Wolverhampton Wanderers. Aleksandar Mitrovic gave Fulham the lead, with Ryan Sessegnon doubling the lead. Tom Huddlestone pulled one back, but the Cottagers, with a midfield of Tom Cairney, Kevin McDonald and Stefan Johansen proved far too strong for the Rams. Derby drew their next two away games ahead of the Easter fixtures, 1-1 at Queen's Park Rangers and 0-0 at Nottingham Forest, as they slipped further away from the top two. The next game at home to promotion chasing Cardiff City was postponed due to 'snow', with Neil Warnock fuming about the decision as there was hardly any snow around the ground. Derby were suffering from injuries and suspensions. I think Warnock had a fair point! On Good Friday, which was the last day in March, Julie and I travelled with Sarah and Austen to Dave Thompson's apartment in La Mata near Torrevieja, for a week's holiday, which was Austen's first flight. We left East Midlands Airport in the cold and rain. Derby were playing relegation threatened Sunderland at the iPro in an evening kick-off. When we arrived at Alicante airport, I found out Derby were 1-0 down at halfway through the first half. I thought to myself, surely Derby can come back and win this. We arrived at Dave's place following the forty-five-minute journey from the airport. I was stunned to find out Derby had been beaten 4-1. The defeat left Derby in fifth place, with seven games remaining. I watched the Easter Monday fixture at a cold, wet and windy Preston North End in tee shirt and shorts, in a lovely twenty-four degrees at the Irish pub Shannon in La Mata. Tom Lawrence's goal gave Derby much needed win. Derby beat Bolton Wanderers 3-0, before facing a daunting trip to runaway leaders Wolverhampton Wanderers. Wolves won 2-0, with Gary Rowett adopting a negative damage limitation approach. Wolves, in my opinion, were arguably the best Championship outfit I've witnessed.

Derby's next game was at the Pirelli Stadium, Burton. Fortunately for me, a friend of mine at work, John Mountford, was renting a house from a Derby County employee, so he managed to get hold of a couple tickets for me. Paul Cannon came with me. We had a beer in the Mill House pub before strolling along the canal to the ground. We sat in the away seating in the Main Stand, with the main bulk of Rams fans on the East Stand covered terrace to our right. Derby's performance, to put it mildly, was shambolic. Liam Boyce gave the Brewers the lead midway through the first half, with David Nugent levelling five minutes later. Luke Murphy put Burton ahead right on half time, with Lucas Akins adding a third with twenty minutes left. It was embarrassing, but to be fair to Nigel Clough, his side played well in their quest to avoid relegation. There was a nice touch at the end when Clough brought on Shaun Barker for the last minute, four years since he injured his knee playing for Derby. Middlesbrough, also in the play-off shake up, won 2-1 at the iPro, making it three defeats on the bounce. The next game against Cardiff City, live on Sky Sports, at home, was an absolutely must win, or Derby's pay-off dreams would be in tatters. Derby put in an outstanding performance and won 3-1, which was a massive boost to their confidence. Callum Paterson put the Bluebirds ahead in the first half, but Derby came storming back with Cameron Jerome levelling with twenty minutes to go. Matej Vydra put the Rams ahead with eight minutes to go. Jerome then added his second and Derby's third in the last minute. With two games to go, Derby were two points ahead of seventh place Millwall. Derby earned a welcome but surprising point at Aston Villa, with Lewis Grabbon's late equaliser denying the Rams three points. Derby, who needed a point in their final game against Barnsley to ensure their play-off place, won 4-1, which relegated Barnsley. The reward was a play-off semi-final with Fulham. In the first leg at the iPro in a carnival atmosphere, Cameron Jerome's good vein of form continued, as he scored the winner with a powerful header from Craig Forsyth's cross. I went to the second leg at Craven Cottage. I drove with Mark Jarrett, Paul Cannon and Gavin Chadwick, on a warm sunny afternoon. We parked up at Stanmore and met up with Nigel and Matt Lee and travelled in on the train. We met Martin Fisher at The Crabtree pub on the banks of the Thames, before walking down to Craven Cottage. The big decision for Gary Rowett, was whether he would play Matej Vydra or go more defensive? He decided to go more defensive, playing Ikechi Anya wide left with Cameron Jerome as the loan striker. We were all in different parts of the ground. I was with Gavin in the Putney End. Derby somehow survived the constant pressure, with Scott Carson outstanding, going in at half time 0-0. Unsurprisingly, Fulham scored two minutes into the second half, through Ryan Sessegnon. Dennis Odoi doubled the lead twenty minutes later, with a near post header from a corner. The Rams could have few complaints, as Fulham were far the better side. Yet another season in the Championship beckoned.

CHAPTER 18

ROWETT LEAVES AND SUPER FRANKIE LAMPARD

2018/19

Mel Morris hinted that there wouldn't be much finance available to Gary Rowett to improve the squad following the Fulham defeat. The squad was ageing, and an input of younger, hungrier players was needed. A week later, Rowett asked Morris for permission to talk to Stoke City about their vacant manager's job. Morris agreed and Rowett moved on. With Stoke newly relegated to the Championship, their spending power would be far greater than Derby's. I wasn't too concerned. Like most supporters, I wasn't enamoured by the Rowett style of football. It didn't take long for the new appointment, with former Chelsea and England legend Frank Lampard appointed as the new manager. Lampard had been linked with Ipswich Town, but he signed a three-year deal at Pride Park on the last day of May. Lampard began to reshape the squad. There were three permanent signings and two season-long loan signings ahead of the season's opener at Reading at the start of August. Brentford winger Florian Jozefzoon arrived from Brentford for £2.8 million, striker Jack Marriott from Peterborough United for £3 million, and utility player George Evans from Reading. The two loans were youngsters Mason Mount and Harry Wilson, from Chelsea and Liverpool respectively. Craig Bryson returned from his loan spell at Cardiff City. Departures included Andreas Weimann, who joined Bristol City for £2 million, with Chris Baird, Darren Bent and Jason Shackell all released.

Derby won their opening game at Reading 2-1, which was shown live on Sky Sports on the first Friday night in August, with goals from Mason Mount on his debut and a last-minute flying header by Tom Lawrence, from Mason Bennett's right-wing cross. On the Sunday lunchtime, Julie and I travelled down to Stansted airport with Steve and Dawn Hallam, for a seventeen-day holiday on the west coast of the USA. We were stopping at a hotel close to the airport for the Monday morning flight. On the Sunday afternoon, we went to the Four Ashes pub in Takely, a taxi ride from the hotel, to watch Stoke City play Leeds United in their first League match since relegation, which Leeds won 3-1. The following morning, we flew to Las Vegas for three nights which was the first part of the holiday. Whilst we were in Vegas, Derby made three more permanent signings. Martyn Waghorn arrived from Ipswich Town for £5 million, Scott Malone joined from Huddersfield Town, and USA international Duane Holmes signed from Scunthorpe United. Another season long loan signing, Fikayo Tomori, arrived from Chelsea. Matej Vydra, top scorer from the previous season, joined Premier League Burnley for £11 million, and Jamie Hanson left to join Oxford United. Vegas was unbelievably hot with daytime temperatures of 45 degrees. In the evenings at 9 p.m, it was so warm outside that we had to go inside to cool down. Vegas must be the best place in the world for hotels, but three nights was enough for me and I was glad when we flew to San Francisco for the next part of the holiday. We stopped in nearby Oakland in Airbnb accommodation, so we had a daily commute into San Francisco by train. We loved San Francisco, with trips to Alcatraz, Fisherman's Wharf, Pier 39, Lombard Street and the Golden Gate Bridge. We also went to Yosemite National Park, but had restricted access due to the wild fires in the area. The weather was a bit of a problem, as Martin Fisher had warned me, with daily temperatures only reaching sixteen degrees. On the Saturday, whilst on the seafront, we found out Leeds United had won 4-1 at Pride Park in a teatime kick-off, but at ten a.m. in the morning in the USA, with the eight-hour time difference. Nick Blackman who had hardly featured for Derby, headed out on loan to Sporting Gijon in Spain. Derby progressed to the second round of the League Cup, with a comfortable 2-0 win at Oldham Athletic. After four nights in San Francisco, we picked up a hire car for the hour's drive down to Monterey for three nights. This is a lovely part of the world. The seventeen-mile scenic route along the Pacific coastline drive though Pebble Beach is breathtaking, with its stunning golf course, which can be seen from the beach at Carmel-by-the-Sea. Pacific Grove was great too and we met an Aston Villa fan who ran a local pub. After Monterey it was then a 200-mile drive down Highway One to Santa Barbara. It was foggy for most of the way, and spoilt the views. Before the drive down, I'd found out Derby had lost 2-1 at Millwall, with Academy product Jayden Bogle making his first start. On the drive down, Stoke City, who were playing a little later in the day, drew 2-2 at Preston North End. Santa Barbara was stunning, with a real Mediterranean feel and was much warmer than our previous stops. We stopped at the Cheshire Cat, a beautiful hotel with great rooms and a lovely garden, with British owners from Cheshire. For the last leg of the holiday, we spent two nights in Los Angeles. We stopped in the Echo Park area. As we were only there for one full day, we went on a bus trip, taking in the touristy parts like the Hollywood sign, Venice Beach, Beverley Hills and Sunset Boulevard. On the bus trip, I found out Derby had beaten Ipswich Town 2-0 at home, with Joe Ledley and Tom Lawrence scoring. The highlight, though, was Santa Monica, at the start of Route 66. We weren't that impressed with LA. It was very sad to see a lot of homeless people on the streets. On the day we were travelling back, during the morning, Stoke lost 3-0 at home to Wigan Athletic. Steve wasn't too happy with the way the Rowett era had started!

The first game of the season I went to was on the last Saturday in August, at home against Preston North End, with Derby winning 2-0, with goals from Mason Mount and Richard Keogh. I'd moved seats from the South Stand to the South West corner, with Mark Jarrett and Dave Hudson. The reason for moving was that the South Stand now was purely standing up all game, and at my age I just wanted to sit! The sponsorship deal with iPro ended, with the ground returning to its original name, Pride Park. Derby then won 4-0 at Hull City in the League Cup second round, beating the same opponents again three days later 2-1, with a late Florian Jozefzoon goal. Derby sold Cameron Jerome at the end of the transfer window to Turkish side Goztepe for an undisclosed fee, with Chris Martin loaned out again, this time to Hull City. I was really disappointed by this move, as I felt Martin would have had a lot to offer, if he linked up with Mason Mount and Harry Wilson, but Lampard must have seen it differently. Following the international break, I was up in Scotland, doing the Three Peaks Challenge with some workmates. We'd completed Ben Nevis and were in the minibus on the long drive to Scafell Pike in Cumbria, when we heard Derby had lost 1-0 at Rotherham United, with Frank Lampard banished to the stands. Derby had a fine win at home to Brentford, with two of the goals scored by Harry Wilson. He and Mason Mount were having a major influence on the team. Derby then travelled to Old Trafford for the League Cup third round. Derby put in a fine performance. Juan Mata gave United the lead but Harry Wilson levelled with a sublime free kick. Jack Marriott scored his first Derby goal with five minutes to go. The Rams couldn't hold on, with Marouane Fellaini scoring a last gasp equaliser. It was to be decided by penalties, and Derby rounded off a terrific evening winning 8-7, earning another plum draw away at Chelsea, and a quick return to Stamford Bridge for Frank Lampard. On the final Saturday of September, it was a trip to Bolton with some of the Michigan 'Old Boys'. It was a real effort to get to Bolton due to a train strike in the area, with Mark Jarrett sorting out the travel arrangements. We got the train to Manchester, then a bus into Bolton town centre. We went to The Spinning Mule for some pre-match beers, before having to get taxis to the newly named University of Bolton Stadium. We sat in the upper tier of the South Stand. Bolton took the lead after ten minutes. Derby dominated possession for the rest of the game, but never troubled Remi Matthews in the Bolton goal. It was a very frustrating afternoon, with Derby ending the month eighth in the table, with sixteen points from ten games, four points behind leaders West Bromwich Albion.

Derby then drew two games, 1-1 at home to Norwich City and then 1-1 away at Queen's Park Rangers. Leaders Sheffield United were then in town for a Saturday teatime kick-off shown live on Sky Sports, with Derby producing a thrilling performance, with Jack Marriott scoring a brilliant right side-foot volley to give the Rams a 2-1 win. Marriott was beginning to look like the player who had scored thirty-three goals for League One Peterborough United the previous season. Marriott scored again in the 4-1 win at West Bromwich Albion as Derby produced another fine performance, with Tom Lawrence, Harry Wilson and Scott Malone scoring the other goals. Derby then absolutely dominated the away game at Middlesbrough, but didn't take the numerous chances they created. Jayden Bogle's own goal six minutes from time denied the Rams the three points. On the last day of October, Derby visited Stamford Bridge for the League Cup fourth round tie with Chelsea. Derby put in a very creditable performance, with Jack Marriott scoring a fine goal but went out, losing 3-2. Derby started November with another good win 3-1 at home against Birmingham City, as they moved up to third in the League, only two points behind leaders Norwich City. Derby came crashing down to earth though the following week, when Aston Villa won 3-0 at Pride Park, who scored three times in the last fifteen minutes. Another blow to Derby was a torn anterior cruciate knee ligament injury to Craig Forsyth for the third time, which ruled him out for the season. After the international break, I went to Hillsborough on the train with some of the Michigan 'Old Boys', for the game at Sheffield Wednesday. Pre-match we went to the Sheaf Island pub again, before getting taxis to the ground. Adam Reach gave the Owls an early lead, but goals from Harry Wilson and

Jack Marriott gave Derby a half-time 2-1 lead which they held on to, earning the three points. Derby ended November losing to Gary Rowett's ten-man Stoke City 2-1, with ex-Ram Tom Ince scoring the winner. Derby suffered another injury blow, with Curtis Davies rupturing his Achilles tendon. Derby started December well, beating Swansea City 2-1 at home and winning 1-0 away at Wigan Athletic. The first East Midlands derby against Nottingham Forest at Pride Park ended 0-0, in a fairly uneventful game. The Rams lost 3-1 at Sheffield United on Boxing Day, but were involved in an astonishing game at Norwich City in their last game of the year. Derby were 2-0 down to goals from Ben Godfrey and Teemu Pukki, but hit back before half time, though Fikayo Tomori and Mason Mount. Pukki restored the Canaries lead with ten minutes to go. With five minutes remaining, the floodlights failed, delaying the game by twenty minutes. When the players returned Florian Jozefzoon equalised and then Jack Marriott scored the winner a minute later. Incredible stuff! Derby ended the year in sixth place, nine points behind leaders Leeds United.

Following Derby's 1-1 draw at home to Middlesbrough on New Year's Day, Southampton were the visitors in the third round of the FA Cup. Frank Lampard gave starts to squad players Kelle Roos and Max Lowe, who had returned from his loan spell at Aberdeen. Nathan Redmond gave the Saints a two-goal lead, but Derby hit back through Jack Marriott and Tom Lawrence, with Marriott missing a golden chance late on when he blazed over. Derby lost 2-0 at Leeds United before travelling to St. Mary's for the FA Cup replay which was shown live on the BBCTV. Lampard sent Max Lowe back to Aberdeen for more experience of first team football. I thought he had an erratic game at home to Southampton. I think he's quite 'loose' as a full-back and if I was an opposition manager, I would encourage my team to 'get at' him. At St. Marys, Derby again played well and won on penalties for the second time in the season at a Premier League ground. Frank Lampard then signed free agent thirty-eight-year-old Ashley Cole on a deal until the end of the season, with Andy King also arriving on loan until the end of the season from Leicester City. Joe Ledley left the club after being released from his contract. In the fourth round of the FA Cup, Derby were drawn away to one of the great names of English football with a trip to Accrington Stanley. The capacity at the Wham Stadium (or Crown Ground as it's more commonly known) was 6,000, so I was concerned I'd miss out on a ticket, as the usual allocation is twenty-five percent, so 1,500 tickets. I phoned the ticket office at Accrington, explained my situation, and they were fine in letting me buy three tickets in the Accrington end. In the meantime, Accrington had increased Derby's allocation to 3,000 so I would probably been OK. On the last Saturday of January, I drove up to Accrington with Mark Jarrett and Joe Rees, for the lunchtime kick-off with the game being shown live on BT Sports. We met Nigel Lee, Matt Lee, Paul Cannon and Joe Cannon at the Crown pub for a pre-match pint. Jack Lawrence, who was stopping overnight in Manchester, also met us pre-match. Jack, Mark Jarrett and I sat in the Jack Barrett Memorial Main Stand, with the Derby fans stood on the open Coppice terrace to our right and in the seating in the Eric Whalley Stand opposite. Accrington, particularly their owner Andy Holt, had done a fantastic job welcoming the Derby fans, erecting hospitality marquees around the ground. In a scrappy game on a difficult surface, Derby won 1-0, with a Martyn Waghorn goal twelve minutes from time. Derby were indebted to a fine save from Kelle Roos, from Billy Kee's late free kick. More of a concern was an injury to Mason Mount who limped off during the first half.

I missed the Michigan 'Old Boys' trip to Preston North End the following Friday, through illness on what was one of the coldest nights of the winter. I was gutted as I've never seen Derby play at Deepdale, and that's one ground I certainly need to do. The game ended goalless, with Preston dominating from start to finish. Derby then beat Hull City 2-0 at home and drew 1-1 at Ipswich Town, before going out of the FA Cup at the fifth-round stage, with a poor performance at Brighton and Hove Albion in a game shown live on BT Sports. The Rams then suffered three League defeats in a row. Millwall won 1-0 at Pride Park, with Jed Wallace scoring a late winner. Derby put in an inept performance in the East Midlands derby at the City Ground, shown live on Sky Sports, losing 1-0 to an early Yohan Benalouane goal in a really toothless display. This was followed by a 4-0 defeat at Aston Villa, with all the goals being scored in the first half, with Frank Lampard making six changes from the Forest game. Derby slipped to seventh in the table, three points behind sixth place Bristol City.

I was in Germany with work at the start of four home games on the bounce. I missed the 2-1 home win against Wigan Athletic, with Mason Bennett scoring a wonder goal. Derby's next two games were drawn against Sheffield Wednesday and Stoke City. The fourth ended in a 6-1 win against Rotherham United, with Martyn Waghorn scoring a hat-trick, with Mason Mount making his first start since he was injured at Accrington

Stanley. March ended with the Rams in sixth place, a point ahead of seventh place, Bristol City with eight games remaining. Two away games followed, with Derby picking up a point in a 3-3 draw at Brentford, but lost 2-0 in a very poor performance at Blackburn Rovers. A Mason Mount hat-trick gave Derby a much-needed win at home against relegation threatened Bolton Wanderers. Going into Easter, Derby were eighth two points behind sixth place Bristol City. The Good Friday fixture at Birmingham City ended in a 2-2 draw. The Easter Monday game at home to Queen's Park Rangers was an absolutely must win game. It turned out to be a very dramatic afternoon. With the game 0-0 and four minutes into added on time, Harry Wilson held his nerve and scored from the spot. Seven minutes later Wilson scored again to settle the nerves. What an afternoon! With three games to go, Derby travelled to Bristol City in a real six-pointer. Derby were back in sixth place, one point ahead of Bristol City who were now in eighth place. The Michigan 'Old Boys' had an away day, but I didn't go for reasons I'll explain shortly. Derby put in a fine performance and won 2-0, with goals from Tom Lawrence and a great finish from Jayden Bogle. Two games to go, Derby were on level points with seventh place Middlesbrough, but had a game in hand and were four points clear of Bristol City. The game in hand was at Swansea City. I drove to the Liberty Stadium with Mark Jarrett, Neil Robson and Bill Brown. After the long drive, we had a bite to eat at the Harvester near the ground, before the short walk to the stadium. We sat in the upper tier of the North Stand, with a good following from Derby for a midweek match. Richard Keogh gave Derby a first half lead, but Wayne Routledge levelled halfway through the second half. With one game left at home to West Bromwich

Albion, who had already booked their play-off spot, Derby needed a win to guarantee theirs. A tense afternoon lay ahead. Derby took the lead with a Martyn Waghorn header, but he then went off injured just before the break. Straight after half time, Stefan Johansen levelled. Derby though struck twice in three minutes, through Mason Bennett and Harry Wilson. Derby had made hard work of it, but had secured a play-off semi-final with Leeds United.

The first leg against Leeds United was at Pride Park. Derby didn't really turn up, and Leeds won with a Kemar Roofe goal ten minutes into the second half. David Nugent played up front, but was now struggling to make an impact, as Waghorn was injured and Jack Marriott was only fit for a place on the bench. I keep on going on about it, but why was Chris Martin out on loan? Derby were up against it as they travelled up to the cauldron of Elland Road, in what turned out to be one of the greatest nights in the club's history. Leeds went 1-0 up, with Stuart Dallas scoring halfway through the first half, with Derby now really up against it. Frank Lampard made a tactical switch a minute before half time, taking off Duane Holmes and replacing him with Jack Marriott. Marriott made an immediate impact, seizing on a mix up between Liam Cooper and Kiko Casilla to pull one back. At the start of the second half, Mason Mount stunned the home crowd by putting Derby ahead 2-1. Twelve minutes later, Mason Bennett was pulled back by Cooper in the box, and Harry Wilson coolly converted the spot kick to give Derby the lead on aggregate for the first time in the tie. Stuart Dallas scored his second on the night with a fine finish to bring Leeds back into it four minutes later, as the game swung from end to end. Gaetano Berardi received a second yellow for a rash tackle on Bradley Johnson, with twelve minutes left. A fine flowing move from Mount and Richard Keogh slipped Marriott in, who calmly finished lifting the ball over the advancing Casilla to give Derby the aggregate lead and sending the travelling support into raptures. Scott Malone received a second yellow in the last minute but Derby survived and booked their place at Wembley. It was certainly an 'I was there' moment for the travelling support, Unfortunately, I was at home watching the drama unfold!

On Saturday 25 May, two days before the play-off final against Aston Villa, I made the seven hour drive up to St. Andrews on the east coast of Scotland for a week's holiday with Julie and Austen. I couldn't miss the play-off final, so I missed the Bristol City game to be able to pay for Wembley, which I potentially knew was looming. On the Monday, I was up at 5.15 a.m. for the fifty-mile drive to Edinburgh airport. The plane left at ten o'clock for the flight down to Heathrow. I met a couple of Derby fans and three Villa fans in Edinburgh, who were on the same flight. On arrival at Heathrow there an issue with the trains, so I needed to travel in by the bus that was provided. I met up with the Michigan 'Old Boys' in the Covent Garden area about midday. There was a fantastic atmosphere on Wembley Way, as both sets of fans made their way to the ground. Paul Cannon did a fine job sorting out the tickets, but it was impossible for about fifteen of us to sit together. I sat with Dennis Ceranic and Mark Jarrett in the North East corner on the front row of the top tier, with a fantastic view. The big talking point pre-match was Frank Lampard's team selection. The supporters wanted him to pick Martyn Waghorn and Jack Marriott, who both weren't fully fit but would probably last for an hour. Lampard saw it differently, and picked Mason Bennett as his focal point. Mason Bennett is a great trier, puts in a shift, but in my opinion, doesn't have the required quality to play that role. For some reason, Lampard took a shine to Bennett from the moment he was appointed.

Villa took the lead right on half time, through Anwar El Ghazi's far post header, which was a crushing blow to the Rams. It was 2-0 when John McGinn headed home following poor indecision by Kelle Roos. To be fair to Roos, he had played very well during the second half of the season since he'd replaced Scott Carson. Derby now had no choice but to chase the game and Lampard made a triple change, bringing on Marriott, Waghorn and Florian Jozefzoon for Bennett, Tom Lawrence and Tom Huddlestone respectively. Derby began to attack as the game opened up and Marriott went close with a left foot shot before pulling one back with ten minutes of normal time remaining to set up a grandstand finish. Derby really took the fight to Villa and finished really strongly, but couldn't get that vital second goal. If the game had gone on a for a further five or ten minutes, I'm sure Derby's pressure would have told. In four play-off finals, I've seen three defeats and one win. Wembley certainly isn't a place for losers. I made my way back to Heathrow for the return flight to Edinburgh, and the drive back to St Andrews for the rest of the holiday. It was day I'll never forget.

CHAPTER 19

LAMPARD BACK TO CHELSEA AND DERBY'S FIRST CONTINENTAL MANAGER PHILLIP COCU

2019/20

Chelsea had parted company with Maurizio Sarri a couple of weeks after the play-off final, with all the talk in the media all about a possible return of Frank Lampard to take over at Stamford Bridge. After weeks of speculation, Mel Morris gave Chelsea permission to talk to Lampard, who was appointed their new manager in the first week of July. This didn't give Derby much time to appoint a replacement, with the new season only four weeks away. Morris appointed former Barcelona and Netherlands international Phillip Cocu as his new man. Cocu had a successful spell as manager of PSV Eindhoven, but had recently been sacked by Fenerbahce in Turkey. Cocu's first act was to join the players in Florida for the pre-season tour. One of his headaches was how to replace Mason Mount, Fikayo Tomori and Harry Wilson, who had returned to their parent clubs. All three had played a massive part in the previous season. There was quite a lot of transfer activity prior to the season started. Craig Bryson's long spell at the club ended after he joined Aberdeen. David Nugent joined Preston North End, Alex Pearce signed for Millwall, and Bradley Johnson left for Blackburn Rovers. Nick Blackman finally left to join Maccabi Tel Aviv and Jacob Butterfield moved to Luton Town. The major signings were Krystian Bielik from Arsenal for a club record £10 million, and Graeme Shinnie, who Frank Lampard had signed from Aberdeen. In coming loans were Jamie Paterson from Bristol City, Kieran Dowell form Everton, Ben Hamer from Huddersfield and Matt Clarke from Brighton and Hove Albion. Chris Martin returned from his loan at Hull City.

The Cocu reign started with an away win at Huddersfield Town, shown live on Sky Sports on the Monday evening, with two fine finishes from Tom Lawrence. The win though was overshadowed by the major breaking news that Derby had signed Wayne Rooney from DC United, with Rooney joining the club in January. Scott Carson left the club to join Premier League Champions Manchester City on a season's long loan. The Rams drew their first home game against Swansea City, before playing Scunthorpe United at Glanford Park in the League Cup first round. I drove up to South Humberside with Mark Jarrett and John Wayne. We met Nigel and Matt Lee for a pre-match pint near the ground before taking our place on the covered terrace South Stand. Krystian Bielik made his debut as Cocu gave some of the squad players much needed game time. In a low-key game of poor quality, debutant Lee Buchanan gave the Rams victory twelve minutes from time with a fine left foot cross shot. George Thorne left the club, joining League One club Oxford United on a three-month loan. Derby drew 2-2 at Stoke City in the next game. That evening, Julie and I travelled to Birmingham for an overnight stop, as we had a 6 a.m. flight to the Greek mainland before picking up a ferry to the Island of Thassos.

With being away, I missed the next home game, a 2-1 defeat to Bristol City. The following morning at our hotel in the resort of Limenaria, I was having breakfast when I noticed a guy in a black Derby shirt. We started having a chat and discussing the previous night's defeat. It turned out the guy, Jeff Sims, lived in Littleover with his wife Dawn, just five minutes' walk from us! Dawn was a big football fan too, with both of us big Chris Martin fans! The next game was at home to West Bromwich Albion. We met up with Jeff and Dawn to watch the game, after Jeff had persuaded a barman on the lovely Limenaria seafront to put the game on in his pub. The game finished 1-1, with West Brom equalising with a Kenneth Zohore penalty five minutes from time after Martyn Waghorn had put Derby in front with an early penalty and then missed another one just before the break. The next day was the day Ben Stokes and Jack Leach's last wicket partnership at Headingley, that saw off Australia. Jeff, very superstitious, didn't leave his sun-bed throughout the partnership. To be honest, he didn't leave it throughout the whole of the holiday! Derby crashed out of the League Cup 3-0 at Nottingham Forest, with Phillip Cocu again playing an under-strength team, as did Forest, to be fair. Some of the Michigan 'Old Boys' went and weren't impressed with Cocu's decision to do this at the local rivals. Jeff used his magic again on the Saturday, as we went to the same bar to watch Derby's game at Brentford. Derby produced a horror show and lost 3-0, with Cocu very critical of the players after the match. The League table wasn't good reading, with Derby sixth-from-bottom with six points from six games in a disappointing start to the campaign.

My first game back from holiday was against Cardiff City, a week after the international break. We met up at the Exeter Arms with the Michigan 'Old Boys' at the Exeter Arms for pre-match food and beers that was very well organised by 'Mort'. The game ended 1-1, with Derby drawing their next game away at Leeds United, with Chris Martin scoring a late equaliser after Leeds had dominated. That day Paul Cannon, Mort and I went to Edgbaston, to watch Derbyshire in their first ever T20 Blast finals day. On a beautiful late September day, we got the train into New Street and had breakfast before walking to the ground. Nottinghamshire played Worcestershire in the first semi-final, with the Pears winning after Notts pressed the self-destruct button. We saw the final stages, watching the game in the pub as it had had shared coverage with the Leeds-Derby game. In the pub, we met Richard Kniveton and Paul Lowe, two lads I'd played cricket with but had not seen for years. Nick Chadwick, not surprisingly, was in the pub too! We returned to Edgbaston for the Derbyshire v Essex semi-final. Essex scored one hundred and sixty on a low slow turning wicket, which was probably above par. Derbyshire lost wickets regularly, despite a good start, with Essex captain Simon Harmer taking four wickets, and were all out for one hundred and twenty-six. Essex went on to lift the trophy. Paul, Mort and I left, and had a few more beers in Birmingham before heading home. It had been a really good day, with the weather completing it. The following Wednesday morning, some staggering news broke. Tom Lawrence and Mason Bennett were on the way home from a night out at the Joiners Arms pub in Quarndon, when Lawrence's car crashed into the back of Bennett's on the A6. Richard Keogh was in the back of Lawrence's car, and suffered a knee ligament injury that would rule him out for the season. Lawrence and Bennett had to complete 180 hours of unpaid work and were banned from driving for two years. Keogh was sacked by the club. A dark cloud hung over the club as they went into their next match at home to Birmingham City. Derby got a much needed 3-2 win, after going 2-0 up, with the Blues then pulling it back to 2-2, before Jamie Paterson scored the winner. In the midweek I went up to Barnsley with some of the Michigan 'Old Boys'. Derby were 1-0 down, but then took a 2-1 lead, before a last minute Conor Chaplin goal earned the Tykes a point in a game Derby should have won. Derby then beat promoted Luton Town 2-0, with keeper Simon Sluga letting a Matty Pearson thirty-yard back pass slip under his foot for an unbelievable own goal. Derby fell to a 3-0 defeat in the capital at Charlton Athletic, before beating Wigan Athletic 1-0 at Pride Park. The following Saturday, it was the first Michigan 'Old Boys' away day of the season at Hull City, on a cold, wet, late October Saturday. We stopped for a breakfast on the way up, and to watch the Rugby World Cup semi-final between England and New Zealand in Yokohama. England won 19-7, and booked a place in the final. We carried on up to Hull, stopping for pre-match beers and playing snooker at the New Walton Social Club, which was a real blast from the past. Derby's away form was becoming a concern. Hull won 2-0, with the impressive Jarrod Bowen scoring twice. I didn't think Bowen would be at Hull long, as he had Premier League quality. He ended up moving to West Ham United in the January transfer window, for a reported £22 million. Derby were sixteenth in the table with eighteen points from fourteen games.

Derby's win at home and lose away theme continued, as they struggled to find any consistency. The Rams beat Middlesbrough 2-0 at home before losing 1-0 at Nottingham Forest, shown live on Sky Sports, following a bad mislaid pass across his own box by Jayden Bogle, which Lewis Grabban capitalised on. Derby won 1-0 at home to Preston North End with a goal from substitute Martyn Waghorn, with Craig Forsyth making his first start after recovering from his third major knee injury. Fulham beat Derby in the next game, with the Rams' third 3-0 defeat of the season in London. The next Michigan 'Old Boys' away day was the away game at Blackburn Rovers, with Jack Lawrence and Gavin Chadwick joining us on the bus on the first Saturday in December. Pre-match was spent in the Fernhurst pub, just down the road from Ewood Park. On a horrible, gloomy, wet day, we sat in the upper tier of the Darwen End with the lower tier empty. Derby were not at the races and never created a chance all game. Adam Armstrong scored the Rovers winner, which Ben Hamer in the Derby goal should have saved. My abiding memory of the afternoon was looking down at the row at Mort who had 'What the hell am I doing here?' written all over his face. Derby drew 1-1 at home to Sheffield Wednesday, but then lost 1-0 at home to Millwall and 3-0 at Reading on the run up to Christmas.

The defeat at Reading wasn't helped by the sending off of Scott Malone in the fourth minute. Worryingly, Derby were seventeenth in the table, with twenty-six points from twenty-three games but the alarm bells were ringing with the string of poor performances. Derby drew 1-1 on Boxing Day away at Wigan Athletic, with Martyn Waghorn's last minute goal, Derby's first on the road since 2 October, earning the Rams a rare point. Derby's last game of the year was at home to Charlton Athletic. Derby recorded a much-needed win, with Jason Knight scoring both goals, which were his first for the club. This was a fine win, despite the early sending off of Krystian Bielik. The start of 2020 started with Wayne Rooney making his debut, and captaining the side in the home game with Barnsley. It was no great surprise that the game was shown live on Sky Sports. It was all rather surreal, seeing Manchester United and England's greatest goal scorer in a Derby shirt. Jack Marriott gave Derby the lead after missing two glorious chances, but Barnsley levelled through Elliot Simoes after the break, following a mistake from Ben Hamer. Martyn Waghorn steered home Andre Wisdom's cross to secure Derby the points. The League table looked a lot healthier, with Derby twelve points above the drop zone.

Derby won 1-0 at Crystal Palace, with a neat finish from Chris Martin in the third round of the FA Cup. Derby gained a point in a 2-2 draw at Middlesbrough, and three in the 1-0 home win against Hull City, as the Rooney effect was bearing fruit. The FA Cup fourth round paired Derby at Northampton Town. Derby were poor and escaped with a 0-0 draw. In the midweek, I drove to Luton Town with some of the Michigan 'Old Boys', with Nigel Lee driving down too. We went for pre-match drinks and food in a town centre pub. We met up with Gavin Chadwick, Jack Lawrence and Nick Chadwick, the latter of whom had jetted in from the US for the game, suitcase and all. We walked to the ram shackled Kenilworth Road and took our place in the Oak Road Stand. Wayne Rooney gave Derby the lead with a deflected effort on the hour, but relegation threatened Luton hit back to take the lead. Chris Martin levelled with a far post header with five minutes left, but Jayden Bogle's own goal a minute later secured the points for the Hatters. Max Lowe was sent off two minutes later for dissent. Derby, in all fairness, had played fairly well, in an entertaining game. Derby ended January with a fine Friday night 4-0 win at home to Stoke City, shown live on Sky Sports, which lifted them to thirteenth in the table with forty points from thirty games. Derby then scored four more, as they knocked Northampton Town out of the FA Cup. The Rams then recorded their first League away win since the opening weekend, as they won 3-2 at Swansea City with Tom Lawrence scoring the winner ten minutes from time. After dominating possession in the away game at Bristol City, the Rams conceded twice before half time. City increased the lead to 3-0 before Martyn Waghorn and Chris Martin scored, but the Rams went home defeated. Derby drew their next two home games, 1-1 against both Huddersfield Town and Fulham, before losing 2-1 at Queen's Park Rangers. Derby then dominated the game at Hillsborough with Tom Lawrence scoring twice and Jason Knight adding the other, with Chris Martin having assists in all three goals, with Derby winning 3-1. The Rams were knocked out of the FA Cup at the fifth-round stage at home to Manchester United, with Odion Ighalo scoring twice in a comfortable win for United. Chris Martin was in fine form during the home game with Blackburn Rovers, scoring twice after Louie Sibley scored with a wonder strike with his first career goal. The Blackburn game turned out to be the last Derby game to be played with a crowd as the

Coronavirus pandemic started to grip the world. Prime Minister Boris Johnson ordered the public to stop at home to prevent spread of the virus.

The season started again behind closed doors with no fans allowed in the ground on Saturday 20 June. Derby visited Millwall in a really surreal atmosphere. Millwall took the lead through a Matt Smith far post header. But Derby came roaring back, with Louie Sibley scoring a brilliant hat-trick with three top finishes to give the Ram a winning start to the 'restart'.

I left Rolls-Royce Wednesday 24th June, following just under forty years of service. I was given a fantastic leaving presentation by Gavin Chadwick, Matt McCormack, Jack Lawrence and James White, who's more affectionately known as 'Rotherham Ron'. Many thanks to Adam Wainman and Andrew Bushnell for allowing Julie and Sarah to attend. I had a very enjoyable time at Rolls-Royce having met some great characters and made some lifelong friends. It certainly has given me a great life. At school, my plan to either work in a bank or do sports journalism. My dad, though, wanted me at Rolls-Royce, where he had spent his working life, and he wouldn't entertain sports journalism due to the lack of opportunities in that field. We had plenty of heated discussions about it, but I have to concede he was right. Parents always are!

Derby then beat Reading 2-1 at home, with Tom Lawrence sent off after the final whistle. A Wayne Rooney free kick gave the Rams victory at Preston North End, as they moved up to seventh in the table, a point behind sixth place Cardiff City. A late Chris Martin effort gave Derby a point in the home game with Nottingham Forest, where there was another sending off due to Martyn Waghorn seeing red, as the Rams began a run of games against teams above them. They lost four games on the trot, as the Lawrence and Waghorn suspensions depleted Phillip Cocu's options. The 2-0 defeat at West Bromwich Albion, 3-1 at home to Brentford, 2-1 at Cardiff City and 3-1 at home to Leeds United crushed their play-off hopes. Derby won at Birmingham City in their final game, but the performances had been very poor after the three wins initial wins following the 'restart'.

CHAPTER 20

FIFTY YEARS OF WATCHING DERBY COUNTY COMPLETED, 'SURVIVAL SATURDAY' AND THE EURO 2020 BONUS

2020/21

Chris Martin was offered a new deal but decided to move onto Bristol City, with nobody coming into replace him, so Derby didn't have a natural target man in their squad as they opened the season against Barrow, who were newly promoted to the Football League, in the first round of the League Cup. The season started on the first Saturday in September, due to the late finish of the previous season. Phillip Cocu strengthened his squad with the arrival of Mike te Wierik from Dutch club Groningen and David Marshall from Wigan Athletic, with Matt Clarke returning on a season-long loan from Brighton and Hove Albion. Mason Bennett joined Millwall for an undisclosed fee, Scott Carson returned to Manchester City on a season long loan, with Scott Malone joining Millwall on the same arrangement. Not surprisingly, Ikechi Anya was released, as well as Tom Huddlestone.

Derby were very poor and look disjointed, with only Jack Marriott as a recognised striker. They managed to overcome

Barrow 3-2 on penalties, after the game had finished goalless. It must have been a tough watch for the neutral fan as the game was shown live on Sky Sports. Full-backs Jayden Bogle and Max Lowe joined Premier League Sheffield United, with Nathan Byrne signing for the Rams from Wigan Athletic for an undisclosed fee, ahead of Derby's opening League game at home to Reading. It was still football behind closed doors due to the Coronavirus, so watching Derby's games was restricted to Rams TV or Sky Sports. Derby were again poor against Reading and lost 2-0, with young Academy striker Morgan Whittaker playing up top with Jack Marriott. Preston North End won 2-1 at Pride Park in the League Cup second round, but it looked like goals were going to be hard to come by. Mike te Wierik was sent off, as he was struggling to come to terms with the demands of English football. Derby then landed their man, with the £3 million acquisition of Polish international winger Kamel Jozwiak from Lech Poznan. He made his debut in the 2-1 defeat at Luton Town. Ex-loanee Jordan Ibe also arrived, on a free transfer following his release from AFC Bournemouth. The Rams finished their September fixtures with a disturbing 4-0 home defeat at home to Blackburn Rovers, who scored three times in the opening fifteen minutes. October started better, as Derby finally got their first win with a Wayne Rooney free kick at Norwich City, with Derby parading their new popular pink away shirt, as the club joined forces with Umbro to donate some of the proceeds to breast cancer. Two more defeats followed, 1-0 at home to Watford and 2-0 at Huddersfield Town. Jack Marriott and Florian Jozefzoon both left the Rams on loan, to Sheffield Wednesday and Rotherham United respectively. Much travelled thirty-four-year-old striker Colin Kazim-Richards joined the Rams, as he was a free agent. Three 1-1 draws followed at Nottingham Forest, in a much-improved performance, at home to Cardiff City and away at AFC Bournemouth. The League table wasn't good reading though, as October ended with the Rams in the bottom three, with six points from nine games. November was even worse, with four defeats on the bounce. Queens Park Rangers won 1-0 at Pride Park, which was followed a couple of days later by news that the club had agreed a deal with Derventio Holdings, who were effectively owned by Khaled bin Zayed Al Nehayan, to take over the club for a rumoured £60 million. The next day, Derby lost 2-0 at home to Barnsley, with manager Phillip Cocu having to self-isolate due to the Coronavirus pandemic. This turned out to be Cocu's last game in charge, as he was sacked during the international break. Mel Morris put Wayne Rooney, Liam Rosenoir, Shay Given and Justin Walker in charge of the team. Things didn't improve, with defeats at Bristol City and Middlesbrough, as Derby slumped to the bottom of the table, with six points from twelve games and a big relegation battle lay ahead. Steve McClaren re-joined the club as Technical Advisor prior to the Middlesbrough game. Rooney was then put in sole charge as interim manager, as the Rams faced two big games at home to fellow strugglers Wycombe Wanderers and Coventry City. Both games finished 1-1, with record signing Krystian Bielik making his first start against Coventry following his long-term injury. A win finally came on the first Saturday of December, with Jason Knight's second half goal giving the Rams a vital 1-0 win at Millwall.

Two goalless draws followed, away at Brentford and at home to Stoke City, before Kamil Jozwiak scored his first goal for the club in an impressive 2-0 win at home to Swansea City. The away game at Rotherham United was postponed at one p.m. on the day of the match, due to an outbreak of Coronavirus in the Millers camp. This was disappointing as Derby were on a good run of form. Derby started the home game well against Preston North End on Boxing Day, but Martyn Waghorn's red card for a crude challenge didn't help Derby's cause. Derby defended well but lost to a goal in added time by Alan Browne. Derby then recorded their biggest win of the season, with a 4-0 win at Birmingham City, shown live on Sky Sports, in the last game of the year. The goals were shared by Krystian Bielik, Graeme Shinnie, Colin Kazim-Richards and Jason Knight. The Rams were still in the bottom three, but closing the gap on the teams just above them.

Derby dominated the early part of the crunch live Sky Sports away game at Sheffield Wednesday on New Year's Day, who were a place below them in the table, but didn't take the chances they created. Callum Paterson's header gave the Owls the three points in a 1-0 win. The FA Cup paired Derby at Chorley, who were in the National League North, which is the sixth tier of the English football pyramid. Derby were struck down with the Coronavirus, so the first team squad and staff had to go into self-isolation. Derby played a team of young Academy players with no first team experience. Chorley won 2-0 in the game at Victory Park, with the game shown live on BT Sports. Derby's next game was another six-pointer at home to Rotherham United. Derby couldn't cope with the Millers' physical approach and were totally outplayed, losing 1-0 to Jamie Lindsay's goal four minutes from time, which was a crucial blow. Derby then ended January winning three games in a row, all by 1-0. Their impressive run against the top teams continued, beating high-flying AFC Bournemouth. This was followed with a victory at Queen's Park Rangers and at home to Bristol City.

The win against Bristol City, though, came at a cost, with Krystian Bielik suffering another anterior cruciate ligament injury that would rule him out for the season. Derby finally moved out of the bottom three, but it was incredibly tight at the bottom of the table, with four points separating seven teams. Wayne Rooney added five loan players to his squad at the end of the January transfer window with Lee Gregory, Patrick Roberts, Teden Mengi, George Edmundson and Beni Baningime arriving from Stoke City, Manchester City, Manchester United, Glasgow Rangers and Everton respectively. All the deals were to the end of the season. Three players left the club. Duane Holmes left for Huddersfield Town, George Evans joined Millwall and Morgan Whittaker signed for Swansea City for £700,000. The next game was the re-arranged crucial away game at Rotherham United. Derby lost 3-0 after Lee Gregory missed a golden chance, with all the goals coming in the last fifteen minutes. Derby were back to winning ways, beating Middlesbrough 2-1 at home, with Colin Kazim-Richards scoring with a wonder strike. This was followed by a big 2-1 bottom-of-the-table win at Wycombe Wanderers, on Derby's first ever visit to Adams Park. Andre Wisdom scored a last-minute goal in a massive 2-1 win. The table was looking a lot healthier as the Rams moved up to seventeenth in the table, seven points above the drop zone. Derby fell to a 2-1 defeat at Watford in a game shown live on Sky Sports, but beat Huddersfield Town 2-0 at Pride Park, with Richard Keogh playing at Pride Park for the first time since his acrimonious departure. Derby 'got out of jail' in the home game with Nottingham Forest, live on Sky Sports, in the last game of February. James Garner gave Forest a first half lead, and to be fair, controlled most of the game. Colin Kazim-Richards, though, hit his second top strike of the month, to salvage a draw which Derby didn't deserve. March turned out to be a really poor month for the Rams. Wayne Rooney rang the changes for the trip to Cardiff City, which ended in a 4-0 defeat. This was followed with a 1-0 defeat at Coventry City, when Maxime Biamou cashed in a poor pass from Nathan Byrne, who had been one of Derby's most consistent performers. Derby got one of their two points of the month in a goalless draw at Barnsley in a dreadful game, on the night I received my first Coronavirus vaccine! The Rams then lost 1-0 at home to Millwall, with Shaun Hutchinson scoring right on half time. Their second point came with a fine second half performance against Brentford, coming back with goals from Lee Gregory, and Louie Sibley's first goal of the season. It was announced that Derby had pulled the plug on the deal to sell the club to Derventio Holdings. It was announced that Mel Morris was in advanced negotiations to sell the club to No Limits Sports Limited, fronted by Spanish businessman Erik Alonso. Another poor defeat came at Stoke City, as the month ended with Derby only two points above the drop zone, as the threat of relegation was becoming a strong possibility.

The Easter Saturday 2-0 win over Luton Town at Pride Park was Derby's first win in eight games and marked fifty years since my first ever Derby game in 1971. It was so disappointing not to have been able to attend, due to the ongoing Coronavirus pandemic. Derby fell to another defeat on Easter Monday by 3-1 at Reading, despite a fine strike by Tom Lawrence. The Rams put in a very spirited performance in against Champions elect Norwich City, but lost to a fine free kick by ex-Ram Kieran Dowell. Three more defeats followed, 2-1 at Blackburn Rovers, 3-0 at Preston North End and a crushing 2-1 reversal at home to fellow strugglers Birmingham City, shown live on Sky Sports, as the pressure on the club and its supporters was becoming unbearable. The fortunate thing for Derby was that Rotherham United, below them in the table, couldn't win their games in hand that had mounted up due to the pandemic. Derby lost 2-1 at Swansea City, in yet another game shown live on Sky Sports, after taking the lead with a Tom Lawrence goal. It was incredibly tight at the bottom of the League with any two of Derby, Rotherham and Sheffield Wednesday certain to join Wycombe Wanderers, who still had a very slim mathematical chance of survival, in League One. Rotherham gained a point in a goalless draw at Luton, which meant it would go down to the last game. The scenario was simple on 'Survival Saturday'. If Derby beat Sheffield Wednesday they would survive, but if they lost, they would be relegated. Derby would survive with a draw provided Rotherham didn't win at Cardiff City. The Sheffield Wednesday match was arguably one of the biggest games in the club's history.

The day didn't start well on a wet and windy November type of day. I went with Paul Cannon to watch the game, shown live on Sky Sports, in the garden at Richard Tapping's house. Rotherham took an early lead at Cardiff, which at that stage meant Derby had to beat Sheffield Wednesday. Things turned even worse just before half time as Sam Hutchinson gave the

Owls the lead, with the game lacking any sort of quality. Derby roared back though early on in the second half, equalising through Martyn Waghorn's header from Tom Lawrence's cross. Derby took the lead with a sublime Patrick Roberts curling left shot, to calm the nerves around the city and county. Derby pressed the self-destruct button as a poor Craig Forsyth clearance fell in to the path of Callum Paterson who steered the ball past Kelle Roos to level for Wednesday. Things got worse as further poor defending, with Derby failing to clear a corner, resulted in Wednesday taking the lead through Julian Borner's close range header. Down in Cardiff, Marlon Pack equalised with two minutes to go. At Pride Park, seconds later, Derby were awarded a penalty when Kamel Jozwiak was hauled down as he raced away from the Wednesday back-line. Waghorn stepped up, showing nerves of steel, to strike a magnificent penalty past Kieran Westwood. The Rotherham game finished in a draw, which meant Derby just had to hold on to a draw to guarantee safety. The Derby game though still had at least ten minutes to go due to added injury time. Derby managed to survive late Wednesday pressure with Curtis Davies defying the medics, coming on form the bench to play the last ten minutes, only five months since having surgery for a ruptured Achilles tendon. What a man! Derby had avoided relegation to League One with only forty-four points, winning only one game since late February. It had been the most nervous, tension filled last few weeks of the season, to endure the most wretched season that the fanbase will never, ever forget. To make it worse we couldn't get in to watch. Football is absolutely nothing without fans in the grounds. I think I'll leave it there…regarding Derby County.

The 2020 Euros were delayed for a year due to the Coronavirus pandemic. Eventually much to the relief of football supporters over Europe the tournament eventually got underway on June 11. England progressed through the group stages topping their group ahead of the Czech Republic, Croatia and Scotland. This set up a last sixteen tie against Germany. The day prior to the Germany game Julie and I were out with Nigel and Sue Lee up in the Sheffield area. Nige was trying to get tickets for the Germany game but was unsuccessful. As an alternative he bought tickets for the semi-final for himself and his son Matt in England's side of the draw. It was a gamble as England still had to overcome Germany which as most football followers know wouldn't be straightforward. That evening Nigel made the Michigan 'Old Boys' on our What's App group chat aware that he had bought these tickets. Paul Cannon, Martin Fisher and Neil Robson also followed suit and bought tickets also for themselves and their sons (and daughter in Paul's case). The following day I also decided to a purchase a ticket together with Mark Jarrett at 4pm just before the Germany game was due to start at 5pm. The tickets weren't cheap at £500 a time but this was possibly a once in a lifetime opportunity of seeing England play in a major semi-final in their own country with the game due to be played at Wembley. In a tense game against Germany, England finally overcame their arch rivals with two late goals from Raheem Sterling and Harry Kane to set up a quarter final tie against Ukraine who had beaten Sweden. England dominated the game against Ukraine and ran out 4-0 winners. Our gamble paid off and we were on our way to Wembley for the semi-final against Denmark.

I drove to Wembley with Mark Jarrett. We booked in for an

overnight stop at the Premier Inn in Edgware, before getting the tube to Trafalgar Square to meet Nige, Paul, Martin and Neil and their 'young ones' at the Admiralty pub at 2pm for a few pre-match beers. We left the pub in good time to make our way to Wembley. The atmosphere on Wembley Way as good as I've ever experienced at a football match. I just wished I had been carrying a bottle to capture it! We stopped for a few photographs before heading into the ground. The ground was absolutely buzzing as the two teams emerged from the dressing rooms for the National Anthems prior to the 8pm kick-off. We were sat in the Upper Tier of the North Stand on the halfway line with the two managers patrolling their technical areas below us. Denmark took the lead through Mikkel Damsgaard's free kick on the half hour which stunned the majority of the 60,000 crowd. England levelled though five minutes before the break when Simon Kjaer under pressure from Raheem Sterling, steered Bukayo Saka's cross into his own net. England made most of the running in the second half as Denmark tired, but they couldn't break down the resilient Danes. The game went into extra time. Sterling was bought down in the box at the end of the first period of extra time. Harry Kane's weak penalty was saved by Kasper Schmeichel, but Kane managed to fire home the rebound to send England through to their first major final since 1966. The noise at the end of the game was deafening as 'Football's Coming Home' and 'Sweet Caroline' reverberated around the ground. England sadly lost the final four days later to Italy, but Wednesday July 7 the date of the Denmark game will live in my memory forever. What a day!

Mum and Dad - Fortunately Dad loved his football and cricket. Mum only ever went to one game and was hit in the face by the ball!

With my lovely wife Julie. We met on the day Derby lost 5-1 at Barnsley in March 1984!

With my gorgeous daughter Sarah, who still gets ID'd in pubs!

King Charlie - No words needed!

Top photo - Derby North End 1978. Ex Ram Graham Harbey on the back row second from right.
Bottom photo – My sister's Pauline, Irene and Lynda. All three not football followers!

Both photos Michigan 'Old Boys'. Bottom photo (left to right) Nigel Lee, Matt Lee, Derek Lee, Mark Jarrett, Martin Fisher, Dave Hudson. Most ex-school mates and top friends

Top photo – The Chap Harriers (left to right) Lee Griffiths, Nick Chadwick, Joe Rees, Gavin Chadwick and Dave Thompson with club legend Roy McFarland

Bottom Photo – With our good friends Dawn and Steve Hallam (Stoke SOS) who loves a rant on Twitter and is King of the Retweet

Top Photo With our good friends Carol and Graham Perry- famous for his meeting with Phil Brown

Bottom Photo My first ever League game v Huddersfield Town in April 1971

Top Photo Carl Smith – who I've been to many games with.

Bottom Photo My nephew Matt Birks who I've also been to many games with.

Top photo Austen, my eldest Grandson, who's football nuts and primarily a Glasgow Rangers fan!